"This beautiful book—accompanied by more than 70 rare and wonderful black and white photographs—recounts the tale of one man's spiritual quest and the finding of his Guide, Sant Kirpal Singh (1894-1974), an authentic Adept in a lineage that traces its roots in distant ages. These ancient teachings were revived five centuries ago by Guru Nanak and Kabir Sahib, and were again given new life and relevance in the 20th Century. It is a teaching that emphasizes service, ethical living, as well as a free, scientific method of meditation which seeks to unite the individual soul with its Divine Source.

The book is filled with the author's inspiring experiences and adventures, along with illuminating converse with his Master and successors. At one place, Kirpal Singh tells him, 'A hungry man is an angry man and to speak of God to an angry man is a mockery. We must serve those naked and hungry Gods moving on Earth.'

Journey to the Lumious is a fascinating story of the trials and ecstacies of the spiritual quest and how the author manifests his mentors' teachings in life through meditation and the path of service. Along the way, Arran Stephens founds the highly successful Nature's Path and LifeStream food companies, which express his ongoing vision of improving the world we all share."

—Carolyn DeMarco, MD,
"Take Charge of Your Body:
A Woman's Health Advisor."

TESTIMONIAL

"One of the great spiritual teachers of our age, Sant Kirpal Singh, in 1967 advised the young aspirant at his threshold to keep a journal of his experiences on the mystic path. Arran wisely took this advice and compiled his journals into an inspiring account of a most fascinating odyssey.

Arran retraces his steps from boyhood farm life in British Columbia, through the tough streets of Los Angeles, encounters with drugs and beat poets, to the depths of despair, and finally to a California monastery where he begins the long road to self-awareness and spiritual insight.

Meeting his destined Master in India lifted Arran's spiritual search to a new level of meaning and commitment. His richly detailed accounts of ashram life, meetings with renowned saints, scholars and teachers—including the mystic poet-Sant Darshan Singh, vibrate with aliveness and soar with vision. In *Journey to the Luminous*, a personal memoir is transformed into a universal story of every heart's search for meaning and truth.

As a successful entrepreneur and organic foods pioneer, Arran has admirably translated his spiritual learning in the physical world. He demonstrates the value of meditation and moderation in our fast-paced western lifestyle, which adds a powerful practical relevance to his book. *Journey to the Luminous* is a remarkable story that reveals both the struggle and rewards of living the spiritual life."

—Rex Weyler, publisher of *Shared Vision* magazine,
co-author of *Chop Wood, Carry Water*,
co-founder of Hollyhock Seminar Centre

Journey
to the
Luminous

with Mystic Adepts
of our Century

Arran Stephens

CREDITS

Journey to the Luminous Cover,
Moth & the Flame, &
Planes of Creation illustrations:
Arran Stephens

Book Design: *Ken McCormick and Arran Stephens*
Editors: *Joan Morgan and Eliot Jay Rosen*

Published by
Elton–Wolf Publishing,
301 – Pier 55 – 1101 Alaska Way
Seattle, WA   98101-2982
(206) 748-0345

Suite 212 – 1656 Duranleau Street – Granville Island
Vancouver, BC   V6H3S4
(604) 688-0345
Web site <www.elton-wolf.com>

ISBN   1-58619-075-X

Library of Congress   99-67485

DEDICATION

To
The Nameless & Formless Creator,
To all Adepts & lovers of the mystic Word—
To Kirpal, Lion of Mercy—whose unfathomable Light sustains me;
To all who walk the way of love, earth-stewardship & service;
To family, friends, &, not least of all,
To you, good reader.

This book—
in the form of its memories,
experiences and message,
was a priceless gift to the writer
which he gratefully passes on.
All net proceeds from its sale
are to be donated to charity.

F O R E W O R D

*I*t was both a privilege and a pleasure to be asked to write the Foreword to *Journey to the Luminous.* I have known the author for over twenty-seven years, and although we live a continent apart on opposite seacoasts, our paths have crossed many times both in North America and in India where much of his incredible story takes place. I write from the perspective of being a long-time student of comparative religion (both East and West) and of spirituality, a teacher of peace studies, and simply as a fellow traveler on life's journey. And what an exciting journey of discovery Arran Stephens has been on, beginning in his teens as he struggled to find life's meaning and purpose.

His early odyssey took him from his native British Columbia to California and New York, as he explored the venues of the artist and the excesses of the times. We relive with him the turbulent era of the sixties and share in auspicious encounters with Allen Ginsberg, Eden Abhez, and others on the leading edge of the counterculture. Then, fueled by an intense inner yearning, Arran embarks on a painstaking search to find a genuine spiritual mentor. After some false starts and promising leads, in 1964, he learns of the great Indian sage and mystic adept, Sant Kirpal Singh Ji Maharaj. That first contact awakens a deep recognition and triggers several profound mystical experiences. As a result, his life undergoes a transformation. After a deep meditation on the 12th of January 1967, Arran "decides" to leave all to visit his mentor in India, but without requisite permission. Later, however, as he departs for the airport, he receives a personal letter from Kirpal Singh dated and mailed on 12th January, inviting him to come! Since then—now over thirty years later, Arran remains deeply involved in the study and practice of an age-old, yet surprisingly modern spiritual path—not as a monastic recluse—but as a civic-minded family man and highly successful pioneer in several natural foods enterprises.

Journey to the Luminous is very much in the tradition of books written by seekers who have turned inwards and eastward to reclaim their spiritual roots, such as Paul Brunton's *Search in Secret India,* Julian Johnson's *The Path of the Masters,* Irene Tweedy's *Chasm of Fire,* and Andrew Harvey's *Journey to Ladakh.*

In *Journey to the Luminous* the reader is introduced to the age-old teachings of the Masters of Sant Mat, which in modern times goes back more than five hundred years to Kabir and Guru Nanak. The twentieth century has seen four great teachers in this tradition, beginning with Hazur Baba Sawan Singh (1858-1948). It was Hazur's spiritual successor who took Arran under his wing and directed his young student to keep a detailed journal of what he saw, heard, and experienced of ashram life and his travels crisscrossing the subcon-

F O R E W O R D

tinent. Over half of the book unfolds in Sant Kirpal Singh Ji's (1894-1974) inimitable presence.

With loving care, Arran weaves the times and teachings of his mentors into the tapestry of his own growth and struggles. The pages overflow with picturesque descriptions of life in India, including details of trips to the pristine Himalayas, to the dusty byways of rural villages, and to shrines and pilgrimage centers. Descriptions of the hubbub of chaotic crowded cities and the contrasting oasis-like serenity of ashram life provide an evocative backdrop for the book's narrative thread. Many of his accounts reveal things which defy explanation by ordinary standards of understanding, including miraculous healings and the sudden appearance of the radiant form of the Masters to individuals many thousands of miles away in times of need.

The reader is provided a rare opportunity to witness the daily activities of living Saints and their interactions with people of all walks of life—from presidents and princesses to simple rural workers. One encounters in action the deep humanity of these servants of humankind, as well as their extraordinary qualities of transvision, protection, and access to inner spiritual dimensions. We are treated to memorable meetings with Raghuvacharya, renowned among the yogis of Haridwar, who late in his lifespan of one hundred thirteen years, became an advanced practitioner of the inner path, and we encounter a wide range of humanity from venerable Tibetan Lamas to two former hardened criminals whose lives had become transformed.

Bereft at the passing of his Master in 1974, Arran plunges into the search for his successor, and, finally, in 1978, is led to the mystic poet Sant Darshan Singh who provides balm for his saddened spirit, as well as a mystic confirmation of the continuing lineage. Over the following years Arran spends many periods in Darshan's presence, and regales us with stories of his spiritual acumen and wit, recounting sublime sessions that often began in the hours well past midnight. As a fellow student in the Sant Mat tradition, I also had the good fortune to be present at some of these sessions. Sant Darshan Singh was an attentive and humble being whose twinkling eyes shed palpable beams of light. He encouraged Arran to publish his recollections. This work evolved naturally to include many profound experiences with Master Darshan, including an account of the latter's conscious departure from this world in 1989.

Sant Rajinder Singh succeeded Sant Darshan Singh as the spiritual guide of the unbroken Sant Mat lineage, now known in the West as the Science of Spirituality. Over the past decade, Sant Rajinder has traveled to every continent, extending his message of love, peace and unity throughout the world to millions of people.

In the book's final chapters, Arran speaks movingly, yet candidly of his times with the present Master in the Pacific Northwest and in India. These accounts reveal Rajinder Singh's extraordinary qualities as spiritual Adept, as well as his basic human goodness. Like his predecessors, he teaches free of charge, a method of inversion through meditation, enabling aspirants to connect with their own divine Inner Light and with the Celestial Sound-current—the source of all creation. This eternal principle has been referred to in many of the world's great religious and spiritual traditions as Word, Logos, Naam, Kalma, Shabd, Sonorous Light, Voice of the Silence, etc. The Adepts of the inner path, ancient and modern, have emphasized the importance of integrating ethical living with daily meditation to ensure steady spiritual progress. A few of the side-benefits of meditation are: stress-reduction, improved memory and concentration, inner peace, and the development of a more loving, accepting attitude towards others.

As the 20th century draws to a close, Arran witnesses the positive response from large numbers of people throughout the world to the teachings of the Mystic Adepts. Besides the rare boon of associating with three highly unique spiritual teachers in one lifetime, the author acknowledges other benefactors. I was moved to read of his friendship with the then elderly Dr. Edmond Bordeaux-Szekely, translator of the Aramaic *Essene Gospel of Peace* and of his meetings with the eclectic Ram Dass.

In *Journey to the Luminous*, the reader encounters an individual's struggle with the apparent paradoxes of the spiritual life: effort and grace, separation and union, death and life, pain and ecstasy. One glimpses the profoundly transformative personal relationship which lies at the heart of mysticism—that of the competent adept and the sincere wayfarer.

Arthur Stein, Ph.D.
Professor of Political Science,
Co-founder of the Center for Nonviolence and Peace Studies,
University of Rhode Island, Wakefield, RI
July, 1999

PREFACE

Journey to the Luminous may be a strange story, but it is true.

At fifteen, my loving parents drew apart and the secure, trusting world I had known until then imploded. Without family or friends, I was forced to scramble for survival and identity on some of the meaner streets of Los Angeles and San Francisco. Two years later, broken in mind and spirit, I took refuge in an unusual monastery near the summit of Mt. Chatsworth, where my spiritual quest was ignited through a succession of baffling encounters with a mysterious inner Light. Burning with questions, I left the monastery and its unsatisfactory theology in search of answers. In the three years that followed, I entered the shadowland of addiction, and the wondrous inner spring dried up. In my darkest hours, suffering and heart-prayers attracted the inner Light yet again, and with an intelligence beyond my reckoning, It led me from the abyss. Through a succession of remarkable and incredibly timed events, I received an invitation to consciously embark upon the journey Home, and to meet the human manifestation of my radiant Guide.

In 1967, at twenty-three, I joyously embraced the relative austerity of ashram life in mystic India, fortunate to have as my mentor, one of the great universal spiritual teachers of the 20th Century. "Write down what you see and hear, that you may not forget," Sant Kirpal Singh Ji Maharaj advised me, soon after I arrived. The diary entries that followed became the genesis of this book. Seven glorious, yet sometimes tortuous months passed in his quickening presence. Fervent, not yet half-baked, I returned to the West in the peak of the hippie revolution, and started a little business based on the principle of service, while carrying on intense spiritual practice.

While shuttling between cultures and continents over the next thirty years, I recorded priceless conversations and teachings of three widely revered Mystic Adepts of our time. Each embodied unique dimensions of what is possible in human evolution.

As artist, idealist and businessman (an admittedly odd combination), I was privileged to participate in the birth and flowering of the natural foods and environmental movements in the Sixties and Seventies, which led to active involvement with various entrepreneurial vehicles that continue to this day. The blessings of wife, family, friends, associates, co-workers and fellow wayfarers have added untold human dimensions and responsibility to the mystic journey. The great poet-saint Darshan once advised me, "the purpose of power is to protect." What a lesson for anyone in a position of authority!

Despite the swirl at the edge, I have sought the solitudes of a hermit in the luminous heart. The mystic heart referred to is not beating in the chest, but radiating behind the eyes. When we reach its sacred precincts, we realize that we are not this changing body, nor the egoic personality, nor the outer world we have become identified with. When the boundaries between Self and the Overself begin dissolving, we discover that we are eternal and very luminous.

The well-traveled and most ancient Path which threads my account is not religious-specific yet honors the essence of all spiritual traditions and all great teachers. In truth, the Way remains beyond description—when experienced, only then can it be known. The message, while very, very old (as old as humanity itself), remains immediate, verifiable, and within reach. Countless, the starting points; myriad, the paths; names of the Nameless resound by the thousands; innumerable, the lovers—but the Destination and Beloved are One. Ultimately, *we* are One. Each awakening to the homeward journey to Oneness is unpredictable, unique and filled with many adventures, at least from a human perspective.

If any wayfarers discover some resonance, a little glow, some fragrance in the pages ahead, then my job is done. The imperfect "pipe" takes no credit, and begs a thousand pardons where his rust has tinted the pure elixir.

> *The Sun is risen! In its vast dazzle*
> *Every lamp is drowned.*
> *- Jalal u'Din Rumi*

Note: About the cover art, the artist has attempted to represent the archetypal tunnel connecting the physical and the Beyond, through which all must pass—either at death, or before—for those who have made the transition through spiritual practice, or by sudden awakening. Entering the vast cave is the separated seeker, propelled by longing for return, connected by Logos; at the end, the Luminous. Along the journey, he discovers the radiant Guide in its various guises, the Protector of the traveler, and realizes his own true nature as soul. As the prodigal soul draws nearer to its distant destination, it begins glowing brighter and brighter, ultimately eclipsing several temporal suns. Its own Light is the very essence the Supreme Being placed there in the beginning of existence.

Along the luminous path, the image of a moth and Flame has often flared in the inspired imagination of mystic poetry. Borrowing Shah Jehan's carpet (adjacent page), I took liberties, crafting the image of a radiant nebula at the center and a seeker-moth at the edge, poised in flight, a creature intoxicated with wonder and ardor in the presence of what it lives—and dies for. Its "death" is not really death, but a transformation of consciousness—like the phoenix that rises from its ashes.

TABLE OF CONTENTS

TABLE OF CONTENTS

"Bolan Pass," Northwestern Frontier, India, 1872.
Watercolor by great-grandmother Agnes Cripps

1

The Radiant Sun of which we speak, never sets;
Our World is upheld by its Light.[1]

The past forms the basis of our present life and the intricate relationships we have with everything and everyone. If we consider our evolution from a spiritual perspective, we may perceive a slow but inexorable progress from the darkness of ignorance towards the fully conscious Light of our real essence. Each is placed in circumstances uniquely critical to awakening, but, like Sleeping Beauty, our soul awaits her Prince.

My parents were farmers and artists—our sixty-acres were caringly wrested from the unspoiled forests of Vancouver Island, with mountains rising on three sides. For awhile we lived in a hand-hewn log-house overlooking the Goldstream Valley.

Lt. Gen. J.M. Cripps

Recollections of My Indian Career, the gilded leather-bound autobiography of my great-grandfather, General Cripps, fired my vivid child's imagination. Its musty pages detailed life in colonial India from 1839 to 1878. *Recollections* contains a number of old photographs and twenty-five exquisite original watercolors by great-grandmother Agnes—of tombs, temples, bullock carts, rivers, and mountain passes in India. Grandmother Cripps was born at Peshawar in India's Northwestern Frontier. In my mind's eye, India's mystery beckoned, like a distant voice from a faded dream.

The author, 1948

In my eleventh year I was sent to summer Bible camp. Religion was a huge mystery to this otherwise unchurched boy, soon to be immersed in resounding sermons, hell-fire warnings, salvation's promise, verse memorization and the love of Jesus. One day the minister called me to his office and asked, "Do you want to be saved from eternal damnation in the name of our Savior?" "Yes!" "Then you are saved!" I was thusly dismissed, somewhat under-whelmed, for I had imagined salvation as supernaturally tangible, and momentarily mourned the vacuum. Nevertheless,

"Fortified barracks at Rawalpindi" watercolor by Agnes Cripps, Northwestern Frontier, India, 1872.

a natural prattle with the divine began in my heart. The old hymn *"He Walks With Me,"* swam in my consciousness as a form of reality, but my askings were mostly confined to finding lost marbles or winning first place in the race.

I felt called to the ministry, to find the best door to God. Learning of my zeal, Dad took me to the pristine forest behind the farm, a place of extreme beauty and peace. *"Arra-boy, this is our church; this is our cathedral,"* he gestured with a sweep of hand as we stood overlooking the verdant Goldstream Canyon at our feet, while firs and cedars towered above. A whisper of distant waterfalls and wind caressed the moment, imprinting it. I then entered his faith of nature-communion. Organized religion, its institutions and ministers, he felt, often imprisoned, rather than freed the spirit. He wrote:

> *The time will never come / When He will turn His face*
> *From rich or poor, or close the door / On any creed or race...*
> *For when you call upon the Lord / It never is too late.* ©

One day two friends and I stood quietly in chest-high ferns in another glade of that sacred forest. An enchanting ringing seemed to come from everywhere, within and nowhere—the Player unseen. When asked if they could hear it too, my pals looked at me blankly. In the years to come I would discover many who listened deeply to this same creational tone. Wordsworth glorified *sermons in stones* and *books in rivulets;* Thoreau attuned to his *distant drummer;* and Plato listened deeply to the *Music of the Spheres.*

Mum had a wonderful way of enabling others to see unnoticed beauties—the pattern in a stone, the color of a leaf, a tiny wildflower springing from emerald moss, water dancing in sunlight, maidenhair ferns waving on a wet canyon wall. She knew by heart the Latin names of every herb and plant in our bio-region. As well, she brought homemade cookies to the abandoned elderly, and comforted the sick. Her strength and character inspired many.

Dad raised unique varieties of vegetables, berries, and fruits. Renouncing modern chemicals

Goldstream Park, 1953

and mechanization, he discovered simple, economical methods to strengthen soil fertility and the health of plants. The message of his life could be distilled into a single phrase; "Leave the soil better than you found it." He extolled the virtues of the lowly earthworm and of mulching,[2] and more than a thousand songs flowed from his pen, despite an inability to read a note of music. In my twelfth year, he took me night hunting on one of the backfields of the farm, where he shot a deer. The next morning, when the doe was recovered and butchered, a remarkably human-looking fetus slid out. Overcome with remorse, he never touched his guns, nor ate venison again.

Goldstream Berry Paradise—our farm—was sold the following year. Along with an idyllic childhood, I was parted from Dizzy, my beloved cat. I called him Dizzy because he would turn like a whirling dervish whenever I circled my finger in front of his face. We were closer than words could convey.

From the pristine Island, we traveled by ferry across the Straits, then by train, south to smoggy Los Angeles, where Dad pursued his musical dreams. At thirteen I soon discovered that gang culture permeated the schools and the streets. A teenager had to become tough and wary to survive.

BEGINNING OF THE BEAT

Several months after settling into our rented hacienda in the Hollywood Hills, one hot afternoon while watering the garden, a lean, orange-white tom-cat walked up the front steps straight towards me. Beneath the grime, there was a remarkable resemblance to my old friend. "Dizzy, is that you?" I whispered. As soon as I circled my forefinger in the air, that scraggly animal started to turn around in circles. Immediately he was purring and blissfully rubbing my leg. I swept him into my arms, and ran to the house, yelling, "Look, everyone, it's Dizzy!" Somehow, he crossed the Juan de Fuca Strait, and traveled 1,500 miles overland to find his boy in the middle of a city of millions.

One of Dad's songs, *The Lord Looks After His Own* was selected as the theme-piece for a feature Disney film, on the condition that all "Lord" references were deleted, but he refused to change what he felt was a true inspiration—and thus the "Big Time" passed him by.

> *When winter creeps down and down the mountains,*
> *Turns the waterfalls to crystal fountains,*
> *the Lord looks after His own...*
>
> *Gone is the glory of the sun, gone is the winter rain,*
> *Though only blue notes fill the air, lovely spring will come again.*
>
> *Though life will bring you tears and sorrow,*
> *All men will share that great tomorrow,*
> *The Lord looks after His own.© —Rupert Stephens*

At fifteen, my secure, trusting world abruptly ended, and our family scattered to the winds, each our separate way. I became a street kid, and struggled to survive as an artist (thankfully, after a short unhappy spell, Mum and Dad were reunited for the rest of their long lives). For several desperate years I identified with the Beat generation and its icons. The beat and the bohemian were a rebellious lot pre-dating the Hippie era. Painters, sculptors, poets, jugglers, musicians, anarchists, and scoundrels, all sought something not quite definable, yearning to break through the self-prison to find, to know, to be fulfilled with purpose, to dance with the muse. I absorbed the best art I could from my contemporaries, in an effort to find my style, if not my self. One of my poems appeared in *The Mendicant—Poetry Journal* (1960).

Substance abuse and wild living characterized the Sixties. Scrawled on Venice and North Beach alleyways and cafe walls were its pagan slogans: "Art is love is God," and "Blessed, blessed oblivion...It's Cool & Cool is everything." Rebellion, anarchy, booze, drugs—soft, hard, psychedelic, uppers, downers, promiscuity, madness and drunkenness were cool, and God was "dead" unless He or She or It existed as a reflection somewhere in a riff of Bird's alto sax or a moment in poetry. The most memorable mescaline insights were back-door, trap-door entries to lower astral, telepathic, ancestral, animal, comic book, surreal stream-of-consciousness places where matter thinned enough to allow some flotsam and jetsam of paranormal awareness to slip through. How many of my peers had I seen consumed by drugs, dragged away and locked up, violated and forgotten?

> *I have seen the best minds of my generation*
> *destroyed by madness, starving, hysterical, naked,*
> *dragging themselves through the negro streets at dawn*
> *looking for an angry fix...*
> *HOWL & Other Poems,* by Allen Ginsberg

The Beat appellation was derived from beatific—as in "beatific vision," and true to form, not all of this generation were on oblivion's path. Kahlil Gibran's *Prophet*, Paul Reps' *Zen Flesh, Zen Bones*,[3] Aldous Huxley's *Doors of Perception*, the Zen reflections of D.T. Suzuki, and Alan Watts offered serene enigmas, some Eastern philosophy, and cool poetry.

I met a few true seekers, and had in fact befriended the reclusive and inspiring Eden Abhez, vegetarian and author of the song *Nature Boy* made world-famous by crooner Nat King Cole. But every hope, each oasis, turned into an empty mirage. The sun might be rising for others, but mine was a furtive life in self-imposed shadows. Often broke, I slept on the beach, drunk on cheap wine or high on drugs, sometimes crawling into a cardboard box to attempt escape from the cold. When hungry, I ate discarded food, or begged. Misery was my companion, relieved and exacerbated by illusive excesses, a course which took but two years to break body, mind, and spirit. Like Rimbaud, I tried to string garlands between the stars and dance, but could sustain neither the tightrope nor the frenzy. Having known hunger, poverty, constant street danger, and addiction, by seventeen I was a haggard alcoholic and drug-dazed atheist who railed against the Author of pain. One day dragged into the next, as my mind grew black as Poe's raven. Jimmy-the-Beard, a derelict poet appeared on the boardwalk and taunted me with a line from E.E.Cummings *"How do you like your blue-eyed boy, Mr. Death?"* And he walked on, cackling.

With no further will to continue my miserable existence, I dragged my feet across the cloying sand and entered the waves on Venice Beach. Pounding, chilling surf frothed up to my neck, push-pulling my rag-doll body through the vortex. *"Soon, no more torment,"* I thought, before succumbing to the cold, cold sea.

As I slipped beneath the waves, inexplicable serenity began to glow within, coupled with an urgent beckoning to discover life's purpose and begin anew. It was not too late! I struggled to disengage from the powerful undercurrents, and emerged at the foaming edge. Shivering, I staggered across the expanse of gray sand and fog. Tormented, yes. But quitter, not.

1. Unless specific credits are given, various sayings, paintings, verses, interpretations and many of the photographs herein are the author's. Photos by the author are identified by (AS); other photo credits are unknown.

2. "My earthworms, in the Utopia I had created for them, worked day and night to improve my soil by burrowing through it, digesting and spreading humus..." *Sawdust Is My Slave* in its entirety can be ordered at no cost from Nature's Path Foods, 7453 Progress Way, Delta, BC, Canada, V4G 1E8 or, downloaded from www.naturespath.com

3. I met the elderly Paul Reps in Vancouver in the Seventies. A close friendship ensued which lasted until his death. Paul confided to me that he had received initiation from the Indian sage, Sant Kirpal Singh in the early Sixties.

2

Despite brief hope, I could not pry away depression's insidious and shadowy fingers. The words of the poet Mayakovsky haunted me: *"I am as lonely as the only eye of a man on his way to the blind."* In a Venice Beach coffeehouse, an equally burnt-out comrade described a monastic retreat, not far away. "'The Fountain of the World' sits near the top of Chatsworth Mountain," he told me. His eyes were bright with hope: "It's free, and we would be welcome, as long as we follow the rules and do some work. The folks there practice brotherly love and walk barefoot!" "Brotherly love? Walk barefoot?" I asked, incredulous. "It has to do with their vows of personal poverty and non-injury to living things. Some of their buildings are built around trees, rather than having them cut down. We can stay as long we like. It's worth checking out!" We packed our few belongings and headed for the hills. Like a wounded dog, I craved a quiet glade, a tree to rest beneath.

The Fountain of the World was high above the smoggy Los Angeles basin, surrounded by tall eucalyptus, poplar, and pine, boulders the size of buildings, and dry sunburnt hills. Almost from the minute we left the car, soft zephyr-like breezes started sweeping away the cobwebs from my mind. Obligatory group sessions called "Concentrations" were held in the main hall each evening, where thirty or so monastics would stand in circles with closed eyes, hands upturned, chanting such affirmations as "Love One, Love One..." or, "Be positive, be positive..." over and over, from very slow and low to very fast and high-pitched. Despite initial feelings of embarrassment and weirdness, I eventually settled into the routine. One week after arrival, I had an experience that profoundly changed the course of my life.

During an evening Concentration I became quite detached from the outer surroundings and entered a condition of heart-flow prayer—a sort of unceasing implore to the Unknown. While gazing with closed eyes into the dark void, I became cognizant of a comet-like light speeding from the distance straight toward the center of my head, growing brighter and brighter with every moment. A wave of circular, evanescent, golden whiteness burst upon my vision. Then came another bright comet, and another, unceasing, rhythmic, and mysterious. It was as though I had entered the living heartbeat of the Cosmos. In that heart of Light I experienced intoxicating waves of unconditional love. The body and the world simply ceased to exist. All that remained was boundless scintillating radiance and awesome energy, proceeding simultaneously in all directions. After what seemed an eternity—perhaps only a few minutes—this reality/vision subsided, intruded upon by the activities of monastic life.

This was the first conscious taste of that intangible something, for which I had been blindly groping. With this illuminating experience came an all-know-ingness, a love freed of egoism. Once separated from that blissful state, however, numerous questions and doubts assailed me.

"Surely Elder Nikona will know," I thought, as I approached the monastery's head. With mixed emotions I asked about my mysterious experi-ence. Elder Nikona admitted, "I do not know what this Light is, my son. But I do know that by it you have experienced a blessing of a very high order." I excused myself to walk alone in the night, lost in thought, questioning, wondering: *To whom can I turn for help? What is this Light? Am I chosen for a higher calling, or have I lost my mind? Who am I? What is my destiny?*

Over the next few days I sought from others but drew blank and unsatisfactory responses, as well as questioning looks.

One night I was awakened in total darkness from a dreamless sleep by a con-stant thundering roar on all sides, as though a gigantic waterfall of sound were pressing into my being. Inability to lift even a finger led to desparate panic. "God! I'm dead! Help me!" I cried, though no sound escaped numb lips. Physical paralysis and lack of bodily sensation was complete. With Herculean effort I eventually began moving fingertips, then toes, and gradually the rest of my alienated body—which seemed nor more than a husk in which the real me lived.

I began to search through the monastery's well-stocked library, and discovered a translation of the *Bhagavad Gita* (The Celestial Song), an immortal discourse between Krishna and his disciple Arjuna, the warrior-prince. The *Gita* examined morality, religion, duty, yoga, meditation, and the goal of human existence, an elusive goal that could be attained by realization of one's higher self. Self-realization led to ultimate illumination and freedom from the cycle of births and deaths.

Something inside began resonating to the Gita's ancient message. One passage in particular whispered to my slumbering memory and set it astir:

> *Let the yogi sit in Sidh-aasan, in a place neither too high nor too low,*
> *...And, fixing gaze at the root of the nose, He should make his mind as*
> *still as a candle's flame in a windless place.*

Hidden from others, I began to sit straight-backed, left leg folded under, right leg folded on top, hands resting upturned on each other, thumbs touching, eyes closed. For some inexplicable reason, this posture seemed like the most natural and obvious thing to do. The burning pain which quickly developed in my westernized legs was excruciating, but with determination the time for sitting was gradually increased each successive day from a few minutes to half an hour, from half an hour to an hour, and longer. Whenever I sat like this, after a few minutes the golden Light would return, imparting a delectable inner state. Each encounter left me strengthened; each plunge into the billowing radiance helped heal the sickness in my heart.

I often slipped from the dorm while others slept, following a long and precarious trail through bushes and rocks to sit alone atop a huge prehistoric boulder over-looking the dark valley below. These late vigils under the glittering stars were rewarded with further joyous and radiant experiences, though phantasmagoria of the lower mind sometimes left me shaken. A cosmic, benign force is always in service of aspiring humanity, but a corrupt power may also assail and test one's resolve. Whenever this happened, as it did from time to time, I persevered in solitary struggle, intensely invoking God's protection, throwing myself at His mercy, even shedding tears. Then, as reward, like candy for a child, the Light would return and banish the phantoms.

Two months passed. Increasing pressure was being brought to bear on me to renounce the world and become a full-fledged monastic brother. This vow meant giving up money, property (not that I had any), family, and friends on the outside, and living a life subservient to a puzzling theology with Krishna Venta, their departed founder, at the top. From talking with his few remaining original followers, and reading magazine articles and mimeographed pages, I learned that Venta, a white American, boldly claimed that he was none other than the long-awaited and final Messiah, the Buddha, Krishna, Isaiah and Jesus all rolled into one. I was neither ready nor willing to surrender life and freedom in blind obedience to anyone. To the questions that dogged my existence, I longed for answers that rang true on all levels.

On the day of my ordination, I decided to leave. Each step through the grounds felt as though immense psychic weights were about my ankles, making movement exceedingly difficult. I looked around and noticed several crones directing their focus upon me. With every ounce of will I struggled up the last few stairs leading to the open road, but once off the Fountain's property, my feet and mind took wings. I ran and ran till I could run no more, down that mountain road.

The Lake Shrine: With high hopes, and no money, I found myself at the gates of the Self-Realization Lake Shrine in the Santa Monica Mountains, founded by the yogi-saint Paramahansa Yogananda. The peaceful, meditative aura and jewel-like beauty of the lake, the white swans, and the bright atmosphere drew me many times over the next few months. I'd hitchhike there from Venice Beach, to meditate and read Yogananda's *Autobiography of a Yogi*, in which I discovered numerous references to the divine Light experienced by saints and seekers of various times, places, and faiths. The accounts of India's great sages, who were like scientists of the spirit, beckoned powerfully. Yogananda was a Christ-like man, but he had consciously died in 1952. Where to turn? I wasn't able to recognize his exalted stature among the kind and helpful followers I met.

Unnoticed and in secret, I spent most of one full-moon night sitting in the lotus posture by the serene lake. Wrapped in silence for many hours, I observed the ever-unfolding panorama within. As I went deeper and deeper, for the first time I began to see radiant visions of great yogis and Saints. How could I reconcile such sublime experiences with my wretched life?

My difficulty, like that of many seekers, was that initial mystical experiences were quite overwhelming, if not bewildering. I had very few reference points. Then there were the claims put forth by a plethora of teachers and followers. How was one to determine their validity and reach? One thing for certain, this new-found Light was the source of good and holy power, perhaps the unseen source of all life and Intelligence in the universe. The Bible speaks of it:

> *The light of the body is the eye.*
> *If therefore thine eye be single*
> *Thy whole body shall be full of light.—Matthew 6:22*

Pythagoras, the Grecian mathematician, philosopher and mystic had referred to the "Science of Light," which, when mastered, can alter the structure of matter. With its aid, Pythagoras demonstrated his mastery of the elements by controlling an eagle and a rampaging bear, which obeyed his higher will.

A remarkable experience involving the power of this same Light befell some friends and me in 1963 in San Francisco. While strolling through a late-night crowd, one member of our party skipped ahead onto busy Market Street and directly into the path of a speeding bus. I was suddenly aware of subconscious gears shifting; the prescient "observer" came forth both to witness and partici-pate. Everything and everyone appeared dreamlike, slowing down. Into this thickness, I felt a sudden rush of adrenaline and cried loudly, "Look out!" A brilliant flash of Light enveloped the entire scene. Everything stopped, frozen in time-silence—the bus, the people, and all sound. In that split-second pause, only the would-be victim was able to break the stasis and move free from the path of certain death. The eerie stillness was replaced with the roar of everything. A brief suspension of time and space became enveloped in Light; a life was saved! A mysterious miracle had occurred, and all who were witness were profoundly thankful.

One refrain I would often hear in the search ahead: The Holy Book, or the body of teachings, was now to be considered as the Master, the Guru. I wanted an unsealed revelation, a living Teacher of the highest stature who could answer all my burning questions. However, my periods of God-longing were short lived and unstable, satellites partly shot through the Earth's atmosphere, only to be recaptured and pulled back by the gravity of desire and attachment. From 1961 to 1964, with one or two exceptions, the springs of Divine Light all but dried up as this prodigal wandered and squandered the spiritual capital that we all come into this world with, and I again sank into the abyss of addiction and despair. The inevitable dark night of the soul engulfed me.

Following a solo exhibition of my paintings at a major San Francisco art gallery (Fall of 1963), I visited lovely Mendocino County, where rolling grassy hills invitingly beckoned. I gladly followed. In long and solitary walks came flickerings of renewal and bonding with the Earth Mother. I marveled at the way the sun's rays filtered through the leaves of a huge oak tree, and then to my eyes, breaking into prisms and rainbows. The Inner Light, which had been lost for two years, began to resurface in the form of myriad sparklings across the wash of external sight. In a poem of sorts, I attempted to capture that fleeting ecstasy:

> *Lending from his splendor, the Sun said,*
> *"Take a little PEACE of me,*
> *And let it be your Light for the night."*

Too soon, alas, the Light dissipated. I was unable to hold to it, but knew that from the Luminous my peace and salvation would one day come, if only I could peel away the layers that separated me from it. For now, my spiritual quest was sullied, and a rude but merciful awakening was speeding toward me like a night train careening around a hidden bend.

Etching by Gustave Doré

3

None is poor, O Bhikha.
Everyone has rubies in his bundle;
But how to open the knot
He does not know,
And therefore he is a pauper.
— Bhikha Sahib (1713-1763)

En route to Tangiers, I arrived in New York's Greenwich Village. By prearranged plan I was to connect with my friend, who had my tickets and traveling money. Snow was falling as I waited by Washington Square where the fountains had already turned to ice. Hours passed with no familiar face in sight. When the last coffeehouse closed, I was on the street, freezing, thinking of my mother, my fate and survival. With suitcase in hand, less than forty dollars and thin clothing, I walked and walked the bitter streets, not knowing where to go.

There was a cruel beauty in the patterns of snowflakes swirling about the cold streetlights. Somehow I survived the long night and those that followed.

According to a Hindu proverb, one uses a thorn to remove a thorn. Suffering was to be the dross-burning fire and my journey's goad. After many difficulties, a spare room and studio space were found. While I prepared works for an art exhibition, the quest, like a smoldering coal under dead ashes, was uncovered by a favorable wind and re-ignited.

In the basement of Weiser Books, I discovered the *Hundred Thousand Songs of Milarepa* by the great medieval saint of Tibet; *With Mystics and Magicians in Tibet* by Alexandra David-Neel; *The Secret of the Golden Flower*—a sacred text on Chinese mysticism; *All and Everything* and *Meetings with Remarkable Men* by G.I. Gurdjieff; Osborne's biography of the silent sage Ramana Maharshi; and other influential texts. While the world outside was covered by an eerie mantle of ever-deepening white snow, alone in my room in the orb of imagination I felt like a yogi perched in a grotto among the crags, the neighboring walls deep canyons, their windows cave-mouths.

After a lapse of years, meditation recommenced. In the absence of a spiritual guide, I developed a simple technique of visualizing two triangles, one above and one below, and would bring them together in my mind's eye. If concentration were unflinching, at the moment of their intersecting a spiritual Light would flood the darkness. After some practice, the radiance began to disclose the presence of a brilliant figure within its center, a form filled with luminosity and power so intense, the features were indistinguishable. This I took to be the illumined Buddha-Christ-Self.

I saw my body astrally transparent, with its multicolored *chakras* revealed. The secret of yogic heat employed by Tibetan yogis, was briefly unveiled as psychic fire from the thousand-petalled lotus (located in a higher dimension paralleling the cranial area) was drawn down in a steady stream into the navel plexus. Upon reaching that center, a glowing heat spread to every part of my body. I tried to capture the transparency of the subtle body with paint and brush on canvas, The results, although interesting, were but crude and inaccurate material representations. At times of detached focus, the room's atmosphere became filled with a ringing thunder. These brief and isolated experiences blessed and lifted me above an otherwise sordid existence.

My paintings were exhibited at the Thompson Galleries in Greenwich Village, alongside two large and rare original oil paintings by Gustave Doré, the nineteenth-century artist. Doré, renowned for his astounding black and white illustrations for *The Rime of the Ancient Mariner*, Dante's *Divine Comedy*, and Milton's *Paradise Lost*, was not known for his oil paintings, which were filled with a sublime use of color, illumination, form, and depth. On the opening night reception, a terrific thunderstorm burst over the city.

Studio, New York City, 1964

Not one buyer or reviewer showed up, even for priceless Dore! The exhibition was a flop. Apart from a few internal glimmerings, the past three and a half years had been a denial of all that was healthy and holy. I had been steeped in darkness, drugs and selfishness and was weary of the gutter. I craved discipline and order. At this crossroads, I was introduced to the local Gurdjieff meetings. The next nine months were spent avidly studying under the tutelage of philosopher-pianist Willem Nyland. During this period, I earned my bread as a grocery delivery boy, furniture-mover, and a waiter at the Paradox, a macrobiotic restaurant, while otherwise exploring new dimensions in art, diet, and intellectual pursuits.

Then in his late seventies, Nyland had spent twenty-four years off and on with the enigmatic George Gurdjieff in France, all while working in espionage for the Allies during both World Wars. Gurdjieff exerted tremendous influence over some of the most renowned writers, musicians, and philosophers of the West during the second quarter of this century. Nyland, in turn, was passing along what he had received, and was the best teacher I'd met so far.

The Gurdjieffian philosophy and "The Work," as his teachings in practice were known, contained traces of Truth gleaned during extensive travels and studies with Sufis in the Near and Far East. His principal teaching was that we are all *"asleep"* and must awaken in a higher sense through various esoteric practices, including self-remembering and "sacred dance." The dance involved movements synthesized from Mevlevi and other Middle Eastern dervish orders, aimed at bringing the participant into harmony with himself and the cosmos.

While benefiting from the practice of "self-remembering" in the context of a support group, an advanced teacher, and in solitude, I felt that some of Gurdjieff's ideas did not hold water. For example, he maintained that the soul perishes with the physical body at death; that man does not "have a soul, but has the *possibility* of *developing* a soul"; that reincarnation and transmigration do not exist; and that eating of meat develops will power. My lack of concurrence with such ideas did not endear me to certain members of the group. Gurdjieff's techniques aimed at shocking his students from their "sleep," but his bizarre methods have often been called into question. I was eventually left high and dry in Gurdjieff's mysterious intellectual desert. Rafael Lefort, one of his direct students later commented, "Gurdjieff was more than a teacher but less than a Master."[1] Who was I to know?

Nine months of intensive study nevertheless rewarded me with sharpened focus. I was grateful for the mental and work disciplines, and especially for a deeper exposure to the mystical verse of Jalal-u-'Din Rumi, a thirteenth century Sufi mystic Adept. I thirsted for living waters, the oasis of a perfected one, which Nyland opined no longer existed. He and others in "The Work" ridiculed my search as pure folly. But truth-yearning had grown white-hot intense. My destiny train was accelerating, and nothing could now derail it.

At this juncture I met Allen Ginsberg for the third time. He had recently returned from India, and loaned me *The Gospel of Sri Ramakrishna*, penned by biographer-disciple Mahendra.[2] This sublime spiritual treasure seriously affected the course of my quest. Its pages unfolded the awe-inspiring life of the nineteenth century Bengali saint, Ramakrishna, whose high degree of illumination was palpably present in his exquisite sayings, supported by the records of his spiritual experiences and affirmed by the subsequent attainments of his direct disciples. As I read on, I learned how Sri Ramakrishna sometimes engendered such a receptive condition in his students that a mere slap on the chest or a piercing glance was sufficient to send them soaring and absorbing into superconsciousness. Ramakrishna's holy and stainless life convinced me of the reality of the spiritual path, the necessity of a living adept as guide, and the requisite discipline of mind and senses. His loving devotion to and mystical union with God in a variety of forms clashed with practically everything I had learned.

A familiar pattern was emerging from my study of Ramakrishna and the lives of other saints. Part of it entailed sublimation of the energy path, directing it away from the senses, upward and inward to higher centers within the mind, and to dimensions beyond. I was convinced that the purity and self-control that Ramakrishna, Buddha, Jesus, Rumi, and others like them embodied were necessary to the path of spiritual success. It would not be an easy undertaking, for the powerful steeds of the five senses continuously drag the attention downward and outward into the world of matter and illusion. This worldly tendency runs counter to the inward and upward centripetal flow—back to our divine Origin.

When I returned the *Gospel* three weeks later, Allen was overjoyed. Practically jumping up and down, he explained, "The night you borrowed Ramakrishna, thieves broke into my apartment and stole my entire book collection. Your borrowing Ramakrishna was very auspicious for me! This is the only book not stolen!" And I thought, "Very auspicious for me, too!"

GLIMMERINGS

In the pursuit of transformation, alcohol, drugs and cigarettes fell away like dead skins. Animal flesh felt unwanted by my body. Meat, then fish and fowl and even eggs were discarded and replaced by the bounty of the vegetable kingdom. Accepting the discipline of continence with help from the constantly implored Divine, I turned from my former life. Because of this new way of living, the vitality of my dissipated body was renewed; various ailments disappeared, and with them, my haggard old-man appearance.

An unexpected meeting on a busy Eastside street with a former acquaintance validated my new course, as I learned the shocking news that our mutual friend, a talented twenty-one-year-old writer, had just been found dead in his flat from a drug overdose. After we went our separate ways, my heart, while saddened, overflowed with gratitude at being spared for the quest ahead.

My search took me to a kind and erudite Swami-monk at the Ramakrishna Vedanta Center, as well as to meetings by devotees of Sri Aurobindo.[3] Echoes of Truth were immanent in Aurobindo's words, in what he called the *"Light of the Super-mind,"* but he too was no more on the earth-plane. These nurturing steps were bringing me closer to the *life* of the Light. For example, it didn't particularly matter what group or spiritual practice I was being exposed to, for whenever I closed my eyes, an engulfing experience of universal Light would come. I went to the Church of Swedenborg to study the teachings of this eighteenth century mystic, and often escaped the busy and noisy streets to pray/meditate in Catholic cathedrals. Though inspired by the great teachers and their messages, like the saints' statuary, these churches were silent and lifeless. My longing heart was broadcasting prayers in all directions: "God, please send me a true Master!"

Where to go? All the great ones were gone from this world. Where was the *living* Master? Was he or she in some unknown monastery or village in Turkey, Tibet, Japan, or India? I had no clue. Since conditions in America did not, to my mind, seem favorable for such development, I looked to the East. I went to shipyards looking for work aboard Orient-bound freighters, but the door kept clanging shut. Resolved not to accept anyone less than a living Christ, a Ramakrishna, or a Rumi, I was determined to search and search until found.

Little did I realize, one doesn't *find* a Master. In the fullness of time, in response to the cry of the soul, *the Master finds you.*

---

1. Rafael Lefort, *Teachers of Gurdjieff* (According to inside sources, Rafael Lefort was the pseudonym for the well-known author and teacher, J.C. Bennett).

2. Ramakrishna, the Bhakta-Saint is not to be confused with the Hari Krishna movement.

3. Sri Aurobindo was a significant Indian philosopher, intellectual giant, authentic mystic and founder of the successful spiritual community, Auroville, in Pondicherry, India.

4

From 1964 to 1965, life revolved around art and the inner quest. After three
years abroad, my brother turned up at my seventh-floor walk-up apartment on
New York City's Lower Eastside. Godfrey's eccentric genius manifested in flowing, semi-abstract totemic sculptures; a boyhood apprenticeship with Kwagulth
chief Mungo Martin served him well.[1] Godfrey's murals and sculptures were
scattered over several continents in coffeehouses, galleries, collectors' homes
and a museum or two. Although hopeless with finances, his macho charm,
remarkable memory for poetry and storytelling made him the life of every
party. I had struggled to blossom in his shadow, but by now I was disenchanted
with the superficial art scene. Former wild and egocentric heroes toppled from
their pedestals, supplanted by worthier ones—the past masters of several spiritual traditions, who represented to me the pinnacle of human development.

One afternoon Godfrey returned with a large, empty leather portfolio found
abandoned in a nearby alley. Neatly printed on the inside were the name and
address of Paul Caponegro, one of the city's foremost nature photographers
who, coincidentally, was being groomed to succeed Willem Nyland. This chance
discovery seemed fraught with implications. I apprehended my quarry at the
dispersal of the next Gurdjieff meeting, and briefly explained my need to speak
privately. Paul laughed and set a time three days hence to meet at his New
York apartment. I anxiously counted the days and the hours.

When I arrived, Paul disappeared into the kitchen to prepare a pot of coffee,
allowing me an opportunity to inspect a collection of fascinating images on the
walls of his well-appointed home. Among studies of rocks and ferns were photo
portraits from a by-gone era. Judging by the subjects' looks and attire I pre-
sumed they were Eastern mystics. A tiny photograph of a white-turbaned man
with a long snow-white beard drew my attention like a magnet. His regal yet
otherworldly face was the epitome of beauty and serenity.[2]

While I stood witlessly staring, Paul entered the room and handed me a photograph of a different, yet equally extraordinary stranger.[3] In the moments that
followed, I stood transfixed before the rugged visage of one who radiated
power and compassion, his eyes aglow with inner bliss. As I held this otherwise
inanimate picture, subtle gears began shifting. The boundaries of matter began
to dissolve, exhilarating currents engulfed me; my spine tingled, and with open
eyes the periphery of vision sparkled. It felt like the top of my head was gently
opening into a universe of Light. Wave after surging wave of diaphanous luminosity billowed forth from the face in the photograph, yet simultaneously from
within my head. The lustrous eyes of the Familiar Stranger were within the

Sant Kirpal Singh Ji Maharaj (1894-1974)
This photograph was the first I had seen of the Master.
During one of his three world tours, an utter stranger approached
him on the street with the words, "Sir, you have the face of a prophet!"

center. I felt loved unconditionally. Then, from far away yet very distinctly, ten words formed in my consciousness: *"If God has a face, He must look like this."*

This was too much for any rational mind to absorb! Struggling for a point of reference, I broke away and recovered my senses. With the picture cradled in my hands, I walked over to Paul and asked, "Is he a Sufi?" "In a way, yes," he answered with a quizzical smile. "Is he still living?" I asked with trepidation, as all the great teachers I had so keenly read about were no more of this world. He nodded in affirmation. *Relief.* "Tell me more," I pried, but Paul changed the subject. Still bathing in the afterglow of my bewildering experience, I could hardly hear Paul's words. On leaving, he handed me a tattered book, and commented, "You may find this of interest." It was written by Kirpal Singh—the one in the second photograph.

I took home my threadbare treasure and read through the night, this detailed biography of a little-known nineteenth-century spiritual Adept who was known simply as Baba Ji (Baba Jaimal Singh). The book was however, far more than a biography. Every page opened up new yet ancient possibilities, explaining spirituality as a universal science, devoid of ritual, dogma, or blind belief. The book was a guide, a map and a genealogy in my search for truth. Levels of mystic experience were explained, affirming my limited excursions yet far transcending them. Kirpal Singh, the author and possibly a real living Saint, spoke eloquently of the teachings of Baba Ji and many other past Master-souls whose teachings were underpinned by deep practice of meditation on the inner Light and Celestial Sound-current:

> *It was, said Baba Ji, the path most economical in effort and the one most rewarding for reaching back to the Primal Source of all life and light. Its secret lay in the insight that if the soul was to merge back into the point from where it had descended, the way of ascent must be identical with that of descent. The Nameless One, when assuming Name and Form, had projected Itself into Shabd, Naam, Kalma or the Word. It was this spiritual current whose primary attributes were melody and effulgence that was responsible for all creation....All sages, in their own different ways, had testified to the working of the Word or Naam Power....*
>
> *The music and glory of the Word spread through all creation and permeated our being. If only the Atman [i.e. the individual soul] could be contacted with it, it could use this "string from the Nameless Lord" to reach His Door. But the soul in its downward descent had loosened the link and had forgotten its real nature. Acquiring the gross coverings of body and mind, it had lost sight of its native home and identified itself with its prison.[4]*

In spite of my peripheral experiences with the Sound and Light of Creation, returning to the Source of it all would require living help:

> Baba Ji indefatigably emphasized the necessity of a living Master for success in the field....The spiritual journey was not a matter of intellectual disquisition. It was a question of practical ascension. Without his enlivening touch the soul could not awaken from its slumber and get attuned to Naam. The Jiva Atman [the embodied soul] was too far lost in the gross material to contact Shabd on its own account.
> Besides, the inner way was not an easy one and even if the soul could transcend physical consciousness and enter the realms within, it could not proceed very far on its own...
> He did not promise spiritual attainment in some future life after death. He gave a taste of it here and now...[5]

As if a bell had been struck, my inner self responded radically to his message. Although he spoke in third person and made no self-claims, his words were redolent with authenticity. The name, Kirpal (pronounced *Kirpaul*) began to revolve in my mind like a rosary. Had I at long last found the Guide? On the last page of his book was an address in India. Taking the plunge, I wrote and asked for a blessing on my life. I was on the cusp of twenty-one.

Poor Paul! I returned to badger him with many a question. He was quick to point out that he wasn't a follower and maintained a healthy skepticism, but he confided, "I attended one of Kirpal Singh's talks on his 1963 world tour, which took place in a large church in Boston. 'Something' happened to me then which I have never experienced before or since. But first let me caution you that there are some Adepts from the East who have developed subjective powers which cannot be rationally or objectively evaluated." "Please continue," I asked, barely suppressing my excitement.

"From where I stood at the back of the church, I observed a sphere of bright golden-white Light above his head. This Light pulsated, spreading wave upon wave across the audience. It was the most extraordinary thing I have ever witnessed." Paul's non-devotee status made his testimony even more meaningful. The puzzle-pieces were falling into place. Meeting the Master in person became my passion. I was just picking up in this life where I left off in the last.

---

1. The Kwagulth are a First Nations people of the coastal areas of British Columbia, renowned for their woodcarving skills.

2. Hazur Baba Sawan Singh Ji (1858-1948).

3. Param Sant Kirpal Singh Ji (1894-1974).

4. Kirpal Singh, *A Great Saint Baba Jaimal Singh: His Life and Teachings*, (Delhi, India: SK Publications, 1993), pp. 85-86.

5. Ibid., p. 88.

5

After an agonizing wait, Kirpal Singh's first letter arrived, sealed in a slim, pale green envelope. Couched within his fatherly words was a tingling grace-current, and with it, a perceptible lightening of ancient burdens. He directed me to attend the local *satsang*, or "truth gathering" held every Sunday in downtown Manhattan.

I was then working as a waiter at the Paradox, an eclectic macrobiotic restaurant popular among the emerging counter-culture. Serving meals to the likes of many people of notoriety, jazz musicians, poets, artists, health seekers, and truth-seekers, I found the Paradox a fertile bed of new ideas. One evening, toward the close of business, I became involved in a philosophical discussion with a customer and Richard, the owner of the Paradox. As our exchange deepened, the customer glibly remarked, "I have heard it said that if you want to see God, close off your eyes and ears." As a soul on fire, I was willing to try anything, and, closing my eyes and ears to the external world, I found myself traveling through a luminous, starry universe. When I opened them two minutes later, I was stunned by the immediacy of a reality parallel to the one we are normally aware of.

The three of us left the following week for Washington, DC, to attend Kirpal Singh's seventy-first birthday celebration (he was in India at the time). Among the hundred or so celebrants, we met T.S. Khanna, an elderly disciple initiated in the 1930's who shared miraculous stories and his experiences with two contemporary Masters.

We stayed the night at Khanna's home, where Master Kirpal had resided a few months earlier on his second world tour, at a time, alas, when I was intensely searching, but unaware that only a few hundred miles away was the living Adept I was searching for. When I bedded down in the darkened living room, Kirpal Singh's full face unexpectedly appeared in front of me, created from particles of effulgent Light. For more than an hour, this remarkable vision remained until sleep drew its veil. In proportion to my experience, my faith in the competency of this Master was growing; I increasingly trusted that he would guide me back to God in this lifetime.

Over the next few weeks I often prayed, "Let me not die without the gift of Naam!" and submitted my written request for initiation. During the period of waiting, the Master-power twice reached down, past the barriers of mind and ego, deep into my dreams where my soul's essence was flung into the beyond. In the first dream-which-became-a-vision, Kirpal appeared, accompanied by his departed Master, Hazur Baba Sawan Singh floating in a royal blue sky. They sat cross-legged, hands folded, dressed in white raiment, knees almost touching, their unwavering gazes focused on me for more than an hour. I became filled with child-like wonder and gratitude as I looked back and forth from one Master to the other, absorbing their serene smiling faces, twinkling eyes, and radiant white beards. Unity flowed between them, to me, and back again. Something of eternity was conveyed, but mere words beggar description. Bliss flowed into my waking state for days afterwards.

In the second vision, my future Guide sat at a distance in rural India. Several devotees squatted before him on khaki-hued sand, under a bright cerulean sky. In his hands was a small pouch containing dust garnered from the threshold of his Master which he was about to pour upon the foundation stone of an *ashram*, or spiritual school. As he loosened the drawstrings and tipped the bag, its contents began to spill. Simultaneously, the dust became incandescent and flew across the distance into my eyes, blinding me with its intensity. Immediately my phoenix soul soared up through layers of ever-increasing brightness and cosmic melody. Later, upon returning to a numb and tingling body, I wept inconsolably, yet with residual inebriation. I had been torn from the bosom of reality, and desperately longed to return![1]

For weeks I lived in the hope of receiving his answer and daily checked the barren mailbox. Then, one happy day his letter arrived, I was accepted for initiation, and on the 28th of March, 1965, the local representative read me the instructions.[2] Preceding two meditation sittings, a detailed description of the inner regions, the ruling powers, and the charged names that allow passage through them—one for inner Light and another for inner Sound, were given. Finally, the rays of spiritual dawning filled the vacuum of my boyhood longing. My feet were on the Path at last.

Initiation has been described as both a re-birth, and an infusion of *attention* of an Adept to an aspirant, independent of the distance between them. While initiation is a foretaste and the introduction to a clear-cut scientific method of meditation and personal transformation, it is not a mere formula. Nor is it a graduation. "Perfection walks slowly and requires the hand of time," said Kirpal; permanent union with the Beloved is attained after a long journey, one which passes through thorns, rugged passes as well as soft flowering meadows. It may take several lifetimes, and *if* awakening ever seems sudden, it is the result of lengthy preparation—possibly the fruit of progress made in past lives, and the touch of a true Adept.

I left for a retreat in northern New England, which allowed a disciplined schedule of meditation balanced by hard physical work. Although some progress must have been made, I soon discovered how little my mind and senses were under control. In the wealth of *Sant Mat* (Path of the Masters) literature, there are frequent references to the various stages of the inner journey. The first great breakthrough is said to occur when the physical consciousness is transcended, and one enters the astral focus between and behind the eyes, and beholds the radiant lightform of the Guide who ushers the soul into higher regions. Continually frustrated in attempts to reach that coveted experience again, I resolved to shut myself in a small closet and not come out until my inner vision was opened. I was determined to storm the gates of heaven, for they would not yield to any ordinary supplication. My resolution, however, dissolved after a few hours, compromised by the need to answer the call of nature! Full of frustrated aspirations, I recalled the prayer of Soami Ji:

> *This noble path of the masters*
> *Shall suffer a great setback*
> *If I succeed not in my endeavors.*
> *I cry from my egoistic reason*
> *And do not resign myself to thy will...*
> *As a branch fallen from the tree,*
> *I am cast away from the Real Home.*[3]

After several weeks, my relationship to the practice gradually deepened. I now felt strong enough to brave the world and revisit my folks on the West Coast. When the bus I was on reached the Canadian border, I was anxious, for in the past I had worked without permit, and was now about to test my commitment to truthfulness. A man ahead of me was pulled out of line and detained. I was intently engaged in silent repetition of my initiation mantra. "How long have you resided in the US?" asked the Customs Officer. I honestly replied, "Five years." Looking over my shoulder, he called, "Next!"

A million lines of Light: After returning to Vancouver Island, I worked at various jobs, and lived in a small wooden shed in my parents' garden. One evening while sitting in meditation, Mum burst through my door crying hysterically. After a few minutes, she became calm and related her strange experience:

"I was in the living room with Dad and Godfrey, when I started looking at your painting of the Master above the mantelpiece. Wherever I moved around the room, his eyes followed me. I asked, 'Kirpal Singh, can you see me as a person?' Then, oh! I can't describe it! A million lines of brightest Light came from every direction and struck me right here!" she pointed to her forehead, in the center between the eyebrows.

I laughed and assured her, "Everything is OK, Mum. The point where the Light struck you is your third eye. Master just showed you that he sees you. He knows and loves you. Don't worry!"

She had been suffering acute attacks of bursitis every morning for more than a year, which were becoming progressively worse, resulting in the loss of use of her left arm. The day after this spectacular experience, both parents volunteered to discontinue eating meat so long as I stayed with them. Coincidentally, the bursitis disappeared and her arm regained full mobility.

However, they were invited out to a steak barbecue, and the following morning her bursitis returned with a vengeance. When they resumed a vegetarian diet, her bursitis was healed, and the arm remained normal for the rest of her life.

Although never formally initiated, Mum was quite receptive. On one of their frequent moves between California and the Northwest, they encountered a fierce rainstorm. Mum was tired and claustrophobic. Surrounded on four sides by large trucks, speeding along in excess of 70 mph, she screamed, "We're going to crash! I'm going to let go of the wheel! Oh God, help me!"

At this point two large, tanned hands appeared and gently covered hers. "They were Kirpal Singh's hands! I recognized them from his pictures," she insisted. Disengaging from traffic, she pulled the Nash Rambler over to the shoulder. Looking to the mountains, she saw the dark rain-clouds part, allowing the sun's rays to shine down in dramatic splendor through the peaks and across the valley floor. Within the center of the brilliant sun appeared the turbaned figure of Kirpal smiling and waving to her.

> *Every time He [the Perfect Master] gives initiation to anyone, He creates [or transfers] an astral image of himself in the disciple. And from then on, the Master never leaves the disciple. The double, or other self, or image of the Master is sometimes what we call the inner Master...*
> *The Master sometimes calls these Doubles of Himself his agents. They do his work, taking care of all his disciples. They have the power to act without limit. They can do what the Master wishes them to do, and they obey his orders. The human side of the Master....may not know what is going on in the life of that person. It may be on the other side of the globe. He will not be aware of the details, but he can know them if he wishes....If the Master had a million disciples, he would have an astral double of himself in every one of them, and that agent of the Master would look after the disciple at all times, reporting to the Master here only in cases of extreme emergency.*
> *—from a letter to a disciple by Hazur Baba Sawan Singh Ji*

All in good time: Two or three months after initiation, I sent my self-introspection diary along with a letter and a list of questions to the Master. I waited, and waited...for *six months!* Finally I received a letter of apology from Dalip Singh, the secretary of Sawan Ashram, for having misplaced the Master's original reply! Enclosed was a copy of his extraordinary five-page, single-spaced letter. After addressing me affectionately, his first advice was the important link between service to humanity with inner progress: "You should progress more on the Path when there will be better chances for your helping others." Then he proceeded to answer a wide variety of questions. Following are a few lines from that cherished missive:

Hazur Baba Sawan Singh,
Painting by the author, 1966, oils on linen, 24"x 30"

The Five Shabds are the varying types of sounds heard within, each denoting the spiritual planes up to Sach Khand. As a matter of fact, the Sound-current is One but there is All-Consciousness, slightly less Consciousness, partial Consciousness predominating [over] Maya, another region where Maya and Consciousness are at par, and the last where Maya predominates and Consciousness is at a lower ebb. The five charged names denote these stages.

Practice makes a man perfect. You can improve gradually by increasing the time of your sittings. The holy meditations should not be a mechanical routine of just sitting for a certain time but it should be of austere loving devotion dyed in a reverential humility when you stand abegging at the Divine Door of the Lord...

Q. *Can even a sinner like myself attain to Godhood in this very lifetime? Sach Khand?*

A. *Yes, even you can attain to Godhood during this lifetime provided you work for it strictly according to the behests of the Master. You have been granted the sacred boon of initiation which is a safe visa to Sach Khand, and it is up to your earnest efforts and steadfastness which would bless you with your wish in due course.*

Miraculous Supplier: Spiritual yearnings constantly smoldered like quality incense, slow-burning, yet perfuming. Despite hard labor and simple living, I couldn't seem to scrape together enough money for an extended trip to India. More importantly, I didn't have my Guru's permission. In 1966, as consolation, I visited the Sanctuary in Anaheim, California. Formerly a Unity Church, with gardens and guesthouse, the Sanctuary had been acquired as the headquarters for the Master's work in the Western Hemisphere. At the outset of my brief stay, I discretely planned to paint portraits of the Masters and donate them to the Sanctuary. One day, I visualized two stretched, primed, fine linen canvasses, various paints, and materials. In the margin of a preliminary pencil sketch, I wrote down the planned dimensions 24" x 30." The next morning, I caught a bus to my parents' place in Santa Monica (they had moved again), about 100 miles north. When I arrived, no one was home, but a large package wrapped in heavy brown paper was stuck between the screen and

Sant Kirpal Singh
Painting by the author, 1966, oil on linen, 24"x30"

front door with my name on it. The sender was identified merely as: *"K. NYC."* According to the postmark, the parcel had been shipped two weeks earlier. I tore away the paper. Inside were two stretched, primed, linen canvases, size 24" x 30!" This was but one of many manifestations to come of what others might call miracles. *When we begin to attune to the higher Self, all the forces of Nature come to help us.*

While working on the portraits of the Masters I did little more than hold the brush. They became alive, and sometimes like a child, I would ask permission, "Excuse me, may I work on your nose? Your eyebrows?" The eyes of the portrait of Kirpal Singh Ji, especially, follow one from any angle, a peculiarity noticed by many.

Returning to Vancouver, I opened a small art gallery devoted to fine art from both Western and Eastern cultures. While painting portraits and landscapes, I lived a spartan life behind a partition in the back of the store. In addition, I worked for the School Board in grounds maintenance. One day a stranger entered the gallery, and demanded, "I was walking by, and some Power dragged me back. What in the world is going on here?" Pointing to Master's photograph, I replied, "He did it."

"Look at those eyes! I belong to a yoga group, and many of us are seeking something higher. If you'd like, I'll introduce you."

A week later, as we entered the kitchen leading to Ananda's yoga center, several people were casually talking. This was unfamiliar territory, and my attention was wholly focused in simran. A young woman walked over and point-blank asked, "Do you mind explaining something? As soon as you entered the room, I experienced an incredible Light all around," she exclaimed, "like someone setting off a flash bulb."

"The Light you have just experienced," I replied in awe, "was due to the grace of my spiritual Master whom I was remembering; it had nothing to do with me. That was just a foretaste..." As a knot of people gathered around, I described *Surat Shabd Yoga*—the Science of the inner Light and Sound-current. Comparing it to several other systems—*hatha*, *raja*, *kriya*, and *kundalini yogas*—I respectfully pointed out the relative benefits and limitations of each. Over the next two years, more than twenty-five came for initiation.

A thousand times brighter than a thousand suns: The Master's letter of August 31, 1966, arrived, answering more questions:

Q. Just how high is Christ?

A. The initiates of the Living Master do meet the form of Christ in their astral travels...It is no surprise if you glimpsed that radiant form within...always repeat the charged names mentally when you see any form within and if that stands before simran know it for certain that it is genuine and friendly; and will be helpful for your inner journey on to the True Home of the Father...The reference of Lord Christ being 'A thousand times brighter than the brightness of a thousand suns' is an allegorical expression of Sat Purusha's divine glory, whose each hair is resplendent with divine light of a million suns put together.

Q. This is a dreaded question and I must ask what will become of me—what will I do if you leave the earth plane forever? To whom should I look for guidance? Who will be your successor?

A. Please rest assured that ever since initiation you are under constant protection...and it will continue till eternity. ...always look within for guidance and all help will be forthcoming from above. You should be happy to know that I do not propose to leave the earth plane so soon as there is still much work to be accomplished, that has been assigned to me by my Satguru. God willing, when I leave this plane, that Power will continue to work at some other human pole, who will be notified in due course, whose company will afford you all necessary guidance outside.

Darshan is a Sanskrit word, and in Sant Mat terminology it means vision internally or externally, of the Lord or a perfect Saint. In eight letters written over these two years, I sought permission to come to India, for I craved darshan, like a fish craves water, but his permission was withheld.

SEEING IS ABOVE ALL!

January 12, 1967: "Leave all and follow Me!" At least, that is how I interpreted a thrilling morning meditation. It was *now* or *never*. I straightway closed the gallery, quit my job, and bought an unrestricted ticket which could allow me to stay for years in India, if necessary. Two hundred dollars remained. Money was the least of my concerns. God would have to take care of me.

January 20th, the morning of departure arrived. "Am I following my Master, or am I following my mind?" Now I was starting to worry! With trepidation, I recalled the saying of Sejho Bai, a woman Saint of sixteenth-century India:

> *If God is displeased with you, reconciliation comes*
> *through the grace of His Saints,*
> *but if the Guru is displeased with you,*
> *then who can reconcile you to Him?*

Until now I hadn't seriously questioned my impulsive decision. I could even be sent back in disgrace, but heart assured the mind, "If Master turns me out, I will stand by the gate and watch him pass by. I will be content with that!" *When was love never a challenge to reason?*

While I packed my old suitcase, heavy footsteps thudded across the outside entrance. I could hear the squeaky mailbox open, a letter falling, the *clank!* of the lid, and steps fading away. I rushed outside and opened the mailbox. Like a nest-egg, a blue aerogram-letter was waiting, addressed to me. On the reverse was the rubber-stamped address of Sawan Ashram, India. With pounding heart I carefully unsealed the envelope and read:

> *January 12th, 1967* [the same day "I" decided to leave all]
> *Dear Arran...if you still desire to come here early, you are wel-*
> come... *Yours affectionately,* (Kirpal Singh).

If I still desired? He *knew;* it was his play all along, exquisitely timed! Thanks flowed like a mantra from my heart as I rushed to catch the plane and the transformation of my existence.

From You I came, to You I shall return...

---

1. I later discovered that this experience coincided with the Master's receipt of my application for formal initiation.

2. Whenever it isn't possible for a Master to be physically present, he may authorize one of his representatives to convey initiation instructions. The representatives merely act as agents; it is the Master who takes over the karmic account of the new initiates, and it is he alone who grants the mystic experience.

3. Kirpal Singh, *Prayer, Its Nature & Technique*, (Bowling Green, VA: S.K. Publ. 1959).

6

The airliner touched down at Palam Airport, disgorging passengers into the chilly January night. I had entered another world, for which nothing could have prepared me. Despite boisterous din and babble, I felt received and embraced by Mother India, as her children know her. I stooped and touched the tarmac with my hand, reverencing this ancient land.

After customs inspection I was greeted by Gyaniji, the articulate silver-bearded ashram secretary; Princess Khukhu, daughter of the Maharaja of Jhind; and Eileen Wigg, an Englishwoman who had lived several years in India.

Khukhu drove her jeep at high speed through the inexplicably familiar, dilapidated streets of Delhi, honking at everything in her path. A mantle of darkness and pungent mist enveloped the city. By the roadside, shawl-and blanket-robed figures clustered around dried cowdung fires for warmth; people on bicycles appeared wraith-like in the jeep's lurching beams. Men and bullocks pulling burdens piled impossibly high on wooden carts appeared sporadically out of the gloom, around which we deftly maneuvered. India was awakening to another day.

I asked my companions if we were near the ashram yet. Hands firmly gripping the wheel, Khukhu turned around and replied, "Every moment brings us nearer to the Master!" Her fierce devotion was proverbial. As we drew close to our destination, I wept tears of the unworthy, and in the flood, the reality of my separation dawned as I was swept towards the infinite Sea.

The car hit a big pothole and I was jolted back to the external environment. Sights and smells exclusive to India impinged upon my senses. Passing through Shakti Nagar and over a clattery bridge, we arrived at Sawan Ashram. The cries of awakening birds greeted us as pink light kissed the dawning sky. Entering the ashram's wrought-iron gates, we rolled through a corridor of banyan and eucalyptus, then turned ninety degrees to the right. On our left were clean white buildings, which served as the living quarters of the ashramites. Several hundred feet further we passed the Master's house, enclosed by a low-walled garden hedged by blooming roses and bougainvillea. I had heard of his fondness for roses. His mother's name was Gulab Devi, *Goddess of the Rose.*

"Master is resting and will see you later in the morning. He has just returned from his Bombay tour. Someone will call you," Khukhu explained, with a proper British accent. After casting a wistful glance toward his door, I was escorted through another fragrant rose garden and on to my spartan room. Once inside, I became aware of tangible energies breathing through me.

At 8 A.M. I was startled from my otherworldly reverie by a knock on the door. "Master will see you now," said a voice on the other side. I was escorted to his residence, heart pounding wildly, fearful. The thought of meeting the Word incarnate was almost too much to bear. *Will this be my beginning or my end?* After removing shoes, I was led through a large screen-enclosed porch to a dimly lit parlor. We continued towards a bright doorway and through it to the *durbar*, or court, of this spiritual king—his modest bedroom study.

There before me was the Master. Although years have passed, that meeting, even the sound of the rustle of his clothes, remains forever imprinted in my heart and mind as though it had existed from the beginning of time. He sat cross-legged on a neat low bed, dressed simply in white cotton kameez shirt and baggy sylvar pants, white turban on his head like a careless crown, dark blue vest with five pens in the breast-pocket, brown hands resting in his lap.

He waved me into the room. "Hello! Hello! Come in! Won't you sit here?" as he offered a Western chair. Instead I sat on my knees on the floor before him, wondering how all this could be happening. Taking my work-callused hands in his soft, strong, brown ones, Satguruji affectionately patted and stroked them. His silent gaze penetrated into the depths of my soul—uncritical, loving, accepting, human-near yet holy-far. Of itself, my head lowered and soon felt his hand atop it, full of the weight and light of the Father. *Merci, mon Dieu, at last!* My battered ship found its harbor, these desperate eyes, their cynosure. I confessed aloud, "I have been a terrible sinner!"

He answered in deep, rich tones, ***"Master is for sinners!"***

A long silence elapsed. "I cut short my Bombay tour to be here when you arrived," he said breaking the hush.

I was dumbstruck, incapable of responding. Why would someone as great as he, one whom countless thousands loved and revered as Master, do so much for such a poor, unlettered, and unproven youngster sitting dazed at his threshold? With the passing moments, such questions became subsumed, answered by love alone. And as he continued holding my hands, I observed up close his other-worldly mien—an essence that photograph, brush, chisel, words or notes could only hope to, but never fully capture.

He smiled and beamed, eyes almost hidden in the folds but for the untrammeled light dancing in their liquid depths. His face, god-like in an Old Testament way, bespoke a universe of meaning beyond my knowing, each line and furrow and a thousand fine waves in his silver beard proclaiming a rugged, yet resplendent perfection.

> *If only the Beautiful One were to take*
> *My wandering soul under his wing,*
> *I would sacrifice all empires*
> *Upon the mole that adorns his face.*
> —*Hafiz of Shiraz, fourteenth century Persia*

Ashram is the Sanskrit word for refuge, a sanctuary, a place of higher learning, a quiet place in nature specifically suited for imparting spiritual knowledge from master to disciple. When the land for Sawan Ashram was acquired, it was a sparsely inhabited wood on the outskirts of Old Delhi. Dedicated in 1951, the foundation stone was laid by Sant Kirpal Singh himself, sprinkled with dust he had gathered from the threshold of his Master's *Dera* or hermitage. (This recalled for me my earlier vision of cosmic dust, and its unusual significance.)

Over the years, an urban tide surged around the ashram's perimeter, and the area became a busy town. However, the moment one passed through the wrought iron gate, beyond the outer babble and traffic's din, one entered an island-oasis, saturated with brightness so palpable that I sometimes chortled, "this charged atmosphere can be sliced, served on a plate and eaten!"

The ashram was an international school of awakening, a nucleus around which innumerable hearts were caused to turn and flare, to orbit in a kind of dervish dance without form. I soon learned, however, that ashram life was not a "piece of cake." Facing and changing mind's habitual tendencies is a formidable task—one often prefaced by intense personal turmoil. But for those willing to sacrifice their lower nature for the higher, there is no better accelerator of inner growth when combined with individual practice of the *Word*. Visitors to this mystic perfumery, whether buying or browsing without commitment, inevitably received some of the Master's fragrance as largesse.

I soon settled into the rhythms of this esoteric community, enjoying it immensely. The experience was an intensely personal one, centered in the Master-teacher/disciple-student relationship. There were profound lessons to be learned from the discourses and informal sessions, if not from just observing the Master in a kaleidoscope of actions and interactions. Trying to put one's deepening understanding into practice during the daily round was a constant challenge. One learned, like King Robert Bruce's persistent spider, that success at any level often requires many a temporary fall.

There was beauty and charm in Sant Kirpal Singh's discourses whether he delivered them in his native Punjabi and Hindi, or in fluent English (which he learned in youth when attending a Christian mission school). He was also well versed in classical Persian, and his knowledge of the world's religious scriptures was nothing less than encyclopedic. He knew *by heart* the 1,400 page Adi Granth of the Sikhs, and whenever he wanted to illustrate a point, freely quoted the Bible, the Koran, Vedanta, and luminaries such as Rumi, Buddha, Bulleh Shah, Wordsworth, Emerson and others. No matter how obtuse a subject, he picked up its universal thread in a way that both scholar and unlet-

Sant Kirpal Singh giving meditation instructions, Sawan Ashram, Delhi, 1967 (AS).

tered could comprehend his gist. His language was simple, powerful and unadorned; his accent difficult to identify. He was fond of parables and maxims drawn from village life. His sense of humor was highly developed, but so subtle and dry, it would sneak up and catch one unawares. Once caught in it one might almost expire from laughter. He once joked, "A saint who never laughs is a sad saint." When someone once asked him, "Sir, how should we address you?" With a chuckle, he humbly replied, "Just call me Mister Zero."

Harish Chaddha, the editor of the Urdu and Hindi *Sat Sandesh* magazines, shared one of his experiences: "I had once again been late with the Master's work; I went to him like a truant before the class teacher. But to my surprise the Master was not forthcoming with the usual reprimand. Instead he started off by talking of the special purpose God has in fashioning each individual object in creation. Then, planting his eyes on me, he ended, 'I believe God made you to serve as a touchstone for testing the patience of a saint!'"

His first discourse that I attended was informally delivered in a local garden on the 28th of January. He spoke of one of the greatest of human frailties, certainly one of mine, that of judging others. Excerpts follow:

> *If we realize that death is certain, there will be a change in our life. We must remain attentive in meditation; if not, the mind will think of others and judge their actions. Instead of the good in others, we take their negative qualities to be our guiding factor. Beware, for, 'As you think so you become.'*
>
> *God has said: 'He is my loveliest child who sees Me in others.' Thoughts are very potent. Have a sweet tongue, honeyed with humility; it should not injure the feelings of others. You aspire to love God, yet you curse those in whom He resides; injuring the feelings of others is a great sin. If you have to face a person with evil qualities, it is better to move to one side. It is easy to seek God, but very difficult to mend yourself. If we realized that God resides in others, would we want to hurt them? If others won't give up their evil ways of hurting, why should you depart from your sweet ways of helping?*
>
> *I have selected the best piece of advice; now it's up to you to follow it or not. God has given us this tongue to glorify Him and to sing His praises; not to hurt the feelings of others. Guru Nanak has said,*
>
> > *'Sweet tongue, honeyed with humility,*
> > *O Nanak, is the essence of all virtues.'*

Whether meeting him one-on-one or in huge throngs, practically everyone experienced an unforgettable loving power emitting from his eyes. Even if that glance lasted no longer than a flash, it seared deep into the psyche. Many, upon seeing him for the first time, would start quaking in their shoes and burst into tears, including those who had forgotten how. His glances would run the gamut of father-stern to mother-tender in the blink of an eye, yet shining through the mask was an immutable theocentric consciousness-raising Light. Like the Masters of ancient time, Sant Kirpal Singh was one with the heart of Light.

8

Knowledge is the child of scriptures,
but it is love which is their mother!

Diary, February, 5 & 6, 1967: For the past few days, human streams have been pouring through the gates from across India to celebrate their beloved teacher's birthday. The ashram's less than three acres seem to swell in order to accommodate the masses that fill every nook and corner. Many poor folk (some extremely so) travel hundreds of miles on foot, bicycle, bullock cart, bus and train, enduring hardships with cheerful resignation. Twelve foreign countries are also represented. As I observe from the sidelines, the Master's happiness is that of a father meeting long-separated children.

The ashram managing committee wants to decorate the grounds for the festive occasion, but Master's expressed wish is to keep it unobtrusive, as he is careful to discourage the start of rituals in any form. However, the persistence of the devotees prevails, and he allows his simple bungalow to be gaily garlanded like a Christmas tree with fragrant strings of marigolds, jasmine blossoms, and hundreds of tiny colored lights.

The *langar* [free kitchen] is crowded with Indian women and men working around the clock, cooking huge cauldrons of vegetable subje, spicy dahl and more than 60,000 chapati flat-breads which fill an entire room to the ceiling! Throughout the crisp February night, groups of villagers sit beneath the stars around fires for warmth, blending voices and hearts in beautiful *bhajans* [sacred hymns of past saints] that continue on and on. My heart is exceedingly glad, and overflows with love toward these simple, good people.

On the evening of his 73rd birthday, the Master addresses a throng that packs the ashram from one end to the other.

> *Since I have met my Master, I have given up discriminating between man and man; there is only soul. It is not the question of intellect or learning which enables us to meet the Lord; it is a question of LOVE.*
>
> *Without earnest prayer from the heart of hearts, no one has realized the Great Reality. Without love, no one has met the Beloved. The Almighty is controlled by the true devotee, I tell you! If you want to go on Haj, or pilgrimage to Mecca, go by way of the sea, not the dry desert. The desert sand is the way of intellect, and the sea—the flow of your tears—is the best way to meet and merge with the Lord in the true Kaaba of the heart.[1]*
>
> *Life is a game like chess; you must be careful how you play. One wrong move and you may forfeit the game. People play stocks, money*

and horses, but here you have to stake your love if you want to attain self-knowledge and God-realization. Kabir says, "Now I want to play the game of chess with God: If I lose, I become Yours; if I win, You become mine."

February 6, 4 A.M. **Meditation of effortless effort:** While the sangat (congregation) chants lyric verses of Kabir, the white-clad Master emerges from a doorway. A ripple sweeps across the sea of 18,000 souls and their responsive singing ceases in mid-verse. After sitting in a half-lotus upon the dais, Maharaj Ji's soul-quenching eyes move across the audience, alighting upon this person and that. Then suddenly his eyes are upon me. Startled, there is a moment of panic. I feel read like an open book, and there is *no* escape. All extraneous thoughts subside. I feel a loving power, electrical, and a taste of bliss as a silent bridge forms between us. Long after his eyes move on, *they remain.* About twenty minutes pass. No one speaks, no one moves. To move even a finger, to break this luminous state, would be a sacrilege to an unwritten, unspoken code. Now that everyone is well primed, Master commences meditation instructions:

> *"Meditation is the process of withdrawing the attention from the world outside, and focusing it at the seat of the soul in the body, behind and between the eyebrows. This point is known as the inner eye, third eye, the single eye, Shiv netra, tisra til, or the divya chakshu. In order to withdraw our attention and focus it on this point, mind must be controlled and stilled.*
> *"Sit in one pose, and move not your head, limbs or eyes. Sit straight but relaxed with no tension in the body below. Sit still, please. To be still does not mean moving!"*

His arms sweep inward, hands contracting to the point between his eyes.

> *"Close your eyes as in sleep, and look sweetly, lovingly, intently into the middle of the darkness lying in front of you. You will see a dark veil. That which sees the dark veil within, without the help of your physical eyes, is the inner eye. Do not put any strain on your physical eyes, nor turn them upwards, for that will result in headache or heat. Pay no attention to the breathing process...let it go on naturally.*
> *"There are two currents working in the body; one of motor-currents or prana or the vital-airs, and the other of surat, or attention, which gives us the sense of feeling. The Saints do not touch the prana currents which govern breathing, circulation of blood, growing of hair and nails. The pranic system of breath-control is the way of yogis and not that of the Saints. The Saints' way is to concentrate surat or attention at the single or third eye while mentally repeating the mantra of five charged names which act as an "open sesame" to the higher planes.*

"As you look within, you will see a sky, or blue sky. If you look minutely into it, you will find it studded with stars, or you may see pinpoints of Light. If so, try to locate the big star out of them, and fix your whole attention on that. Then you may see the inner sun or moon. If so, focus all your attention into the middle; it will break into pieces, and you will cross it. Beyond you will see the radiant form of the Master or his Master..."

He continues with the esoteric instructions, until everyone is absorbed.

"...Become the eye itself. Go on looking constantly without a break. Those who are initiated, repeat the five charged words, one by one, very slowly, mentally, internally, at intervals, so that your inner eye is not disturbed. Those who have not been initiated, just sit in sweet remembrance of God...repeating with the tongue of thought any name of God or Saint which you hold dear. Any effort on your part stands in the way; let yours be an effortless effort, and you will find that your soul will be withdrawn from the body as easily as a hair is drawn from butter. It is by the grace of the Guru that we see."

Stillness and a supernal harmony wash over the assembly. *I am a bubble in a cosmic sea, moved by wave after wave of bliss. Whenever mind begins wandering, the silent mantra brings it to heel.* An hour passes, punctuated by the Master tapping the microphone. "Leave off meditation. Those of you who saw the *Guru Saroop* [radiant form of the Master] in meditation, please raise your hands." Several hundred arms shoot up around me. He asks, "Those who saw both the form of the living Master and his Master within..." Over a hundred raise hands in affirmation. An advanced disciple of Hazur Baba Sawan Singh, by the name of Baba Bela Singh raises both hands, exclaiming*"Sacha Padshah, Sacha Padshah!'* [True King, True King!]. Bela Singh is a retired railroad official—tall, straight-backed, snow-white beard, in his seventies. Another disciple of Hazur stands, a blind man in his forties. His clothes are poor and worn. Trembling and unrestrained, a high-pitched wail emits from his throat, forming the words, *"Saaawaan Kiirpaaal! Saaawaan Kiiirpaal!"* Shivers go up and down my spine. I look to the Master's face to see his reaction, knowing his aversion to external show, but all I see is compassion.

In the preliminary stages of development, a few experience uncontrollable ecstasy upon seeing the radiant Master within, unable to differentiate between God, the Light of God, the God-Man, or even their own self. This state has been referred to in Sufi literature as *mast*, and the person who experiences it *mastana*. Like Saint Paul, one identifies with his or her Master: "It is I, yet not now I, but Christ who liveth in me."

Speaking over the microphone a third time, when he asks if we saw inner

Light of any description, thousands of hands rise, about 80% of those present, including several who later admitted they had come only to scoff. As one old Sikh emphatically expresses from the crowd in colloquial Punjabi, "*Wha Wha!*" (Wonder! Wonder!), his long graybeard waggling.

Throughout the day, government leaders, saffron-clad yogis, Orthodox and Namdhari Sikhs, Sufis (Bhikh Sahib and Nizam-u-din Nizami), Tibetan Lama Bakula, and numerous others sit on the platform with the Master, drawn by his universal spirit. It is highly unusual for different religious leaders to sit together in such an assembly. Several of India's renowned mystic poets, including the Master's son Darshan Singh, recite their sonorous compositions in Urdu and Punjabi. Sacred hymns from Sikh scriptures are sung by the famed Chelaram singers to the accompaniment of *vina*, harmonium, cymbals, and heart-throb-like *tabla* drums. Only twice a year does Master allow musical instruments to be played at the ashram, his focus being on the inner "unstruck melody." The soulful beauty of such divinely inspired outer music ignites the spirit and unites the people.

During the long celebrations, a sturdy farmer rises from the audience asking permission to speak. When Master assents from the dais, he relates:

"Brothers and sisters, I was confused after Great Master Sawan left this world in 1948. There were many theories and conflicting reports, so I kept to myself. One night, two years ago, my village near Amritsar was invaded by hostile Pakistanis shooting guns and looting homes. Several tried to grab me, but I ran for my life. They followed, hot on my heels, and bullets whizzed past my ears. While running across a field, I stumbled and fell headfirst into an irrigation ditch. I was fearful that my end had come, and started praying fervently to my Master.

"You can imagine my amazement when Hazur appeared in the company of this Great One we see sitting here before us today. These Masters took hold of my arms and carried me bodily beyond danger's reach. Then they disappeared—but not before Hazur disclosed the identity of Sant Kirpal Singh and where I could find him. O, my brothers and sisters, it is a great blessing to be enjoying the same grace and love which I used to experience in Hazur's physical presence."

He folds his hands and bows, tears of gratitude rolling down weathered cheeks.

Bowing back to the disciple, Master smiles and adds "It is all Hazur's grace and benignity. Miracles are the result of the operation of hidden laws of nature, with which we are not as yet conversant. A devoted disciple sees many a miracle operating in his or her life. The hidden hand of the Master looks to their welfare in difficulty and danger, wherever they may be."

Following satsang, the multitudes are organized into lines and fed. It is my joy to join my brothers and sisters in serving this bounty, ladling lentil dahl from serving pails and passing out thousands of chapatis. The plates are made of big leaves pinned together with tiny twigs. After all eat their fill, the leaf-plates are gathered and fed to grateful cows outside the ashram walls. Perfect recycling!

In the evening, Master speaks again for two hours. I have gleaned a few gems from his mine of wisdom to share with posterity:

A hungry man is an angry man, and to speak of God to an angry man is a mockery. We must serve those naked and hungry Gods moving on Earth.

Hindu scriptures describe the beautiful hansa (swan) of paradise, which feeds only on pearls, whose beak separates milk from water. This hansa is an allegorical reference to the realized soul. When you rise up into super-conscious awareness in the Fourth plane, you are none other than He; soul then cries out "Sohang," or as Mansur, in a state of unity declared "Ana'l Haq" [I am the Truth], or as Christ said, "I and my Father are One." You have been designed by the Creator to feed on the pearls of Naam; you have been endowed with Vivek [discrimination] to separate the milk of truth from the water of Maya [illusion]. You were meant to differentiate right from wrong, truth from untruth. Realize that your true abode is far beyond the trinkets and trash of this impermanent world. Unfortunately, you have become like a scavenger crow consuming the excreta of the world and yet you do not care to leave it for the truth.

Once a shepherd found a lion cub and brought it up with his flock of sheep. In due course the cub identified with the sheep and would bleat and chew grass just like the rest. After many months passed, another lion came along and saw what had happened. He took the young lion who thought he was a sheep to a pool of water and forced him see his true reflection therein. Then the lion roared and bade the other to also roar, so that he might know he was the king of all other creatures. When he roared, the flock of sheep panicked and ran away. The Master is the lion that comes to show us what and who we really are—that we too are lions in the company of sheep.

It is easy to find God, but difficult to become a human being in the true sense of the word—a wholly integrated human. Become a true human first; then it is not so difficult to realize God. A realized one is like a sound, fully cured brick; when placed in a building's foundation, it gives strength to the entire structure.

1. *Kaaba, also known as the "Black Stone of Abraham", is enshrined at Mecca—the focal point for practising Muslims—and about which the faithful prayerfully circumnambulate.*

N A A M   I N I T I A T I O N

9

Search for the Sun which never sets,
Listen to the Music which lasts through eternity.
- Jalal-u-'Din Rumi

Diary: *Early morning, 7th of February:* Sunlight penetrates the damp haze
and an occasional crow caw drifts across the courtyard. Outside, the ordered
chaos that is Delhi awakens throughout its labyrinthine and smoky streets.
Within these walls of plaster and brick, four hundred sit in a screened-off area
near the *langar* (free kitchen) anxious to be amongst those accepted for initiation.

Today is the first time I observe the Master in person giving initiation. He
arrives and deftly moves through the orderly rows of candidates, countenance
serious, his eyes hidden behind furrowed brows. Inwardly concentrated on
what for him must be a transparent spectacle, without hesitation he singles out
approximately fifty individuals and motions for them to leave. A Master knows
who and *when*, as he receives inner direction in this selection process from the
God-power—the Source of all knowledge. In an earlier heart-to-heart session,
he revealed, "Master can see the lives of those coming to him just as one looks
at the contents of a glass jar, whether it contains pickle or jam, salty or sweet."

When several of the rejected protest and weep, he assures, "Sister (or brother), it is not yet time. Attend more satsangs and study the teachings of the
Saints. Abide by the vegetarian diet a while longer and avoid all intoxicants.
God will help you." Two separate individuals actually manage to change his
decision with their sincere pleas and promises. I learn that the Divine Will that
works through a living Adept is flexible, especially when a cry comes from the
core of one's heart. Kirpal is fond of quoting this Rumi verse:

> *Even if an arrow has been shot from God's bow,*
> *The Murshid (Godman) has the power*
> *To turn it from the half-way mark,*
> *Back to the quiver whence it came.*

Now, 347 remain, including a young man blind from birth. Detailing a wondrous cosmology of the five spiritual regions which begin only when the body
and its chakras are transcended, the Adept proceeds to reveal to the initates
the five sacred names of power. This *mantra* acts as a password to the inner
regions and acts to protect the initiate from negative influences.[1] As he drills
the new initiates in the memorization of the Names, the atmosphere becomes
electric. After the names have been learned by all, detailed meditation instructions are given.

At the close of one hour's silence, the Master meticulously makes a written record of the various inner mystical experiences reported by the novitiates. I am in awe as the blind man relates various details of the Master's features, the color of his coat, the shape of his lotus-like eyes, the position of a mole on his face. Brij Mohan, my translator tells me there are many others like him.

Thirty minutes of *Bhajan*, a special sitting for listening to the celestial Sound-Current, follows. At the conclusion, he moves closer to the new initiates. Orderly rows dissolve and re-congeal around his wicker chair, as he enjoins them to keep a spiritual record of all failings in thought, word, and deed, as well as detailing their experiences and any difficulties experienced within.[2]

"Please send your diaries to me every three months for further guidance where necessary. Initially, you may find failings increasing; actually your failings may not be increasing, but awareness of them increases. Only by becoming aware of shortcomings can you uproot and replace them with their opposite ennobling virtues. When you develop receptivity, and fill out your introspection diaries with love and regularity, you will find the Master in front of you.

Attend Satsang regularly, and give the bread and water of life to your soul before you give food to your body...Leave hundreds of important works to attend Satsang, and leave thousands of important works to sit for meditation.

When you are initiated by a true Master, his astral form takes its abode in your third eye. He's an Unpaid Counselor both in this world and in the beyond!" he chuckles. *"Don't forget: in this human body, the true temple of God, you can progress one hundred times quicker than after death—so make hay while the sun shines!*

*The initiates have a great concession: at the time of death, your Master will come to receive you, and not the angel of death. He usually appears several days or weeks before death to advise you of your coming departure from this world. I'm talking now of those who keep the precepts! For those who do nothing with the gift of Naam, he may or may not appear before they leave the body! But regardless, Master **is** responsible for your ultimate liberation. Those who are not initiated are taken by the angel of death to the Lord of Actions (Dharam Rai) who metes out punishments and rewards strictly according to past actions. That is why Krishna has said, 'Bad deeds are like iron chains, and good deeds are like gold chains.' Both are binding, and both are the cause of further rebirths. We have to become neh-karma, or karma-free, by attuning with and absorbing into the Sound-current.*

*"In your final moments, and much beforehand if you have gained proficiency in meditation, Master's radiant form will take you to a higher stage where you can make further progress. **At the time of death, the initiate will be as happy as a bride on her day of marriage!***

He may then place you in the first, second or third stage, or may take you direct to Sach Khand. In some cases, where worldly desires and attachments are predominant, he will allow rebirth, but in circumstances more congenial for spiritual growth.

This is purely a spiritual practice and not an 'ism'! Remain in your societies and in your religions and learn this as a science.

*You are my children, and I have love for the soul in you, the God in you. Be regular in your practice, keep in touch, and **go jolly!** The Master-power will always be with you."*

Initiation for the children: Separate from the adults, ninety boys and girls aged five to fourteen are given permission to meditate with the Master on the celestial Sound Current. This in itself is initiation, a seeding of consciousness, albeit half the usual process.[1] The children are lined up, squatting in orderly rows; with the simplest of words and gestures, Master instructs them in the correct posture for hearing the Unstruck Sound. Amazingly, most of these normally energized, playful fidgeters manage to sit as instructed for forty-five minutes! Gurudev then slowly walks between the lines and lightly taps each child on the tops of their heads with his forefinger, then helps them to stand. Several require momentary support while sensory currents gradually return to their bodies. One by one they shyly confide remarkable experiences; about sixty report the inner vision of the Master or his Master within. One twelve-year-old Hindu boy, beads of perspiration on his forehead, with gaze inwardly focused, whispers: "I had darshan of Issa Massi on the cross. His body and face were filled with Light."[3] Another boy blurts out, "I saw you, Maharaj Ji![4] You showed me my report card, which is due next week. With your grace I passed all subjects with good marks!" As Master looks around, his eye catches mine, and a beautiful smile lights his face.

Several report seeing the Master discoursing to multitudes on the astral and causal planes ("as above, so below"), and hearing mystic melodies ranging from jingling bells, Big Bell, Gong, Conch, Thunder, Drums, Sitar, Violins and Flute. Like a doting grandfather, he pats his charges before they scamper off to proud parents watching from the sidelines. So effortless and spontaneous his positive mysticism! When the innocence of a child is combined with the spiritual power of an Adept, the inner vision and audition are opened to a greater degree and in less time as compared with most adults. The Masters teach young and old to receive the Kingdom of Heaven in an innocent, trusting and childlike way.

I see in Kirpal a perfect innocence. *Child is the father of man.*

Sant Kirpal Singh giving initiation to children. Photo by Lucille Gunn

1. These names, if given by anyone other than the true living Master or his authorized agent, or if learned from reading spiritual literature, would carry neither charging nor protection.

2. Sant Kirpal Singh devised this unique chart at the beginning of his mission after analyzing the self-introspective and self-correcting habits of past Saints.

3. The term Issa Massi (Master Jesus) are widely used throughout India, Pakistan, and Afghanistan. Thomas, a direct disciple of Jesus, traveled through these countries and established one of the oldest Christian communities in the Indian State of Kerela.

4. When the child comes of age, the second half of initiation is given—meditation instructions and a sitting for inner Light. This done with the permission of the parents and at the discretion of the Master.

5. Maharaj Ji (pronounced *Maharajee*) means "spiritual king," and is a term of great respect.

10

Towards the celebration's close, I wandered over to the Master's house where I noticed a quiet man in his forties, with welcoming deep-set eyes, dark beard, pale green turban and western clothes. I recognized him as Darshan Singh, the Master's son.

"Hello, dear brother," he said softly in excellent English as he smiled and took my hand in both of his. Pleasantries exchanged, I inquired, "What was it like to have been raised in the home of a perfect Master?" The following anecdotes emerged as Darshan responded with a humble demeanor, yet with great devotion and enthusiasm:

"Master brought me to Hazur at an early age. You have probably read that when he was searching for the truth, God in the form of Hazur Baba Sawan Singh Ji appeared in his meditations in 1917, actually seven years before meeting him in person at Beas in 1924.

"In 1926, at the age of five, I approached the Great Hazur on my own, 'Sir, will you kindly give me Naam?' Hazur smiled and said, 'I will give you a very sweet *enaam* (enaam means 'reward'),' and he gave me some sweets, which we call patassas in Punjabi. After I went away, I realized that this couldn't be the same Naam my father was having in his meditations!"

We shared a laugh, and Darshan continued, "So, I again approached the Great Master, and remonstrated, 'Hazur, I want the same Naam my father practices!' Then Hazur made me sit down, and put his finger on my forehead.

After a few minutes he asked me, 'What do you see?' 'I am *seeing* the inner sky. I am crossing the sky. Now I am seeing a big bright star in the heavens.' Hazur said, 'That is enough Naam for now.' I ran up to my respected father, and breathlessly exclaimed, 'Bau Ji, Bau Ji, How far have you got Naam? I have got it up to the stars!' So, I was blessed with initiation by Hazur, as was the Beloved Master.

"My respected father was very strict, yet so loving. He would not let us take our breakfast unless we had given adequate time for meditations. As strict as the beloved Master was, he would provide everything for me, without my asking for it. It was a home filled with awe and love.

"When I was a university student I kept a photograph of the Master on the wall of my room, taken when he was in government service. Under it, I inscribed the caption, 'My Father.' Now I have another recent picture of the Master which I have entitled, 'Universal Father,' for he has become Father to the entire humanity. He sees all and treats all as his own sons and daughters.

"As a young lad studying in the College of Lahore, I would return home from my studies to find the Beloved Master either working late into the night writing

Hazur Baba Sawan Singh, Sant Kirpal Singh and Darshan Singh
Ji, circa 1939

his magnum opus, the '*Gurmat Siddhant,*' or sitting cross-legged, immersed in deep *samadhi,* where he would remain the entire night. And when I arose for my meditations at three or four in the morning, Master would still be sitting there, working on the manuscript or in meditation. At one time these sleepless nights of his went on uninterruptedly for more than six months.[1]

"During the day the Master worked dutifully in a responsible government post, overseeing hundreds of subordinate officers and their staff. It was not until he retired as Deputy Assistant Controller of Military Accounts in 1947 that he turned to devote the rest of his life to spreading the spiritual mission of our great Hazur under his orders."

At my request, Darshan recited one of his recent poems, carefully translating each verse as he went along. His spiritual stature seemed to grow. The final verse bespoke a lyric union of the soul with the Lord.[2] It was a very shy disclosure, a secret unbragged. Maybe, I thought, the 'union' spoken of was just a poetic metaphor. Darshan's glistening eyes briefly rolled upwards as the faintest expression of ecstasy crossed his face.

He later presented me with a book of his recently published poems, *Talash-i-Noor (Quest for Light)* and inscribed the following words, "With loving regards to my dear brother—(signed) Darshan. 6-2-67." Kirpal Singh had written the Foreword praising both Darshan and his universal vision of brotherhood.[3]

Inspired by the reminiscences of his super human endurance, I asked Master Kirpal that evening, "If we attempt to meditate all night, will we be sustained in our worldly activities during the daytime?"

He explained cryptically, "This is the Bread of Life!"

I persisted, "But it would only be possible with your grace."

"Grace is already there. It is up to your steadfast efforts to have it. A strong man revels in his strength, and a weaker man wonders how he got it! This strength cannot be attained in one day. You have got to work for it, you see. Rome was not built in a day; time factor is necessary."

---

1. A man is known by two things; desire, and need for sleep. A Saint is one who is freed from both. "What is God? Man *minus* desire. What is Man? God *plus* desire."—Kirpal Singh

2. Eleven years later when this same poem was again read to me by Darshan, it resolved a huge enigma regarding his level of spiritual advancement and triggered in me an explosion of awakening (chapter 54).

3. This may have been the only time the Master wrote a Foreword to any literary work.

KARMA, HELL, SIDDHIS, AND HEALING

II

*Everything in the universe is the fruit
of a Just Law, the Law of Causality, the Law
of Cause and Effect, the law of Karma.*
—*Dhammapada of Gautama Buddha*

One often hears the word *karma* bandied about, but the average understanding of this immutable principle is casual at best. The law of karma, or action and reaction, plays a major role in the evolution and devolution of life. Karmas have been classified by the Saints of the Sant Mat tradition into three distinct categories:

Sanchit: The storehouse of karmas going far back into innumerable incarnations from the unknown past.

Pralabdha: Fate, or destiny, or that portion of the sanchit [store-house karmas] that constitutes our living present from which there is no escape however we may wish and try.

Kriyaman: The karmas we perform as free agents in our present life, and by which we make or mar our future.[1]

When one is initiated into the inner science of spirituality, the *Word* aspect of the living Master resides with the initiates in their third eye—the seat of the soul, located between and behind the two eyebrows. For want of a better word, this *Master-Power* begins the process of guiding the initiate in the present and the future, while winding up old karmic debts. The pralabhda or fate karmas that created this present life and which govern major events such as birth, intellect, health, sickness, wealth, poverty, status, marriage, children, etc., are left in place, and when fulfilled, the individual has no choice but to leave this world at the time of death. The souls of initiates, once freed from the trammels of the earthly body, are not subject to transmigration into lower forms (below the human form), but are taken to higher spiritual regions as merited by their conduct, devotion and practice. From the inner planes, such souls evolve and joyously progress back to their Original Home.

While pralabdha or fate applies to all who are born, in the case of the initiates, the severity and duration of difficult karmas are considerably toned down, like a minor injury or illness in exchange for something far more serious. In this context, one of the past Masters described the mitigation: *"Sooli ka kanda, hogia"* [*"a pinprick for the gallows"*].

The formation of kriyaman or day-to-day karma is reduced by the cultivation of ethical virtues, self-introspection, simran, satsang and meditation. According to the Adepts, the ratio of *pre-destination* and *free choice* is approximately seventy-five/twenty-five percent.

Sant Kirpal Singh Ji often came down with a mysterious fever following the giving of initiation, with Christ or Buddha-like solicitude. Masters assume the karmic burdens of many lifetimes of their initiates, burning them in the abstract fire of Naam. Sometimes they transfer karmas to themselves and suffer vicariously without a murmur. As mysteriously and suddenly as the symptoms of illness may manifest in the body of a Saint, they also disappear when the debt is paid. If the sanchit karmas were not assumed, there would be no way for the jiva or individual soul to become totally free. The immutable law of justice, endless sowing and reaping, endless birth, death, and rebirth, are circumvented through an Intercessor who represents the merciful and tenderhearted aspect of the Divine.

In a letter to his first Western disciples, Dr. and Mrs. Brock, Baba Sawan Singh Ji has stated:

> *No initiation is possible without payment of karmic debt. People may be thinking that Saints lead a life of ease. They have crowds of followers and so forth and so on. But the Saint's duty is most difficult. He carries a heavier responsibility than a captain of a ship in a storm. This sea has a bottom and shores, but compare it with the sea of existence through that Saints guide the soul and make it one with the One. The more your soul is elevated, the better your service. There is no doubt that pretenders, in the garb of Saints, have done enormous harm, but such is the case in other walks of life as well....*[2]

Sometimes, like Baha'u'llah, Christ, Guru Arjan, Tegh Bahadur, Mansur al' Hallaj, Milarepa, and Shamas Tabriz, the Saints may be called upon to make the ultimate sacrifice at the hands of orthodox fanatics and political schemers who are ignorant of their genuine spiritual stature. A consciousness unfettered by pain, fear, anger, or retribution is capable of calmly blessing even an executioner, as did Jesus when he prayed for his crucifiers: "Father, forgive them, for they know not what they do." Guru Arjan, when being tortured and boiled alive, responded, "Sweet is Thy Will."

Astral Hell: Not long after arriving at the ashram, a boil formed inside my left ear. The pain was excruciating, unlike anything I had ever known, but I struggled to accept it as a gift, an opportunity to repay some old and ugly karmic debt. What seemed to intensify the suffering was a constant, very loud inner sound coming from the left side of my head. Unable to escape from its screaming intensity, I was mindful that the Master often told us never to listen to inner sounds from the left side, as they have their source in the Negative or *Kal* power, and as such are debasing to the soul. Only the inner sounds emanating from the right side and from above are from the

Positive pole, or *Dayal (the Merciful)*, the current that draws the soul back to its Source, its center and Unity.

During the second night of steadily progressing agony, I had an incredible excursion into an astral hell. In the past, I had often wondered if "hell" was merely a fairy-tale or a fabrication created to scare people into behaving in a socially acceptable way, or if "hell" referred merely to the sufferings of this physical world. I was curious because all the founders of the world's major religions referred to a hell or hells as well as a paradise or paradises. The Masters in the Sant Mat tradition teach that astral heavens and hells exist as temporary abodes of the spirit, wherein good and evil karmas are reaped. Once the accounts are cleared, the semi-purged souls are then returned through the womb-door and into a fresh incarnation, to spin and reap again—and not necessarily in a human form. The chains of iron wrought by bad deeds, and the chains of gold, formed of good deeds, both bind the soul and perpetuate existence in the wheel of transmigration—termed in the Sant literature as *Chaurasi Lakh* or the Wheel of Eighty-four Lakhs [8.4 million species].

In this experience, the Master allowed me to enter the astral inferno and view it from a safe vantagepoint. I saw great numbers of souls in basically human shape, suffering in intense fire and anguish. Some were immersed in burning lakes while others were contained in places of unspeakable filth and degradation. Some were moaning; many were crying for help. The Master protected me in an impenetrable bubble, impervious to the heat, suffering, and stench of that place. I saw for myself that hell indeed does exist, and that certain souls do go there to pay off heavy crimes and misdeeds. Fortunately, it is not a permanent place, for once the karma is paid off, these souls are released to pursue a higher and nobler path in their spiritual and ethical evolution.

When I returned from that surrealistic inferno, I had to face my own physical hell in the form of an ever-intensifying earache. When I could withstand the pain no longer, I dragged my ball-and-chain body in the direction of the Master's residence. As it was after midnight, I didn't want to disturb him and decided to turn back. I had been taking a homeopathic remedy given by Dr. Moolraj, but it didn't seem to have any effect. Not long after returning to my room and torture chamber, it felt as if a cannon exploded in my head. The boil had burst, and the blood and pus that drained out from my ear over the next few hours soaked two towels.

By 7 AM the pain again reached unbearable proportions. In desperation I again dragged this body back to Master's house and asked if I could see him. Edna Shinerock who saw me go in later said that I looked like "death warmed over!" Master was sitting cross-legged on the bed. He beckoned me to him and asked, "Why didn't you come to me sooner?" "I didn't want to disturb you," I replied. "There's no question of disturbing. Hmmm...."

Master turned to his big black medicine case about the size of two briefcases, and looked through the hundred or so small glass vials in it, which contained homeopathic remedies. He finally came up with a big white aspirin-like tablet, looked at it intently for a few moments and then asked, "Would you like?" Still in great pain and clasping the bloody towel to my left ear, I nodded slowly and opened my mouth, while he placed the pill on my tongue. In that instant all pain disappeared and the bleeding stopped. I thanked him from my heart, but the Master would take no credit, humbly deferring to the medicine.

I asked, "To whom do *you* turn when in pain?"

He pointed to his third-eye location between the eyebrows and replied, "I turn to my Higher Self."

I naievely asked, "Is the Higher Self one's own Satguru?"

"*Higher Self is God!*" He responded emphatically. "You see, sometimes pain does arise even with Masters." He then added, "It was the homeopathic medicine you took earlier that drew the boil to a head. In future, come to me sooner."

I bowed to the one from whom my relief came. How many ugly karmas had just been washed away? I should always give thanks for adversity, for troubles are gifts of absolution in disguise.

Siddhis (supernatural powers): The Masters have all powers, but they hold them in abeyance. Whenever they employ spiritual powers, it is under exceptional circumstances and then only to save, help or awaken the disciple. Ability to perform miracles is not the sign of a true Master, and is considered to be a lower power.

> *It is necessary here to give a word of caution regarding riddhis and siddhis, or the supernatural powers that one very often comes to acquire in the practice of yogic discipline. They are to be scrupulously avoided, as they are positive obstacles in the way of true spiritual progress and the attainment of self-realization and God-realization....*
>
> *These temptations assail one in the second stage of the journey, but prove of no avail to one who adheres to the Path, and is firm and steadfast in his sadhna [spiritual practice].*[4]

I had earlier overheard the Master stating quite bluntly, "Miracle-seekers are not truth-seekers," and he added the Biblical quote: "*Seek ye first the kingdom of heaven, and all else shall be added unto thee.*" On learning that one of his older initiates had taken to mastering lower powers with the help of mantras, the Master wrote to congratulate him for having regressed from college to primary school! Upon receiving this ironic reprimand, the initiate was filled with remorse and gave up dabbling with such practices.

Spiritual Healing: Related to *riddhis* and *siddhis* is the subject of spiritual healing, widely embraced by numerous New Age enthusiasts, occult societies, and several mainstream religious groups. The Masters of Sant Mat view spiritual healing from a very different angle of vision:

> *"Sufferings demanding spiritual healing fall mainly in the domain of physical troubles, that may include mental agonies such as a nervous breakdown, etc. These being the reactions of the past, karmas demand adjustment and as such are to be borne by the victim. The healer conducting this service takes the karma on his head, to be borne by him at a later stage. The bit of spiritual attainment he has achieved in silencing his mind is dissipated. Moreover, this process of healing is administered on weaker minds, which usually fall prey to their own sentiments or tendencies. What can ordinarily be cured by undergoing a bit of suffering and medicine, is exchanged for spiritual dissipation, and the debt remains standing, awaiting adjustment at a later stage....*
>
> *The Masters advocate right living and right thinking. A simple and truthful life will lead to happiness and joy. If, however, some suffering due to the evolution of past karma comes, its severity and duration is greatly toned down by the intervention of the gracious Master Power, like a penny for a pound, or a needle prick for the gallows....*
>
> *The healing administered by Jesus and other Masters was of a higher quality. When you merge in cosmic awareness and lose your identity you become so spiritual that even thinking of a person or a touch of the hem of the garment will induce healing.... You have not to exert on your part to heal others; it is faith that cures.*[5]

1. Kirpal Singh, *Wheel of Life: The Law of Action and Reaction* (Delhi, India, Ruhani Satsang, 1965), pp. 11.

2. Sawan Singh, *Spiritual Gems: Extracts from Letters to Seekers and Disciples* (Beas, Punjab, India: Radha Soami Satsang, 1965) p. 43.

3. Kirpal Singh, *A Great Saint: Baba Jaimal Singh*, (Delhi, India: S.K.Publications, 1993), pp. 72-73.

4. Kirpal Singh, *Crown of Life—A Study of Yoga*, (Bowling Green, VA: SK Publications 1961).

5. Kirpal Singh, *Spiritual Healing Circular*.

12

After considerable pestering, Dalip Singh, the elderly ashram secretary-treasurer eventually allows me the privilege of typing up some of the Master's correspondence while not meditating my usual five to six hours per day. Dalip Singh has quite a reputation for being very strict and abrupt, but with me he is always loving. Each evening he presents the ashram's account transaction ledgers to the Master who carefully scrutinizes every entry and column.

"During his official career, Master was so careful in his outer behavior," Dalip Singh divulges one day, "that he would empty the ink from his fountain-pen before leaving his government office. He did not consider that ink his own; it belonged to the company. Early in his accounting career, a wealthy contractor put a pile of silver rupees on the young Kirpal Singh's desk in order to assure approval of his contract. Kirpal informed the contractor that his application would be handled sequentially. Then, with an edge in his voice, he told the contractor to take back his money! He continued working but the contractor, thinking the bribe insufficient, added even more coins to the pile while ingratiatingly asking for the favor. The poor fellow didn't know whom he was up against! Kirpal Singh swept the coins onto the cement floor, which crashed and jingled throughout the office, startling everyone from their chairs! His peers tried to convince him that accepting bribes was acceptable and that if he didn't his career would be in jeopardy. Kirpal adamantly refused, and although initially he suffered for his virtue, his honesty, hard work and equanimity were ultimately rewarded with promotions to the highest government positions of trust and responsibility. Our Master retired with honor in 1947 as Assistant Comptroller of Military Accounts where he oversaw a staff of six hundred."

When commissioned to continue the spiritual work of his Master in that same year, Sant Kirpal Singh lived on his government pension. He never accepted money, food offerings or gifts for his own personal use, with one exception that I know of. Shortly after I arrived in India, an elderly widow dressed in ragged clothes arrived at the ashram. I learned that she had worked hard at a very poor paying job, sewing and mending clothes. With her savings of a few meager paisas (a paisa is India's smallest coin, worth only a fraction of a cent), the widow bought a packet of sweets, and took the long bus ride from her village to the ashram. Her ruling passion was to offer these sweets to her Guru. She wanted nothing else. Hunkering down on the ground at the back of a crowd of several hundred, she became overwhelmed by a sense of unworthiness in the Master's presence and quietly wept. Rising from his wicker chair, Master rushed into the throng and took the bag of sweets from her hands, asking: "Please dear mother, may I have some?" He ate a piece and returned the rest to her as *parshad.*

Adjoining the Master's apartments is a porch, a large airy terrazzo-floored white room enclosed by screens facing gardens on three sides. From early morn till past midnight a never-ending stream of aspirants comes and goes. Master frequently moves between his bedroom-office, an intervening living room and a white wicker chair in the porch, which creaks delightfully whenever he settles into it. There he meets and listens, advises and blesses. Several times throughout each day the Master distributes huge handfuls of *parshad* to devotees who gather here. Even chipmunks, sparrows and finches flit in and out with parshad that spills to the floor. Parshad means divine grace, freely given without consideration of the beneficiary's effort or virtue. Any food or flower freely given from the hands of a person of realization becomes tangible parshad, if not a catalytic meditation-booster. In the past few weeks I have received such a huge quantity of puffed rice from his hands, I add buffalo milk and eat it like breakfast cereal.

Here on the porch, one gets an intimate glimpse into the Master's mission. I often witness him opening his wallet to those whom fate has dealt a cruel economic blow. Usually the truly needy are too shy to ask for help, but he always seems to know the ones in real need. The Sikh scriptures sometimes refer to an ideal Saint as Gharib Niwaz—literally, "Home of the Poor." I also see the materially wealthy, the politically powerful, and learned scholars humble as dust, all seeking alms of grace from this great equalizer. All kinds come to his door, seeking marriage blessings, names for babies, a physical cure, advice on this or that, consolation to the bereaved, comfort for the injured and ill, and to offer thanks for blessings already received. A blessed few seek improvement in meditation, to have doubts resolved, or to ask forgiveness for some dark deed.

Stigmata and the Buffalo Boy: One night on the porch I ask, "Master, your disciple, Mrs. Gordon Hughes of Kentucky, with whom I have been corresponding, has purportedly received the stigmata or wounds of the crucifixion on her hands and feet, which bleed at Christmas and Easter. I have also read accounts of other stigmatics such as Padre Pio, Saint Francis, and Theresa Neumann. How and why is this?"

His answer is most revealing: "As you think, so you become!" And he continues, "Once a seeker went to a Master. The Master asked him, 'Whom do you love most?' He replied, 'I love my buffalo most!' His Master then told him to go into a room and think only about his buffalo. Two days later the Guru returned and told this fellow, 'Alright, come out of the room now.' He answered, 'I can't, my horns are too wide for the doorway!'" His face wreathed in smiles and soundless laughter, Master continues: "But you see, this degree of identification and concentration is very rare. *As you think, so you become.*"

I venture another: "How can we be rid of the ever-asserting ego?"

Scrutinizing me with soul-piercing eyes, he replies: "It is only when you rise above the three planes—physical, astral and causal—and become One with the Controlling Power of the Universe."

Chaddha Sahib asks, "Why do you never spare yourself, Maharaj Ji? Why are you ever rushing here and there, giving satsangs, neglecting rest, regardless of the cost to your personal health or comfort?"

"I am simply carrying out the will of my Master," he replies. "He has assigned to me certain tasks to accomplish, and as long as even a single breath remains, it is my duty to complete them. How else can I show my face before the Almighty?"

Earlier I saw a humble devotee wandering about the yard expressing his feelings in song, which brought a smile to my heart. It is impossible to translate the subtle tones, rhyme and meter; only one phrase I understood:

> *Doctor Kirpal has entered the hospital of Sawan Shah,*
> *And the joy of the afflicted knows no bounds.*

Consoling a disciple who complained of increasing deafness, the Master said, "Why do you worry about it? Deafness is a blessing! You are saved from thirteen percent of the sense impressions, but more than that, you don't have to listen to other people's complaints!"[1]

Diary, February 12: Master plays with Mary Howard, an angelic six-month-old baby with golden curls, while her American parents look on adoringly. Two weeks ago Master had coaxed Mary into taking her first steps.

Master holds aloft a bright yellow film canister. From a squatting position Mary reaches, but Master moves it toward himself. She stands, and toddles closer, hands outstretched. He now holds it higher. Only after continuous effort does he give, and rewards her with a touch on the top of her head, and Mary's smile rivals the sun.

Such sweet fun between a Master and disciples is referred to as *leela*—or "divine play." Everything within these sacred walls is a thinly veiled play of consciousness. Under his expert guidance, our inner Light-child emerges, learns to crawl, walk, reach and fumble for Godhead. Once the Adept's company is reached, he steps back, as if to say "go higher." If lucky enough to reach the first or second stage of the inner journey, we are exhorted ever onwards to the next!

Instilling a sense of urgency combined with the inculcation of patience and perseverance in the quest for inner realization, a true Master continually nurtures a deepening awareness of the higher Self, drawing us back to the Source.

The Master and Baby Mary, on an Indian train, 1967.

And many are the exquisite moments which hang on the pauses between the words and actions of the fully awakened being, where time stands still:

> *Love burns the lover, and devotion burns the one you are devoted to;*
> *he has to take care of everything for you when you are devoted. Love*
> *seeks happiness for the Beloved, not for the self, mind that...*
>
> *So, devotion seeks blessing from the Beloved, but love seeks to shoulder*
> *the burden of the Beloved. And devotion throws the burden on the*
> *Beloved! Love gives; love does not require the presence of the Beloved*
> *in order to love. One who loves, he loves, that's all...a lover is never*
> *alone...The Beloved resides in him. They are one, whether near or far.*
> *So devotion asks, and love is silent and sublime, devoid of outward*
> *expression. Such is the ideal of love.*
>
> *...I am giving you the best of all I have come to know, and that is*
> *love. You must become conscious of yourself. God is Light and*
> *Consciousness, but that Consciousness is now enveloped by matter. You*
> *are not matter. You are sparks of Light. Be one with the great confla-*
> *gration of Light!*[2]

Ashram Characters: the colorful cast of ashram characters intrigues me. This is just a partial list, and some will appear later in my story:

Ganga Dhar: He's in charge of tape-recording the Master's discourses, and fiddling with the electric cables, batteries and microphones. He and his assistant have humorously been dubbed Wire-Das—"Servants of the Wire." Ganga Dhar organizes large ashram construction crews, and gets them moving with his shouts of *"Chello! Chello!"* ("Move! Move!"), so he is also nicknamed Chello-Das. He meditates regularly. A Westerner approaches him today and asks, "Ganga Dhar, you must have made a lot of progress in meditation," to which he replies with a humble smile, "Sahib, I am like a tree without any leaves, and cannot give shade to anyone. And I'm so rooted in the ground, I cannot even whip myself up to God!" *Oh, Ganga—you speak for me...*

Ram Saroop and *Mohan Singh,* respectively, are the drivers of the ashram cars—a 1957 Champion Studebaker stationwagon, and a new Ambassador. More about Ram Saroop later on. Mohan has become my friend, and he is a strong, devoted servant of the Master. He was initiated at an early age by Hazur, and lives with his wife at Sawan Ashram. Mohan has had many wonderful experiences with Master Kirpal.

Gyani Bhagwan Singh is a learned and highly articulate gentleman, a long-retired Indian Railway official who was initiated by Hazur in the 1920's. He is on the ashram's managing committee, and serves as general secretary.

Edna and *Stanley Shinerock* have lived at the ashram for several years. She has a reputation for firmness. Stanley, an accountant, works for the Canadian Embassy, and Edna assists foreign visitors in adjusting to ashram life.

Gursharan plays classical Indian bamboo flute—beautifully, I might add.

Ram Ji is a delightful fellow around my age, who comes from a very poor family. His job is to clean, cook and serve. Each time we pass each other in the hallway, we make a game of the Indian tradition of touching the feet of one's elders, laughing like crazy in our display of mock subservience.

Ayat: In his late teens, Ayat also comes from a poor background. Master brought him into his service—cooking, ironing, and cleaning. There would be many millionaires and rulers who would gladly trade places with Ayat, but not the other way around!

Master Pratap: He is the Music-Master, whose story will come later.

Dalip Singh: Ashram Secretary-Treasurer. A scrupulously honest, elderly and trusted co-worker of the Master. Dalip Singh takes me under his wing to help with Master's correspondence.

Harish and *Bimla Chaddha:* The Chaddhas have long resided at the ashram, serving the Mission in various ways. Harish is a newspaper correspondent, an editor of the Master's monthly magazine, *Sat Sandesh—The Message of the Masters*—in Hindi and Urdu, and author of several publications including the full-length Hindi book, *Pita Poot* (Father and Son), which is an account of the Guru-disciple relationship between Hazur and Sant Kirpal Singh.

Princess Narendra Kaur Narendraji, daughter of the Maharaja of Jhind, came to the Master after her husband died in a jet plane crash. Fiercely devotional, she lives in a small house within the ashram with her daughter.

Bibi Hardevi Raja Ram (a.k.a. "Tai Ji") is a prominent devotee of Hazur, elderly widow of Raja Ram, and major domo about the ashram. She is mentioned in Dr. Julian Johnson's book, *With A Great Master in India.*

Pundit Dhani Ram Sharma: A distinguished and devoted sevadar of both Masters. Pundit Ji is in charge of book sales and initiation records.

There are hundreds of inspiring disciples from all religions, castes and differing socio-economic status who come regularly to the ashram to attend the talks and darshan sessions. They serve the Master's mission, but live and have full-time careers in their own homes, beyond the ashram walls. Some whom I have come to know personally are: Sethi Ji—Master's personal secretary; Brij Mohan Sharma—devotee and businessman; Bhadra Sena—author and correspondence secretary; Dr. Vinod Sena (Bhadra's son)—head of the English Department of Delhi University; Darshan Singh Ji and others.

---

1. According to the Masters, we receive thirteen percent of our sense impressions through the ears (sound), approximately eighty-four percent through the eyes (sight), and the remainder through the nose (smell), tongue (taste), and skin (touch or feeling).

2. From a tape-recorded talk between Kirpal Singh and American disciples.

13

Lead us from the unreal to the Real,
From darkness to Light,
From death to immortality!
—The Vedas

Although my life's meager savings were spent coming to India, I considered that even five minutes in the company of a true One were worth more than all the treasures one could accumulate in this faithless world. As time passed, a subtle love began to permeate my consciousness, profoundly altering my perceptions. My former life seemed but a distant dream. I had been free from the influence of drugs and alcohol for several years, yet nothing could remotely compare with the divine intoxication I now experienced. The presence of the Master was like a perfume which engulfed all who drew near. The sweetness it awakened far surpassed the pleasures of sense, intellect, accomplishment or fame. Recently, in satsang, the Master stated *"God is an Ocean of intoxication."*

Since arriving at the ashram, I hadn't noticed any particular progress in meditation, which dissolved my preconceived notions of attaining samadhi within a short time in the Master's presence. On this subject, I approached Father one morning. "It is due to your attachment to the outer form of the Master," he chuckled, putting me at ease, and added, "The other will come in due course!" I thanked him and took leave.

"Brother, Master wants to see you right away!" exclaimed a breathless sevadar who found me on the far side of the ashram a few days later. I ran over to the porch and entered the inner sanctum. "Why are you walking about with such a long face?" Master demanded. I was unable to respond. "Long face! Long face! Why the long face?" Startled by his blunt prescience, I struggled for words. "Maharaj Ji, I'm running out of funds, and have to return."

His mouth dropped open and ample eyebrows raised up incredulously, "What?! Don't think of the future and don't think of the past. Make best use of the living present and put in maximum time for meditations. You are a dear child of the Father and are to stay here with me!" He pulled from his pocket a big roll of rupee notes, and removed the rubber band which held them all together. "If you ever need anything, come directly to me!" While thanking him, I declined his kind offer. Master then warned, "They're not all saints here, mind that!" There was nothing I could hide, for I had imagined that many of the ashram's colorful characters were on some higher plane, and he wanted to disabuse me of this fantasy. In a recent satsang he warned, "The Master is like a cow who loves to give her sweet milk to the calf which comes from a distant pasture, but the ticks living on the udder only drink her blood."

Several days later, I unexpectedly received a $100 money order from my mother. I timidly approached the Master and asked if I should borrow some money until I could cash the draft downtown, as otherwise my pockets were quite empty. He peeled off some notes, asking, "Will this be enough?" and insisted I accept it. I cautiously accepted 20 rupees and returned the rest. Two days later, I proceeded to Master's house, absorbed in the idea of settling my debt—as if such were possible. How could a slave of the mind ever repay the emperor of the heart?

After an anxious wait, he suddenly emerged onto the porch, smiling and greeting. I stammered, "Master, here is the money you kindly loaned me." He chuckled and pushed my hand away. I insisted, but again he refused. As he turned his back, I sneaked the rupees into his coat pocket! But, while looking in the opposite direction, he omnisciently caught my hand in his right, suddenly turned, and lightly slapped my face three times. He disappeared into the crowd, leaving me stunned, my ears ringing, and the impression of his huge, beaming countenance in my mind.

In a most vivid dream that night, Mohan, the driver appeared and conveyed a message; I was being called upon to help spread the Master's teachings in the West. Suddenly I was wide awake on the inside. The Satguru appeared in the distance dressed all in white, clearer than daylight. Without moving his limbs, his form seemed to accelerate straight towards me; now he was directly in front. His right hand moved back as if to strike, then swung with full force towards my face. When his hand connected, there were a few moments of exploding-imploding lightning. He was all that remained, and his holy visage began to glow brighter and brighter with an incandescence eclipsing the sun, a vortex of stupendous luminous power. I was dragged into and through its center, then catapulted into the Beyond at great speed, over vast distances, becoming a mote of freed awareness, momentarily part of and one with an Ocean of ecstasy and grace. Angelic music and wondrous beauty flowed through everything. This Ocean had no water, edges, bottom, nor end. The word "ocean" was no more descriptive than "sky" or "infinity." Love-consciousness abided, and my actuality was no more than a tiny bubble floating in titanic majesty.

Alas, my dip into the Cosmos was not destined to last for long. As the elements of ego-self began to re-congeal, trickster mind was crying for my return somewhere far below in relative darkness. Against my will, I was sent back, for my consciousness was unacclimatized and contained impurities incompatible with these higher realms. Descent took place with great speed, and from every side came a high pitched keening—a kind of musical friction as soul plus mind skidded down through successive layers, until softly and silently re-entering a supine, barely recognizable body through a vertical aperture in the forehead. Upon return to the prison of physical existence, I wept again. Although separated from that Life of Life, indescribable bliss saturated my awareness for the next few days.

God comes to His lovers in many ways, in many forms. To me He came in the guise of my Guru's slap, which conferred a brief taste of Eternity, an advance installment from which to draw strength whenever weak, dry, uninspired, or in trouble. Greatly fortified, I prayed that I might someday be worthy of serving him and the creation in some small way.

Left to right: Paathi-ji or "Master-Ji" (Music-master) and Master Kirpal, Sawan Ashram

14

Early Spring, 1967: Maharaj Ji and his caravan of two crowded Ambassador cars prepare to leave Delhi for a two week tour of Agra, Indore, Baroda and Ajmeer. I am left behind, extremely weak from amoebic dysentery— euphemistically called *"Delhi-belly."* I want so *badly* to go! Just before getting into his car, Master pauses and waves me over, saying: "If you feel better by this afternoon, you may come to Indore with Master-ji by train."

'Master-ji' is the nickname of Partap Singh, a widely acclaimed master of classical and devotional Indian vocal music. He is also called *Pathi-ji* (The Singer). It is his task to sing soul-stirring bhajans (hymns) of the Saints, around which Master Kirpal bases his discourses. Master-ji has incredible built-in volume control, and whenever the electricity fails, rendering microphones useless, as often happens in India, Satguru Kirpal will give him the nod. There is something almost supernatural about Master-ji's beautiful voice, which without loudspeakers, can carry across the huge crowds, even up to a mile away. Partap Singh stands a little over five feet, and the white beard which frames his noble face is about a third as long as he.

Against the insistent advice of several well-wishers and Dr. Mool Raj, I decide that I cannot bear to stay in the empty ashram; I simply *have* to be with my beloved Guru. Master-ji and I hire a three-wheeler, broken springs and all, to take us to the train station. I grit my teeth, as every bump and jolt from the pot-holed street sends sharp pangs into my gut. Most auspiciously, all cramps disappear the moment we board our "Gandhi-class" (third-class) coach. Even though we sleeplessly pass the next night and day in a sweltering, over-crowded berth—jolted, jostled and covered with soot—my elf-like companion and I spend most of our time in blissful meditation. Master-ji lies on the bare metal floor wrapped in a thin muslin sheet (his unwound turban) like a moth in a cocoon, meditating, while passengers sitting on benches above try not to put their feet on him.

At one point, Master-ji's face emerges from his shroud, emanating serenity and beatitude. In lovely broken English, he says, "My Master Sawan with me all night. He ve-r-r-y beautiful, ve-r-r-y bright! Face like full moon! I love, He love. You love, a-a-l-l-l is Love!" We both laugh a long time, like drunkards in a tavern.

After some gentle prodding, Master-ji shares a little of his life:

"I was chela [student] of Shahanshah. He wrote many God-songs, and taught me all *ragas* [modes] of Indian classical music. Shahanshah once great champion wrestler of Punjab, then became vairagi sadhu [a renunciate]...spiritual wrestler! You know I many times sing bhajans of

Shahanshah in satsang. Master very much love and respect. Very powerful meanings in his bhajans. Shahanshah also came to Hazur Baba Sawan Singh, many times. He see Hazur one with God... and the beauty of God, both! I came to Hazur maybe thirty years ago, and took Naam. I also see Master Kirpal with Hazur many times; he already most great disciple of Hazur. Baba Kirpal already Saint, he like older brother to us. Hazur give hukam [order] to Master Kirpal to sit by his side, conduct satsang and help sangat [congregation]. Once he sit by Hazur at big initiation. Hazur give order, 'Kirpal Singh, you give them Naam!' All see Light and hear *shabd dhun* [Sound Current]. Big *shakti*! [spiritual power]. I there."

"How did you come to this Master?" I ask.

"When Hazur left chola [physical coil] I verrry upset! No want live this world! My born name, Partap Chand, from Hindu family, but then I decide not to shave, not to wear shoes until I find Hazur and happiness again. Not go anywhere! Hazur say to sangat, 'Kirpal Singh my very own self.' But I not care. Then Master Kirpal write me letter: 'Master-ji, come and visit me in Delhi.' I not listen. Again he write, but I not answer. Third letter said, 'If you don't come to me, then I will have to come to you!' I think, 'What I lose in going to see?' and take train to Delhi. When I reach Sawan Ashram, I see Hazur Baba Sawan Singh sitting in Master Kirpal's chair. I no believe! I rub my eyes! Hazur still sitting there, so I bow head to his feet. When I get up, look at him, Master Kirpal there! He say 'Stay here with me. Serve Hazur and sangat.' I call wife and son from Punjab, and never leave!"

I notice that Master-ji is now wearing shoes.

15

How can the love between us sever?
From the beginning of time,
'till the ending of time,
there has been love between You and I.
—Adi Granth

The timeless plains, farms and villages of Madhya Pradesh roll by as the train's clickety-clack, clickety-clack continues for the next twenty-five hours. There will be an occasional stop here and there, while hordes of colorful passengers scramble in and out. "Garam chai! Garam chai!" call out the chai-wallas at the stations, who hold up clay pots (disposable and recyclable) of steaming hot, cardamon-fennel-fragrant, milky, sweet tea under our faces, peering through the open, but barred train windows. For a mere 25 paisa coin, they part with this stimulating beverage, then the steam-whistle blows, pistons and wheels turn, and the train lurches forward again.

Tired and begrimed with soot, Master-ji and I arrive in the clean and orderly city of Indore, lovingly greeted by several local organizers. We are escorted to Ram Krishna Dharamshala, a combination community center, Hindu temple and hotel complex where we will stay for the next few days. Expectancy is visible in every face as Master's arrival is overdue.

After an exhausting journey in searing heat, including a busy program in Agra, Maharaj Ji and his dusty party finally arrive by car at sunset. I have never seen him so weary as he slowly labors up two flights of stairs. With his hands, he lifts each uncooperative leg, step by step, his face wincing with pain. When I move toward him to offer help, he brusquely waves me away. After reaching the top, he enters his room, pulls a curtain and reclines on his bed. Wrenched by his physical condition, I retreat to my room and in seclusion, quietly weep for him. Fifteen minutes later, Master emerges, countenance youthful, pink-cheeked, bubbling with life and radiance. He meets crowds of seekers late into the night, far surpassing the endurance of those half his age. While the merciful Saints inhabit a corporeal form, they have frequent and practically instantaneous access to an inexhaustible life-sustaining reservoir.

He often says, "One can only know a Master to the extent that he chooses to reveal himself." To truly see a Master can be its own form of awakening, although *seeing* is not quite the same as *becoming*. As his transcendent nature is intimately linked with our own, a true Adept "waits" to ignite the "tinder" within us—but only when it is ready.

The evening discourse takes place in an open park before thousands of Indori citizens, including many of her leaders. A large fancy silken cushion is placed on the platform, but when the Master mounts the dais and notices the cushion, he frowns, picks it up and flings it far into the night before settling down on a plain unpadded sheet. He is disdainful of pomp and show; he is simple and humble, yet fully empowered.

While poignant verses from Kabir and Arjan Dev are chanted, Gurudev casts handfuls of marigolds into the delighted audience. Seated at the front, blossoms from his hand strike my face and torso. If my body is a harp, each flower's impact is a thrumming of its strings, and the resonance continues for the duration of satsang. His gentle voice pours like honey into the collective consciousness, and the silence between phrases vibrates and enfolds everything. To know, to experience this bliss, foretells of some future pain of separation. But, as Longfellow said, *"It is better to have loved and lost than never to have loved at all."* Later, I collect thirteen fragrant marigolds which struck me earlier—some in my lap, some on the carpet. I wouldn't trade these for pearls.

Tonight, many witness the Master physically changing into the form of his Master and back again as he discourses. While riding back from satsang I ask about this noumenal manifestation. From the front seat of the car he replies, voice redolent with humor, "What's that? There must have been something wrong with your eyes!"

In the state of divine Unity, no differentiation exists; essence flows back and forth:

> *'Whoever knows the mystery of the numeral One,*
> *becomes One with Him.'*

If lucky enough to find such a doorway, one may experience the Formless essence personally aspected as Father or as Mother, giver of the milk of pure White Light and True Knowledge. A hymn of Guru Arjan Dev sings of the multifaceted Godman, the embodiment of tender humanity with divinity:

> *Thou art my Father*
> Tu mera Pitta
> *Thou art my Mother*
> Tu hai mera Mata
> *Thou art my Brother*
> Tu mera bhandap
> *Thou art my Kith and Kin.*
> Tu mera bhrata
> *O my Protector, Thou art within me,*
> Tu mera Rakha sabni t'hai
> *And nothing do I fear.*
> Ta bhao kayha Akhara jio

Satsang with Swamis— Gita Bhavan, Indore, 1967 (AS).

In the morning we visit sprawling, but immaculate Gita Bhavan on the out-skirts of Indore; its director, Bal Mukunda, a recently initiated disciple, shows us around this large temple-complex, dedicated to several dieties of the Hindu pantheon. Inside the main ornate structure, Master Kirpal shares a white marble dais with about twenty-five orange-robed renunciate swamis. After very lengthy introductions and speeches by others, the capacity audience is finally treated to his discourse on the Path of Naam, while polychrome statues of Krishna and other dieties stand sentinel behind. From the perspective of a God-realized Adept, there is no paradox in religious diversity, for such a one sees the cosmic dance of Unity behind the veil.

> *"Life is a dome of many colored glass*
> *which stains the white radiance of Eternity."*

Before leaving, we visit a newly built eye hospital which is blessed and inau-gurated. It is most encouraging to see intelligent men and women of various religions and societies drawn to this path without breaking with their own faith, family, customs or rituals. In this context, Jesus assured his listeners, "I come not to break the law, but to fulfill it." As students advance on the path of love and gnosis, rites and rituals may fall aside like husks. Once one has tasted the kernel within, ritual becomes non-essential, but an option that is exercised for those who wish to maintain socio-religious observances.

Pritam Das of Ujjain: We make a side-trip to Ujjain, a large town, fifty miles from Indore. Several thousand attend satsang beneath a colorful canopy. From there we flow (that's how it feels) to the ashram of a local holy man, Baba Pritam Das, to eat and rest. For the next three hours, the Master and Pritam Das sit on a couch to the side, holding each other's hands, sharing sweet memories of Hazur, from whom both received their spiritual treasure. Pritam Das, with his snow white beard and acquiline profile, has a remarkable physical resemblance to their Master. As the day draws to a close, Pritam Das escorts everyone through the Sahaj Yog Ashram, surrounded by fruit trees, vegetable gardens and wheat fields. We are given stalks of fresh green chickpeas to peel and chew (delicious!) as well as fresh papaya. It is rare to see Master so care-free as he leisurely inspects various crops and plants without hordes of seekers crowding him.

The Indian sky has turned all shades of gold, vermilion and crimson. Master and Pritam Das stand together under the mango trees, bathed in the sun's setting glow. A thick peace lies over the land. We bid farewell and motor back to Indore, just in time for evening satsang.

After the public talk, hundreds follow the Master to the dharamshala, where he sits in an armchair in a large room jammed with people from wall to wall. Many are the pairs of eyes and ears, but they are like one big eye, and one big ear, straining to catch every glance, to hear every word. One after the other, seekers new and old come forward.

One asks, "Maharaj Ji, what benefit might a stranger have if he happened to be passing by and overhears part of the initiation instructions or surreptitiously learns the five charged Names?"

"When this same question was asked of Hazur, he replied, 'If a dog happens to run through a cotton field, does it mean that he will come out wearing a three-piece suit?'" Laughter fills the room.

A new man makes his way, close to the Master's knee: "Maharaj Ji, may I trouble you?" he asks in excellent English.

"Yes, to the best I know."

"For the past ten years I have been searching for a God-man, but all in vain. I have been to Rishikesh, Hardwar, Banares, Himalayan hermitages and several other holy places. I have sat at the feet of many Gurus and received various initiations."

"Did you see Light?"

"No, Master, all I ever received were empty promises and never any higher experience. No Light have I seen. I performed many practices and yoga techniques but still the inner veil has not been rent! I am totally lost if I cannot find God!" While he weeps, Master lays his hand on the man's shoulder.

The seeker continues, "I had almost given up the quest for Light as a will-o-the-wisp. Having your darshan, I confess great attraction. I do feel some

Power. Will you please grant me the holy Naam?"

Master asks him, "Haven't you already received initiation?"

"Yes, Guruji" he replies, "several years ago I took Naam from another teacher in the Sant Mat tradition, but even though I put in three to four hours daily for meditation, I have never experienced anything within."

"Why don't you go back to him and request experience along with the Names?" Master urges.

"I tried, Maharaj Ji, but it isn't possible to get near enough to speak or ask questions." He starts to cry, because he thinks Master is refusing him.

"Dear friend, don't be disheartened," Master comforts. "First of all, *don't row in two boats*. Don't mix up spiritual practices; do one thing wholly and solely, with full attention! Leave off the past. Have respect for your former gurus; don't condemn them. I have all respect for them. If you find someone who can practically open the inner way, you should follow him with single-minded devotion. Kabir says *'Unless I see with my own eyes, I cannot even believe the words of my Master.'* That's a very rare qualification! If others can give the inner way, by all means go to them. If not, you are welcome here. If you are thoroughly satisfied, you are welcome to come tomorrow morning and have a sitting along with the others, and if you receive anything, it is all due to the Grace of God and my Master working overhead. There is nothing to be disheartened about, mind that!"

The next morning he and a hundred others are internally connected and started on the El Camino Real. In the months to come, I am to see this poignant scene reenacted in many places.

Eyes Like Lightning: I happen to walk past the room where initiation is taking place and peered through the slats of the wooden shutters on the unglazed window, curious as ever. I can barely make out the Master in the dim light, sitting on a low wooden platform facing in my direction, with the new initiates before him. He is repeating aloud the five Holy Names, helping the new initiates learn the Gur Mantra. He notices me spying and fixes his piercing gaze on me for a few seconds. Suddenly, a blinding beam of Light shoots from his eyes to mine, physically bowling me over backwards. In utter awe and exhilaration, I hide behind the wall, heart pounding!

Although only four days have passed at Indore, a profound bonding has occurred, evidenced by the tears shed by hundreds on Master's departure. Several touch their foreheads or hands to the dust where he passes, and I, the dry Westerner, envy such spontaneity and simplicity. It is not my destiny to always be dry.

16

*Shabd is the Guru,
and Surat, the disciple.* —*Nanak*

Master-ji and I board a rusty, worse-for-wear, twenty-two-seater bus, bound
for Baroda, a long ride towards the south-west of India. Scorching heat is mag-
nified by the bare tin roof and more than sixty passengers. I soon conclude that
its unpadded metal seats were designed in hell for the long-of-leg! The bus
stops in a deserted barren region to pick up four loin-clad tribesmen who wear
hunting slings wrapped around their headgear. The one closest me suddenly
vomits on the floor. I attempt to accept the heat and other trying conditions as
gifts of the Lord. Suddenly, Master's car passes on our right. From this
moment on, I close my eyes and enjoy a cool mystic breeze which magically
transforms this rickety, sweltering bus into a luxury coach.

It is past 9 in the sultry evening when we reach Baroda, a sprawling city of
several million. As the bus roars away, leaving us in a choking diesel cloud,
Master-ji suddenly exclaims, "Oh, oh! I forget Baroda address of Maharaj Ji!"
We laugh and agree that somehow the Master-power will guide us to our destination. By pedal rickshaw we proceed to a famous temple built over the very
place Guru Nanak visited five hundred years earlier. From a granthi [Sikh
priest], we obtain permission to stay. There we meditate, eat, and rest.

In the morning, the granthi gives me a lesson on the *vina*, a traditional
stringed instrument with a long fretted neck and two large dried gourd sound-
chambers attached to the underside. The vina's haunting if not beautiful note-
bending sound has no parallel in western music, and its timbre and tone is
said to resemble the sound-current in the third spiritual region. Master-ji has
gone for a walk in a nearby bazaar and returns with Kartar Singh—a gentle
giant, prosperous merchant and the local satsang leader who was purchasing
vegetables for the Master's free kitchen when he and Master-ji literally bumped
into each other!

He delivers us to a palatial residence once occupied by the Maharaja of
Baroda, then ushers us into a huge room, where the Master is resting upon a
canopied bed. Seeing us, he sits up, perfect feet peeking out from under baggy
sylvar trousers, skin color like honey-golden amber, unlike any other. I find it
impossible not to bow before such unpretentious majesty. "You have the Indian
disease!" he jokes, referring to my bowing. "People were out looking for you
until after 1 a.m. I was not worried." His eyes are giving sport as he adds, "but
others were!" I'm one big smile.

In the evening, a mammoth crowd gathers to hear the Saint from Delhi:

"*God working through the Guru can connect you to That which has no mother, no father, no brother, no equal. A genuine man of realization never calls Himself a Master. When Nanak was asked, 'Who is your Guru?' he replied, 'Shabd or the Eternal Sound Principle is the Guru, and Surat [the Attention] is the disciple.' A true Master considers himself to be the servant of servants.*"

In this vein, during his third world tour in 1963, Sant Kirpal Singh was invited to speak at the Grand Mosque of Paris. After listening carefully to his enthralling message, the Grand Mufti (head priest) requested a memento. The Master gave him a photograph of Hazur Baba Sawan Singh which he then personally inscribed in Urdu, "*Ghulam-i-Ghulama, Jamal*" ["*The slave of Thy Slaves, Jamal.*"] Jamal was the Master's pen-name.

It is the morning of initiation and departure. Of sixty new seekers, only one man cannot hear the sacred inner Sound at the first sitting. Even when put aside for a second sitting, he experiences nothing. Master frowns with *apparent* impatience, *seemingly* in a hurry. He touches the new initiate's right ear, and after less than a minute, taps the top of his head. The meditator opens his eyes and with a stunned expression, reports hearing loud ringing bells within.

According to the Adepts of Sant Mat, the internal sound of the big bell is the first important level of *shabd* or Sound-current heard within which is able to exert sufficient magnetic attraction upon the listener, thus drawing soul's consciousness into the astral plane. Regions above and beyond this astral heaven reverberate with even finer and more compelling melodies. These realms are filled with radiant scenes of such exquisite beauty and grandeur that the beholder is overwhelmed and enraptured. There is no earthly parallel.

When humble Francis of Assisi took shelter in a cave from a raging storm and opened his heart to God, he received profound illumination in a vision of Christ accompanied by the loud pealing of church bells in and around him.[1] While engaged in deep prayer, St. Theresa also heard God speaking to her through the medium of inner bells, although initially she was fearful of them and her sanity. The prophet Mohammed heard the inner bells, transforming into the voice of Gabriel, which dictated to the unlettered shepherd boy the Holy Koran.

The inner sound has nothing to do with the medical condition known as *tinnitus*, although several who have heard unbidden strains of the music of the spheres within initially sought help from doctors. There is, however, no cure for God but *God*.

The more I travel with the living Master, it becomes obvious to me that he, in his time, is in harmony with the Divine Will and thereby in control of the cosmic tap—for those who seek the inner way.

Five centuries earlier, Guru Nanak taught the helplessness of ego-centered attempts to realize the Divine, before Whom one must be humble as dust:

> *You have no power to speak or to be silent,*
> *No power to ask or to give.*
> *You have no power over life or death,*
> *No power over wealth or state*
> *For which you are ever restless.*
> *You have no power over spiritual awakening,*
> *No power to know the Truth,*
> *Or to achieve your own salvation.*
> *Let him who thinks he has the power, try.*
> *O Nanak! none is high or low, but by His Will.* [2]

---

1. As related in an out of print Catholic publication, *Four Saints Who Changed the World.*

2. Kirpal Singh, *The Jap Ji: The Message of Guru Nanak*, (Bowling Green, VA: SK Publications, sixth edition 1981).

17

*I seek a physician who knows the secret
of this world and the next,
That I may tell him of my condition
and be cured of the malady of transmigration.[1]*
—*Mira Bai*

Our caravan exits Baroda, rolling north up the Grand Trunk Road. The GT Road spans the sub-continent, from the mighty Himalaya down to India's southern tip, one of the important contributions of the former Mughals and the British Raj, 'though the GT can also be a hair-raising adventure:

> *In built-up areas, you move at a snail's pace through crowds of men and women, schoolchildren, cows, pigs, goats, water buffalo and camels; three-wheel taxis, bicycle rickshaws, buses and trucks are hooting all around you. In the country-side, the road surface is not wide enough to take two cars at once, so your driver will play a game of chicken, counting on his opponent to move aside at the last moment. Ours combined prudence with daring. That such skill was not universal was demonstrated by the number of over-loaded trucks lying upturned by the roadside....[2]*

It is my uneasy privilege to ride in the same car with the beloved Master. Uneasy, not because of the road hazards, but because I have the unmistakable sense that he is peering inside my innermost mind, aware of every uncontrolled thought, every secret. As I experience this tension, somewhere between fear and gratitude, he unexpectedly turns around from the front seat, gives me a quick look and comments, "Until one can meet the Inner Master and converse with Him at will, outer guidance is necessary." His sudden words transform into a mantra, a prayer that repeats itself over and over. My yearning for "at will" communion increases with each breath, each heartbeat.

In the afternoon we stop for lunch by the roadside, beneath the cooling shade of a huge banyan tree that spreads its protecting arms overhead while sending vines—airborne roots, actually—to the earth below. Vivid sap-green wheat fields, patches of bright yellow mustard flowers, and rows of tall sugar cane march into the distance, fenced by spangles of pink and red blooms on cactus hedges. *Basant!* Indian springtime! Beauty abounds in everything!

The Friend carefully peels and cuts a cantaloupe, then personally serves everyone; only then does he himself eat a thin sweet slice. There are no words to describe the presence of *Hu-Dost,* (Persian: *Friend of God*).

At dusk, our caravan pauses briefly for chai and leg-stretching in the medieval Rajput city of Chittor. Across the cobbled road and behind the tents of the bazaar, high, orange-red sandstone ramparts of ancient fortresses are gilded by the setting sun. These walls, which once held back mighty armies, now resound with the twitters and cries of thousands of roosting birds. Calling me to him, Master leans out the car window and asks, "Do you know that this is Chittor, the place where Princess Mira Bai lived? You know of Mira? She overflowed with love and intoxication of God. Her Guru was Ravi Das, the cobbler-Saint."

Having already learned to sing two of Mira's hauntingly beautiful Hindi bhajans, Master's history lesson assumes special meaning for me. Mira's songs are among the most poignant and lyric in the rich Sant tradition. The story of her God-inspired life is even part of India's multicultural school curriculum, where children of all religious backgrounds learn her devotional songs by rote.

Master continues, "Due to her devotion and worldly indifference, members of the royal family sought to kill princess Mira. Her sister-in-law put a poisonous snake in a basket of flowers and sent it as a gift. When Mira accepted, it is said that the snake emerged, bowed before her, and said, 'How fortunate am I to meet a true lover of the Lord.'

"Mira's brother-in-law starved a wild lion, then set it loose on the secluded path Mira walked every day—the path to the temple wherein she sat for meditation. Upon seeing her, tradition says, the lion bowed his head on her feet; 'At last I have found a true devotee! Now I have attained much benefit from having your darshan!'"

Master chuckles, "This is the outcome of true love for God. Such love has great power, you see. Such love can perform wonders!"

Sang sweet Mira:

> *O All-pervading One, I am dyed in Your color;*
> *When other's sweethearts live in foreign lands,*
> *They write letter after letter,*
> *But Mira's Beloved lives in her heart,*
> *And she sings happily day and night.*[3]

Ajmeer: We reach Ajmeer late at night. The morning sun uncloaks and gilds ancient palaces, temples, mosques, low mountains, Anasagar Lake, and Ajmeer's generous people. Sere desert, thorny shrubs, and rocky hills surround the city that is so typical of Rajasthan. After returning from a long exploratory walk, I find the Master sitting at ease in the sun-dappled shadows of a towering mango tree within the spacious walled garden of our hosts.

Only a handful are present and the conversation is relaxed. I watch as a two-year-old girl plucks a marigold and toddles near. The Master accepts her flower with sweetness and attention, then lovingly returns it.

In a disciple's garden, Ajmeer, 1967 (AS)

"I am wondering why so many Saints kept unshorn hair and beards," I ask.

"Saints are the worshippers of Nature!" Master responds vigorously. "Nature intended man to have a natural appearance. Nature is beautiful except when tormented by the hand of man. The beard was provided as protection. Those who keep it rarely experience throat or chest ailments." He emphasizes, "I'm not advocating or starting any new religion, mind that! Nor am I encouraging anyone to change the society or religion to which they already belong."

My mind is an open book to him. I have been secretly wanting to follow the Master's example and keep my own hair unshorn, perhaps even wear a turban. I then express curiosity about the biblical Samson, about whom it was inferred that he derived his superhuman strength from his unshorn hair and his chastity. When he lost both to Delila, he also lost his tremendous power. Master replied obliquely, "If a man were to keep his hairs unshorn in the West, he might find employment a problem," and adds, "Whatever is cut grows again. Even a man who shaves can have progress within, is it not so?"[4]

He discloses the beliefs of certain yogis that uncut hair conducts a subtle energy essential to the practice of *kumbhak yoga*—an obscure practice involving withdrawal of the vital airs or *prana* from the chakras below up to the *sahasrar*—the thousand-petalled lotus in the astral plane. The fruit of this practice can result in a state of suspended animation, super-human strength, and prolonged life. There are documented cases of kumbhak adepts supporting the full weight of an elephant or a truck on their bare chests. Some have been buried alive for long periods—for weeks and months, then revived. Through kumbhak yoga or even judicious use of breath, one can extend one's lifespan.

"Your *days* are not numbered; your *breaths* are numbered," he adds. "By regulation of breath, life can be prolonged. Conversely, by wasting breath through acts of dissipation, one's lifespan is shortened."

In contrast to several yoga systems, Sant Mat or the *Surat Shabd Yoga* involves withdrawal of the *surat* or attention altogether, by-passing the treacherous path of breath-control and kundalini (the path of serpent energy—which lies dormant at the base of the spine). In addition, there are no requirements to shave or not; the practice of anything of a potentially harmful nature is eschewed. The path of the Adepts may be practiced by the physically fit or unfit, the old or young, or by those of any religious background—the "isms" are left in place.

> As a river springing from the snowy peak of a towering mountain flows toward the sea, it undergoes many changes of setting, shape, motion, and appearance, and yet its waters remain the same. If one could discover this audible life-stream within oneself, if one could discover its lower reaches, one could use it as a pathway leading inevitably to its source. The currents might at certain points enter gorges and rapids but nevertheless they are the surest way on the upward journey. Be a range howsoever unscalable, the waters will have cut a pass and carved a passage, and he who will avail himself of their guidance would never fail to find a way. And since this Naam or Word-current springs from the Anaam or the Wordless, he who holds firmly to It will inevitably reach the starting point, transcending plane after plane of varying relativity until he arrives at the very source of name and form; thence to merge into That which has no name or form.[5]

Chisti's Tomb: Ajmeer is renowned for the memory of the great saint, Shaykh Mouinudin Chisti (1136-1236 A.D.), an early Sufi preceptor of *Sultan-ul-Azkar*, as the path of the Celestial Sound-current was then known in the Middle East. Chisti, who was born in Sanjar, Persia, received initiation from his spiritual Master, Khwaja Uthman Haruni in Nishapur. From there, the Saint made a lengthy journey on foot to India, eventually settling in Ajmeer, despite initial opposition from orthodox Hindus.[6]

Between satsangs, I have the opportunity to visit Chisti's tomb with Santokh, who serves as my guide through the old city. Many legends and miraculous stories concerning this great Master survive to the present, some no doubt having grown with the telling. Because of his love for the downtrodden, Chisti was known as *Gharib Niwaz, "the Abode of the Poor."*

With the passage of centuries, an elaborate mosque and esoteric school was established over Chisti's humble tomb. The twentieth-century Sufi mystic, Pir Inayat Khan, also lived and taught here. Khan was familiar with a branch of the inner science, palpably evident in *The Mysticism of Sound*, one of his many published books in the English language.

Santokh and I walk barefoot through the beautiful multi-arched ancient sandstone and marble buildings, aware of a lingering spiritual presence. We inspect two gargantuan iron cauldrons ten feet wide and fifteen deep in which tons of rice are cooked every year and sold to hordes of pilgrims who trek from all over India and abroad to attend the celebration of the anniversary of Chisti's birth and death days. The death anniversary is termed *Urs* (literally, "Wedding Day"), as death, to the lovers of God whom have achieved union with Him, removes the final veil from the face of the Beloved.[7]

The extraordinary devotion of our Ajmeeri hosts Kartar Chand, his wife, and sons is evident in every detail. Kartar, a prosperous sugar merchant, is a shaven Hindu though his sons have been brought up as Sikhs.[8] The example that this harmonious family sets has inspired hundreds of all faiths to traverse the path. Our words, if not backed up by practice, have no power.

The day before leaving for Jaipur, our next stop, Master asks me in jest, "Would you like to return to Delhi by elephant? You'd like? Just say, and I will arrange!"

The next morning I find myself astride a great tusked beast, with dark, gentle eyes. As brother elephant lumbers ponderously up an incline to the gateway of the Jaipur fortress, a strolling musician serenades us with his violin-like sarangi. When the ride is over, we find shade under a cluster of *peepul* trees. In their branches, we are entertained by a family of wild acrobatic monkeys, who win our applause and payment in bananas.

From the graceful pink sandstone redoubt on the promontory above, a handful of brave Rajput warriors held back Emperor Aurangzeb's hordes, bent on subjugating all of India. After a valiant struggle, the Rajputs were no match for the huge armies and perished to the last. The Rajput women committed suicide rather than surrender and be violated. These beautiful fortresses whisper a rich and tragic past of patriots, martyrs, and heroes.

It is the Saints, the Masters, who have sustained and nourished India's soul throughout the chaotic millennia. Their wisdom and message of individual salvation has spread to all countries of the world. I know that spirituality is not bound to any physical locale, but whenever I see a map of the Indian sub-continent protruding from the great landmass above it, down into the Indian Ocean, I cannot help but ruminate on her vaguely heart-like shape. Does our planet of elements have a *heart?* If fortunate enough to become attuned to the Infinite, one may feel its pulse everywhere, yet here in India, perhaps more than anywhere. She may be over-crowded and burdened with great difficulties, but India's spirituality endures. It permeates the dust, the centuries-old dust trodden by the Saints and lovers of the One.

---

1. Darshan Singh, *Streams of Nectar*, Wiley Eastern Ltd, New Delhi 110 002, 1993, p. 145.

2. Denis Healey, Former Chancellor of the Exchequer in Britain, fondly writing of his travels in India, *Toronto Globe & Mail.*

3. *Women Saints of East and West*, (London: Ramakrishna Vedanta Centre, 1972,) p. 56.

4. Kirpal Singh was born into a Khatri Sikh family whose custom was to let the hair grow unshorn all through life. Although he became a universal man, Kirpal Singh continued to respect and observe the outer aspects of his traditional faith. During his period of search, he studied and mastered many forms of yoga. In the biography *Pita Poot*, author H.C. Chaddha chronicles in Hindi hitherto unknown incidents, spiritual practices and experiences from Kirpal Singh's extraordinary early life prior to his first contact with his Satguru. In one such example, Kirpal, in his tireless attempts to realize God, spent many winter nights from dusk to dawn meditating while standing in a frigid pond, water up to his neck. Mr. Chaddha related to me, "'Maharaj, that was a very great *tapas* [austerity] you performed.' He replied, 'That was no austerity; it was the only way one could withstand the inner fire of kundalini.'" Kirpal Singh was also a firm believer in regular exercise, fresh air, pure diet, and continence to restore and maintain good health. Even into his sixties, he could perform the most difficult of yoga exercises. He wrote, "The curative power is already within the body; doctors merely help to clear the way...."

5. Kirpal Singh, *The Crown of Life: A Study in Yoga* (Delhi, India: Ruhani Satsang, 1970), pp.144-147.

6. John A. Subhan, *Sufism, Its Saints and Shrines*, (Lucknow Publishing House, 1960).

7. Shaykh Chisti's successor was Qutub-uddin (1186-1237), whose successor in turn was the famed Baba Farid (1173-1266), known as Shakar Gunj, or "Storehouse of Sugar." When just a young boy, Farid would sit for daily prayers with his devout mother. She would hide a piece of candy under her son's prayer mat, and after prayers were completed, he would reach for the candy Allah always gave him. One day his mother forgot to put the candy there. Realizing her forgetfulness, she became afraid that her son might lose his faith in Allah when he discovered her simple ruse. But Farid's heart was so pure, and God so in love with him, the treats miraculously appeared. Thus his saintly reputation spread.

8. Until the early twentieth century, it was the custom of many Hindus to bring up their first-born sons in the Sikh form, a carry-over from the seventeenth and eighteenth centuries when India was plunged into an uprising against the Mughals. During that period, with the exception of the Rajputs, Marwars, and Mahrattas, Hindus generally carried on commerce, administration, and agriculture. The majority of male Sikhs went into the military, ostensibly as defenders of Dharma or righteousness, earning distinction as courageous warriors, even during World Wars I & II.

VILLAGE DANTAL AND THE LORD OF PETROL

18

Diary: Ajmeer is several hours behind us. There is no sign in evidence as the car suddenly veers off the highway to the left. The Master and his party are expected at Dantal, a farming village, some fifty miles west across a tortuous, road—what amounts to nothing more than a rutted dirt path. Dust plumes kicked up by our lurching car rise high into the cloudless air, a signal to all within sight that someone special is on the way, for cars rarely pass here. Thick dust covers our windows, and as it shakes free, we glimpse the ancient land.

Here and there are sudden out-croppings of rocky terrain, dark islands in the dun-colored sand. New wheat covers fertile and irrigated patches with rich green. Farmers behind wooden plows are pulled by black, horned oxen or leathery camels, manuring as they plod along. The men of this region uniformly dress in white cotton dhoti and shirts, but their heads are crowned with bright orange, purple, or red turbans. The women who work at their sides are dressed in vivid ghagra choli—long flowing red, green, blue, yellow, and purple skirts with tiny mirrors sewn onto them. Their blouses and scarves are elaborately embroidered, their wrists and ankles bedecked with silver bangles—colorful splashes punctuating the starkness of the land.

Plunging deeper into the countryside, our caravan grows as peasants drop plows and run toward the cars. After four long years, Maharaj Ji has returned! Turning back to peer through the dust-wake, I see scores of laughing, bobbing heads, perfect white teeth, dark skin, turbans and veils askew, joyous families running enmasse. Lurching along the crests and falls in the path, we arrive at last at Dantal nestled at the foot of a hoary mountain. The beauty of such an unspoiled place thrills this refugee from modernity.

In no time, the car is surrounded. Mohan says in broken English, "This whole village, all Master initiates, five hundred! Only very few no initiated, one or two peoples. Very simple peoples! Very much love Maharaj Ji!"

We drive the final leg through a narrow road choked alternately with tangles of banyan and mango tree roots, slow-moving cows, and blithely unaware pedestrians. Finally the narrowness and incline bar further passage. Master alights to greet his beloved children, many of whom try taking the dust from his shoes. I am almost swept away by the noisy river-like human mass and have to push and squirm to keep up. With obvious difficulty, Master labors slowly up the steep rocky path between a narrow corridor of buildings, the mountain towering directly overhead.

Before a little house, he pauses for breath and mounts a flight of stairs, entering a tiny, darkened, two-room dwelling. I barely squeeze through the compacted crowd outside. After adjusting to the darkness within, I see Master holding the hand of someone lying under mosquito netting. The veil drawn aside, I see a man with a strong, broad face, split with a huge smile and perfect teeth; deep love glistens in his eyes. Master turns to me and says, "See his rosy cheeks? See how robust he looks? You would never suspect that he has been bedridden for so many years. You see, he is paralyzed from the waist down."

As a silent interchange of loving glances passes among us, the man says something in Hindi. Master translates for me, "He says, 'It is due to my bad karma that I am bedridden, but it is my good karma that Master has come!'" Some karmic debts must be paid before final liberation can be received. Only a strong few can accept them so graciously.

Pundit Ghansham Das is a learned disciple of Hazur. The success of Master's mission here is greatly due to Ghansham's exemplary influence. Before taking leave of this dear brother lying physically helpless but spiritually awakened, Master reveals, "It is for his sake I have come all the way here! Even the slenderest strands of love are stronger than ropes of steel!"

Master bids him adieu and amazingly *jogs* down the rocky hill to where more than a thousand villagers wait, chanting Mira bhajans beneath a brightly patterned canopy. For two hours, the Master pours his heart into these lovely people, who drink each word, each gesture, each glance, enraptured. Strong tides are flowing! A handlebar-mustachioed farmer sitting near is wholly lost in the sight of his Beloved, and a smile stretches from ear to ear as he rocks back and forth, tears streaming his cheeks. I glance around for a moment and notice that ecstasy has swept the crowd. Today the tears are not of pain, but of loving joy.

Late in the day as we take leave of Dantal, the car is again pursued. With eyes sparkling, Master Kirpal turns to address me from the front seat, "These people are simple," (pause) "God is simple, and *He* is simple too!"

"How many from this village saw the Radiant Form at Initiation?" I ask of him.

"Ninety-nine out of a hundred. There was only one man who could not see."

Astounded, I ask again, "The Radiant Form of the Master?" (In the West, ten to twenty-five per cent might have this experience at the time of initiation.)

"Yes. When I first visited Dantal four years ago," Guru Ji continues, "several hundred came for initiation and were given a sitting. Meanwhile another seventy-five arrived and asked to be initiated also. They were given instructions, the Names, and put into meditation separate from the first group. More from outlying districts arrived, also requesting Naam! This third group was also given a sitting. Then the first and second groups had to be attended for Sound. A fourth group arrived, but as it was so late they had to be turned away."

Time, which bears heavily on modern society, means little to those who live by the seasons, by the rising and setting of the sun. Here, no newspapers, no

Dantal Village satsang, 1967 (AS)

cinemas, no radio or television, no billboards, no rushing and pushing pace, no noise, no pollution, no hospital, no jail. These are the hewers of wood and drawers of water, their faith deeply ingrained from cradle to pyre. Religion and spirituality are as much a part of their life as food and water.

The Lord of Petrol: "Forgive me, Maharaj Ji, but I forgot to get petrol (gasoline) for the car, and now we are out," confesses Ram Saroop. The highway is still fifty miles distant. Master rebukes Ram Saroop for being so careless in his duties. Master then does a strange thing. He begins praising petrol like anything: "Petrol is one of the wonders of the world, it is the proverbial demon carrying the load of industry and commerce, it runs great factories and propels cars, ships, and airplanes. Petrol has helped annihilate distance....petrol has lightened man's burdens...." In no time it seems the car reaches the main highway safely, a span of fifty miles on an empty tank!

Ram Saroop, realizing what has happened, folds his wizened hands and bows before the Master. "Maharaj Ji, you have saved us again!"

"What?" Master replies, "I have done nothing. I have only praised petrol, and petrol has helped us!"

Heart to heart with the Master—Rajasthani village. (AS)

19

*Love is both the beginning and the end of the path.
In this way, God's love and our own are identical, for one
who has divine love has reached God.—Kirpal Singh*

15th March, 1967: Another ten-day tour begins—this time, Western Rajasthan: In this hot, thorny land, many seek respite from the sorrows and uncertainties of worldly existence. The simple and the sophisticated, young and old, the sheep and the tiger, all drink from the same well to find quickening in the company of the One for whom there is no stranger and no enemy.

While traversing the narrow, pocked road south of Delhi, the rear tire of our overloaded Ambassador car blows out on a deserted stretch. The mission's old blue Studebaker passes by and stops a little ahead. Out steps the Master to inspect the damage and tire-change while I stand idly by, watching him. Turning, he rebukes me firmly, "Why don't you sit and meditate!" I back away and immediately sit in bhajan beneath the shade of a kikkar thorn-tree. The reprimand of the Friend is a jolt, an awakening, as self begins to dissolve into the celestial Sound-current. My truest ally is the Word; my enemy the lower mind. Mind seeks separate existence, whereas the Friend, union. Whether in his presence or deep in the bliss of meditation, even the most skeptical, agitated monkey-mind finds a "peace" which "passeth understanding."

Hanumanghar, March 15. The white-clad One sits in a wicker chair facing an open courtyard, conversing with twenty or so fanned out before him. I emerge from my room, still in the afterglow of meditation. "You sing bhajan for Master?" Tai Ji asks. Confused, I think she means *listening* to the Unstruck Sound, for bhajan has more than one meaning. She corrects with a giggle, "No, No! *Sing* bhajan!" This hymn of Guru Nanak flows from my heart to his, and fills the nighted courtyard:

Santa Jana Mila Har Jas Gayo
In the company of Saints, glorify the Lord,
Kota Janama kaye dukha gawayo
And in exaltation, find relief from all sorrow,
Jo chahata soi mana payo
Where every wish is fulfilled;
Kara Kirpa Haar Naam divayo
O Merciful One, bestow the gift of Naam...

Sara Basukha Haar Naam Berdayee
Supreme, unalloyed bliss-giving Naam.
Gur Parshada Nanak Mata Payae
By Guru's grace, Nanak hath attained Knowledge Divine.

Night descends suddenly in Rajasthan. Like the sparrows, most people have left for their homes. Only the Master, Mohinder—the local group leader, Dr. Lal Singh, and myself remain. A deep detachment from the world has taken root, and I long for a life of meditation in seclusion, free from distractions. Some of my Indian brethren might say my inclination is a result of *sanskaras* or impressions carried forward from previous incarnations. My Western friends might think I am seeking an easy way out. I have no inkling of the intense life of action and responsibility awaiting me.

"Master," I ask, "should I give up all worldly ambition and spend full time meditating in an effort to reach the Goal in this life?"

"Hazur did not give Naam to yogis who lived from the offerings of others," he replies, "but if they were truly after spirituality, He would give it only after extracting their promise to meditate at least six hours daily—three hours for themselves and three hours for the people from whom they begged! Everything must be accounted for. Even a glass of water, if given out of devotion, has to be paid for. The person who gives has some motive behind it, and if you accept, your account is debited. If you have little or no spiritual capital, then you become bankrupted.

"If a soul is really in earnest, God has ways of taking care of their needs so their devotion and spiritual practice remains unbroken. Such cases are rare. Practically all Masters except for one or two earned their livelihood by the sweat of brow and were householders. Work with detachment as much as will provide for basic necessities. Whatever is left over should be shared with others, and devote your spare time to meditation."

I ask, "How much time did Master meditate?"

"I used to put in a maximum of sixteen to eighteen hours a day," he replies, "in shifts of four to eight hours at a stretch; five to six hours a day minimum as a householder, under the orders of my Master."

After bidding good-night, I retreat to my unlit room, pondering his attainment while simultaneously trying to fathom my direction. Intellect soon exhausts itself, and soul is launched into the living, luminous void—a moth fluttering toward the Midnight Sun.

In the morning, Maharaj Ji addresses the open-aired assembly:

"One who knows will never say that He knows. Who does not know will always brag, 'I know!' A true Master will never say he is a Master, for he sees

Rajasthani temple architechture (AS)

God as the Doer of everything, Who knows his knowing, and that he of himself knows nothing."

After initiation, our two-car caravan departs, pushing for hours across arid Rajasthan. Sand dunes, bright turbans, and camels flash by as I keep my head partly outside the stationwagon's window in a bid to minimize the suffocating 120° F heat. Twelve of us are crammed into this improbable space. Farmers eke subsistence from the parched and barren soil. Cactus and thorn-bush fences contain thin cattle while keeping out thieves. Flat lands, empty sand, reddish hills, black rocks, red stones, majestic buttes, thatched huts, patches of bright green, water-holes, hundreds of temples—huge temples and tiny one-person temples—life in the slow lane. Lakes and wells are few and far between. Where there is water, there is life; where there is life are people, and among the people, there is always a tiny handful hungry for the higher way.

Padampur. Diary: March 18. For three days we are guests of Jagir Singh, a wealthy farmer and village chieftain. Upon freshly plowed fields, hemmed by mango and guava groves and high adobe walls, more than 3,500 villagers listen to the Satguru from Delhi. Late in the afternoon, Jagir Singh and family take our party on a guided tour of their large mango and guava orchards. I discreetly follow with my old eight-millimeter movie camera. While filming, Maharaj Ji walks right up to the lens as I'm peering through. "What is this?" he asks. I am tongue-tied as usual, and hand it over, not knowing if he is pleased or displeased.

"I want to take your picture too!" he says with a chuckle, aiming the camera at me and then around at the gathering crowd. Soon, the film is exhausted. Although I normally wouldn't admit it, I'm really overjoyed to be in the picture, thinking, "Now, I'll have something to show back home, taken by none other than him!" To my chagrin, however, when I open the camera, the entire film spills out, exposed and ruined. Diwan Chand laughs, "Oh-ho! brother, Master wants you to use the camera of your third eye!" *Whatever.*

Ganganagar, Diary: March 22-24. After brief satsang stops in Karampur and Fathui villages, we arrive in Ganganagar, a dusty frontier town surrounded by fertile fields and a grid of tree and pampas-lined canals. We take up residence in a large dharamshala. Our first night is to begin with Master's discourse in a large canopied square in the center of town, but the air turns unseasonably cold. Strong winds shake and lift the overhead canopy while we chant before the empty dais. Thunder and lightning suddenly shatter the atmosphere and a few heavy raindrops fall, followed by a roaring downpour, filling the roads with dancing rivulets.

Satsang shifts to a large Hindu temple attached to our dharamshala four blocks away. Several hundred of us run, laughing, slipping, and jostling through the muddy thundering lanes. The raging storm knocks out the city's power. Candles and lanterns are lit as we file into the eerie temple and sit cross-legged before an ornate altar. Every sound echoes beneath cavernous vaulted ceilings; candle flames cast weird shadows across an eight-foot high milk-white marble statue of Ram Chandra, Avatar of Vishnu.[1]

Whispers cease. We become aware of the unmistakable sound of Master's footsteps crunching sand against the marble floor, echoing along the walls. After removing his shoes, Maharaj Ji sits cross-legged on a low wooden table next to the altar. For the next half hour, he looks penetratingly into the audience without speaking or moving, while candles and lanterns accentuate his haunting beauty. Outside, the storm continues to rage. Next to the Master, who, as always, is oblivious to distraction, a temple priest nervously mutters prayers and waves candles before his mute white idol.

Ram Chandra was a Hindu incarnation of the *Preserver* aspect of the Divine. Tonight, Master describes the four phases of Rama, the function of *Kaal* (Time, also termed the Negative Power) and of *Akaal*, (the Timeless, or Positive Power):

Coming to the aid of the devotees of his era, Rama incarnated into this world to wash away all the unhappiness that the sages, the rishis (meditating forest-ascetics), and munis (sages) were suffering at the hands of evil forces; this is the work of the Avatar. When any country is badly run and riots begin, control is put into the military's charge and when the trouble is corrected, rule returns to civil administration. So it is on a larger scale, when the world retrogresses to a state beyond its own control, God's Power manifests in the form of the Avatar, who settles chaos and misery and restores righteousness.

Tulsi Das, author of this great epic, tells of the two manifestations of the same Power, which are superimposed upon each other. However, there is a vast difference between these two: the Master's Rama and the world's Rama.

> One Rama was the son of Dasrath,
> One Rama is vibrating in each being,
> One Rama is Creation's play,
> One Rama is distinct from all.

The main comparison is between Rama which manifested in the Avatar Ram Chandra, and the Rama which is different from or above all other powers. The Avatar, Ram Chandra, or Lord Rama, who is stated to have been the incarnation of Lord Vishnu, the Preserver, was born the son of King Dasrath and was competent in fourteen supernatural powers.

Avatars are like benefactors who come to give decent food and clothing to the prisoners, to temporarily alleviate their sufferings, yet in spite of this they are still bound in the prison of the world. The Masters come to free us forever from this prison and escort us back to the heavenly abode of our Father.

Naam is the Maker of both Avatars and Masters. Somewhere this great Power is working in the Avatar like a commander-in-chief of an army, and somewhere It is working in the Master like a viceroy. Both are expressions of the same power, but with different functions.

As Kabir has said, "God has made Negative and Positive, for He wanted to enact the play of creation." Both are God's great Power, which He uses in His own design of creation. That Power is the Sustainer of everything—It is the background behind everything; Its methods of working are varied, that's all. Avatars punish the sinners and reward the righteous; Masters free the attention from the prison of mind and senses and rejoin that attention or soul to its Source. The Avatar's job is to restore and maintain order in the world that it may remain inhabited by souls; the Master's job is to uproot souls from worldly habitation, pull the soul above mind and senses, and connect it to Naam Itself. So Negative and Positive both draw their Power from the One Lord.

The morning following the storm, a frail elderly woman is carried up the steep narrow stairs to our dharamshala's roof, where Master holds court. Pouring forth a tale of woe, she weepingly implores him to release her from the miseries of old age. Although an old initiate of Sawan Singh, she has lost contact with the inner Light and Sound. Master asks directly, "Mata Ji, do you really want to die?" She croaks, "Yes." The Master smiles and walks over to her chair, puts his thumb on her wrinkled forehead, and commands her to close her eyes. Master's brow is furrowed in concentration; he then asks what she sees inside: "A star! A great bright star in the inner sky!" After removing his thumb, he says, "Learn dying while living," impressing upon her the need for preparation before the final change. After reassuring her of Hazur's constant protection, he returns to his room where others wait.

Among the new aspirants is a venerable sadhu with dreadlocks piled high on his head. In his fifty-year search, Bhagat Ram performed austerities such as *Panch Taap* (the austerity of five fires, i.e. sitting between four fires, with the hot sun overhead); standing on one leg continuously for several years, meditating in the jungles and in icy Himalayan caves like Shiva; wandering penniless across the sub-continent from one pilgrimage spot to another. And, like the seeker from Indore, he'd received initiation from several teachers but until today, he was still bereft of the treasure of Naam. Later, when describing his initiation experience with Master Kirpal, an inner bliss transforms his wrinkled old face, for Bhagat Ram secured the radiant form of the Guru Dev, and his glistening eyes proclaim, "I will ever be bound by your Love!"

Only five are unable to hear the Unstruck Melody. When Maharaj Ji has them sit again for listening, while standing over them, he closes his own right ear with his thumb. I and several others sitting in the room copy his example. At the end, when he asks of their inner experience, the result is unanimous; everyone, including those who heard nothing at first, now report clear, loud pealing of the big bell in their body-temple. When he turns from the new initiates to ask what the spectators experienced, three attempt to describe inner flights beyond relativity to *Par Brahm*.

Diary: March 24. On the open road once again, the direction of our compass is God—Who is in all directions. During the five hundred mile return journey, the old Studebaker breaks down ten times in the heavy rains. Each time she coughs back to life again as toothless Ram Saroop coaxes and supplicates her in the strangest mixture of Hindi and English. Twelve of us share this ride. I sit between him and Mool Raj. Hand firmly on the wheel, Ram Saroop addresses me, "O Sahib! 1955 Champion Studebaker, American car! Master Power, Ram Power, Guru Power, very great! O Sahib, God Power very great." Having exhausted his English repertoire, Ram Saroop lapses into singing the Ramayana:

Ram Naam, rattan amolak, Gupat khajana,
Pita ji, mooay varney do.
The Name of God is a priceless jewel
O my father, let me be betrothed to Him.

To keep from sleeping at the wheel, Ram Saroop sings from the Ramayana's endless verses at the top of his lungs, his sparkling dark eyes inebriant, godly. En route to Delhi, our hearts and voices spontaneously join in singing various hymns of the Saints. We stop occasionally for *"pachees meel chai"* (25 mile tea), strong enough to keep Ram Saroop going another twenty-five miles, or *"pachaas meel chai"* (fifty-mile chai), very strong tea indeed!

The Beloved Master, who had gone ahead in another car, is waiting for us with open arms when our weary caravan straggles into the Delhi ashram.

I have the unshakable sense that every detail of our journey has already taken place on a higher level of being. Even in dreams, it is the same as waking, *it is always He*. In every face, everywhere, it is *His* face.

Silent and effortless communion goes on for several days continuously. Only when taken for granted does this special grace dissipate, leaving me stranded and longing in the world of opposites and dis-clarity.

---

1. Rama's heroic exploits are captured in Sanskrit verse in the ancient religious classic of Hinduism, the *Ramayana*. The original Ramayana was composed thousands of years ago by the forest sage, Valmiki, purportedly centuries *before* Rama was even born. Many spiritual truths lie hidden in the pages of the Sanskrit *Ramayana* and its more contemporary Hindi predecessor, the *Ram Charitar Manas*, written by Goswami Tulsi Das. The fantastical and supernatural tales of both scriptures are beautiful allegories, containing deep mystical teachings on the devotional path. But, what was meant to be literal is usually taken as figurative, and the figurative as literal. Nineteenth century Tulsi Sahib of Hathras, a great mystic Adept, divulged that in a previous life, he was Tulsi Das, and had come again to clarify and demystify his teachings, which he recorded in the *Ghat Ramayan [The Inner Ramayana of the Body]*. The Ghat Ramayana is a powerful esoteric record of Sant Mat teachings written in the common language of his time and place.

20

His feet shone as burnished brass...

March 27: It was my good fortune to find the Beloved Master completely alone this morning, sitting cross-legged on his bed, working on fat bundles of correspondence. Approaching cautiously, I ventured to ask a question that had been on my mind for over two years:

"Hello?"

"Yes, what is it, please?"

"I have read in your writings that both Baba Jaimal Singh and Baba Sawan Singh had the *padam rekha* or lotus line on their feet as a physical sign of spiritual mastery. I wonder if Master would please....?"

Wordlessly smiling, he glanced down at his right foot resting on his left knee, and pulled off the white sock.

Looking very closely at the sole of his bare foot, I saw a very long, deep, slightly curved line running along the center, starting about three inches from the heel. Joining this central "stem" near the ball of the foot (at the solar-plexus point of reflexology) was a flower-like constellation, where many lines joined together in a large star-like lotus, radiating finer lines up and outward to each toe. Maharaj Ji traced his index finger along the central line to ensure that I understood. Unconsciously, I moved closer in order to see better. A sweet delicate perfume, like perfect jasmine after a rain, was emanating. Like the *chakor* bird, my head felt pulled closer and closer until finding repose on his foot; ecstatic bliss suddenly surged into my consciousness.[1]

"Let me see your foot," he asked after I came to. When I bared my foot with the intention of showing him my usual non-lotus lines, they somehow had now disappeared. The sole of my foot was quite blank, and I felt intensely exposed and unformed.

"If one is born without the lotus, can it ever develop?" I managed to ask. His answer was silence, while gazing on me with compassion. As there was nothing left to discuss, I tried to thank him and took my leave.

Over the next few months, I experienced many unusual manifestations in the Master's presence, and when comparing notes with others at the ashram, I was not alone. For example, on his broad forehead, three radiant vertical lines often appeared. At other times the natural forehead creases coalesced into crescents, orbs and the sanskrit OM sign. Sometimes, in his presence, all thoughts of body and of self would go. His form would then begin glowing, increasing with every heartbeat. On occasion, Kirpal Singh—the man, would actually disappear, leaving only a sphere of boundless Light spreading in all directions. This lent profound meaning to his self-deprecating reference he once or twice made to himself as "Mister Zero."

Such manifestations appearing in the visage of past Saints are mentioned, though rarely, in several ancient texts and scriptures. Mystic yoga treatises refer to three *nadis* or subtle energy channels: *ida, pingala,* and *shushumna,* which, while present in everyone, lie dormant, waiting their awakening. These conduits allow energy to pass between higher spiritual regions and the corporeal body through the *tisra til* (third-eye) center, and downward to the lower *chakras* or ganglionic centers at the throat, heart, navel, generative organ, and rectum. However, only in the central channel, between and behind the eyes, in the *shushumna,* can the Celestial Melodies be heard. Through this aperture, the distilled and etherialized spirit rises up, drawn towards its Source.

Another stage on the soul's journey comes when an archetypal vision of *luminous feet* manifests within the meditator's steady gaze, a prelude to meeting the complete image of the Adept before it descends from the astral plane above. As fantastic as it may seem, a golden dust-like brilliance emanates from the Lotus Feet into the seeker's awareness. This "dust" has been referred to by various mystics as an *elixir of life* and the progenitor of higher knowledge.

> *Take care to retain attention*
> *within the two eyebrows;*
> *Purifying mind and body,*
> *fix gaze at one center;*
> *Penetrate then the Beyond,*
> *Behold Reality face to face;*
> *Where, O Tulsi, the dust of Saints*
> *spreads a wondrous carpet of Light.*
> —Sant Tulsi Das

This mystical experience is not exclusive to the East. In the Revelations of St. John we find:

> *His head and his hairs were white like wool,*
> *as white as snow;*
> *and his eyes were as a flame of fire;*
> *And his feet like unto fine brass,*
> *as if they burned in a furnace;*
> *and his voice as the sound of many waters...*
> *and his countenance was as the sun shineth in his strength.*

---

1. The Indian chakor bird becomes mesmerized whenever a full moon comes out. The chakor remains motionless, but its head slowly follows the moon across the night sky, until it bends and finally rests backwards on the ground.

Throughout the ages the line of Gurus has been in existence.—Gurbani

Spirituality has enjoyed numerous flowerings within the world's great religious traditions, underpinned by the illuminations and revelations of individuals. The Realized Being, in whose person the fullness of mystic experience fuses with gnosis or spiritual knowledge, appears in most if not all of these traditions. Such ecstatic heroes embody a kind of theosophy of Light based on receptivity to the *Word* or *Logos*, the *Naam, Shabd, Udgit, Kalma,* or *Sarosha*, as the God-into-expression power is called in various languages. As the seeker makes progress, he or she comes to fathom the true meaning behind the revelatory utterances of saints.

Christianity and Islam, although not initiatory in their official exoteric forms, contain such streams. Although the great Church attempted to substitute itself in the place of individual prophetic inspiration, spiritual hermeneutics emerged from time to time in individuals like Meister Eckhardt, Jacob Boehme, Emmanuel Swedenborg, St. Theresa, and others.

Sufi and Shiite streams within Islam have acknowledged and honored a divine anthropomorphism manifesting in human form, which draws practitioners toward their own celestial assumption. Some of the brightest stars in the Sufi galaxy include Mansur, Shamaz Tabriz, Hafiz, Rumi, Najmuddin Kubra, Mueenudin Chisti, and Bulleh Shah.

In the Buddhist tradition, India's Bodhi-dharma and Tibet's Milarepa appear. The Jewish Balshemtov of Russia was a transcendent example of the mystic knower. Spirituality in India flourished under Mahavira of the Jains, in Mira and in Ramakrishna. It emerged in the Chinese Master of *Tao*, Lao Tsu, in the Persian prophets Zoroaster and Mani, and numerous others.

As the Word, Logos, or Tao is blind to outer labels, it often moves across religious and family lines. A keen seeker would pay scant attention to the external religious form, nationality or genetic race of the enlightened, just as the shape and color of a bottle has little relevance to what is inside, form being merely a vessel to contain the essence.

As I am about to accompany the Master on his forthcoming tour of northern India's Punjab, my heart picks up a beat. I have long contemplated the peerless quality and variety of this region's heritage of spiritual sons and daughters, and their relationship to the present dispensation.

Punjab actually means "five waters," and the fertile province is defined by the Beas, Ravi, Satluj, Chenab, and Jhelum rivers. Aryan, Greek, Afghan, Persian, Mongolian, and Turkish armies poured through Himalayan passes into this rich and fertile region, bringing with them new religions, ideas, and arts, cross-pollinating local culture, customs, and bloodlines. Despite invasions and tyranny, the Path of the Masters took deep root here and managed to survive prevailing orthodoxy's frequent efforts to restrain or eliminate it.

Sixteenth-century India was witness to two great spiritual teachers of universal scope: Kabir Sahib of Banares, and his contemporary, Guru Nanak of the Punjab. Their teachings focus on the perfect science of inner Light and Sound—as well as to outer expression in compassion and selfless service to all creation. Both Saints taught the limitations of idol worship, rites, rituals, fasts, pilgrimages, and casteism. They were much more than social reformers as some historians have dubbed them.

The Sikh Saints: Nanak (1469-1539), considered *Guru* to Hindus and Pir to Muslims, was first in a lineage of illumined Masters known as the Ten Sikh Gurus. Nanak traveled widely on foot, north to Tibet, east to China's borders, south to Sri Lanka, and west to Mecca—an incredible feat, considering the absence of trains, cars, and airplanes. His contemporary, Kabir Sahib (1399-1519), taught in and around the pilgrimage city of Benares and was also embraced by Hindus and Muslims alike. Although it is taught that Nanak was born spiritually perfect and had no need of any Guru, his prolific writings proclaim the need for such in almost every verse. Some believe that in his youth, Nanak encountered the great Kabir Sahib with several other sadhus where he realized the "True Bargain of life" (*Sacha Sauda*), although there is no external proof other than the important and striking fact that their teachings are identical in every important aspect. Whether this historical issue will ever be resolved is less important than the fact that both lived and sang the unity of the One Creator, of the One Divine Light immanent in all forms, realizable within. Both spoke of the five spiritual regions and of the five holy names. Both emphasized the importance of finding a perfected living teacher or Satguru. Both advocated the transformative power of satsang, the receiving of ethical and spiritual instruction, and of meditation on *Sat Naam* or the True Name. Although dialects differed, their terminology and cosmology were identical. Their original styles both found prolific expression in sacred poetry and song.

In the Sikh lineage, Angad followed Nanak, Amar Das followed Angad, and Ram Das followed Amar Das. In 1604 AD, the fifth Guru, Arjan Dev, completed his compilation of the *Adi Granth* or *Granth Sahib*, comprising approximately 1,400 large pages in *Gurmukhi* script. This remarkable scripture contains the writings of six of the Gurus, all of whom used the *nom de plume* "Nanak." Thus they came to be known as Nanak the First, Nanak the Second, Nanak the Third, and so on. Included in the Holy Granth are the verses of many other saints of realization, belonging to various religions and castes. By far the largest selection belongs to Kabir Sahib. In it, we also find the verses of

Dhanna the farmer; Saina the barber; Sadhna of the butcher caste; Nam Dev the calico printer; Ravi Das the cobbler; Shaykh Farid a Muslim divine; Raja Pipa, a king; Ramanand the Brahmin; Ramanuja the Reformer; the blind poet-saint Sur Das; Trilochan; Beni; Bhikan; Jai Dev; and Parmanand. One of the earliest original versions also contained a hymn of Mira Bai.[1] (Many beautiful verses of the Ninth Guru, Tegh Bahadur were later included by his son and successor, Guru Gobind Singh. The Tenth Guru included none of his own.)

In Guru Arjan's court were many of India's greatest scholars and musicians who spent years collecting, sorting, and copying verses by hand. Under his inspired guidance, each of the *Granth Sahib's* thousands of verses was designated one of thirty-one different classical musical measures, or *ragas*, so that future musicians could know which melody would be best suited for each verse. Kirpal Singh referred to this inclusive scripture as "a banquet hall of spirituality" because of its rich diversity of Saints from all backgrounds, prevailing religions and professions.

The Sikh scriptures occupy a unique position in religious history. They represent not only the first deliberate attempt to present the oneness of all religions, but are composed in a language that is still alive and not a thing of the past. Hence they have lost none of their pristine freshness and have not been wholly buried under the debris of theological interpretation. Being mainly in the form of devotional lyrics, their appeal is not merely expositional. They speak of the whole man, singing of his problems, his weaknesses, the vanity of the world and the eternity of the Absolute, beckoning him on to greater and ever greater effort, towards his divine home.[2]

Guru Arjan Dev's fame as saint, scholar, and patron of the arts spread far and wide. Even the emperor Akbar the Great (1542-1605) twice visited Guru Arjan and became a pious admirer, donating a large tract of land surrounding Amritsar for his work. Arjan's great learning, humility, and universal vision endeared him to the masses, but also earned resentment from the narrow-minded orthodoxy. When the Guru was later falsely accused of undermining Islam and Hinduism and brought before Jahangir, the fanatic son and successor of Akbar, he was asked to change the *Adi Granth*. Guru Arjan replied to the emperor:

"I regard all, whether Hindu or Muslim, rich or poor, friend or foe, without any hatred or partiality....As to the erasure of hymns in the Granth Sahib, I cannot erase or alter even one iota. I am a worshipper of the Immortal God, the Supreme Soul of the world. There is no monarch save Him; and what He revealed to the Gurus ....is written in the holy Granth Sahib. The hymns which find a place in it are not disrespectful to any Hindu incarnation or the Prophet Mohammed, blessed be his name. It is certainly stated that prophets, saints, and incarnations are the

handiwork of the Immortal God, whose limit none can find. My main object is the spread of truth and the destruction of falsehood; and if, in pursuance of this object, my perishable body must depart, I shall account it great good fortune."

The gentle Guru's enemies concluded that he would yield to no ordinary threats, so they put fetters on him and began to torture him in various ways. He was ordered to sit on red hot-iron plates, super-heated sand was poured upon his head, and boiling water was spilled over his holy body. Not once did the Guru utter a cry or beg for mercy.

When his friend, the Muslim mystic Hazrat Mian Mir, witnessed this torture, he wept and begged permission from Guru Arjan to use supernatural powers to bring down a rain of fire upon the Guru's tormentors. Guru Arjan replied that although it also was in his power to do this, the way of the Saints was in submission to the will of God.

"I bear all this torture to set an example to the Saints of the True Name, that they may not lose patience or rail at God in affliction. The true test of faith is the hour of misery."

He then uttered the famous words,

"Tera Bhana Meeta Lagay.
Sweet is Thy Will."

After the martyrdom of Guru Arjan, Nanak's dispensation continued unabated through Hargobind (1595-1645), Har Rai (1631-1661), Har Krishan (1656-1664), and Tegh Bahadur (1622-1675). The number of their disciples steadily increased. Tegh Bahadur also received a martyr's fate at the hands of Aurangzeb, the last of the Mughal emperors, who ordered his beheading. Before his tenth year, Gobind Rai, the son of the martyred Ninth Guru, was already fully God-realized and cognizant of his divine mission.

Aurangzeb ruled India with an iron fist and forcibly converted all in his grasp to Islam. Those who resisted were crushed or enslaved. Over the next three decades the Guru infused courage into the terrorized populace to rise up, defend and reclaim their freedom and dignity. Thus, in 1699, when tyranny was at its zenith, the Tenth Guru established the *Khalsa*, or brotherhood of the Pure Ones, to protect the weak and innocent.

Gobind functioned as both Saint and Avatar by exhorting his followers to be *Sant sipahi* or warrior-saints—chaste, fearless, ethical, fair, honest, and compassionate. He created and organized a defensive army, and never took the role of an aggressor. He claimed neither territory nor possessions won in battle, nor would he allow his followers to loot, rape, or pillage as was a common practice. Among his followers were a large number of Muslims whom he loved and respected, encouraging them to keep their distinctive customs, dress, and names. The Guru was indefatigable in his efforts to liberate the people from hatred and superstition. He enjoined worship of one Supreme Being—the *Akaal* or *Timeless*—through daily meditation, selfless service, and a pristine code of ethics that has endured to the present time.

The achievements of the Tenth Guru were extraordinary. He was a prolific mystic poet and author of several important works; brilliant general and military strategist, master archer, undefeated swordsman, and a competent spiritual Adept who had fully traversed the inner planes of creation. Thousands sought his guidance and protection. Many maharajas and maharanis, even enemy soldiers and Muslim generals like Budhu Shah, Saiyed Khan, and Saiyed Beg who initially opposed him on the battlefield, became his most ardent disciples. Historians have described famous battles when the Guru's non-professional army comprised of farmers and tradespeople beat back hardened armies ten times their number. They were like Galahads who declared, "I have the strength of ten, because my heart is pure."

I was present when a pacifist asked Master Kirpal how it was possible for Guru Gobind Singh to have been a Master and also take up arms. "Look here," he responded, "if someone were to come here to kill you, should I let them? I will be the first to lay down my life for you!"

The punjabi word "Sikh" is the language equivalent of the Sanskrit *shishya* or "disciple"—one who learns. The outer religion and Sikh rituals only developed *after* the departure of the tenth Guru. Sikhism is the most recent of the major world religions, claiming approximately 20 million adherents. The writings of the Sikh Gurus, Hindu Saints, and Muslim Divines incorporated in the *Adi Granth* have not yet been altered, but they have been inadequately interpreted and translated. The Gurus themselves embodied religious tolerance and love, making no distinction between Sikh and non-Sikh.

> *The highest religion is to rise to universal Brotherhood;*
> *Aye, to consider all creatures your equals.*
> *Conquer your mind, for victory over self*
> *Is victory over the world.*[3]

After Guru Gobind Singh: One of Sant Kirpal Singh's many significant contributions to posterity was that he provided important, otherwise missing historical linkage between the Gurus and the spiritual lineage of Sants of the twentieth century:

> *Guru Gobind Singh traveled widely, penetrating the Himalayas in the North and going to Deccan in the South. During his extensive travels, he met and lived with the ruling family of the Peshwas and initiated some of its members into the inner Science. It is said that one Ratnagar Rao of the Peshwa family was initiated and authorized to carry on the work by Guru Gobind Singh. Sham Rao Peshwa, the eldest brother of*

Baji Rao Peshwa, the then ruling chief, who must have contacted Ratnagar Rao, showed a remarkable aptitude for the spiritual path and made rapid headway. In course of time, this young scion of the royal family settled in Hathras, a town thirty-three miles away from Agra in Uttar Pradesh, and came to be known as Tulsi Sahib (1763-1843), the famous author of the Ghat Ramayana, *the Science of the inner Life-Principle pervading alike in man and nature. The vita lampada of spirituality was passed on by Tulsi Sahib to Soami Ji—Shiv Dayal Singh (1818-1878).*

The link between Tulsi Sahib of Hathras and Soami Ji of Agra is likely to be overlooked, but there can be little doubt of the same. From the manuscript account of Baba Surain Singh, the Jeevan Charitar Soami Ji Maharaj *by Chacha Partap Singh, and the book entitled* Correspondence with Certain Americans *by Shri S.D. Maheswari, we learn that Soami Ji's parents were the disciples of the Hathras Saint and frequently visited him at his home for his darshan, and attending discourses whenever he visited Agra. It was he who named their son, Shiv Dayal Singh (Soami Ji). Before the birth of the eldest child (Soami Ji), he (Tulsi Sahib) prophesied that a great Saint was about to manifest himself in their home; and after his birth, he told the parents that they need no longer come to Hathras, for the Lord Almighty had come in their midst.[4]*

The Hathras Saint took a keen and lively interest in casting the life of Soami Ji in his own mold. He initiated the young child at a very early age; and Soami Ji, on the last day of his life, told his disciples that he had been practicing the inner Science from the age of six.[5]

Shiv Dayal Singh (Soami Ji) of Agra was the Master of Baba Jaimal Singh, (Baba Ji.) After Baba Ji attained realization, he returned to the Punjab and settled on deserted land overlooking the banks of the Beas, where he spent a great deal of time in meditation whenever he was not engaged in service. In due course, Baba Ji found his great disciple in the person of a handsome young engineer by the name of Sawan Singh Grewal, and empowered him to carry the spiritual torch into the twentieth century. Sawan Singh became known as Hazur, the Great Master, and the size of his following became enormous.

---

1. Max A. McAuliffe, *The Sikh Religion* (New Delhi, India: S. Chand & Co., 1963).

2. Kirpal Singh, *Crown of Life - A Study in Yoga* (Bowling Green, VA: SK Publications 1985), p. 220.

3. Kirpal Singh, *The JAP JI - The Message of Guru Nanak* (Bowling Green, VA: S.K.Publications, 1987) p. 113.

4. In 1986, Sant Darshan Singh shared with me unique details on the life of Sham Rao (Tulsi Sahib). These were his words as I recorded them:

Baba Jaimal Singh,
Sant Sipahi—the Soldier Saint
1838 – 1903

"Sham Rao Peshwa was born in 1763, the crown prince of the Peshwa dynasty, but, like
Gautama Buddha, he was indifferent to kingship and the intrigues of courtly life; his heart
was filled with detachment. On the evening before his coronation as king, a great dust storm
arose in answer to his prayers. He mounted his horse and rode off into the raging storm, never
to return, with orders that none should follow him. He traveled widely, eventually settling in
the north at Hathras where he became known as Dakhani Baba (Sage from the South).

  He was also known as Tulsi Sahib, as distinguished from the earlier fifteenth-century Tulsi
Das. In addition to his famous *Ghat Ramayana* (Ramayana of the Body), he wrote the
Shabdavali and *Ratansagar* (The Jeweled Ocean). There is sufficient circumstantial evi-
dence that *Ratansagar* was named after his Guru, Ratnagar Rao, who was initiated by
Guru Gobind Singh Ji. His younger brother, Baji Rao the Second, who ascended the throne
at Poona, gained great renown for his brave struggles and victories against the corrupt
empire. Before Tulsi Sahib departed this world in 1843, he passed the torch to Soami Ji of
Agra. Tulsi Sahib stated that he was Tulsi Das in a former life, and because the latter's
Ramayana was so greatly misunderstood and interpreted in a literal rather than a figurative
or allegorical sense, he came back again as Tulsi Sahib. His *Ghat Ramayana*, especially the
sections on *Balkand* and *Uttarkhand*, explain in detail the true significance of the spiritual
allegory in such a clear manner that there can be no room for equivocation."

5. Kirpal Singh, *A Great Saint: Baba Jaimal Singh - His Life & Teachings* (Bowling Green,
  VA: S.K. Publications, 1993), pp. 7-8.

Picnic in Sirsa, Punjab, (L. to R: Tai Ji, Master Kirpal, Krishan Lal, & Dr. Lal Singh.

22

Diary, 6 AM, April 4, 1967: Myriads of small-bird twitterings and raspy crow caws resound from the ashram trees as Mohan and Ram Saroop rope piles of luggage onto the roof racks. "Take your seat, please!" Master points me to one of the waiting cars, while he bids farewell to the gathering crowd, closing in like bees to honeycomb. Soon, engines will cough to life and carry us northward to the Punjab.

I came here for God, but as an unexpected bonus, I've gained entry to India's sacred heart—her people, history, and shrines. Exiting Delhi's teeming labyrinth, we embark on the narrow cobbled road which passes through hundreds of farming villages and towns. In several places the way is lined with those who have been patiently waiting in the sun for hours, just for a glimpse from the Satguru's eyes. I ask, "Mohan Ji, without telephones or other means of communication, how do these people know when or where Maharaj Ji is coming?" "Some advanced souls talk with Master in meditation," he replies. "They know Master's plans." I wonder if our dependence on gadgets has rendered us less receptive to such subtle realities.

Patiently, expectantly, the villagers salute their Preceptor with hands prayerfully joined or open, wafting over their faces and heads palpable glances sent their way. *Darshan* is an active but silent process where the eyes become cisterns of a higher, devotional existence. "The tongue of Love is dumb and mute," Master says to me from the front seat. Then, in the Guru's sustaining *"bread and water of life"* aspect—reminiscent of the Christ—he adds, "They eat and drink me!" Here and there, as we slowly pass, I hear a few plaintive sighs through the open windows. Many who are passed, run again to the front, darshan after darshan. There are some for whom the Light is dimmed neither by the darkest night nor by physical distance.

Chandighar—City of the Moon: By mid-afternoon, we arrive in Chandighar, Punjab's modern capital, which lies at the feet of the blue Himalayas, visible to the north. Chandighar ("City of the Moon"), was designed by Le Corbusier, whose unique imprint is evident everywhere in massive curving, almost surreal concrete structures, housing projects, parks, gardens, and wide, tree-lined boulevards. The great architect has captured India's past and translated it into a contemporary city of beauty.

Evening satsang is held on a field in the town center. A multicolored canopy hoisted on twenty-foot poles, billows overhead in the gusting wind. Ten thousand have gathered to see and hear the Saint from Delhi. I jot down a few moments from his two-hour discourse:

> *"This body is a wonderful house in which we live, but we have lost the Indweller. There was a simple man who had his horse stolen. When the theft was discovered in the morning, he exclaimed, 'Thank God I have been saved!' People asked in amazement, 'Why are you so thankful? Haven't you just lost your horse?' 'Oh, had I been riding that horse, I would have been stolen also!' The people laughed at his foolishness. But, truly speaking, he was very wise. Do we not lose the rider while saving the horse of the body? We are the rider, the Soul, a conscious entity, a drop from the Ocean of All-Consciousness."*

After some time, tears begin flowing down my interpreter's cheeks and all translation ceases. The words, *pyar, prem, mohabat, ishq,* and *bhakti* pepper the Master's discourse, and I know these denote various stages of divine Love. The audience sways and ripples like a wheat field in a breeze, and a shimmering network of Light like an inverted golden basket covers all, permeates all. Without interpretation, nothing remains to distract the luminous presence. As the chanter sings from the *Adi Granth*, each of the verses' hidden meanings are unfolded. Both are intuitively synchronized—one singing a line, the Master commenting, with never a moment's hesitation between them. The charged atmosphere reaches one plateau after another, reminding me of a performance

I once witnessed between two classical Indian virtuosos—Ravi Shankar on sitar and Allah Rakha on tabla. *This*, however, is on a higher level altogether. Later, the interpreter rediscovers his tongue:

> *An oyster is valued when a pearl is found within its shell. Similarly, our life is highly prized only when we have realized the priceless pearl of Realization.*
>
> *Where there is reality and genuineness, you will also find imitators who are like the flowers of the seemul tree which bloom but carry no fragrance. Like the bagla [a small white heron, indigenous to India], they dress in white, seemingly meditating, but as soon as they spot a frog or a fish, it is in their beak! Such imitators prey on the unwary, and inspire lack of faith...Did not Christ in His time chase the moneylenders from the Temple, saying "Go ye out, Pharisees! Ye have made my Father's House a place of business!"*

April 5, 8:00 AM: Hundreds are put into an hour's silent meditation. When he walks through the sitters, Master happens to brush my sleeve. Intense spiritual currents surge through my body and inner vision.

"Leave off meditation please!" he asks, but one fortunate woman has gone so deep, nothing avails in bringing her soul back. Only after Master directs Sheila Massi to massage her neck in a certain way, does the lady's attention partially descends to the eye-focus. Absorbed in super-consciousness, the return to the gross and dross of physicality causes her to weep.

Speaking of tears, it is a sight to see—tall, strong, proud tillers of the soil, disciplined soldiers, police officers, merchants, new brides, old wise women, and complete strangers, becoming undone in the presence of the Friend. Surely the garden of divinity is watered by tears, for whichever way I turn I see stoics and skeptics, professors, doctors, lawyers, illiterate peasants, the wealthy and poorest of the poor, powerful and powerless, Easterner and Westerner, Hindu, Muslim, Sikh, Christian, Buddhist, Zoroastrian and Jew—all leveled by *love*. Kindness, charity and a helping hand are some of its visible manifestations. And, tears are the distillation of our body, mind, and soul. In a single tear, there are a thousand verses, songs and sacred books.

*April 6, **Kalkaji:*** We leave Chandighar in the morning's half-light for the moun-tain-ashram at Kalkaji. Embarking from the vehicles, we climb on foot to the top of a high hill and traverse a narrow footpath down into a luxuriant ravine. In grassy meadows stands a solitary, simple white building with billowing awnings spread out for shade. Over a thousand wait below as Master-ji's thrilling voice echoes across an encircling amphitheater of mountains. Three or four long-sepa-rated disciples break ranks and fling themselves before their Preceptor.

Nimbly side-stepping the would-be feet-touchers, he mounts the white dais. His words bear the weight of attainment. The verdant hills, the smoke-blue mountains, and azure sky form a perfect backdrop. The world elsewhere is oblivious of this simple king—though no potentate of worldly domain is he, this emperor of hearts.

In the latter part of the nineteenth century, Baba Sawan Singh, as a disciple, stood at the side of his Master, Baba Jaimal Singh in the Murree Hills. Sawan expressed appreciation of the beautiful scenery to Baba Ji, who replied, "My child, you do not understand. *You and I were here before these hills were even formed.*"

Pinjore Gardens: We depart Kalka around 11AM and by mid-afternoon arrive at the fabled Gardens of Pinjore. I sit cross-legged on cool marble in the shade of a sandstone cupola, eyes riveted on the Friend nearby as he partakes of a small meal.[1]

My eyelids close of themselves, as wave after wave of bliss wafts from his direction. Somewhere along the way, mischievous Tai Ji places an ice cube against my forehead, testing my concentration. After a few minutes, I become dimly aware of giggling at the periphery. Eyes open and refocus on the Master, staring back at me from ten feet away.

With a sweeping arm, Master gestures to the stairways, descending terraces, fountains, and buildings flanked by troop-like ranks of lush mango and lichee orchards laid out in perfect symmetry spreading for miles into the valley below. Under his breath he mutters, "There are *five* levels." I wordlessly ask, "How many levels are there in your words?"

Majori Village: We reboard and traverse a dusty, pot-holed road for several miles. After a sharp turn up a wide path, hedged by thorn-topped mud walls, we reach Majori. The artist in me is enamored with the congruity of the bright landscape and the adobe architecture. Baba Lehna, the village chief, rushes forward to bow respectfully but instead is embraced affectionately by the Master. We are led through narrow corridors past fat, sleepy buffaloes, and arrive at Lehna's place. Seeing me unmindful in the high-noon blaze, Master calls me to his side in the shade. Hilarious Punjabi tales are swapped, and the air is filled with intoxicating laughter. After a while these rustics beseech Father to bless their humble homes, and thus begins a walking tour where babies, sweets, fruits, and scriptures are blessed. They offer everything, which he accepts for a moment and returns. Their grateful and brilliant smiles aren't easily erased from the slate of my mind. What I experience in his presence makes me want to dance and shout from rooftops, *"He who sent us into this world has come to* *take us back!"* But legs stumble and the tongue is dumb.

> *A saint is an ocean of love and when tides rise in it, even the people*
> *sitting on the seashore get drenched. If you want to cultivate love, you*
> *must associate with a Master-soul, for then you will both see and*
> *experience great overflowing tides of love in his eyes.*[2]

We return to Chandighar for three days, where I am boarded with the Hastir family. Vishwanath Hastir is a well-placed civil servant, and a homeopathic doctor who never charges for his effective diagnoses and medicines.[3] My hosts anticipate every need with such cheerful generosity that I am ashamed for my past selfishness. I resolve to emulate their example. "We believe," he said, "that the *guest is God.*"

On our last evening, Vishwanath finds me an eager listener:"As a university student in 1936, I often visited the house of Sant Kirpal Singh in Lahore during the time he was writing his magnum opus, *Gurmat Siddhant* *("Philosophy," or "Wisdom" of the Masters).* In fact, we lived on the same street, Ram Galli Lane. Ram Galli means the Lane of God, and because we had such a great Saint living next to us, it seemed that God was indeed near! Master detailed his son Darshan, who was also my close friend, to research relevant verses from the scriptural treasures of Persian and Arabic mystics for inclusion in *Gurmat Siddhant.* I was also given some service collecting quotations. When completed, *Gurmat Siddhant's* approximately two thousand pages were read before Baba Sawan Singh in the presence of many others."

I interrupt, "Were you there?"

"Yes, I had the good fortune to be there also, at least for part of the reading. When the recitation was completed, Baba Sawan Singh reverently placed *Gurmat Siddhant* on his head and proclaimed, 'This is the greatest book on spirituality written in centuries; listening to it has the same uplifting effect as attending satsang. Although published in my name, Kirpal Singh is its author.'" Following a Guru-disciple tradition of yore, Sant Kirpal Singh signed his work in the name of his Master.

"To give some idea of the size of Hazur's satsangs at Beas towards the close of his mission, and of the enormous quantities of food cooked and served freely to all who came, the daily quantity of salt alone was more than seven hundred pounds." I calculate that if the salt content were 2%, then the total food, including chapatis, which are salt-free, would have been in excess of 60,000 lb. per day.

April 7: Of the many initiated this morning, more than twice as many women than men witnessed the luminous form of the Master within. Five women and four men experienced total sensory withdrawal from the physical body. Later, when I specifically ask why some bodies collapse on the ground when the soul-currents temporarily withdraw, Master answers that if one sits erect, falling over is avoided. In response to another of my questions, he says that initially, because of their devotional nature, women often progress faster than men. And, "When sitting in the bhajan posture (for inner listening), the soul withdraws from the body faster than in any other position."

Gobind in the Guru: At high noon we bid adieu and are on the road again. Twice our caravan stops along the winding, hilly highway as hundreds of villagers seeking blessings surround Master's car. In the middle of a deserted stretch of hilly jungle, Maharaj Ji suddenly tells Mohan to pull the car over. A second later, a jeep speeds past from the opposite direction. Its driver suddenly slams on the brakes, sliding into a 180-degree turn. Out leaps a Sikh in the full dress uniform of an army Major. Master, in the back seat, opens his door and the Major runs over and flings himself on his feet, blurting, "My Lord, when driving past, I saw Guru Gobind Singh Ji appear in your form. Who are you, Guruji?" The Major had never seen or heard of Sant Kirpal Singh Ji before. The prescient Master replies, "I am only a humble servant of the Guru."

We have just passed Baba Sawan Singh's Dera at Beas. The golden domes of the Satsang Ghar shimmer in the distance, and gradually disappear as we move along. This remarkable building was designed, and its construction supervised, by Sawan Singh himself, who by profession was a gifted engineer. Through half-closed eyes, I glimpsed Hazur's ghostly image riding a white horse, keeping time with our car. I turn around to look at Master. He is silent, his eyes brimming with a million remembrances.

Sant Kirpal Singh giving discourse in the presence of Hazur, Beas, Punjab, circa 1940

Kiratpur is our next halt. Ancient, rugged dun-colored hills ring the town on three sides. Kiratpur gained great sanctity throughout the Punjab as the sixth Guru, Hargobind, and his son Har Rai, the seventh, lived here. A local family generously vacated their home for our use. I'm given a bed on the rooftop, but when a light sprinkle begins to fall, I am moved under the verandah just three feet from the Master whom I can see and hear through the unglazed window. Until past midnight, eager young Sikhs come seeking answers and the removal of doubt.

April 8: Around 3 AM, I rise for meditation; Master has been resting for the past two hours in the darkness, close enough for me to hear his rhythmic breath. My meditation is re-channeled as I become aware of a faint rustle of sheets. The Master sits up, near yet unseen. Unexpectedly, and barely audible, I hear him whisper-singing some verses. Honing in on his voice, I recognize lines of the *Jap Ji*—the sacred verses composed by Guru Nanak five hundred years earlier:

> *Ek Onkar, Sat Naam...*
> *There is One Reality,*
> *The Unmanifest-Manifested;*
> *Ever existent, True Naam—Conscious Spirit,*
> *The Creator; pervading All;*
> *Without fear; without enmity;*
> *Timeless; Unborn, Self-existent,*
> *Complete within Itself.*
> *Through the favor of His true servant, the Guru,*
> *God may be realized.*
>
> *Truth was when there was nothing,*
> *Truth was before all ages began,*
> *Truth exists now, O Nanak,*
> *And shall exist forevermore.*

The Jap Ji's thirty-eight stanzas, one flowing into the next, portray a beautiful lyric tapestry of the macrocosm, leading to the finale:

> *Air is the Master, Water the father, and Earth the mother,*
> *Day and Night are the two nurses in whose lap*
> *the whole world is at play.*
> *Our actions: good and evil,*
> *Will be brought before His court,*
> *And by our own deeds, shall we move higher*
> *or be cast into the depths.*
> *Those who have communed with the Word,*

Their toils shall end.
And their faces shall flame with glory,
Not only shall they have salvation, O Nanak,
But many more shall find freedom with them.[4]

Master finishes, and the silence begins to resonate. In the ringing thunder, my soul skirts the awesome chasm between death and life. The Adepts—and Master Kirpal is unquestionably one of these—wing far beyond, administering to countless denizens on the inner planes. I marvel that while emancipated from the husks and shells of rituals, he still observes and respects the traditions into which he was born. The Sikh scriptures tell us, *"The true Master is also the true Disciple."*

While taking tea and fruit with him at 7 AM, Gurudev solicitously inquires after my welfare, to which I reply that I am very comfortable and very happy! By eight, Pathi-ji's thrilling voice, amplified, echoes off the crenellated hills. Kiratpur's entire populace sits before the Master who proclaims the purpose of existence. He moves amongst them, an ageless Messiah in an ageless setting. The camel and ox, palm trees, adobe and stone buildings, bearded patriarchs, wise mothers, and bright-eyed children adorn the scene; this is a page torn from the Bible. I pluck a few pearls from his talk:

> *If even a dog will clean the ground with his tail before sitting, how can we expect God, who is all purity, to sit in an unclean place? If God's image is not reflected in us, it is because the mirror of our heart is not yet clear.*
>
> *Naam is the true paras, or Philosopher's Stone, reputed to have alchemic property of changing base metal into gold. Once, a man saved the life of an alchemist and as reward, was gifted with the fabulous paras for one month only. Our man went to the market to buy iron so he could change it into gold. "The price of iron is too dear. I will wait for its price to drop." He waited until the next day, but the price, instead of dropping, had risen sharply. And thus, everyday thereafter, the price continued rising. He kept procrastinating until the month had passed. The magician returned to claim his stone. Had the foolish man bought the iron, even at a high price, he could have turned it into gold. Similarly is the case with the disciples. What you have received is far more. While the Philosopher's Stone may turn iron into gold, a Saint can turn you into a Saint! But if you continue putting off your spiritual practices, procrastinating, frittering away valuable time in outer pursuits, you will find this precious life gone. Then it will be too late. Don't put off till tomorrow what you can do today. Make hay while the sun shines!*
>
> *Paramhansa Ramakrishna was a simple bhakta (devotee) and didn't pose like other sadhus; he had experience of transcendent Reality. When asked by Naren, (Swami Vivekananda), "Master, have you seen*

God?" Ramakrishna replied, "Yes, my son. Not only have I seen God, but I see Him even more clearly than I see you!" At another time Ramakrishna held open his hand before Naren, saying, "If this is a plate of honey, and you are a bee, how will you eat it?" Naren replied, "I will come to the edge to eat it, so that my wings may not become immersed in the honey and I drown." Ramakrishna said, "This is the sea of Immortality! You will not die! Plunge headlong into it!"

If the Master cannot give you experience by opening your third eye then he too cannot see. Go to an able person. If a teacher is only matriculate, he cannot give you a Master's Degree, but do not degrade lesser teachers, respect them. My advice is to go to someone of the highest degree, who not only sees and knows the Reality in all its phases, but who can also make you see That.

Remember: wife without husband, elephant without tusks, bird without feathers, body without eyes and calf without milk is just like a soul without a Master. The barren land, which receives no rain, is no different than a human being bereft of Naam. A well without water, a house without light and an orchard without fruit are like a soul cut off from God's divine Light and Melody.

April 10 **Guru in a Hurry:** Kanpur is a sleepy little village at the end of a long dusty road, where lies the rustic beauty and soul of ancient Bharat. From the top of a three-tiered brick house, I look across golden-green fields spreading into the distance, hemmed by blue-purple mountains. Peasants bend and labor in patches of alfalfa, wheat, onions, barley, bright yellow mustard greens and sugar cane. Directly below, hustle and bustle is heard in the langar as devoted hands prepare spicy lentil dal, curried cauliflower, and potatoes, pakoras (vegetable fritters), rice pilau, and chapatis. With an advance party, I arrived two hours ago. More than a thousand sit beneath awnings on a newly harvested field. Responsive chanting echoes across the ancient land.

I'm startled from my reverie by exploding firecrackers, signaling arrival. Several of us follow Master to the second-floor. Photographs of Saints hang on the walls. Pointing to one of himself, he asks me, "Who is that fellow? *Do you know who he is?"* I smile, unable to reply.

While tonight's satsang concludes with a bhajan from Kabir, plaintively rendered by Pathi-ji, Master's lion-like eyes half close, then turn up in their sockets for several minutes. He is like Aslan; C.S.Lewis' "Narnian lion," in whose roar the universe manifests and unmanifests.

Later, when alone with him in his room, I express a troubled observation: "Why is it that in so many places we have visited, the followers of _____ have tried to disturb your satsangs and spread negative propaganda? I have seen them tearing down your tour posters."[5]

"During the time of my Master," he answers, "there was much opposition from the Akalis (an ultra-orthodox segment of the Sikh religion). They would say, 'Don't look into the eyes of Sawan Singh. He's the Negative Power.' But whoever was against Hazur, after seeing him, became his staunchest follower. Once, when Hazur visited my home village of Sayyed Kasran, Akalis came and threw stones in the satsang. Hazur said, 'Thank you for your kind reception!' And on these words, they were changed. Just see the angle of vision he was coming from!

"It is also happening like that, except now, opposition is from____. They also say, 'Don't look into Kirpal Singh's eyes! He'll mesmerize you. He's the Negative Power!'" Master smiled, "But whoever comes here gets first-hand experience of what they cannot get elsewhere. Hundreds come to me where they have *something* with God's Grace. The cat will be out of the bag, I tell you! I received one letter from their forerunner in the West, who wrote me, 'If any man has inner experience of Light and Sound at initiation, his life-span will be cut short by two years.' Can you imagine? Now their followers are afraid of asking for any experience. Would you like your life to be cut short by two years? Has your life been cut short?"

I reply, laughing, "No."

"In the letter, he asked, 'Does this experience affect the nervous system?' I said, 'No, one becomes fresher. Light and Sound are the Bread of Life.' That letter is with me in the Ashram. Further, they quote from scripture which says: 'It is Satan-ish for the disciple to be in a hurry,' that 'hurry is the work of the negative power.' Yes, the disciple should not be in a hurry...But can the disciple complain *if the Guru is in a hurry?!*" His laughter is filled with Light.

It was often the practice of Masters of antiquity to bestow initiation upon

only a select few and even then not until the probationers had passed through extremely difficult trials testing their sincerity and faith. But in the present age, with its particular needs, time limitations and human frailties, Masters have opened up the floodgates, making true spirituality more accessible than at any other time in history.

I have started tying a turban, letting my hair and beard grow, in emulation of the Master. He looked at me oddly earlier today, but made no comment. I am admittedly impulsive, infatuated, and twenty-three.

Every Saint has a Past and Every Sinner a Future: Ludhiana is one of
Punjab's major cities. The ashram here—one of sixty throughout India—is
managed by Gobind Ram. As I get to know this colorful disciple, I discover one
totally motivated by loving zeal.

"Gobind Ram, tell me your story," I ask my grizzled friend.

"Sahib, you don't want to know!"

"Yes I do! Please tell me so I can learn." After some coaxing, he heaves a
sigh, "*Aachaa* [all right]. Before I came to Maharaj Ji, or shall I say before he
picked me from the gutter, I was very, very bad. I was a gambler and a smuggler.
I was addicted to drinking, opium, and *ganja* [marijuana]. My temper was
uncontrollable, and everyone feared me, including the police. In broad daylight, I used to yank the gold necklaces and nose jewels from wealthy women.
Although I had hoarded up a fortune, I was miserable and restless; my con-
science never allowed me a moment's peace, thinking of all the suffering I had
caused, but I was helpless to change. As I grew older, I began to pray for
deliverance, knowing I would have to pay dearly.

"A few years ago Maharaj Ji came to Ludhiana. What a Godly beauty! What
a power! If I could find any mercy in this world, I knew it would come through
him! I pleaded, 'Maharaj! Give this worthless sinner your Naam!' He said,
'Yes, you can be initiated providing you mend your ways. You must return all
your ill-gotten gains, or you will never be free. Devote your life to serving the
needy and to the spiritual practices, which will be revealed to you.'"

Gobind Ram continues, "Not knowing from whom I had stolen, I stuffed all
my ill-gotten money and valuables into a big sack and went to the center of a
busy intersection where I dumped it onto the ground. I called out as loudly as I
could in all directions, 'Come and take according to your karma!' The rush of
all those people was a sight to see!"

I have met another ex-dacoit, whom I will refer to as Daku (not his real
name). In 1959, the Master gave a discourse in Daku's home village, the
subject of which was the redemptive grace of the Sant Satgurus. Historical
examples were given—Mary Magdalene, the prostitute, saved by Jesus; Sajjan
Thug saved by Guru Nanak; Valmiki, a robber who became a Saint, and the
author of the original Ramayana—to show that change is not only desirable,
but possible, even for those who have trespassed all moral boundaries.

"There is hope for everyone, providing they are sincerely repentant and
desire to change," but, Master added, "Not even God can change one who
doesn't want to be changed...Only that sin is forgiven which is done no more!"
However, Master declined to initiate Daku at this time.

After a few weeks the repentant Daku arrived at Sawan Ashram accompanied
by all the members of his gang. They were initiated and completely changed
their lives. In time, a place known for evil became known for good. Master

often referred to Daku, "Now he is putting in six hours of meditation a day. Even robbers can become Saints! Every saint has a past, and every sinner a future."

A few weeks ago at the ashram, Daku came down with a case of acute appendicitis. He was in obvious pain, and the doctors advised he be operated on immediately, but Master advised waiting. Another day passed, and Daku's suffering increased. Again the Master's advice was sought; again he demurred, "Wait until tomorrow." That morning, an herbalist arrived, and went straight to Daku. He pierced the middle of Daku's left ear and tied a loop of thread through the hole. He then brewed a strong tea of *neem* (margosa) leaves, prized for their antiseptic healing qualities, then immersed a towel in the tea and applied poultices to his ear. As predicted, a large amount of pus discharged over the next few days and the swollen appendix returned to normal. Daku was completely healed. My mind speculates on the karmic dimensions of this case, of suffering and grace, and the unorthodox ways of the Saints.

Book learning vs. Reality: Speaking of the vast difference between academic knowledge, and direct, immediate experience, Maharaj Ji tells the story of Kabir and Sarbajit:

> *Perhaps you have heard the story of Kabir and the pundit? After reading many books and winning many debates, the pundit announced, "I am now to be addressed as Sarbajit, the Invincible!" He went to his mother and declared, "O mother, call me Sarbajit now. I have gained so much knowledge that nobody can defeat me in religious debate!" His mother, who was very wise, said, "Go to Saint Kabir and if you can win him over, only then will I call you Sarbajit." So, the vain pundit loaded up a bullock cart full of books and went to the house of Kabir Sahib. When Kabir asked about the purpose of his visit, the pundit replied, "Either you give me in writing that I am Sarbajit the Invincible, or enter into debate with me."*
>
> *Kabir Sahib humbly acquiesced and gave him in writing, "Sarbajit is the winner and Kabir the loser." But when he took this paper home to show his mother, it read, "Sarbajit is the loser, and Kabir the winner." Sarbajit became very angry and returned to Kabir with his demands. Again Kabir wrote, "Sarbajit is the winner and Kabir the loser." Sarbajit ran home to show it to his mother, but again the paper read, "Kabir is the winner and Sarbajit the loser." A third time he returned to Kabir, but Kabir flatly told him, "O Pundit, you speak of what you have read and studied, whereas I speak of what I have experienced; the two can never agree. If you have some inner experience of Reality, only then come and talk with me."*

*April 13 - **Faqir Chand of Hoshiarpur:*** Master lets me tag along in his car to a holyman conference in Hoshiarpur, about an hour's drive from Ludhiana. Sadhus in saffron robes, and other representatives of Hindu and Sikh faiths, gaze out upon an audience of several hundred from a large dais. Master Kirpal, as the guest of honor, is warmly received. Among the holy men is Faqir Chand, head of this ashram and the successor of Maharishi Shivbrat Lal. Rai Saligram, who was a disciple of Soami Ji of Agra, initiated Shivbrat Lal. Faqir Chand was linked to the same path of Light and Sound, but through a different lineage than that of Baba Ji and Master Sawan.

While smoking a hookah, Faqir Chand launches into a colorful discourse. In his description of the inner spiritual regions, I take notice when he mistakenly reverses the experiences of the third and fourth planes.

After leaving Hoshiarpur, Master carefully cuts and peels an apple and passes the pieces around. From the back seat I ask, "Maharaj Ji, what is the fate of those disciples of a lesser Master who has advanced spiritually to, say, the second or third stage, but not the ultimate Goal [Sach Khand, the Fifth Region]?"

"Their progress will stop," he answers. "They will not be able to go farther than their guru."

"Will the people who follow them derive lasting benefit?"

"No." End of discussion.

Questions & Answers: We return to the Ludhiana ashram late in the afternoon. Hundreds have been waiting, meditating and singing bhajans. After a brief rest, Master invites questions. A woman describes her difficulties in stilling the mind.

M: "Do you keep the diary?"

Woman: "No, I am illiterate."

M: "Do you give fifty rupees instead of five?" Woman: "No." M: "If you can count up to fifty and know the difference between five and fifty, why can't you count your mistakes?" Master chuckles. "Keeping the diary means keeping track of the impediments and imperfections in our lives; then weed them out! If you don't check your lower tendencies, how can you go up in meditation?"

An old grandmother slowly rises to her feet. "I don't see anything in meditation now, but I used to see a lot before."

M: "You are not meditating accurately now. There is something lacking in your concentration. There is a cure for not seeing, but there is no cure for not meditating. Meditate regularly, with single-pointed attention in the manner already revealed to you, and the inner way will be opened again."

An elderly man stands with folded hands. "Master, I am a disciple of Baba Sawan Singh Ji. For many years I haven't been able to sit in bhajan due to severe pains in my hips, but now that you have come, I can sit and, with your blessings, the inner vision has opened again."

Master humbly replies, "It is all due to Hazur's grace that people are benefiting. I am only a puppet in his hands."

A white-bearded sardar comes forward to confess: "Maharaj Ji, forgive me, I have started drinking. Please forgive me, I will never drink again."

M: "O' Baba, it is pardoned, but don't drink again, and see towards your white beard. Your white hairs are a sign that the angel of death is approaching. What are you doing in your old age?"

Recitation without Naam: A renowned Ragi[6] once came to Baba Sawan Singh and asked, "Hazur, I have been reciting the scriptures most of my life. Pray tell me, what is the benefit of this as compared to the Naam which you give? "Hazur asked him to fill up a piece of paper with zeros, and when he finished, Hazur asked him, "Bhai Ji [respected brother], what is the value of the zeros?" The Ragi replied, "Nothing. They are just zeros."

Hazur asked him to put "one" before the zeros and asked, "Now what is the value of what you have written?"

The Ragi replied, "Hazur, it is inestimable. No one can count that high."

Hazur concluded, "Bhai Ji, singing the scriptures without Naam is just like all the zeros. It has little value, but when you get Naam from a perfect Saint, it is like putting One before them all. Then your life becomes infinitely precious."

The reformation of an alcoholic: An alcoholic was initiated in Ludhiana on the '67 tour. While half-heartedly agreeing not to imbibe again, within a few days his old craving overpowered both will and reason. Two years of steady drinking and deterioration ensued. As much as he wanted to reform himself, he was helplessly caught in the grip of addiction. One day he overcame his shame, and traveled to Delhi to seek the Master's help before whom he pleaded: "Maharaj Ji, please don't make me promise not to drink for I know I haven't the strength to keep it. I do not want to be false to you. Please help me reform, for my life is in ruin, and my family is badly affected. I cannot change by myself." And he fell on his Satguru's feet, crying. Pleased with his confession and honesty, Master told the fellow, "All right, you may drink, but promise me jut one thing." Master looked at him with a mixture of sternness and compassion. "Promise that you will never drink in My presence!" After giving his solemn word, the man returned home and kept the bottle at bay. However, after a couple of weeks the old craving began tormenting him again. He remembered his promise, but since Kirpal Singh was five hundred miles away, he reached for the bottle hidden under his bed. With trembling hands, he poured a glass, but as he raised it to his lips, he had the shock of his life, for the Master was standing across the room looking at him. He rubbed his eyes, but the Master's form remained. He really wanted that drink! To avoid the Master's gaze, he closed his eyes and quickly raised the glass. Before the liquor was in his mouth, he received a tremendous slap. From that moment on, he never touched liquor again.

A drunkard, a lover and a moth begin their circling of the Flame;
Friend, I found a great bargain, the sacrifice of mine and wine.
Trading, I found the inebriate eyes of the Beloved
Dancing me in the tavern of the Timeless.

Raho, Bersian & Nawansher: From Ludhiana, we motor to Raho, birthplace
of the grandfather of Ram Chandra. By the 17th century, Raho had become a
flourishing Mughal center, renamed by its rulers as Sirhind. Guru Gobind
Singh's two young sons were cruelly bricked up alive inside a wall by order of
Sirhind's ruler. Within two decades, Sirhind was razed to the ground by the
forces of Banda Bahadur, and its original name restored.

The ashram here is situated in a large building more than four hundred years
old, one of few that escaped destruction. Overgrown mounds of ancient bricks
and rubble remain scattered throughout the largely abandoned town, mute
reminders of the past. Nearby flows the lazy Satluj River, where my ancestor
General Cripps almost lost a decisive battle against the armies of Maharaja
Ranjit Singh. We spend the night here on the ashram's roof beneath the stars. In
the early morn while meditating, a small bird alights on my head. After breakfast, we move on to Bersian, where satsang is held in the fields of a cultivator.

At its conclusion, an old man stands in the crowd and addresses the Master:
"Maharaj, my name is Amar Chand. Hazur blessed me with Naam in the
1930's. Several weeks ago, my only son, Chanan Ram became deathly ill. He
did not have the benefit and protection of initiation." His voice quivers with
emotion as he continues, "While sitting by his side, I closed my eyes and Hazur
suddenly appeared, in your company. Your radiant form came closer and you
gave the clear order to convey the secret of the Five Charged Names to my son,
as his soul was about to depart from the body. I therefore directed him to close
his eyes and repeat the five names mentally. After a few minutes, he opened his
eyes and mouth and repeated, 'I am seeing the light-filled images of Hazur and
Maharaj Kirpal. They are telling me, "Prepare to leave this world. It is not
your permanent place. You have to leave now." And so my father, I bid you
farewell.' I was satisfied. He then closed his eyes, and his soul took flight into
the Beyond." Grateful tears roll down Amar Chand's weathered cheeks as he
concludes, "As I am an initiate of Hazur, now my son is yours. The almighty
power is One and we are bound in it forever."

In the fierce heat of the afternoon (120 F. in the shade), I am invited upstairs
to take rest in the Master's room. Mysterious cool breezes waft through
through. Initially I am fearful that my thought patterns, so apparent to him,
might defile the super-sublime atmosphere. While lying upon the bare floor
with my head towards the nearby reclining Master, my anxiety subsides as
grace-currents allow my attention to quickly withdraw from the external world
and the senses.

Later, I muse, "How can a frail bulb withstand the Power-house? How may a broken cup contain the Ocean? It is said of him, *'He drank the seven seas and yet his lips remained dry,'* whereas I can hardly withstand a few drops."

In the golden ripeness of late afternoon we drive a few more miles down the tree-lined road to the town of Nawansher. As we settle in, I attempt meditation in the room given to me, but so much loud talking and commotion goes on outside my door and window, I am driven to my wit's end. A large crowd has gathered to gawk at, test my patience, and continuously bang the door, laughing and chattering. I lose my temper and shout, *"Chello! Chello!"* (Go away!).

The commotion draws the Master from his room across the lane. He sternly warns, "The sahib has come for bhajan, and if you don't cease your noise-making, I will leave and stay at Raho instead!" Blessed silence comes and the spoiled "sahib" is allowed to meditate in peace—except for the disturbed vibrations of his own mind.

On the following day, Master speaks of gratitude and remembrance:

> *"There are so many mountains and trees on the face of the Earth, but she does not grumble. Once she was asked if there was any burden which was too great to bear. The Earth replied, 'Yes, the only burden I cannot bear is an ungrateful heart.'*
>
> *"My Master, Hazur Baba Sawan Singh used to say, 'For those who remember the Lord in their dreams, I am prepared to make shoes from my own skin for their feet.'"*

---

1. In an early undated hand-written memo to himself, Kirpal Singh outlined his personal dietary, sunbathing and yoga exercise regimen. He allowed himself only six to eight ounces of food per day. This original memo is on display at Sawan Ashram.

2. Kirpal Singh, *Portrait of Perfection,* (Delhi & Bowling Green, VA: S.K. Pub., 1981), p. 285.

3. Homeopathy is widely accepted and practiced in India, England and Europe.

4. Kirpal Singh, *Jap Ji—the Message of Guru Nanak,* (Delhi & Bowling Green, VA: SK Publications, Sixth edition, 1981)

5. I was taken aback by organized opposition to the Master and his mission of love and peace.

6. Ragis are professional singers of Sikh scriptures and are held in very high regard by members of that religion. The most sublime outer music may take one to the threshold of the spiritual world but nevertheless, it is powerless to effect further ingress within.

23

One evening, Tai Ji (Bibi Raja Ram)—the influential lady in charge of Master's food and clothing (who often sent me platters from his kitchen on tour)—began remembering her golden days with Hazur. Dr. Julian Johnson had written of her sight being restored through divine intervention in *With the Great Master in India*. Her story of "Two Towels" illustrates the depth and magnitude of Kirpal's devotion, and Hazur's reciprocity to his great disciple:

This goes back to about 1940. I had purchased some very good quality towels from the bazaar and felt like giving two of them to the Great Master, Hazur Maharaj Sawan Singh. My husband and I drove to Beas with those two towels, and when we reached there I placed them at his lotus feet and said, "Maharaj Ji, please take these two towels for yourself." He said, "No, child, I don't need them. I won't take anybody's things." I said, "All right, you may pay for them then!" But Hazur deferred.

"No, please take them," I insisted. "You can give me the money, whatever they cost, but you must take them." Hazur kept silent for some time; finally he said "All right, I can do one thing. I will take these towels on one condition—that you take two of my used towels in exchange for your new ones!" "What else do I want!" I replied. So he called one of his attendants, Bibi Ralli, and said "Bibi Ji, go in the bathroom and bring two towels." I placed the new towels at his lotus feet and the Master gave me his, which I placed on my head in reverence. Baba Sawan Singh said, "All right, child, I am giving these two towels to you, but first promise me that you won't give them to anyone else." "All right, I won't give them to anybody."

"Even if your husband asks you for them, will you promise not to give them to him?" "Achaa, okay, I won't give them to him."

"So this is final?" "Yes, final."

"All right, you take them."

Afterward, at about 4 PM we started from Beas to go back to Rawalpindi, about seventy-five miles away. On the way, my husband said "Let's see Sant Kirpal Singh when we pass through Lahore." So we went to his place, but I begged my husband, "No, please don't go there, because he may want to take my towels!" He assured me "No, no, he won't do anything like that." When we reached there my husband went in, but I hid myself and would not face Sant Kirpal Singh. When he was in one room, I would run to another, so as not to face him.

Bhapa Ji—as we used to address Sant Kirpal Singh then—asked "What's the matter with Bibi Ji? She is not facing me today. What's wrong with her?" My husband said, "Oh, she has got something, but she is hiding herself so that you will not ask what it is and take it!" Bhapa Ji laughed and sent his wife, Bibi Krishna Wanti, to fetch me.

He asked me "What's this? What have you got with you? Did you bring something from Beas, from our Satguru?" I had to admit, "Yes."

"Alright, then please show me."

"No, no, I won't." Bhapa Ji asked why. "Because I made a promise with my Master that I wouldn't give it to anyone."

"Well, don't give it to me, but at least show me."

"Alright, I'll show you." I pulled those two towels from my handbag and, while holding them, showed them. Bhapa Ji asked, "Just let me see them." He took those two towels in his hands, placed them on his head as a token of respect, and then touched them to his heart and wept. Afterward he asked us to stay for the night, but I said, "No, no, you might take these towels!"

"Oh, no, you just relax for the night," he said, so we agreed. That night he asked, "Until morning—while you are here please loan these two towels to me." He took those towels to his room and lying there alone, he placed them on his heart and began to shed tears in the sweet remembrance of our Master Sawan. During the night he composed a poem concerning those towels, and in the morning when he got up he said, "Before you go home, please do one thing for me. Take this poem, go back to our Satguru at Beas, and then go to your place." My husband used to pay great respect to him, and agreed to return to Beas.

We took that poem back to Maharaj Sawan Singh Ji. When we arrived in Beas, Maharaj Ji said, "You were here yesterday. What brought you back again?" I said, "Master, I am in trouble. I feel very bad." "Why? What happened?" he asked.

I answered, "We went to Kirpal Singh. My towels were going to be snatched away, but I saved them."

"You did a courageous thing. I thought Kirpal Singh would snatch them from you!" "Master, he is not such a torturer!" my husband said, "Maharaj Ji, she has done a great injustice to him. Kirpal Singh was placing your towels on his head and heart, and weeping inconsolably." Hazur Maharaj said, "Oh, I could have given him towels too! Why did you make him weep?" I said, "How could I give him the towels after promising you that I would give them to no one? All I can do now is give you the poem he has composed."

Then Hazur said, "All right, come on, first sing the poem he has sent to me." Then I sang that song.

After hearing the poem, Hazur said, "It's a great pity, he has felt too much. Now you should go back to Kirpal Singh and bring him to me." I said, "No, no, I won't go now. He may take my towels again. I must keep them here. I won't go!" Then my husband said, "Well, I'll go." He went to Lahore and brought Kirpal Singh Ji back to Hazur again. I was sitting in the Dera at that time and again opened my bag to see that the towels were safely kept. When they came, it was late at night. Restrictions for others at Beas did not apply to Kirpal Singh or my husband, as Hazur loved them so dearly. They might come at midnight or 1 AM and nobody could bar their entry to the Master.

All together we went back to Master Hazur. Sant Kirpal Singh bowed before Hazur, who said, "Look here, Kirpal, she was really sympathizing with you." Bhapa Ji replied, "She did not sympathize at my home." Then Hazur said "No, she felt it when you cried, but she could not give the towels to you. But why did you cry? I would have given so many things to you. Come on, Kirpal Singh, what do you want? Tell me, sit down!" And he sat down with folded hands, saying, "No, Master, everything is fine. I want only you."

"But I've got so many things I'll give you." Then Hazur said to me, "Why did you come now? You have your towels with you." I said "I have come to see what things you are going to give him." Master Hazur said, "Come on, Kirpal, tell me what you want!" And he, sitting with folded hands, said, "Master, I want you only." Then Hazur took Kirpal's hand and, placing his own hand upon it said, "Now I give my own self to you." At this, Sant Kirpal Singh Ji became very happy and bowed before his Master.

I said "Oh, Master, you have given everything to him. It is too much! You gave me only towels!" Then Hazur called Bibi Ralli and said, "All right, you go and bring my sweater that I was wearing at night." She brought the sweater and Hazur gave it to Kirpal Singh, saying, "I used it this night and last night too. It's not washed, but you can wear it." And again he said to Bibi Ralli, "Go and bring the cotton shawl that I use when I sit in meditation." Then he gave that shawl to Kirpal Singh and said "Look here, Kirpal Singh, I am giving my most precious thing to you today, this shawl; there is some secret concerning it." But his great disciple never asked what the secret was. I was just sitting there, watching everything. Then Hazur himself said, "This cotton shawl was given to me by my Satguru Baba Jaimal Singh. I have kept it as a very precious trust; tonight I hereby give it to you."

This is not the end of the story; it is still to come. After a while we took leave of Hazur Maharaj and returned to Sant Kirpal Singh's residence in Lahore. Bhapa Ji took those gifts from his Master to his room and kept them where he used to sleep. Thereafter he never slept on that bed, but down on the floor where his bedding remained. At night, from another room we saw him before his bed, sometimes laughing, sometimes weeping, sometimes just bowing out of respect before those things.

Such was the love of Kirpal for his Master that his unspeakable reverence was transfered even to the objects associated with Hazur.

The Disciple and his Master, circa 1938

Kirpal Singh was thirsty for knowledge from childhood. He voraciously read through an entire library, but at the end of every book of religion, biography or philosophy, he penciled the words, *"No way out."* During this period of intense search and pining, his pillow often became drenched with tears.

His innate compassion expressed itself towards the suffering of others. He served the sick and dying in hospitals, as well as in the streets during virulent epidemics, with no regard for his own safety. These were the days before antibiotics were available. His capacity for hard work was legendary, and he had an intrinsic inclination towards spiritual practice. His ability to foretell events even as a child is well known and documented, but he prayed that this gift be held in reserve.

When his father Hukam Singh suffered a debilitating stroke and consequently lost his memory, Kirpal patiently taught him to speak again. Around 1917, he suffered a second stroke and memory loss and once again the dutiful son taught him to speak. When fully recovered, Hukam Singh addressed him: "Pal, I am extremely pleased with you. Ask for anything you want—wealth, children, fame and the like—and if a father's blessings have any effect, you will certainly have what you desire."

Kirpal replied, "I do not want earthly things, I wish only to meet God in this lifetime." His father said, "I have not seen God, but if there is God, you shall certainly meet Him!"[1] Shortly thereafter, Kirpal began having visions in meditation of a radiant being whom he took to be Guru Nanak. For the next seven years, this luminous form conversed with him, took his soul to higher planes, and bestowed many revelations. During this period, Kirpal composed several poems in praise of his radiant Guide, although he remained unaware of Its living physical counterpart on Earth.

In 1924, Kirpal, who was fond of rivers, took a train to the Beas River station about thirty miles from Amritsar. When he asked for directions to the riverbank from Bua Das, the train-master, the latter asked if he had come to see the Saint of Beas. Always keen to meet with the holy, Kirpal took directions and walked three miles to the Saint's dera or hermitage. Hazur was inside taking his meal when Kirpal Singh arrived, and not wanting to disturb the Sage, he sat and waited outside. When Hazur at last emerged, Kirpal was wonder-struck to see the same majestic personage who had been guiding him within for the past seven years. He asked, "Maharaj, why this delay in meeting You?" to which Hazur replied, "This was the most opportune time."

"The Guru appears when the *chela* is ready—even to the most skeptical mind," Kirpal reminisced of his first meeting. "Perhaps none of you have been so skeptical as I was. I was afraid lest I go to somebody who had not met God, then my life would have been spoiled."

The 24 year mystic bond between Sawan and Kirpal that followed was unique in the history of Masters and disciples. Some have found a parallel in the depth of their relationship to that of Shams Tabriz and Rumi, or Guru Ram Das and Arjan Dev, but all comparisons fall short.

On June 11, 1939, Baba Sawan Singh wrote his beloved disciple:

> *May the compassion of the Lord of thy soul be with thee,*
> *May the Lord of thy soul help thee ever and anon.*

Dear Kirpal Singh Ji,
 Radhasoami.[2] *I have received your loving letter and am happy to read its contents. My dear, saints inherit discomfort in life.*

> *"When the crown of love was placed on my head,*
> *Sighs were given as cash grant, and desert as property."*

> *"We are puppets in the Lord's hands,*
> *We are dragged by our destiny;*
> *We go wherever we are ordained to,*
> *Nanak, how true it is!"*

We have come into the world to serve the Lord. Keep yourself engaged in meditation and complete the course of spirituality. But the service of His creation is equally essential. Look at me; I remain engaged in the service of humanity from morn till night. Sometimes I do not get sufficient time to do meditation, but Hazur Maharaj (Baba Jaimal Singh Ji) used to say that service to humanity is no less important than meditation. And, if you feel that people do not pay as much attention to our love as they should, we do not expect any compensation for our services to the satsang.

All sorts of people come to satsang. There are some whose hearts are overflowing with love and they are ready to sacrifice their all—body, mind, and money. There are also some that indulge in tall talk and calumny; they are ever ready to slander. But our duty is to love all. If they do not give up their wicked ways, why should we leave our noble ways? My advice to you is that you should do satsang while fulfilling your official duties honestly and also complete your course of bhajan and simran. I am greatly pleased with you. You are serving the Lord with all your resources—body, mind, and money.

Convey my Radhasoami to Bibi Krishna and love to children.

Yours, (signed) Sawan Singh

Within a few short years of initiation, Kirpal Singh, who had already accessed the first two regions, assiduously cultivated his Master's gift and crossed the remaining higher spiritual realms. When the union of his soul with the Supreme Being was consummated, his inner and outer perfection was complete. Throughout their 24 year relationship, Kirpal Singh devotedly served his Master's mission.

The Last Days of Hazur: According to the Master Kirpal's own words, on the morning of October 12, 1947, Hazur summoned him to his bedside:

> *"Kirpal Singh! I have allotted all other work but have not entrusted my task of Naam-initiation and spiritual work to anyone. That I confer on you today so that this holy and sacred Science may flourish." My eyes were filled with tears, and afflicted as I was, I beseeched: "Hazur! The peace and security that I have sitting at Thy feet here cannot be had in higher planes..." My heart was filled with anguish, I could not speak any more and sat staring—Hazur encouraging and caressing me all the time.*
>
> *After this whenever I had the privilege to be in seclusion with Hazur, He talked about the interior affairs of the Dera and instructed me how to act when he departed forever...*
>
> *One night Hazur, mentioning his inner esoteric experiences, remarked, "The sun has risen high. Can the people of Jullunder [a city in Punjab] also see this sun?" Those sitting nearby were ignorant of this secret expression. The opinion of the doctor in charge was, like the others beside him, that Hazur's brain did not work properly on account of illness. A little later at night when I went to him, Hazur repeated the same question, addressing me, "Kirpal Singh! The sun*

Hazur's original letter to Kirpal Singh

has risen high. Can the people of Jullunder also see this sun?" I replied, "Yes Hazur, the sun has risen high—and not only the people of Jullunder but also those living in England or America who will traverse to inner planes can see this sun."[3] Thereupon Hazur said: "You have correctly answered my question."

Similarly Hazur made mention of several hidden secrets but those around him were hardly able to grasp what he was hinting at—this being a subject familiar to those only who are practical inlookers and spiritually skilled. What, therefore, could other poor fellows know about them? Surveying the surrounding occurrences and events, Hazur observed:

"It's a pity that the followers of Sant Mat also are becoming a prey to misconception. The teaching of the Saints is 'See with your own eyes. If you do not see with your own eyes, do not even believe your Master...'"

On another occasion Hazur said: "Kirpal Singh! The people will flock to the place where they would find the riches of Naam. When Baba Ji came from Agra, he brought with him neither money nor followers. He fetched within him only his Guru, and through his blessings the present Dera came into existence. You obey the orders of your Guru. If an obedient wife acts according to the bidding and wishes of her husband

and the people call her bad names, let them say so. You have to carry on
the mission under the orders of your Master...Tell everybody to meditate
fondly and invert within to reach the astral form of the Master."

Consequently, during Hazur's lifetime and in strict conformity with
His wishes, in November 1947 a proposal for "Spiritual Satsang" was
laid before Him, the main objects of which were solely the ethical and
spiritual benefit of mankind in general, irrespective of caste, color, or
creed—which was heartily appreciated by Hazur, saying: "I am wholly
and solely at one with thee in this endeavor," and directed me to give it
practical shape...to present spirituality to mankind in general in a
lucid and scientific form...

The subject of illness of Saints too, no less, is a perplexing event. The
fact of it is that this illness of Hazur was the result of the weight of
karmic debts, of the deeply heaved sighs and tears of those afflicted
among us. Outer dealings of Saints also set the best example of the
exalted human standard of living and character. They voluntarily take
upon themselves the burden of their own initiated souls without a murmur
or mentioning a word of complaint, and this becomes their usual task.

Every day Hazur grew weaker and weaker in body. From the night of
March 29, 1948, to the morning of April 1, unusual restlessness and
visible "fluttering" was seen visiting his physical frame. This symptom
was also created for putting to test those surrounding him. Throughout
the period of His illness Hazur said many a time, "If a person proficient in bhajan and simran sits by me, I feel comforted and relieved.
Therefore those who come to me or sit near me should do simran."
Accordingly, at the time of appearance of this symptom of "fluttering of
the body," Hazur again spoke several times in these words, "If the person who has to do the work of spirituality after I depart comes and sits
by me, my trouble will be gone."

To comply with this evidently last wish of the Master, the near relatives of Hazur came and sat in bhajan and simran one by one, by the
bedside of Hazur, but there was no relief whatever...

On the morning of 1st April, 1948, it was extremely benevolent of
Hazur to afford a chance to this humble servant...through the assistance
of a lady[4] in nursing service of Hazur—to be by the side of Master, in
seclusion, for about ten or fifteen minutes. At that time with a heavy
heart I sat near His bed and prayed to Hazur: "Master! Thou art
above body and bodily influences, unconcerned to comforts and
discomforts, but we humble and helpless beings are afflicted hard and
cannot endure the sight of Hazur's thus suffering bodily. Thou hast all
powers. We would be extremely grateful if Hazur very graciously
removes this indication of disease on His body."

It is true that prayer succeeds where all other human efforts fail.
Hazur with His utmost benevolence accepted this prayer...When I

Hazur's funeral procession at the Beas River, April 2, 1948.
Kirpal Singh is seen in center-right with his hand raised.

opened my eyes, Hazur's body was in a state of perfect repose, [his]
forehead shining resplendently. He opened His mercy-showering lovely
eyes...and cast a glance at my humble self—both eyes gleaming with
radiance like a lion's eyes. I bowed my head in solemn and silent
adoration and said, "It is all Hazur's own benignity."

Hazur steadily kept gazing for three or four minutes into my eyes,
and my eyes, in silent wonderment, experienced an indescribable
delight which infused a beverage-like intoxication down to the
remotest pores of my entire body—such as was never before experi-
enced in my whole life. Then those mercy-showering eyes closed not to
open again. In his last moments Hazur was all peace.

When he breathed his last, I put my head upon his feet and said,
"The sun of divinity which had risen has set, and I have no words to
express my grief."

Thus in His 90th year, on the morning of 2nd April, 1948, at 8:30,
this brilliant Sun of Spirituality, after diffusing His Light in the hearts
of millions, disappeared to rest below the horizon at Dera Baba Jaimal
Singh.5

It was a time of great bereavement for the devotees left behind. Sant Kirpal
Singh accompanied his Master's body to the banks of the Beas where it was
cremated. In the crowd and clamor, he watched in silent grief until the last
ember had cooled. Someone froze a moment in time in a photograph of him
standing with bowed head before the bier. Hazur's sacred ashes were immersed
in the flowing waters, as darkness of night covered the land. Then, in confor-
mance to his Satguru's wishes, Hazur's Gurmukh disciple quietly departed for
Delhi, and shortly thereafter, the Himalayan mountains, to prepare himself for
the great mission ahead.

Kirpal Singh, standing center, hands clasped before the funeral bier—April 2, 1948

1. "Pal" was the affectionate name that he was called by his family. In this regard, Kirpal fondly told his disciples of the power of parental blessings.

2. *Radhasoami*, or *Radhaswami*, is another name for the Supreme Being or Anaami, introduced by Soami Ji of Agra in the late 1800's. This term was used as a greeting and farewell by Baba Sawan Singh Ji. *Radha* signifies the soul, and *Soami* the Lord, thus "Lord of the Soul." The name Radha Soami contains a clue to the spiritual science:

   > *Radha aad surat ka naam, Soami aad shabad nij dhaam*
   > *Radha is the name of the primal soul current (surat);*
   > *Soami is the name of the primal source of shabad (Word) -*
   > *Sar Bachan - Prose (Beas, India: Radha Soami Satsang).*

   As the name Radha Soami became contentious and even litigious with various groups claiming its rightful use, Sant Kirpal Singh rarely referred to it.

3. Guru Nanak, when nearing his earthly end also spoke of this sun to his son (who was ignorant of it) and his devoted follower—Angad who understood it and succeeded him.

4. Bibi Ralli went to Kirpal Singh and implored him, "Hazur's condition is precarious, and you had better come." Then she took him to the bedside of the ailing Hazur.

5. Excerpts from *A Brief Life Sketch of Hazur Baba Sawan Singh Ji Maharaj*, (Delhi: Ruhani Satsang, 1949, Darshan Singh, *Portrait of Perfection - A Pictorial Biography of Kirpal Singh*, (Bowling Green, VA), 1981.

Sant Kirpal Singh emerging from samadhi.
Ganges River, upper Rishikesh, 1948. Photo by Darshan.

25

Following Hazur's mahasamadhi and in compliance with his wishes, Kirpal Singh left for Delhi. For the seeker and the lover, only Truth and the Beloved count. On April 13, 1948, the new Master held his first satsang at Darya Ganj, Delhi, wherein he gave a humble description of his role:

> Just as the commander of an army grows old and sits in a tent and keeps a boy as an orderly to send his messages to the outside—so this is my position, that of an errand boy.
> Each Saint has his mission in life and comes with a definite instrument of instruction. As soon as he completes his job, he retires from this world and goes back into the spiritual ocean from which he sprang, leaving the work of further reorientation to his successor. Even if the predecessor has to do something for his followers, he does it

through the living successor to whom he entrusted the work on retirement; and only the latter, as a brother-in-faith or Gurbhai may help his brethren on the physical plane...

Our physical life is destined by the Almighty and each one of us must play his role as allotted. I have no choice in the matter...I am a puppet in his hands and a flute through which he plays.[1]

Shortly thereafter, Kirpal Singh went to Rishikesh, a secluded place in the foothills of the Himalayan Mountains. He said, "In the wilderness, I would put in sixteen to eighteen hours in meditation..." The Master's favorite spot was a large rock in the middle of the Ganges River, just above the town of Rishikesh. On that bare, rugged rock he would sit, uncushioned, immersed in samadhi, awaiting further orders from his Master.

He rented accommodation in a house called Rani-ki-Kothi on the northern banks of the Ganges. It was here that his wife Mata Krishna Vanti, son Darshan, daughter-in-law Harbhajan Kaur, and young grandson Raji, Mangat Ram, Madame Hardevi and a few other disciples joined him for several weeks. He sometimes put them into meditation for six to eight hours at a stretch. In the breaks between, he went for long walks around Rishikesh, a renowned pilgrimage center. He sometimes took along members of his party and visited the sadhus and holy men in the area.

He ate simple food—a meal in the morning and another in the evening. One day he said, "Now let me make some chapatis for you," and then he prepared chapatis for all. He then told his family and those with him, "I am cooking chapatis for you today, but in the future you may not be able to get the same amount of time from me."

He shared some of his encounters:

I went all over Rishikesh. I met intellectual wrestlers and those performing the elementary steps: postures, saying prayers, rites and rituals. Most of them were doing hatha yoga practices, which are very arduous and beset with difficulties and dangers. The pranas, or the vital airs, have to be controlled, regulated, and directed properly, which is not easily done. For an average householder it is very difficult and time-consuming. The saints do not recommend such practices in this age; people are not physically fit to undertake this type of yoga.

The transcendence of physical consciousness that a yogi pursuing the path of pranas achieves only after a long and arduous discipline is attained by practitioners of the Surat Shabd Yoga sometimes at the first sitting at the time of initiation.

It is the quality of sehaj, or naturalness and ease that makes the Surat Shabd Yoga accessible to all. The music of the divine Word is vibrating in all alike, and he who follows its path needs no special requirements, whether physical or intellectual. It is as much open to the old as to the young, to the sinners as to the saints, to the simple as to the learned, to women and children as to men. It is the highest form of yoga, which takes the soul to its Source.

In Rishikesh I met only one man who was rising above body-consciousness, Raghuvacharya. That man's habit was so kingly that he would never stand to greet anybody. When he saw me coming at about two hundred yards, he stood up...He loved me and I loved him. In our talk, it came out that Raghuvacharya went to the first plane, Sahansdal Kamal...He said, "What I learned by going through all the Shastras, Vedas, and Upanishads, you speak of from inner experience."

In between meditation and walks in the foothills, Kirpal Singh kept meticulous diaries of his inner experiences and dialogue with the ascended Masters, including Hazur, Baba Ji (Jaimal Singh), Jesus, Kabir, Nanak, Zoroaster, Guru Gobind Singh, Tulsi Sahib, Rumi, and others. These notebooks were written in a coded language of the Master's invention, which he employed for the sake of secrecy. They contain scores of margin notes in English in his own inimitable handwriting.[2]

After more than five months in Rishikesh, the new Master received orders from Hazur and Baba Ji to return to the world and begin his great mission of liberating souls from the bondage of mind and matter.

---

1. *Portrait of Perfection - A Pictorial Biography of Kirpal Singh,* Bowling Green, VA: S.K. Publications, 1981, p.50.

2. These secret diaries remained hidden away for thirty years and were discovered in 1978. A complete photocopy is in the writer's possession.

Dr. Harold Brock and Sant Kirpal Singh, California, 1955

26

In the year 1911, Kehar Singh Sasmas, a learned disciple of Hazur, traveled by steamship from India to Vancouver, Canada. Due to his education and fluency in several languages, Sasmas was hired as an interpreter for the Canadian Pacific Steamship Lines, and later for the Canadian Pacific Railroad Company, when large numbers of Indians—predominantly Punjabis—migrated to work the sawmills and timber camps in British Columbia and northern Washington.

Kehar Singh often discoursed to largely Caucasian audiences in churches and other meeting halls in Vancouver, B.C., Seattle, Port Angeles, Portland and northern California. His understanding of Christian, Hindu, Muslim and Sikh religious teachings, and his references to the possibility of someone living on earth in this very day and age who could actually connect the individual with the Light and Sound of God, created considerable stir wherever he went.

A Port Angeles dentist, Dr. Harold M. Brock and his wife Genevieve, attended one of these early talks. After the lecture, Mrs. Brock, a very spiritually receptive individual, approached Kehar Singh and asked him about the man with the white turban and snow white beard whom she saw hovering above him. Kehar Singh realized that it was the subtle form of his Master she was seeing. In due course, the Brocks, who had been seeking the Truth for many years, became Baba Sawan Singh's first western disciples, later functioning as his initiating representatives. In those days, there was no Sant Mat literature available in English, and the magnificent and in-depth letters of Hazur served as the only source of the Master's teachings in the West.

In his letters to the Brocks in the early 1920's, Sawan Singh predicted:

> *We are expecting much from America... The day will come when your people will turn to Sant Mat (The Path of the Masters)... Some day the Great Work there will assume much larger proportions. You may look confidently for it, in your own time. Be ready for it.[1]*

And again,

> *One point is not to be overlooked at this time. In America every man and woman who is initiated is selected by the Sat Guru under the direction of Sat Purush (the Supreme Being in Sach Khand) for a definite, two-fold purpose:*
>
> *First, that the disciple himself might be free from the bondage of the wheel (of transmigration) and taken to his own home in Sach Khand.*
>
> *Second, that he may perform a definite service in laying the foundation and carrying forward the work intended by the Father for Sant Mat in America. There is a very great possibility there, and we hope and expect much from all of you.*
>
> *If anyone selected falls by the wayside and fails to carry out the work intended for him, that is his great loss. He will one day see how much he has lost by his failure.*
>
> *But those of you who remain faithful and go on working to the best of your ability must one day realize how great is the work you have done and how great is the reward which awaits you. It is my wish and hope that each one who is fortunate enough to get Naam in your country may be useful in the hand of the Supreme in doing this very great work.*
>
> *Keep always love and harmony among yourselves and allow nothing to sidetrack you. Hold fast to the Sound Current, and let no fancy scheme of the Negative Power draw anyone aside. Above all, be faithful to your Bhajan and sit with mind fixed upon the center. It is thus you will all get strength enough to withstand every assault of the opposing powers. You will carry on until victory is attained, and thousands in your country will see the Great Light.[2]*

The Brocks wrote Hazur asking about spiritual succession after one's Master leaves the body.. In his letter dated December 17, 1925 Hazur replied,

> *Your question as to whom to look to for guidance if the present Master goes out of life is very appropriate. The Master leaves the physical*

form in time like other people, but remains with His devotees in the astral form as long as the devotee has not crossed the astral form. All internal guidance will be done by him and it is he who will come to take charge of the soul at the time of death. And in case a devotee rises above the eye-focus now and meets him daily, he will meet him inwardly there as usual. He will continue to discharge his inward duties of guidance as before, only he cannot give instructions outwardly for the simple reason that he has left the physical vehicle. The functions which would be performed through the physical frame only, will now be done by his successor. All outward guidance will be done by the successor, and the devotees of the Master that is gone will love the successor no less. They will get the benefit of the outward instructions from the successor. Correspondence will be done with the Successor, and you will know who it is.[3]

Finally, in 1955 Dr. Brock met Sant Kirpal Singh in northern California on his first world tour. During a morning meditation at Santa Barbara, Master Kirpal placed his hand on the head of the elderly doctor, and the latter, who by his own admission, had never experienced much in the way of spiritual visions, was suddenly blessed with the radiant *saroop* of Hazur within for the first time in his life.[4]

Let me first introduce myself... I am eighty-three years old and have been in the practice of dentistry for fifty-five years. Mrs. Brock, a very gifted woman, died about ten years ago.

It was in the year 1910 or 1911 that Mr. Kehar Singh Sasmas came and told us of the then Living Master, Sawan Singh. We were given the initiation by Mr. Sasmas under the directions of the Master. In our correspondence, I at one time asked, in case he passed on before I did, would I know who the new Master would be? And he said I would.

So I was quite satisfied when Mr. Khanna put me in touch with Sant Kirpal Singh.

India has a background of thousands of years of recognizing the spiritually enlightened ones, while to us in this country the coming of such a one is new and of great importance, and we hope to have the Master back again, at an early date. In Sant Kirpal Singh, I think every one recognizes the unbounded spirit of love that permeates Him and everything He does, regardless of who or what people are or may have been...[5]   Port Angeles, WA Feb. 2, 1956

Dr. Brock, devoted pioneer of Sant Mat in the West, peacefully passed away as he approached the century mark. He was held in great esteem by both Masters and their disciples.

1. *Spiritual Gems—Letters of Maharaj Baba Sawan Singh to Disiciples*, Radha Soami Satsang, Beas, India, page 262

2. Ibid., p. 281-282.

3. From the author's copy of a collection of Hazur's letters to the Brocks.

4. According to T.S.Khanna and others who were present when the Master asked all present to describe their individual inner experiences.

5. Bhadra Sena, Editor, *As They Saw The Master*, Delhi, India, Ruhani Satsang publications: 1956. p. 18-19. This remarkable out-of-print book contains 101 impressions from those who met the Master for the first time on his 1955 world tour. These include extraordinary testimonies from a number of Sawan Singh's first American disciples (now deceased).

27

May 16th, 1967: During my brief Indian sojourn, I have been deeply moved to observe the great love that exists between the older disciples of Hazur and the living Master. I had grown fond of one of these, an elderly man with noble-bearing. Mangat Ram was tall, straight-backed, elegantly dressed in dark Nehru coat, white churdidar pyjamas and white turban, Punjabi-Hindu-style. Whenever we met, we always greeted each other with a Namaste-bow, or a hug. Mangat Ram just left this world. The night before I spent several hours with him, giving massage and alternately sponging his fevered face.

In the early morning I retreated for meditation to a nearby room. Unbeknownst to me, Master had physically come to Mangat Ram, just as his soul was withdrawing via the third eye. Tai Ji called into his ear, "Mangat Ram! Has Maharaj Ji come yet?" Mangat Ram whispered "Hanji...yes. I am going and not returning. Hazur and Maharaj Ji are here and are calling me to come Home." Master laid a gentle hand on Mangat Ram's forehead, and all restlessness in his body ceased. His spirit was never to be troubled by its limitations again.

At the time of Mangat Ram's passing, I was sitting in bhajan. A message came, unsought: *"the bird is released from its cage."* Roused by sounds of lamentation nearby, I shuffled with benumbed legs in the direction from where all this noise was coming. In a different room I found the Master, standing behind a bed upon which was lying a still form draped in a white sheet. Quite jolly, he asked, "You want to see the dead body?" I nodded. When he withdrew the sheet covering Mangat Ram's head he said, "See how peaceful he is? Just as if he were asleep." It was the first time I had ever seen death up close. Mangat Ram looked peaceful, if not beautiful—a slight radiance was on his brow.

Accompanying the funeral procession to the cremation grounds, I saw a tiny bundled form of an infant lying on an unlit pyre, next to that of old Mangat Ram, reminding me that just such a graphic sight of life's temporal nature inspired Prince Siddhartha to renounce the pleasures of royalty and seek enlightenment.

After the pyre was ablaze, we sat near the Master under the shade of a banyan tree. Many of the deceased's friends and relatives were weeping, although his devoted wife was calm, knowing that her life-companion was released from mortality.

Mangat Ram led a virtuous life, rarely lost his temper and spoke little. Every morning, as he walked several miles from the ashram to his silk shop, he would take a great stack of chapatis and distribute them to all the homeless cats and dogs in the neighborhood.

While I write, the pyre burns and the relatives wail. Master poignantly remarks, *"Even the dogs and cats will be weeping for Mangat Ram."*

May 18, 1967: A new visitor arrives from San Francisco seeking spiritual consolation. In her sharing, Sandra allows me to record her words:

> *"The first time I met Master was in San Francisco on his 1963 world tour...Although my mother expressed doubts whether she could maintain the diet due to her illness, Master initiated both of us the next morning anyway. Although I never ate meat again, Mother did and abandoned meditation. She was very sick and in pain for the next eighteen months. One day, out of the blue, Master appeared to Mother and told her, 'In three weeks you will leave the world, and I will take you back to your True Home.' He also told her to to be loving...boy, was she ever difficult to get along with! And he told her to discontinue eating meat, and to put in maximum time for meditation.*
>
> *"I was amazed at the change. From then on, Mother became wise and loving. When she spoke, it was as if Master was speaking through her. She meditated a great deal, and threw out all the meat and alcohol in the house, and all her pain vanished. As she grew weaker, I called in our priest to administer Last Rites, but Mother told him, 'I don't need any Last Rites! Master has come to take me back to God, and there is nothing to hold me here now.' The presence of peace and radiance surrounding her made such a deep impression on the priest that he wrote to the Great Master asking for initiation.*

The Major and the Frenchman: A physical education instructor has just
arrived from France, seeking initiation. While he had read translations of the
Master's works, he understands only a few words of English, and the Master
speaks no French! There are some hilarious attempts at sign-language, and
eventually an interpreter is located in Delhi. Normally, initiations are given on
the first Monday of each month, but Master decides to make an exception. An
Indian army major also wants to be initiated, and both are invited up to the
flat rooftop of his bungalow. The translator, myself and Brij Mohan are also
present. While seated on a cot, the Master conveys the sacred mantra, asks the
Frenchman and the Major to close their eyes and gives out instructions for
meditation. I look at my watch; it is 11 AM. The Master lies down, and immediately begins snoring. Being the naughty one, I have to suppress the giggles,
an inclination that is quickly overwhelmed by intense spiritual grace coming
from above.

About an hour passes in this manner, while the Master softly snores *the
entire time.* When I break off meditation and glance to my watch, the second
hand moves to 12 noon exactly. At that very moment, the Master gives a little
snort, and quickly sits up, swinging his feet to the ground. "Leave off, please.
Alright, what did you get?" The Major and the Frenchman, if not everyone
present, has had the similar experience of seeing the huge Red Rising Sun of
Trikuti. Hismanner and methods are inscutable, powerful and mysterious.

Two days later, the Frenchman becomes very unhappy because since initiation
he hasn't been able to see the Light again. He interupts the Master in the middle
of an important meeting with Muni Shushil Kumar, the renownedJain sadhu,
along with several other prominent religious leaders. I happen to be present, off
to the side, a silent witness. When his insistence gets the Master's attention, he
complains miserably, "Maitre, no light see. Noir. Nothing!" Master reminds him
of his experience at initiation, but the Frenchman is adamant. Master sits him
down on the floor in front and bids him to close his eyes. Master then places his
forefinger between the man's eyebrows, holding it there for the next 15 to 20
minutes. Otherwise ignoring him, the Master carries on normal conversation
with the dignitaries in the room. A couple of humorous and lively exchanges
ensue with the Master waving his other hand around. For the entire period, he
never removes his finger from the man's forehead. During a brief lull, Master
looks at the fellow sitting before him as if for the first time, and pulls away his
finger. Suddenly, the Frenchman leaps up in the air, crying, "Oh! Oh! Very
much lumiere! Brilliance! Extraordinaire! Oh! Oh! Merci mon Maitre!"

God helps those who help themselves, but He also helps those who *don't*,
won't or *can't.* The sun shines on everyone, and grace is without limits.

28

In the third week of May, a caravan of several carloads departs for fabled Kashmir, leaving behind the crowds and sweltering plains. With a party of nine, I leave via sleeper-train, and arrive at the hill-station of Pathankot at ten the next morning. We transfer to a rickety old bus, a belcher of black smoke, and begin ascending a narrow road which leads over high mountain passes with hairpin curves. To the left is a sheer drop-off, at least a thousand feet straight down; to the right, steep rock walls. Less fortunate twisted and rusting hulks litter the bottom of the gorge. With tightness in the stomach, one prays, one accepts! Twice, our driver has to go back and forward to maneuver hairpin corners...and only our Maker knows what lies around the bend. At places the road is supported by cantilevered logs and rocks jammed into crevices hand-hewn into the sheer cliffs; rock and scree are held back by a not-too-reassuring basket weave of willow saplings. One can only surrender; there is no turning back.

We stop for the night in the alpine village of Batote, perched high on a promontory. The view in all directions is magnificent. Raj Kumar Jain, a Supreme Court advocate, his wife, and I go in search of clean water to bathe away the journey's grime. Hiking across boulder-strewn terrain, we locate an icy spring. Nearby, three Ladhaki mountain men prostrate westward towards Mecca, reciting *Namaz*—the prayer of faithful Muslims. Watching from a respectful distance, I am struck by the beauty of their faith. The Koran enjoins: *"Those who remember Me, I remember them."* And, *"I am closer to thee than thy jugular vein."*

After the Muslims depart, we take our icy ablutions. In the course of conversation, Jain tells me, "I worshipped God in the form of universal Mother, and practiced a form of meditation. Sometimes Mother blessed with her visions. When Master came to Indore three years ago, I attended satsang and was profoundly affected. The next day, I went to the temple for worship, as was my habit; lo, before me, instead of the stone statue of the goddess was the radiant form of the Master. From that moment on wherever I looked, I saw him in front of me, a constant blissful vision unaffected by eating, sleeping, walking, or bathing. I became like a madman, but mad after God! After three days, Master's subtle form disappeared, unfortunately. Now we hope to live always at his feet, serving the mission."

The Jains are a minority in India and don't consider themselves Hindus. Jains follow a lineage of Buddha-like Saints. Mahavira, the founder of Jainism (500 BC), roamed the forests in a naked state, practicing austerities and intense meditation until attaining enlightenment. Like Buddha, Mahavira established a spiritual path that included ethical living, non-violence, vegetarianism, selfless service, renunciation and meditation. By and large, Jains have been very successful in business, but those with ascetic inclinations become monks, nuns or sadhus. Of these, the most rigorous become *digambar*, or "sky-clad," renouncing family, property, wealth, name, desire, everything, including their clothes.

The following morning, I sit next to Anita Bhenji, the articulate principal of Panipat's largest girl's college. In the course of conversation, Anita shares her extraordinary coming to the path: "I had been searching for answers to the riddle of existence, and had strong spiritual yearnings from childhood. Several months before meeting the living Master, his radiant form would come to me during my prayers. One night, he transmitted to me the first three initiatory Names, and then took my soul to those higher regions. My prayers to meet him in this world were answered when he came on tour to Panipat. Brother, what is your experience?"

Srinagar—Venice of Asia, 21st May: After crossing the last great mountain pass, the long descent into the Vale of Kashmir begins. In wonderment I gaze upon the exquisite panorama. In all directions, sparkling snowy peaks form a protective phalanx about a fecund valley which, in its immensity disappears into the hazy distance. The base of every mountain up to within several hundred feet of the snow line has been terraced, the result of hundreds, if not thousands of years of toil. These fertile beds are filled with water, iridescent green rice shoots and other assorted produce. From the distance, as we move along, sky and clouds, apricot and mulberry trees, water and paddy, reflect in myriad terraces which appear to move as we do, kaleidoscopic-like shattered mirrors. Columns of tall, straight cypress and poplar line the road and the clear babbling streams. Kashmir is famed for the quality and flavor of its fragrant rice, grapes, raisins, walnuts, mulberries, almonds, pine nuts, apples, peaches, pears, apricots, cherries, saffron and strawberries!

We pause to rest by a mighty spring, the source of the Jhelum River. From a natural subterranean tunnel in the mountain rock, purest water gushes up into a huge roiling pool, full of tame fish which eat from one's hand. In perfect symmetry, this emerald pool is surrounded by ancient trees and gracefully arched medieval pavilions of marble. A stone tablet carved in Persian glyphs echoes a sixteenth century emperor, understandably blinded by beauty, *"If there is Paradise on earth, it is here! It is here! It is here!"* Downstream from Jhelum's cradle, we wash away travel-grime in the clear, bitingly cold water.

Lovely Srinagar, the 'Venice of Asia' greets us. Canals interlace this city of steep gabled wooden buildings, while merchants and tourists ply waterways in graceful boats. We proceed to the sprawling estate of Sardar Jaswant

Singh Chabbra, whose family operates a chain of dry cleaning stores. Jaswant Singh is much more than a businessman, he is munshi, or scholar of Persian literature, and his eyes reflect a heart intoxicated with God. We are treated with generous hospitality and treated like family members.

The thorned rose—August 24: A woman humbly offers a sheaf of red roses to our Gurudev. He separates the blossoms and hands them out to all the surrounding disciples. On the third rose, he winces from a thorn's prick, and comments, "No roses without thorns." Is it that love's beauty is never without pain? When he hands the wine-red rose to me, I pray, *"Never let me be a thorn in your side!"* At his gentle bidding we enter meditation. It is in these blessed hours that the real meaning of communion is revealed.

The Five Dacoits—August 25: While attempting meditation, I drifted off and dreamt of being attacked by five cobras, each a different vivid color. A long and desperate battle ensued, in which I was armed with a sword, but as soon as I succeeded in cutting one serpent, another would attack, and one severed would rise up again as two! They were winning, but I fought on. Eventually they gave up and went away. After waking, I went to Master for guidance, assuming that I did the right thing. As soon as my description was finished, he censured, *"Why didn't you do simran?!"* Each cobra represented one of the five deadly passions which can only be vanquished by the holy names. The next morning, after a long sitting in a room I was sharing with several others, I fell asleep, and was overcome by unworthy desires. Disgusted with myself, I went in search, and found the Master sitting in the garden:

"Master! I feel I am being torn in half. Master is pulling on one side and the Deadly Five (lust, anger, greed, attachment and ego) are pulling on the other."

Leaning forward, fixing his penetrating gaze on me, he says: "Look here! Master is stronger than these five. Keep your eyes on Him and not on them. They obey Him. Say you want to go into a bungalow but there are five vicious dogs guarding the entrance. How will you enter? You simply call for help to the master of these dogs. He will say a few kind words to them; they will obey and let you enter safely.

"Sometimes certain desires may not even be your own. They may be thought-transferred by others. Be like a rock, not sand. Even big waves strike a rock, and bounce back, whereas sand absorbs them. Since you want to make spiritual progress, as an unmarried, it is better not to remain alone in the room with the opposite sex."

Shalimar and the tears of the dog: Later in the day, about thirty accompany the Master to the fabled Shalimar Gardens built four centuries earlier by Moghul kings. Eyes drink deeply as we climb an enchanting path beside a splashing stream. Overhead spreads the leafy arms of gigantic, barrel-trunked

Kashmiri maples. There is a mystical play between the beauty of Nature and the beauty of the Master. As I muse thus, he turns and catches my eye, sweeps his hand in the air and quotes Guru Nanak:

> *Everything in this world will one day perish.*
> *Be not attached to its ephemeral charms.*

We pause awhile and Master sits in sidh-aasan upon a large stone platform straddling the stream. We gather 'round to watch and receive handfuls of fresh cherries from his hands. In the distance downstream, I notice a stray dog trotting in a deliberate straight line, slowing only when he is within six feet of our group. Ignoring others, the dog looks humbly up at the Master, who returns a compassionate gaze. Amazingly, the dog then lays his head upon the Master's feet. Never have I known a dog to weep, but tears begin rolling from the eyes of this conscious entity in a mongrel's body, who has come only for the Satguru's darshan! Master gives him parshad and a touch on the head. Fulfilled, the animal sadly departs. Who knows? perhaps to die and return as human, for only in human form can soul find liberation. Did this neglected cur once inhabit a human form, but through some dark deed, forfeit it? All I know is that the Master's compassion embraces all, and accelerates evolution.

Pahalgam: We leave for the mountain resort of Pahalgam, one of the world's most beautiful jewels. Beneath a flawless azure sky, hemmed by lofty peaks, we arrive and follow Master on foot up a grassy slope. He sits on the living emerald carpet; tall whispering deodar pines stand sentinel behind. He removes his turban and sets it by his side. For the first time I am seeing his dome-like forehead; his hair at the sides is long and tied in a knot at the back, like Rishis of yore. While gazing upon us one by one, we are stopped in our tracks at different levels on the slope, and unbidden, sink to our knees. Nothing is spoken, no one moves. As celestial gears shift,

Sant Kirpal Singh Ji, Pahalgam meadow, Kashmir.

blissful radiance fills the air, billowing in and around the Master's physical form, passing back and forth between he and his disciples. Magically, all phenomena of nature vanishes. Only the jewel in the Light remains. There is no *Kal.*

A thousand thousand suns
Aglow and rising,
Shattering, engulfing, uniting;
And here the Formless dwells in a man.

Mind can never grasp Pure Essence in its totality; it can only fiddle around at the edge. A wakeful night passes; a single blanket and love's glow are my only protection. My small room has an inward view, and a layer of ice has formed in the sink. At seven in the morn, Master puts his disheveled crew into contemplation. He himself sits with us for two charged hours. This meditation takes my soul deeper and farther than ever before, again attesting to the power of his proximity.

The morning air is still at the freezing level when the sitting is over. He asks, "Are you not cold?" I reply, "Thank you, Master." "Well, are you hungry?" "I'm fine, Master." He chuckles and says, "Love knows no heat and no cold. You even enjoy your hunger when you are with me!"

Another Miracle: Several miles beyond Pahalgam, our caravan wanders through grassy meadows and evergreens. We stop to enjoy the scenery, the quietude, and the rushing river. A shepherd passes with a large flock of brown and white sheep. Master walks off by himself and I follow at a distance. How rare that he is free from the clamoring crowds. He stands on the sward, breathing affinity, innocence and purity towards all life.

The river frolics behind us. Master reclines on a blanket to the front of me, his body apparently sleeping. High up the mountain, I see three young men from our group recklessly racing down the steep slope. I gasp as heavy-set Kapoor loses control and falls head-first at full speed about fifteen feet through the air, landing hard on the rock-strewn bottom.

Master is apparently asleep, gently snoring while Kapoor is airborne. At precisely the moment of impact, Master rolls over, stands up facing me, and slaps his side by the ribs three times, precisely at the same spot of Kapoor's certain injury. Kapoor, however, stands up, completely free of injury and pain. When I approach the Master with mouth agape, he brushes off the entire incident. I only convey what my eyes have seen.

Jesus may have lived in Kashmir: Many of Kashmir's original inhabitants are of Jewish ancestry, and are known as "the People of the Book." Moses first led them to this *land of milk and honey*, they believe. The Ahmadia Muslims of the region recognize the special prophetic mission of Jesus (as does the Koran), and vehemently insist that Jesus visited Kashmir. The mountain trail from Afghanistan, which passes into Kashmir, is called *Issa-i-Maidan* or the

Meadow of Jesus. Legend has it that Jesus tarried there a while. In the old quarter of Srinagar is a shrine revered by Muslims—*the Rozabal*—commemorating the sojourn of Hazrat Issa almost twenty centuries earlier. *Hazrat* is the Persian equivalent for Lord, and *Issa*, the Aramaic for Jesus. This, and ancient scrolls in an old Buddhist monastery in Leh, appear to corroborate his visit to the region.

Departure: Mrs. Chabbra laments, "When Master was staying in our house, we were so happy. It was just as if God was here with us. But now that he is gone away, our house will seem so empty!" She and her husband Jaswant were married in the presence of Hazur in the late forties, an event documented on color film. The grandeur of Hazur, with his snow white beard and regal bearing were captured for all times. How this movie came to Master Kirpal is very interesting. The film's owner happened to visit Kirpal Singh Ji in Delhi, but did not accept him as the Master. Master very lovingly offered his brother-in-faith anything his heart desired if he would just allow a copy of the movie to be made, but he refused. Sant Kirpal Singh continued in his loving way, when suddenly the visitor remarked, "If you can give me the grace to glimpse our beloved Hazur once again, I will gladly make you a copy." Kirpal Singh touched him on the head, and immediately the departed Hazur appeared to the visitor's inner gaze. The grateful disciple immediately handed over the film.

Pahalgam, Kashmir, 1967

29

Diary, June, '67: "Please make yourself ready. We are leaving for Haridwar and Rishikesh tomorrow morning!" Master announces. Currents of joy and soaring expectation fill me. Since my teens when I first read Brunton's *Search in Secret India*, and Yogananda's *Autobiography*, I inwardly longed for those sacred haunts where rishis and yogis of yore pursued divine knowledge with singular zeal.

We set out at the crack of dawn, our cars paralleling the mighty *Ganga* (Ganges) upriver, arriving at Haridwar by noon. This ancient religious city teems with ochre-robed swamis, pundits and pious pilgrims. Incense, mantras and temple bells fill the air; statues of Ganesha, the elephant-headed god; Shivji, the blue-throated Himalayan yogi-deva; Sheshnag, the thousand-headed serpent representing the support of the physical plane; Lakshmi, goddess of prosperity; avatars Rama and Krishna, Hanuman the monkey-king—all invite devotees to worship. Vast stoneworks and marble terraces, endless stairs and ornate shrines line the river, where crowds perform ablutions, offering water eastward to the souls of departed ancestors.

Absorbing this remarkable spectacle, one is reminded of Guru Nanak's Haridwar visit 450 years earlier. After observing similar rituals, Nanak began scooping water in his hands, throwing it to the West in the opposite direction. A large crowd gathered, and their priest spokesman demanded an explanation. The great teacher replied, "Oh, I'm watering my fields in the Punjab." They chided him, "That's ridiculous. How is it possible for you to water your fields five hundred miles away?" Nanak replied, "If your offerings can reach the souls of those long departed, surely this same water will reach my fields in the Punjab!" By Nanak's simple example and his highly charged presence, his audience realized the ineffectiveness of outer ritual, and the process of their awakening began.

For centuries and even to this day, pilgrims held the belief that a bath in the holy Ganga will wash all sins away. Kabir in his time reminded pilgrims that if the fish which spends its entire life in the Ganges does not lose its bad odor, how can man think that by such a bath his *soul* will be cleansed? Investiture of miraculous properties to physical objects is the common practice of the priest-craft. Kabir, Nanak and other divine mystics speak of an inner purifying water, found only in *Daswan Dwar*, the third spiritual region: when the soul reaches this stage and bathes in its nectarous waters, the karmas and sins collected from innumerable lifetimes are cleansed. Thus purified and uncovered, soul radiates with a brightness exceeding twelve suns. She then may proceed to the higher spiritual regions in the company of the Guide.

A white bridge spans the wide river over which we cross to the uninhabited side where *Ganga Mayi* (Mother Ganges) flows clear, swift and cold from the Himalayas down to the vast Gangetic plains. As life-provider for India's millions, Ganga is indeed a mother-sustainer. While immersing my feet in the cold currents, Master sits nearby in *sidh-aasan* beneath a towering neem tree, giving *darshan* to several sadhu-renunciates. Above and beyond the hodge-podge of temples and ashrams on the opposite shore, jungled foothills stretch into the bluish distance. I ponder the possibility of having lived here before.

Master shares a glimpse of his earlier life: "I came to Haridwar more than thirty-five years ago, to meditate in solitude on this very bank. Then Haridwar consisted of only a few temples and ashrams, and people were afraid to cross the river to this side [now a beautiful park]. It was then all jungle, infested with snakes and scorpions—but they never bit or harmed me. I found it a good place for meditation. Now Haridwar is commercialized and noise-some." He walks to the river's edge, recounting times when he would swim and allow the current to carry him several kilometers downstream.

Between Haridwar and the smaller, less commercialized village of Rishikesh upriver, we pass more ashrams and temples. Milling crowds of sadhu-mendicants of all ages, male and female, some with long matted hair, prayer *malas*, shiva-tridents and ash-besmeared bodies, beg for alms. Some sadhus engage in incredibly austere forms of yoga. Various sects are delineated by yellow, orange, white or red robes. Some have shaven heads, some are bearded, some have white forehead markings, some red, some are learned and renowned scholars. Some are genuine, most are engaged in elementary stages of yoga. Some are shameless pretenders, preying on the unsuspecting.

From the front seat, Master shares more of his own history:

"In 1948, I went to Uttarkashi, up-river from Rishikesh, and I invited all hermits and sadhus from their retreats. When they gathered together I asked, 'Brothers, who can give experience of Light?' Only one man came forward who had that competency. He could give inner Light to others but his method was to concentrate on the flame of a candle. After one or two years of practice others would begin to see the light inside. You people are given Light the very first day."

Raghuvacharya: We drive to an embankment high over the Ganga, stopping at the Darshana Mahavidyalaya Ashram and Sanskrit School, founded by the venerable scholar and sage, Sri Raghuvacharya. We descend a flight of steep stone steps to a cluster of whitewashed buildings overhanging the sparkling river. When the 111 year old Raghuvacharya emerges from a door, we have the rare opportunity to witness an authentic *Yogiraj*,[1] and a Saint, meet and embrace.

Master has also come for the sake of Mangat Ram's widow, to be present at the immersion of her husband's ashes. A Pundit leads a procession to the river-bank where Vedic rites are performed, prayers intoned and ashes poured upon the water. Not more than a few hundred yards upstream is the rock upon which the Master practised intense meditation for several months in 1948.

Three of us escape the sweltering heat and swim in the slower, deeper waters of the river, despite crocodile warnings. As I swim to the far side, I turn and see Master watching from the cliff.

In a large room of the hermitage, we eat, then rest on the smooth cool floor. The supine but lordly one is a few feet away, attention totally withdrawn and absorbed in the inner spiritual regions. All breathing, all movement of his body slows until entirely still, like a marble carving, and remains so for the next 20 minutes. At this sight I am chilled and alarmed. I whisper my anxiety to my friend Brij Mohan. "Dear brother; not to worry," he assures. "This is usual course for Maharaj Ji. He will return after a while. You don't know these things. This is his mystery." It's a mystery I'd love to know.

Yogishwar, an Englishwoman and disciple of the late Swami Sivananda, is my guide to Rishikesh. She has short-cropped silver hair and is dressed in renunciate's robes. I ask how she came to be here.

Yogishwar answers, "In 1963, I was practicing sadhana [spiritual discipline] in London under the guidance of my guru, Swami Sivananda. One night I entered a deep meditative state, and within brilliant spiritual Light a great Master appeared, with incomparable beauty and power. He was in the Sikh form with long white beard and high turban. Next, another being of Light appeared. The first Master gave me detailed directions to go to such and such a place in London and meet the Living Master. I had no idea who these beings were but I had learned to trust my inner direction. I went to the indicated place and met Sant Kirpal Singh (then on his second world tour and in London). He informed me that Swami Sivananda had just left the body that day. Naturally, this news came as a great shock!

"When I saw a photograph of Baba Sawan Singh Ji, I recognized him as the great Master who had first appeared in my vision. I was initiated that very morning by Sant Kirpal Singh. Again Sawan Singh appeared; this time revealing much more of his transcendental immanence. And again Master Kirpal appeared. Hazur then said to me directly, 'Kirpal Singh is my Spiritual Son. He will take care of you.'"

I ask, "Why have you continued to wear the saffron robes and shave your head like a renunciate, when that is not our Path?"

Yogishwar explains, "I have taken life-long vows of renunciation under the instructions of my guru Sivananda whom I continue to honor and love, but my spiritual salvation and passport through the higher planes is in my relationship with Master and his Sant Mat lineage. Master Kirpal is my spiritual Father, and is fully aware of my aspirations and attachment to Swami Sivananda. He respects my unique relationship to the Divine."

After putting me in my place, Yogishwar invites me to Sivananda Ashram, a stone's throw down-river from Raghuvacharya's. She points out a universal worship temple and samadh (tomb) of its revered founder. We peer inside the door of a decrepit cell where Yogishwar spent years in yogic practice. She jokes about the rats and bugs who kept her company, stating that spartan Sawan Ashram is pure luxury by comparison.

When we return, we find Raghuvacharya and Master up and talking. The sprightly Yogiraj is in an effusive mood: "Before meeting Maharaj Ji in 1948, I had, by rigorous practice of Patanjali's Asthanga Yoga, traversed beyond the six chakras and inner stages up to Sahasrar—the Thousand Petalled Lotus of Light. Sahasrar is headquarters of the astral plane and the final stage of most forms of yoga. Other Yoga systems and their practitioners are unaware of the existence of anything beyond Brahm—the causal world, or second stage. Since meeting Master, he showered grace on this soul, taking it beyond what is possible through yoga."

The venerable sage continues, "Twelve years ago, I became very ill and 'died.' When surat (attention) withdrew from the corpse into higher planes, I saw Hazur, and before him was Maharaj Kirpal requesting Hazur to extend my life another fifteen years, as he wanted more work from me! Hazur nodded his head in acceptance, and thus I am here today!"

We move to the stone courtyard outside, directly overlooking the shimmering river. Raghuvacharya asks to see Master's right palm which he indifferently extends while looking into the eyes of each of us, and not without a twinkle of humor. After careful examination, Raghuvacharya becomes animated, hopping from one foot to the next like an excited adolescent. Speaking aloud in a deep, booming voice and tracing his index finger along the Master's palm he exclaims, "Never have I seen such a palm! Come, see for yourselves!" All surge forward to see Master's flawless, deeply-lined palm. In rich tones, Raghuvacharya declares, "Not even Rama and Krishna had such a hand. You have the hands which belong to God! Whomsoever beholds such a palm is blessed!" In vain he stoops to touch the Master's feet, but is restrained by him.

"Maharaj!" Raghuvacharya implores, "stay with me; rest a while in my hermitage! Six months here will rejuvenate your body and add years to your precious life!" But Master gently laughs and demurs. He has no luxury of time, for the flock he has demands nurturing and the ones yet to gather beckon; the harvest is rich, and the laborers, few.

I had studied Chiero's scientific system of palmistry prior to my coming to this path and my irrepressible curiosity wants to see what Raghuvacharya's

Master Kirpal and Sri Raghuvacharya, Rishikesh.

palm reveals. The venerable yogi proffers his hand. I'm pleased just to hold his hand in mine, and do not seriously analyze it. Physically, Raghuvacharya stands 5' 6", about 140 lb. with deep-set eyes under betel brows. His beard is white and his sparse long hair is swept back and tied in a knot. Possessed of humor, wisdom, and *ojas*—the power which accrues from long celibacy—Raghuvacharya radiates a veritable halo of light.

> *The illumined Raghuvacharya passed away in 1971 at the age of 113. His body was discovered sitting upright in a full lotus posture. Sant Kirpal Singh Ji personally ignited his funeral pyre.*

---

1 Yogiraj translates as 'King of Yogis.'

30

12 June 1967: Rishikesh fades into bright memory as the serpentine road takes us over low mountains covered in lush tropical forests. Night is falling by the time we reach the Master's old foothill estate, a few miles above the town of Dehra Dun. Turning around in the front seat, he fixes me with a twinkle in his eyes, "This is lion country...and there is one Lion in these hills they haven't caught yet!"[1]

Master acquired the 207 Rajpur Road property in the early fifties. Similar spacious estates, many now crumbling, line both sides of the highway. Rajpur provided the English sahibs respite from the relentless summer heat of the plains. It was in this tranquil setting that Kirpal Singh penned his many books.

After taking food tonight, I voice appreciation of the meditation-conducive surroundings, mercifully removed from noise and pollution. Over the chorus of crickets and frogs, Master comments, "Here it is not yet spoiled, 'though the poison of the cities is approaching. Nature is beautiful except when tormented by the hand of man!" I ask of Emerson, Wordsworth, Blake, and Thoreau, mystics in their own right. Compressing volumes into a few words, he answers, "Poets are half-Saints, I tell you! Poets go up rarely to where Saints *come down* rarely!"

At Rajpur, my daily schedule is to rise long before dawn, meditate for several hours, take fruit for breakfast, have darshan, and then hike alone in the mountains, returning to the residence before late afternoon. On my third day, Tai Ji warns of lions and snakes in the jungle. I do not share her fear, although I did meet a wolf in the forest and came across the lair of a large carnivore. From his wicker chair, Master comments, "I used to sit in meditation down there on the irrigation canal," pointing through the huge mango trees towards the jungle. "Cobras often came and stood before me, for hours together." Master raises his forearm, hand down, imitating a hooded cobra. "Then they would just sneak away. Once a cobra slithered into the satsang at Delhi, reared up on its tail and spread its hood before me. The people got up and cried, 'Snake! Snake! Let us kill it!' But I told them, 'What harm is there if a snake has come? Let him listen and enjoy the satsang.' For one full hour the snake stood there and after satsang was finished, he just went away without harming anyone. This is the result of love.

"I tell you, if you have love for God in your heart, nothing can harm you. Nothing can sting or bite you." After a pregnant pause he continues, "It sometimes happens that one whom you have harmed in a past life is reborn as a snake to repay an old debt."

The Goddess of Rajpur: One of my morning hikes takes me up along the uninhabited jungle-covered mountain ridge directly behind the Master's sylvan retreat. At its summit I discover a small solitary temple with a tall pointed dome, a mute white sentinel overlooking the green valleys below. It is noon-time and very hot, and a heavy stillness hangs in the air. Although the building has been recently whitewashed, its plaster surface is cracked and in disrepair. As curiosity gets the better of me, I leave my shoes outside, unlatch an iron chain, and crawl through a Lilliputian door, wary of snakes. Inside the tiny vaulted chamber it is cool and dark. As eyes adjust to the gloom, I notice several smoke-stained niches set in the walls. These contain incense-reddened images of Ganesh and a goddess, possibly Kali or Durga. An eerie feeling pervades the chamber.

Being a devotee of That which is beyond form, I am not attracted to man-made idols or deities of the illusory astral plane. At the same time I am on their territory and do not wish to disrespect divinity in any of its many forms. Sitting firmly in the lotus position, I remove my watch and lay it on the floor. Eyelids drop, closing off the external world as I slip into a meditative state.

After an hour or so, rustling sounds outside rouses me. My tender feet consider the countless thorns and sharp stones littering the mountain path, so I squeeze through the tiny door to the outside to gather my shoes. I am startled to see a large troop of wild hanuman monkeys squatting along the embankment, observing me warily. After latching the door, I cautiously approach them. Suddenly, as one, they leap into the gum-trees, swinging from one flexible tree to the next, rapidly descending the mountain. I run after them down the hill at break-neck speed like Mowgli, the wild wolf boy in Kipling's *Jungle Book*—forgetting my watch in the temple. The next morning I climb the ridge again, to reclaim my timepiece. The latched door is exactly as I had left it, but the watch within is gone. In the evening, I share my adventures with the Master.

With a playful smile he exclaims, "The Goddess of Rajpur has stolen your watch!" Seeing my curious expression, he elaborates, "This valley was once haunted by a goddess who caused great mischief. The temple on the mountain was built to propitiate her, and she has taken your watch!" I laugh heartily at his joking.

Later that night, upon returning to my unlit room, the apparition of the goddess manifests before me, emanating strange green, yellow and blue crystalline energies. Remembering that *simran* of the five charged names not only helps withdraw the sensory currents to the eye-focus, but also wards off any apparitions of the negative power or mayaic illusion, I begin to voice aloud the sacred *mantra*. The subtle form of the goddess gradually disintegrates into the ether.

Renunciation vs. Marriage - *17 June 1967:* Here in Rajpur, a sense of deep detachment and spiritual yearning has possessed me. "Master," I request, "I don't want anything of this world, or the astral, or causal planes. I want to be one with the Lord." He replies, "When the devotee desires only God, God does not refuse him."

I have observed strict continence for several years after a dissolute adolescence and proved for myself the Master's words, "A lamp burns splendidly when it has oil within, but if all the oil is leaked away, how can there be light?" But there are times when the carnal mind troubles me and behaves like a fly on a dung-heap. When I approach him about my common dilemma, he advises, "Always keep the mind occupied with something useful, such as mentally repeating the five charged names. Keep it occupied, as a vacant mind is the home of the devil! And secondly, avoid looking into the eyes of others. Something is passed through the eyes. The eyes indicate what color a person's soul is dyed in."

Seeking clarification, I ask, "Master, in the West, if you don't look into people's eyes, they think there is something wrong with you, that maybe you are dishonest, whereas in the Orient, looking into the eyes of others may be considered impolite."

"In that case, you can look *towards* them, but not *into* them. If you are stronger, you will influence them, but if they are stronger, they will influence you. If you feel lusty thoughts entering your mind, then come into the presence of the Master. If you look into the eyes of a higher soul, that is another matter. Two-thirds of the teachings are passed through the eyes, and the remainder through word of mouth."

I express the desire to remain celibate for the rest of my life, to retreat to the forest to devote full time to meditation and realization. His response surprises me deeply. "Marriage is no bar to spirituality...One needs a life companion in weal or woe to help each other realize the ultimate Goal. Outwardly renouncing and running to the jungles cannot overcome desire. While living in the forests, you will find distractions there too...from birds, animals and insects. There is also the question of where your food will come from. Renunciation is the negative way. Mind is like a donkey; if you pull it you will be resisted. But if you push it backwards, his inclination may be to go forward in the direction you want it to go. If you renounce the world outwardly, desires will still creep in. It is better to be in the world, but have your mind in the forest, renounced at heart. In other words, be in the world, but not of the world. Let your boat remain in water, but let not water enter your boat.

"Once, missionaries went to a certain country and preached, 'Thou shalt not beat thy wives—this is a sin.' The people asked among themselves, 'Do they beat their women in America?'—And as a result they began beating their women. This is the negative way, you see; mind works this way. Not all the Masters have lived totally celibate lives. Not everything is bad, mind that! There is a legitimate use for everything, but one should not misuse it. For example, if you go to a garden and sit beneath the shady trees and enjoy the fragrance of the flowers, the garden-keeper says nothing, but if you spoil the garden or uproot any plant, he will turn you over to the police. If you live a completely celibate life, never marrying, still the desires and sensuous urges arise. Many desires have to be liquidated in this life."

Letting that sink in, he then gives a special antidote for the wiles of the mind: "Put in more time for meditation sweetly and buoyantly and, when you sleep, go to sleep in the lap of the Master-power."

Everything he says is profound, but it hits like a ton of bricks. Marriage? *Me?* The next morning, I ask, "I have been mulling over your advice about having a life-companion, you know, a wife."

"Yes," he leads me on.

"Well, I was wondering, if I marry, I would want it to be for life. Since I'm afraid of the high divorce rate in the West, maybe my chances there wouldn't be so good," I am having a hard time getting the next part out: "Would it be all right to marry an Indian girl?" I have nothing against Western women, but I am being propelled along tracks already laid.

"No harm," he answers. *Whew!*, I sigh inwardly in relief.

I haven't the faintest idea how to go about getting a wife, especially an Indian wife! I also express guilt over not paying my way while with him. With a shake of his massive head, he dismisses my misgivings: "You are one of the family and there is no need to feel any imposition whatever. And perhaps some day you may be instrumental abroad with His grace." I mumble with gratitude, "Thank you Master...I'm just a puppet." He continues, "All these things come from God overhead..."

I then comment about meditation sittings sometimes being utterly sublime, yet at other times barren, dry, and uninspired; sometimes overtaken by sleep or mental garbage. He advises, "Your meditation should not be a compulsive automatic thing of duty only. You should sit in meditation *like a Prince.* Be jolly and full of joy!"

"Meditation is invariably best when sitting in the Master's presence," I interject.

"That is because of *my* charging." He then quickly deflects personal credit and adds, "That is *His* charging Presence. When you sit with Him, are you then doing so out of compulsion? No! Quite buoyant! So, when you sit, sit buoyantly like a Prince!"

18 June: Master points his finger to each one of us, "Perhaps you may become ambassadors of the Golden Age." What does he mean, I wonder? This reference is the first (but not last) time I hear him give promise of a more enlightened era to come in human affairs. With his impulse comes a sense of individual responsibility to assist in some small way.

19 June: "Did Guru Nanak have a Master?" I ask.

"Some come with a degree, and others attain it while here. What difference exists in their attainment?" he answers. After a long pause, he adds, "Guru Nanak and Kabir were contemporaries." From his remark, I surmise that Master is alluding to a spiritual connection between these two great beings—even a teacher-disciple relationship, despite the absence of adequate historical proof. By tapping within, the Masters can know everything about the past, present and future, but it may not be in full accordance with popular history.

Mussourie & Sakya Trezing Rimpoche—19 June: I join a party of seven for a long hike to Mussourie, an old tourist town perched atop the big mountain directly to our north. One can drive fifteen miles along a switchback road, or take the steep seven-mile mountain path, mostly up. After getting the Master's blessing, we leave on foot.

As the day progresses, temperatures exceed 100 F. We arrive in Mussourie around two in the afternoon, weary from heat, thin air, and the strenuous climb. From our vantage, the magnificent snow-covered Himalayas of Tibet—"the roof of the world"—hover in the blue distance. Refugees from that mysterious land operate a number of stalls throughout the Mussourie markets, selling traditional silver, coral, and turquoise jewelry, *t'hankas* (intricate hand paintings on paper or silk scrolls depicting mandalas, saints, and deities for external concentration), and other arts and crafts. Sales to tourists and collectors help support these gentle refugees and their threatened ancient culture.

As we enter Mussourie, we pass a prominent sign in Tibetan script outside a large, handsome building. Prayer flags flutter in the breeze along the top of the walls and roof. Ever curious, I halt our troupe and poke my nose into the courtyard. A warmly smiling, red-robed Buddhist nun appears from a doorway, bowing and inviting our climbing party within. We gingerly follow. Once inside, we are introduced to the highly venerated nineteen-year old Sakya Trezing Rimpoche, spiritual leader in a nine-hundred-year-old tradition. The Sakya lineage, I am informed, is the second largest Tibetan Buddhist sect, wherein succession passes through an unbroken bloodline. Along with the Dalai Lama and more than ten thousand of his countrymen, Rimpoche fled his beloved homeland and was granted asylum in India. Once formal greetings are over, the educated and articulate Sakya Trezing and I discuss some of the inner traditions of Buddhism and its Tibetan variants. I recall lines from the *Tibetan Book of the Dead:*

> *O nobly born, when thy body and mind were separating, thou must have experienced a glimpse of the Pure Truth, subtle, sparkling, bright, dazzling, glorious, and radiantly awesome, in appearance like a mirage moving across a landscape in springtime in one continuous*

stream of vibrations. Be not daunted thereby, nor terrified, nor awed.
That is the radiance of thine own true nature. Recognize it...
Within those radiances, the natural sound of the Truth will reverberate
like a thousand thunders. The sound will come with a rolling
reverberation...Fear not. Flee not. Be not terrified. Know them
(i.e., these sounds) to be [of]...thine own inner Light.

It is late afternoon when we bid farewell. After wandering through the
Mussourie bazaar, we realize that the sun is rapidly sinking beyond the
mountains, and the enveloping darkness will surely make our steep descent
along the twisting path precarious. Striding through the busy thoroughfare, we
bump into Karam Singh, the Master's carpenter. We exult at this improbable
meeting. With a laugh on his strong face, Karam announces, "Master send Ram
Saroop for you. Waiting down hill, around corner!" Then, as mysteriously as he
appears, Karam moves off into the foot-traffic and disappears from sight before
we have time to question further. Sure enough, down the road and around the
bend waits Ram Saroop—beaming a warm, toothless grin, exclaiming loudly,
"God-power, Christ-Power, Ram-Power, bring me! Champion Studebaker!"

Master, children and Studebaker, Rajpur

After we disembark at 207 Rajpur, I retire to my dark room for meditation. This night, I am beset with an unsought visitation, a seemingly endless pantheon of larger-than-life Tibetan deities in full color; wrathful, flaming *Herukas*, serene Buddhas and Tibetan saints appear in a procession within the void. *Simran* surrounds me with a protective shield. My experience appears to have been triggered by the contact with an authentic mystical lineage embodied in the Sakya Rimpoche. As these archetypes emerge from the astral plane, they are submerged into the Light of simran, not to return.

23 June: *Every* morning and afternoon meditation sittings are given for the Dehra Dun initiates and those visiting from Delhi. Most of the sittings are followed by informal question and answer sessions. An elderly woman complains, "Maharaj, I cannot see anything within, because my attention is distracted by my arthritis."

Gesturing with a pointed forefinger to the crook of his other arm, Maharaj Ji says, "When you go to a doctor for an injection, you look away and divert your attention so that you will not feel the pain of the needle. Similarly, fully direct your attention to the Third Eye-focus; you will see the Light, and the pains of the body below will not be felt. It is a matter of controlling the attention."

He speaks of Bhai Mani Singh, an advanced disciple of the Tenth Guru, who was captured by imperial Mughal forces and condemned to death by dismemberment, joint by joint, beginning with the fingers. When the executioner became impatient with this tedious process, he began to take a shortcut by cutting off an entire arm. In the midst of his torture, Bhai Mani Singh withdrew his attention from bodily awareness and laughed at the executioner, exhorting him, "Follow your orders, and cut these limbs joint by joint!"

Rajpur Gems—24 June:

> *Always reserve a place in your home for worshipping the Lord, even if it be only the corner of a hut. That body is beautiful in whom God is remembered; wherever such a one sits, that place becomes beautified. The Guru himself may be poor and without fine clothes, but with him you will enjoy bliss and peace of mind. If we have his company and are given hard work, if we have to sweep the floor, wear coarse cloth and sleep on a sack, still that is far better than the company of the affluent who are far from God. Simple living, fewer desires and high thinking make a real man. That place where we get sweet remembrance of God is the best place, no matter if it be in a poor hut. All our wealth and possessions will someday be burnt. Therefore, we should spend time to seek eternity in the company of a Sadhu or Saint. If God is with us, love is with us—and then, even dust is gold.*
>
> *Once Lakshmi, the Goddess of Wealth, was asked why there was no hair at the back of her head and none on the front. She replied that the hair at the back of her head was pulled out by the worldly people—and the hair on her forehead was rubbed away because she had been pressing her forehead at the feet of God's Saints, but they would not accept her.*

Learning is a Garland of Flowers—26 June: Dan M, philosophy professor from the University of California at-Berkeley, and his wife, are on sabbatical and happen to stumble upon the Master in Rajpur. I'm present as the learned professor volleys question after speculative question. After patiently answering, Sant Kirpal Singh relates the following parable:

"Once two seekers went to a Master. One was learned and the other was illiterate. The teacher said to the illiterate man, 'I will charge you my usual fee, but for the learned man I will charge double fee.' The learned man asked, 'Why charge me twice as much? I am already learned.' The Master replied, 'I am charging twice as much because I have to first make you an _unlearned_ man!' We have to unlearn everything we have learned. But, mind that, I don't charge any fee...it is Nature's Gift, like sunshine, water, and air. If you tell an intellectual man to climb the stairs, he will begin questioning, 'Oh, how many steps are there? What if I fall? How high is it? Why should I climb?' Now, take a simple man; tell him to climb and he will go right up. The house of our body is on fire and what we must do is not ask why it is on fire, but get out of it, the sooner the better. You can ask later."

The professor then stresses the importance of intellectual development and education.

"Dear friend, I fully agree," Master replies. "Education helps to develop inner faculties for having a right approach to life's problems. Learning is a garland of flowers round the neck of a practical man. He will explain many things from the vocabulary at his command, but a man of learning without a practical life is like a beast of burden that has loads of books over his head! Bookish knowledge is all a wilderness and gives no way out. A learned man without experience revels in the pudding like a spoon and gives to others but is unaware of its taste. An unlearned man with a practical life does enjoy the taste of the pudding and gives examples from daily life with the limited vocabulary at his command. Both the learned and the unlearned have to tread the same path of withdrawing from outside to rise above body-consciousness. The ABC of higher learning begins there. Then he sees the Light of God in all and becomes a conscious co-worker of the Divine Plan."

The professor's wife, who has been silent most of the time, speaks up. "If God is within us, why do we need to seek the help of an intermediary?"

"The God in you is asleep. In whom It is awake, He is competent to awaken others. Light comes from Light and life comes from life."

27 June: While I'm strolling down Rajpur Road to the post office, three Sikh youths greet me and I them, although we are complete strangers. These university students have walked more than three hundred miles from their home in the Punjab, seeking adventure. "May we ask why you have come from such a prosperous country all the way to India, adopting our customs and dress?" I tell a little of my story, and invite them to meet the one who drew me. They eagerly follow to the Master's room, where they receive parshad from his hands and paternal guidance.

In the midst of their conversation in Punjabi, Master turns and remarks in English, "Once a special foot-race was held in India between men of different diets. The race was more than two hundred miles in length. One man was vegetarian, one was fruitarian, and the others were meatarians. The fruitarian finished first and won the race. The vegetarian was second, and of the many who started, the meatarians who finished were last."

I relate the story of Dr. Moore from England who walked non-stop from California to New York when she was well into her fifties. When asked what her "fuel" was, she replied, "Grass!" Master comments, "Grass is very strong. Just look at elephants, horses, and oxen. I knew a doctor in Lahore who had very simple living and eating habits. He would eat only one item a day, and every day it would be different, but always vegetarian. He never mixed his food nor ate four or five different courses at a meal. He proclaimed 'I will never die by old age.' He was a good man and his prescriptions were always effective. Every day he bathed in a cold stream and on the way back home, he gave money and free medicines to the poor. He lived to reach a very great age. He was killed in an accident a few years back, and thus he never died from old age!" Master chuckled.

Amritsar Within: Every afternoon at about three, after days of clear blue sky and sunshine, clouds gather above the Rajpur mountains, quickly followed by lightning, thunder, and sudden rains. The monsoon is upon us. Today, a small group of us meditate with the Master for two hours under cover of the open verandah, while the rain performs its ritual dance.

A six-year-old meditator sits rock-still for the entire session. Tapping the top of his head, Master helps him to stand. *"Kya Dekha?* What did you see?" he asks. The boy's attention remains withdrawn, as indicated by his eyes partly upturned. With folded hands, his eyes focus on the Master and he then divulges in great detail his wondrous mystic journey. Brij Mohan translates: "...and I reached a region dominated by a shimmering lake with many bright flames burning along its edges. In its center was a great Temple of Gold, with tall spires and shining domes. When I entered that Pool and bathed in it, I became filled with happiness and wonder, such that I cannot describe. I then proceeded beyond the lake, along a shining marble path. A huge sun appeared, rising high in the heavens, its light far brighter than many suns of this world." At a loss for further words, the little boy places his head on the Master's feet, who pats him lovingly. "This is the Amritsar located in the third plane,

Daswan Dwar," he shares. "When soul bathes in it, the karmic slate is wiped clean; then it is ready to proceed further into the Beyond." Mortals seldom attain such an advanced stage, yet here before us a young child has traversed it within the space of two hours, clearly by the grace of his preceptor.

After a pregnant silence, the Master adds: "Every moment try to learn something. Every day I am learning, even from children...All through life I have been a student of the Mysteries...Whoever thinks, 'I have attained something, I have become something,' has lost everything. Who can boast that he has learned everything? Newton said, 'I am merely picking up pebbles from the seashore of knowledge.'"

A young Westerner moves up to his chair and confides, "I saw a large bright sun-like light. It burst, giving way to a golden-red rising sun; a radiant figure appeared in its center, but I couldn't make out his features—all was Light! This form stood before simran and transformed into Master's face, except you weren't wearing a turban."

"Sometimes the inner Master is seen wearing a blue coat or a white coat. Turban or no turban, surely you can recognize your Friend!"

Question: "Do the huge radiant orange sun and the radiant white moon I am seeing within belong to the astral plane or higher?"

Answer: "The huge radiant sun belongs to *trikuti* [the causal, Brahm, or second stage], and when one breaks open this sun, one meets the Master there. He manifests on all higher planes. Whatever he is seen doing outside, the same he is doing on the inner planes also. The moon you refer to is in *Daswan Dwar* [in the third spiritual region]. Always keep attention fixed at the center of the Light and let it not stray away. Don't look at the waves emanating from the Light, but keep to the center. In this way, Light will burst to let you pass through it. When all attachments are removed, the inner form of the Master manifests of itself; he will speak to you and reply to any question you put to him."

Question: "I'm wondering...does the inner form speak just like the outer form? For example, when you reveal your holy self within, there is a kind of thought emanation from the inner form that solves all problems, but is the inner speech which you refer to something different?"

Answer: "*Spiritual emanation!* Sometimes also the Inner Master's lips move and clearly worded answers are given to questions put to that form when receptivity is developed. Look intently into the middle of his forehead or his eyes or whatever you see before you, and relax completely. You will find that the spirit will be withdrawn like a hair taken out of soft butter, with little or no effort on your part."

Question: "Is all criticism, even of frauds, to be eschewed?"

Answer: "Never with resentment, malice, or hatred. Take those aside to correct if wrong. Never in public."

Question: "If one is forced by circumstances beyond his grasp to tell others an untruth, yet to his own self he is true, will he suffer spiritual setback?"

Answer: "Don't tell lies, but in certain cases, half-truths are alright. If a man is running from someone who wants to kill him, and the killer meets you and asks if you saw where he went, you could tell him something to the effect which would not give away the intended victim."

"I have a terrible problem, Master," I confess.

"Terrible? How terrible is your problem?"

"I am a complete slave of my mind."

"Who is there who is not a slave of their mind? If you abide by the rules of your teacher, you will become the most beloved pupil. But we follow only to the extent our mind allows us. If mind is surrendered, then it is easy to see God; there is no doubt about it."

A few days pass. After listening to a discourse on the various aspects of service to the needy, poor, and sick, I get fired up with zeal and approach the Master: "How may I serve you?" There is such great intensity in his eyes as he focuses his attention on me, that I become paralyzed, afraid. The tension is broken by his two-word reply. Just two words, **"Do Bhajan!"** while his eyes gleam like a lion's.

Despite the commission each Master has, the magnitude of their gift of Naam-initiation, initiates are not relieved of their responsibility to act ethically in executing their duties in the world. They are expected to earnestly strive to advance within through regular meditation. In innumerable ways, the Masters help their beloved disciples. Individual spiritual practice and effort lessen the burden of self and the world, if not the Master's load.

Like a child, I ask too many questions—helpless to stop, yet eager to learn. He is kind and never refuses. "How can we help the Master?" I ask.

"One can help the Master spiritually only after rising beyond the three worlds [physical, astral, and causal]; by submerging the individual ego and becoming one with him—a conscious co-worker of the Divine Plan. Such cases are rare, of course."

The Humility Message, *Rajpur:* Master beckons me over to where he stands beneath the arched verandah, and hands me six 5" x 7" cards. "You may please type up," he says. Grateful for such a task, I retreat with my treasure. Once alone, I examine the cards closely. Each are covered on both sides with his beautiful penmanship in microscopic size, complete with crossed out words and changes. For the next two days I struggle to decipher this approximately 2,400-word message, sometimes pondering a particularly difficult squiggle for a long time until it becomes clear. When the typing is completed, the copy is personally examined by the Master and approved without changes for release.

(Several years later, I met Reshad Field, Sufi teacher and author of *The Last Barrier*. After taking my hands in his, Reshad confided, "Not a day goes by when I do not read this most inspiring message." He pulled out a well-worn wad of paper from his breast pocket; I recognized it as Kirpal Singh's timelessly inspiring *Humility Circular*—the very same one transcribed from those six 5" x 7" cards. "It has been my constant guide," Reshad affirmed.

The following is a brief excerpt:

"Humility," says Lacordaire, "does not consist in hiding our talents and virtues, in thinking ourselves worse and more ordinary than we are, but in possessing a clear knowledge of all that is lacking in us, and not exalting ourselves for that which we have, seeing that God has freely given it us, and with all His gifts, we are still infinitely of little importance."

So the truly humble man may accept sometimes the praise which men give him, and quietly passes it on to God, keeping nothing for himself.

The man who is not truly humble behaves in a very unnatural manner when not praised by men. He becomes upset, loses his patience and even becomes angry. He repulses them with his irritation and creates an awkward situation. Sometimes he suppresses his feelings and remains silent; but he cannot forget the things that are said about him; they haunt him again and again, and do not give him peace of mind.

The humble man makes no fuss. He is at harmony with himself and others. He is gifted with a wondrous feeling of peace. He feels safe and secure, like a ship in harbor, unaffected by howling storms and lashing waves. He has found refuge at the Lotus Feet of the Lord and the storms of changing circumstances have no power over him. He feels light as air. The burdens, which we carry, all our life—the burden of the self and its desires—he has lain aside, and is ever calm and serene. Having given up everything, he has nothing to lose, and yet everything belongs to him, for he is of God, and God is in him. Having broken the bondage of desire, he is as happy with a piece of dry bread as with a sumptuous meal. In every situation and circumstance of life, he blesses the Name of God.

He who would be humble regards himself as a student. He learns many new things, but what is more difficult, he unlearns many things.

Sant Kirpal Singh speaking with disciples, Rajpur

... A scholar came to a Saint and said, "O Seer of the Secret, tell me what I may do to live the life divine." And the Saint said to him, "Go, unlearn what thou hast learnt and then return and sit before me."

He who would walk the way of humility must renounce his earlier ways of living... the opinions he has formed, the standards to which he is accustomed... The things the world would worship are to him of no value. His values are so different from those of other men. Rich food, fine houses, costly dresses, positions of power and authority, the applause of men, honors and titles no longer attract him. He feels drawn to a life of simplicity. He is happy in living a hidden life in the Hidden Lord.

He is dead to the world; he is alive in God. At times he actually behaves like one dead. Yes, the truly humble man is, in that sense, the "dead" man. He has "died." God alone lives in him. His self has been annihilated. His self has vanished into God, and only God remains. God works in him and through him, and God emits in his eyes. God speaks in his words. On his feet, God walks the earth; and through his hands gives His benedictions to all.

Such men are the real strength of the world—its illumination and inspiration. To see them is to commune with God, for God dwells in them. They are the living, moving Temples of the Lord. They are the ones who keep the world intact, though they do not know it themselves. The whole earth depends on them without anyone being aware of it. Their hearts and minds are in tune with the Great Heart and Mind of humanity. They are in complete accord with all that lives. They give their love to all living beings, as though they were the sons of the one sweet Mother. They have broken all fetters and entered into the freedom of the children of God. God does their will, because they have merged their wills in His. God fulfills their least desire, for it is He Who desires all their desires. They are the little saviors of humanity.

Mother's Love—*Rajpur Diary:* Cool moonlight spreads through tree gaps, causing the whitewashed stone path-markers to glow in the dark. Around 11 PM I quietly steal through the shadows, along a path I have come to know intimately. Standing unnoticed beneath the over-spreading foliage of giant lichee trees, eyes drink the sight of the white-clad Father, resting on a *charpai* in a small clearing amongst the roses. Brij Mohan bends over the sleeping Master, applying compression-massage to his legs. In my heart of hearts I often craved this *seva*, but felt much too impure and timid to ask. I creep silently on tiptoes until very close. Brij Mohan looks up, noticing me. "Shh!" I gesture with finger to lips, then point to Master's limbs, making massaging motions in the air, then point back to my chest. Brij Mohan smiles knowingly. Understanding my wild wish, he steps aside. So, with heart in my throat, I lean down and begin pressing Master's legs, copying Brij Mohan's technique. The moment my hands touch his legs however, Master whirls around and confronts me with "Eh?" I am scared out of my wits!

"Oh, it is you." He lies down again and fulfills my wish. My very hands become intoxicated with the touch of his holy form—an intoxication that will remain throughout the night and part of the next day.

After a few minutes, he speaks, "Two letters have come for you. Did you get them?" I reply in the affirmative.

"That's alright."

"One letter was from my mother. She and my father send their loving gratitude."

"What does your mother say? Does she love you?"

"Yes, Master."

"Does she want you to come home?"

"She is happy that I am happy."

"No. Does she ask you to come home? She must miss you."

"Yes, she misses, but doesn't ask me to come back, though she probably wants me to. Since my sixteenth year I have been mostly separated from my parents, so they are used to my being away."

"But you are changed now. How old are you now?"

"Twenty-three."

"Hmm. Seven years. Does your mother love you?" he asks again.

Again I reply in the affirmative, and add, "At one time I was so strongly attached to my mother and father, I thought that if they were to die, it would also kill me."

"And now how do you feel?"

"Now I know they are in your care."

"A mother's love is very strong. My mother loved me so much... Once when I returned to my parents' home in Lahore, my mother, who was upstairs, heard my voice. She ran to the balcony and fell down from there to the ground. She loved me very much." I am amazed, as his words seem laden with human emotion. After all these years, he still enshrines a deep love for his mother. This indeed is a lesson for me.

"When do you plan on going back?"

"Whenever you send me back, I will go."

"That's all right; you'll always be with me... Your mother must love you?" This is the third time he asks this question. I am puzzled why he keeps asking.

"Yes, Master, she loves me very much."

"Then tell your mother her son will be coming back soon." In this way he breaks the news that my days in India are numbered.

I am choked, and reply, "In you, I have found my true parent."

"Yes, that is true, but according to the flowing pen of God you have been joined to your family, and as such you have some responsibility toward them." There is a long pause, as I continue to massage his feet.

Again he repeats, "My mother loved me so much...instead of coming down the stairs, she fell from the balcony upon hearing my voice..." *Long silence.*

"In her letter, my mother described a dream/vision she had," I mention. "In it, she boarded an airplane, but as she got on, she had a premonition that it would never return. When she was seated, and the plane was aloft for some time, she looked around and saw that there were no other passengers. Then the engines began to fail, and the propellers were sputtering to a stop. Dark ocean waves could be seen far below, but she was not very afraid. She looked to the cockpit, to the pilot. The pilot turned around, and the pilot was you, Master! You then took her by the hand, and led her out through the window in front. While the plane crashed into the ocean below, you led her into a glorious rising Sun. That was the last thing she could remember. She now knows that you will take her across the ocean of existence."

"Alright, when you write," he says, "send my love to them, and tell them that their son is returning soon."

The next morning I stand pining outside his house, tears dropping into the dust. The knower of hearts comes out, concern written across his brow. With heat in my breast, I blurt out; "I never want to leave you!"

He replies forcefully, *"I'm not leaving you!"*

Omnipresent Master—Rajpur Diary:

Each morning before sunrise at Rajpur, I walked into the garden, following the narrow path and the irrigation canal, past towering mango groves, past the fragrant jasmine bushes and the guava trees, down into the valley where the furthermost edge of the property runs. There my vigils for the divinity within were kept, wrapped in a blanket until dawn slowly unfolded; bursting with the song of life as it does in Rajpur. On several unforgettable mornings as I sat there alone, I heard unmistakable footsteps coming closer and closer, sharply crunching the gravel path.

> *Do I hear some sound?*
> *Is it the footsteps of the Beloved?*
> *Or am I being tricked*
> *By the beating of my heart?*[2]

I would gladly abandon meditation, everything, just to watch him once again, shaking off his black loafers and sitting quietly atop the stone wall, ghostly radiant in the moonlight, not more than ten feet away. He accepted my presence—never a word passed between us.

On a morning such as this, after he had retreated to his house and the sun spread its roseate glow upward over the eastern foothills, I emerged from meditation. While the Light lingered on, my heart was being squeezed by thoughts of separation and with it, unspeakable sadness. In a swoon, I stumbled down the path into a tangled ravine where the wild jungle begins. "Is this heavenly dream coming to an end so soon? Without you, O' Master, life will have no meaning. You have taken my heart..." Grief blurred my sight.

Sorrow soon gave way to a subtle tingling descending on all sides from an invisible source. Sparkling radiance and joy-bells flooded awareness as I turned in the fluid atmosphere, beholding the cosmic Master in front of me. In slow motion, I lifted my eyes to the sky, and he was there! His transparent mien and blissful Light were in the trees, the stones, and the hills. Whichever way I turned there was the form of the omnipresent One! Unspeakable delight overflowed as I giddily retraced the uphill path, my loving Lord preceding, echoing the eternal Christ:

> *I shall never leave thee nor forsake thee.*

---

1. "Singh" means "lion." Master Kirpal was humoroulsy referring to himself as the lion not yet caught.

2. One of Darshan Singh's poems from *A Tear & a Star.* No words could better capture the delicacy of such moments.

We return to Delhi and time is running out. The Omnipresent Master is elusive, and the great joy, which came towards the end of my stay at Rajpur, is scuttled by the dread of leaving. Each day weighs heavily, despite good meditation. For nearly seven months I have been daily spoon-fed on the ineffable-incomparable. Like an addict I wonder how to survive withdrawal.

July 16: While alone in my room, divine love's sweet anguish becomes a poem, a song. In the morning I approach the Master: "I have written a song that I would like to sing for you."

"Then sing it to your own self!" His stiff reply acts like a Zen koan, throwing my mind into a swirl for hours, until it falls back upon itself, at peace. Much later a few of us sit cross-legged on the lawn around him in the garden as night's sable veil enwraps us. An electrical power failure followed by unusual silence spreads throughout Delhi. Out of nowhere Master says, "All right, you may sing your song now." A plaintive melody accompanies the madly devotional lyrics:

> *Every breath and every heartbeat,*
> *Intensifies my thirst and longing—*
> *For a vision, for a vision in the Light.*
> *In the night I weep for thee, O' Lord,*
> *When will you come to me?*
> *Kirpal, Kirpal, Kirpal Gurudev, Sataguruji.*
>
> *Now at last thou hast heard my cry,*
> *Filled with Light before my eye;*
> *Yearning for the Lord to meet,*
> *At last I have found thy lotus feet...*
>
> *My life, my truth, my everything,*
> *It is for thee my heart does sing,*
> *Lifted by the sight of thee,*
> *I know that thou hast set me free...*
>
> *All who live by the outer sun are blind, O' Lord,*
> *But they who live by the Light of thee, only they can see...*
> *The Sun of Truth shines in splendor,*
> *For they who at thy holy feet surrender, Sataguruji.*

The full moon has risen overhead, bathing everything with its soft luminescence. Breaking the delicious silence, I ask, "Master, please say a few words on Separation..." He is silent for a while.

"In the Punjabi language there are many words of such expression not found in English. The Tenth Guru expressed in Punjabi verse,

'Mittera Piarey nu, Haal mureeda Kahenna...'
[O beloved Friend, tell us of the condition of your poor ones.]

"*'Bhingh, bhingh'*..." Interrupting himself, he asks, "In your country I believe the butcher simply cuts the neck of the cattle, is it not? But in India he first picks up the sheep or goat by the legs and then throws it down on the ground, full force before cutting its throat—and if the knife is not sharp, then...?" Master proceeds with the verse, "*'Bhingh, Bhingh, Kasai-an t'ha Saehna.'* Just like that goat in the hands of the butcher, is how I feel in the pangs of separation from Master!'" *Sawan. Kirpal.* Tears fill his eyes but do not fall...*long pause.* "And the Tenth Guru says, 'We are drinking anguish from a cup covered with thorns.' But you see, there are no words to convey the beauty of the original."

Buddha, or Buddhist: An orange-robed Burmese Buddhist monk asks, "Help me to become a better Buddhist."

Master replies, "I wish you to become *Buddha,* not *Buddhist!*"

I share a dream from the night before in which the Master told me we were old friends. He comments, "We are *all* old friends, you see."

I then relate the plight of a yoga teacher who has written me from Rishikesh—a refugee from tyranny experienced at two prominent yoga schools. "Master, he would like to meet you, but he's extremely cautious about entrusting his spiritual welfare to anyone."

"Tell him the real meaning of Yoga is to *yoke,* or *reunite* the soul with its Source." Master advises. "We don't entrust our spiritual welfare to any *person.* That belongs to God alone—but where His Light is manifest in man, we should feel no hesitation to go there and learn the mysteries of the Beyond from him. Perhaps what keeps us from going is the ego.

"God is already residing within you. God is also in the poor beggar. He can appear in him. NamDev, a great Saint of the fifteenth Century, was so poor that he had no more than four farthings, but he was actually the richest of men. I would say he is now a millionaire!" (laughter)

"Once Hazrat Mian Mir met with Akbar, the great Moghul King. Mian Mir was outwardly very poor, but spiritually awakened within. When Akbar asked him, 'Who are you?' the Saint replied, 'I am Moghul!'

"'How do you say this?' the Emperor asked. The Faqir replied, 'Because I have met you!' When you meet the Master fully, you also become the Master; you imbibe His nature and attributes. St. Paul said, *'It is I, yet not now I; it is the Christ that liveth in me.'* And Hafiz has said, *'I am no more Hafiz; I am He that lives in me.'*

"So whatever you have received here with His Grace," (Master plants his eyes upon me) "you should take back to America and share it with others. Because you have experience, you will not be repeating parrot-like what you have learned. What you say will only affect others if you have experienced it."

Kneading the clay: At evening darshan, the Master bluntly asks Jim, a newly arrived policeman from New England, "Why have you come to India?" Jim innocently replies, "To have you mold me like clay, Master."

Master retorts gruffly, unpredictable: "Then become clay first! Then I'll knead and mold you like clay!" An electric silence fills the room. His face suddenly breaks out in a gracious laugh, and he stretches out his arms, making a kneading motion with his fists towards Jim and then in a circular movement to everyone in the room, uttering, "Kneading, kneading, kneading!"

India's Independence Day—*August 15:* Today's satsang is so large, it has to be held on tented grounds outside the ashram. Using the theme of India's Independence, the Master asserts the need to become independent from the tyranny of the mind and the five dacoits of lust, anger, greed, attachment, and ego. Five minutes into his discourse, a torrential monsoon storm bursts over Delhi, and the canopy begins leaking like a sieve. "This is the time of your examination!" he announces over the microphone, "Your clothes will be wet, but you will be quite safe."

He pushes away an umbrella held by an attendant, for those sitting before him are not provided such comfort. For two full hours, the Master delivers a matchless discourse punctuated by thunder and lightning. Miraculously the loudspeakers keep up, though they too are soaked in the pounding rain. But for a mere handful, the soggy audience remains. I find the rain transubtantiated into particles of Light. The vast congregation is transported into a state of bliss, evidenced by their eyes and faces. As Master finishes, the physical sun breaks out. With a chuckle, our Gurudev pronounces, "*Now, your examination is over!*"

Pages of notes made with fountain pen in my diary have been obliterated by the rain. However, these few lines are still barely readable:

> *Most of the time has already passed.*
> *Little time is left.*
> *If you are just sitting, stand up immediately.*
> *If you are just standing, start walking.*
> *If you are walking, start running fast.*
> *Don't look to the left or the right.*
> *You are running a race toward God!*

32

O' Cupbearer, your frowns are far fairer
Than the smiles of this faithless world.

When a lump of iron is forged into a sword, the smithy applies intense heat from his forge until the metal glows white-hot and softens. Skillfully and painstakingly he hammers the pliant mass over and over, folding and pounding it into shape upon the anvil. Many a time will he heat the forming blade to incandescence, only to repeatedly plunge it into a pail of cold water. The smithy is not afraid of the violent and noisy steam, nor the sparks, clamor, and heat that rise up around him. He does not shirk the danger of his profession, for he has forged countless blades, in myriad shapes and sizes. By layering, tempering, purifying, and strengthening the steel, he produces a sword that can cut through other steel and withstand many a battle-blow.

In the interests of the student, there are times when the great Teachers apply similar disciplinings, temperings, and trials. The reprimand or displeasure of a fully conscious being is no less than an expression of corrective love.

A true lover is sustained as much by a frown as a kindly look; while everyone feeds on the latter, not everyone can withstand the former. Even the passing of a test is in itself a gift, a grace upon the student, a merit that cannot be claimed. Within my own limits, I was dimly aware of my Smithy's workings, and more than once entered the fire of transformation and became uncomfortably familiar with the heat, the hammering, and the tempering.

There were times when, out of foolishness and pride, I displeased him. There could be no worse punishment than the turning of his back or the drawing of a veil over the inner vision. The outer Master didn't have to say a word! As he once casually remarked: "Outwardly my hand is soft and gentle, but beneath the glove is a hand of steel..." He was compassion's essence, but a great disciplinarian nonetheless. I was to earn his displeasure, discover the steel, and eventually be brought closer.

An important meeting was called at Sawan Ashram, attended by many distinguished and learned Indian initiates, including the managing committee. The Master invited presentation of their original ideas on how to best further the spiritual mission. During their learned dissertations, I was mentally criticizing: 'Oh, he doesn't meditate....This one doesn't keep a diary....That one doesn't even see the Light... How can they hope to further the great cause?' Towards the end I was unable to restrain my impetuosity and asked to speak a few words. When Master nodded, I stood, heart pounding, and announced,

"All these fine talks and lectures are very well and good, but unless we practice what we preach, unless we go within and experience the divine Light and Sound ourselves on a regular basis, up to and including meeting the Radiant Form, I doubt we can effectively further the Master's Cause."

While there may have been a grain of truth in that, my delivery smacked of pride and intolerance. I did not take into consideration the fact that divine Power works through many people for noble ends, regardless of inner access. *So what* if one were blessed with a taste of a vision if pride stole away its sweetness? And if the tongue became harsh with others? Such a person would not measure up to those who were noble, kind, humble, and good, but perhaps somewhat deficient in meditation. (Sometimes the Masters may withhold inner experience, in the best interests of the initiate, for they know the time, the place, and the measure.) My insensitive pronouncement had the effect of dropping a bomb on the august assembly. I had made a serious blunder and was about to pay dearly.

Master stood. He said, "It appears our Western friend is not in the full know of things." That was the understatement of my life!

He was not pleased. After speaking briefly in Hindi, the meeting abruptly adjourned.

What had I done? Under which rock could I hide?

When I fell from your grace
I left the dream of eternity;
Tho' waking to this world
Your fragrance lingered on.

Oh revive the splendor of the night;
I'll be its willing sacrifice.

THE WEANING

33

For three interminable days and nights following my blunder at the meeting, the physical Master turned his back. Not once did he look my way even if I walked near him or sat right at the front in satsang. Perhaps I no longer mattered or existed, and heart wilted like a sapling deprived of water, light, earth—everything. Behind the indifference of the Beloved there is always a higher purpose, but there is little solace in such knowing when one is caught in the wringer, when adolescent faith is pushed to the wall.

No matter how hard I reprimanded myself for such unmanly behavior, I had no control over a constant flow of tears. I stood in a corner of the porch, repenting, looking toward the One who refused to return my yearning gaze. In satsang today, unbeknownst to me, he said in Hindi, "The sahib weeps for me out of love—how many of you weep for the Master?"

As a past recipient of much attention, I felt that I was especially loved—a claim which could be made by practically everyone who spent some time with him. He was now showing me how his love could be impersonal. He was wearing away resistant ego and leveling the clods of pride. Like a master physician, he knew the malady and the cure. My ego-disease was chronic and deep-rooted, and a certain aspect of it required immediate, if not dramatic treatment, like the lancing of a boil.

On the night before my leaving India, Master was smiling and ebullient while scooping handfuls of parshad from a large basket to an amorphous cluster of devotees. One by one they left, full of happiness. Finally I stood alone before my Maharaj, half bowing, cupped hands timidly, uncertainly stretching towards him. He had just scooped up another big handful, then fixed me sternly with his gaze and dumped it back into the basket, commenting icily, "Nothing for you." Turning on his heel he walked to his inner rooms leaving me shocked and ignored. I spent the balance of the night in turmoil, alternating between calm faith and writhing in despair; one moment surrendering to the test, the next rebelling. I desperately clung to sweet memories and the living Light. The long night dragged on and on.

When morning finally arrived, I wandered helplessly to his door, remaining there unmoving from eight onwards, but nary a flicker passed from him to me! A continuous procession of fortunate others passed through that portal and were lavished with affection. Returning the same way, I envied their ecstasy, their shining eyes. I thought, *"Though I am a thorn in your side, please never cease loving me. Forgive my prideful tongue! How may I regain your favor? Keep my faith intact. Lord, let me not leave India like this!"*

By eleven, all hope had drained away, and I, little more than a hollow shell, was still waiting, vainly hoping. Master looked up from where he sat on the rug, not more than twenty feet away. He seemed to be looking at me; a huge, jolly smile lit up his face.

"Hello! Hello! You are there? Come on. You will be leaving India soon? Here, you would like some parshad?" *Did he mean me?* I wondered, and glanced over my shoulder, but no one was there. When I incredulously pointed to my chest, he nodded and waved me in. Before time to think, I was there, bowing, grateful this terrible ordeal was over. I held out my hands as he scooped handful after handful of puffed rice parshad into them until it over-flowed onto my lap and over the floor! He was God-intoxicated and God *intoxicating*, unmindful of the spillings. He then dropped several large squares of burfee, my favorite sweet, on top, knocking more puffed rice to the floor. Leaning forward, he said, and so lovingly, "I am giving a special talk tonight and I want you to be there!" *Cloud Nine!* After he left, I gathered up all the crumbs.

Accompanied by a tape recorder, I returned around 3 P.M. Maharaj Ji was sitting on his bed surrounded by thick bundles of correspondence files, head bowed over a particular letter, brow furrowed in concentration. After several minutes he acknowledged my presence.

"Yes?"

"Master, I was wondering if you would consider sending a taped message back to the West."

He took the mike, furrowed his brow in concentration, and communicated the following on August 19, 1967:

> *Dear Arun[1] is coming back to the United States after a period of seven months which he spent here developing in the spiritual way.[1] I send this message of love and best wishes to each one of you over there. You are all dear to me, whether you are working in the east or the west of the United States, Canada or South America. We are all working for the same common goal and I wish that you make progress as quickly as possible.*
>
> *We should do our best and leave the rest to the Master Power working overhead, who will extend all feasible help and protection unasked for. Blessed are they who have been taken into the custody of the Master, through whom God has condescended to bring you back to your Real Home, in this earthly sojourn. I wish each one of you to introspect your lives daily and weed out all imperfections, so that your mind may become as limpid as water—which may reflect your True Self and the Overself. If you take one step Godwards, God will take millions of steps to receive you.*
>
> *You have all been on my mind, and really I love you all, so it is but*

natural that we reciprocate the same....and feel separation... and wish to meet physically as early as possible. God willing, it may be early next year when I may be among you and glad to see you all in person. Many things cannot be conveyed through words—it is heart that speaks to heart. Simply turn your attention towards Him who is always over your head. If you don't transgress the commandments given by Him, you will be nearer to God and there will be nothing to be afraid of in the Three Worlds [physical, astral, and causal].

"I wish you all to love one another so that people may know you are coming to the Master, who wishes to cement you all in the silken bonds of love so that you may not feel any duality whatsoever. We are all one in God, but that unity is unfortunately forgotten. There are two ways to come out of that oblivion: one, weed out all imperfections through self-introspection; and the other, devote time to meditation in the accurate way as prescribed—with all loving devotion. Good action will result in good fruit, but unless the little ego is eliminated from within, we cannot have oneness with God. If you eliminate the "I" from "w.o.r.l.d." that leaves "Word":

> **Word** *was in the Beginning,*
> *Word was with God, and the Word was God.*
> *Without the Word was not anything made that was made.*

You are in Him and He is in you, so I wish you all speedy progress on the Way. And that you can have only when you do your best and leave the rest to the Master Power overhead. The more you will put in time for meditation—by weeding out all imperfections by self-introspection—the sooner you will reach your Goal. I send you all again my best wishes and love, and wish each of you progress on the spiritual way. Kirpal Singh.

After a minute or so of pregnant silence, the Satguru continued, "Some prayer here, you see—I'll just recite a prayer which will give you uplift in your own way:

> *O' Love, who is it who can do this, but Thou?*
> *O' the lifter of the lowly, the Lord of all creation*
> *Who hath made me the object of esteem by all;*
> *He whose touch defileth others,*
> *On him too is Thy mercy, O God.*
> *Yea, Thou makest the low great and mighty—*
> *and feareth not anyone...."*

The tape recorder came to the end of its reel, but I was immobilized; even if able to move, by some unwritten code, movement would have been tantamount to sacrilege. His spiritual grace made visible mighty and cosmic suns continually rising up through his corporeal body as the veil thinned. Though Master added several more lines to the prayer, they escaped into eternity.

Evening Satsang was given at the home of Sheila Mata, a devoted elderly disciple living in the district known as Rajinder Nagar. As soon as we arrived, rain began falling and satsang shifted indoors. The crowd crammed into three smallish rooms plus verandah, pushing me from behind closer and closer to the Master. Soon, his feet were under my legs, his knees within inches of my face. The exquisite discourse seemed to be directed at me—although I'm sure others would claim the same—and we'd all be correct! Whether it was heaven or heaven-on-earth, I could not tell. Being so close to the Source, my head was spinning with intoxication. Somewhere a mystic knower has said it: *A thousand barrels of wine flow through the eyes of the Beloved.* Afterwards, I could hardly stand and needed support to walk.

After returning to Sawan Ashram, I was summoned and the Master gave the following advice:

"Firstly, one by one weed out all imperfections through self-introspection. Only then can you be truly happy. It is easy to seek God, but very difficult to become a Man. When you become a Man in the true sense, then, I would say, God Himself will run after you like anything. He will seek you.

"Secondly, become humble and speak humbly—sweet tongue honeyed with humility is the essence of all virtues. Humility, humility, humility! We must be extremely careful not to be proud and egoistic. Never think you are perfect.

"So, eliminate your own shortcomings. If you sow a bad thought, word, or deed, that will multiply a hundredfold. If you sow a loving thought, word, or deed, you will reap that reward. But still you have to be rid of egoism. Only by contacting the Light and Sound regularly can the ego be subdued. Take this message back to your country."

I said, "Although anyone could say anything to you or about you, you remain unaffected, but imperfect ones like me are affected by what others say, and often react adversely."

Admonishing this argumentative mind, he replied with urgency, "But you have to become perfect!"

"I will try my best."

Master: "Try? Try? 'Try' is the word of an intellectual man. 'Try' is only an excuse. You have got to *DO* if you are to succeed."

His words reverberated across all levels of my being and I felt bewildered by the enormity—if not impossibility of the task. His attainment was my only hope.

"You will be leaving me physically, but He will be with you always. The

Master Power will be extending all feasible help not only within, but outside also."

Leaning forward, understanding my longing to remain forever with him, Master raised his forefinger and commanded, "Put chains on the legs of time!" Soft, barely audible, but blindingly intoxicating mutual laughter elevated these moments to the heights. The prayer, "Please never leave me," escaped my lips. His visage glowed, a life-giving sun, a vortex, magnetically in-drawing while from his mouth came another assurance, *"I am not leaving you!"*

I bowed to capture and hold forever that perfect image behind the eyes, to inscribe his promise in the book of life. Facing him and backing out of the porch, I returned in solitude to my room to pack. Exactly seven months to the day had passed since arriving in India.

At 1:30 AM the taxi came to take me away. Like an angler's line, my hungry glance was cast across the courtyard, wishing, wishing again to draw him out, to see him just once more. The ashram was quiet but for the car-motor, a few crickets, and a distant barking dog. I espied a flickering light behind the shutters of his darkened bungalow, moving from room to room towards the door. My wish-fulfiller emerged, torch in hand, striding quickly to where I stood outside, dumbfounded. Patting the top of my head he said, "Good-bye and God bless you."

From the Ocean's bubble this sound arose,
That you and I are not different;
Do not think I am separate from you,
You and I are not different...
Hide not the fairness of your face from me,
Yes, remove the veil and come,
You and I are not different.

—Rumi

---

1. Master always pronounced my name "Aroon," a fairly common Sanskrit name meaning, "dawn-light."

34

The twenty-four-hour flight disgorged its passengers into La Guardia Airport. New York City's raw energy, decay, and conspicuous materialism flowed past in jarring kaleidoscopic clips. Combined with travel fatigue, I was experiencing mild shock. India's grinding poverty and overpopulation were eclipsed by her great spiritual wealth and enduring family traditions, a sharp contrast to this inner destitution. Yet a hidden glimmering, even here, begged awakening in myriad hearts. One could hear it with the ears of the soul.

The words of the Nazarene emerged, re-voiced and empowered by the living Master: *I am the Vine, ye are the branches...*

Jonas Gerrard, a commercial artist in his early twenties, drove me to meet and speak with groups in New York, Boston, and New England. Filled with the intense ardor and conviction of one who had just returned from seven months' immersion in the presence of a Godman, I exclaimed, "Our Master is so great that if he wished, he could appear even here and now!"

The power of the moment encapsulated us. As we barreled along the freeway at seventy miles an hour, the transparent, shimmering form of the Master began to manifest, smiling and standing upon the hood of the car. Was it a hallucination or reality manifest? "Gerrard, you see? Fifteen thousand miles are nothing; nothing at all. If we cannot bask in his physical aura, this is the next best thing!" Again the Christ-words echoed through my mind: *"Whenever two or more are gathered in my name, I am there."*

The long journey across the United States to Vancouver was made by car and Greyhound bus, sharing with small groups along the way. Low-key centers were scattered across the continent. One of the highlights of this American pilgrimage was my meeting with the legendary Mrs. M. Gordon Hughes of Kentucky. [Apparently no one knows her first name.] For more than two years we had exchanged correspondence and we were eager to meet. One of the first Kirpal initiates in North America, she was also a poet and painter extraordinaire.

David, a fellow-initiate who drove me all the way from New Hampshire, turned down the quiet Louisville street, shaded from the heat by tall elms. After ringing the doorbell of a very old house, I was greeted by a stout woman nearly six feet tall, eighty years of age, and crowned with frizzy reddish hair, not exactly as I had pictured her. "Welcome, Honey", she drawled. "Why, 'ah knew you win you wuz a tadpole, and 'ah wuz a frawg!"

She showed me to the living room where a beautiful portrait hung over the fireplace. The portrait was a younger Master Kirpal, probably in his fifties, with a Ryder-esque moonlit sky and ocean behind him. Mrs. Hughes had painted this picture entirely from an inner vision several years *before* having heard of the Master, when he was yet unknown in America. Her spiritual pilgrimage is beautifully expressed in her own words:

It was in the year of 1928, springtime in Kentucky, April, the month of the brightness of yellow daffodils and white narcissus. For two years and seven months I had been very ill. All the physicians and all the specialists I had consulted for my pain-wracked body said I could not walk again, that I could not even sit up again.

It was the hour of midnight. I lay there in the solemn weirdness, desolate and alone. I felt that I had come to the brink of the crossing into the Great Adventure. I was trying to think. I was trying to go back through my past life, endeavoring to live it once again. I did not want to die. I had so much, seemingly, that I wanted to do. The awful darkness seemed to close in all around me. I seemed to be suffocating. Desperately, I tried to move. Frantically, I tried to call someone. This seemed utterly impossible. I was in an agony of loneliness and despair.

Suddenly, a Great Luminous Brightness appeared in one corner of my room. It grew brighter and brighter. Within the center of this radiant Light, a form appeared, the most glorious Being I had ever seen. He stood there, tall, slender, magnificent. His beard was white and glistening. His vivid blue eyes were filled with divine compassionate flawless love, glowing as an angel standing in the sun. His glance was penetrative, inspired and keen. His robe and turban were white, pure and softer than that of the rarest edelweiss on the alpine snows, and yet emitted myriad scintillations of Light and color. The palms of his beautiful hands were clasped together and held against his heart. I thought this must be God. I stared at Him in amazement. He stood there looking at me kindly and graciously. Then, He walked slowly toward me and passed into my emaciated body.

The next morning, instead of finding me dead, as they probably expected they would, my family was astonished to see me rise from my sickbed, entirely healed and every whit whole.

At this time, I had never heard of a Great Master, but then and there I started a worldwide search for some information about this divine Being. Leaving the Episcopal Church, I took up the study of Christian Science, the White Brotherhood, Self-Realization, Rosicrucianism, the I AM Activity, the Baha'i Movement, and so on and on, year after year, turning wearily away from them all. I studied; I searched; I investigated. I spent hours and days in libraries looking through religious books. I could not find anyone who could give me the information I so earnestly desired.

Twenty years passed, and again in April in the year of 1948, I saw this Being before me again and again, and often in company with another Great Son of Spirituality. There were times when I soared into the Beyond, and saw there two beings, one tall, slender and blue-eyed, the other sturdy and strongly-built and with dark eyes as of a dove, and the two of them talking to another Being whom I later learned was Guru Nanak, the first Guru of the Sikhs.

I continued my search.

Another April! It was springtime in 1952. One morning, a friend tele-phoned me. She was passing through Louisville from Los

Mrs. M. Gordon Hughes with portait of Sant Kirpal Singh— painted by her in the 1940's before she had heard of him.

Angeles, to Florida. She asked if I had heard of Dr. Julian Johnson, who was born and reared in Kentucky, and who had gone to India in search of the Great Master. I had not heard of him. She told me about his books, and in time I received The Path of the Masters *from India. I read this book and felt that at last I was on the right road.*

In due course of time, I discovered Mr. T.S. Khanna of Washington, D.C., and on September 29, 1952, I went to the Capital City and through this blessed soul, I took the Great Master's initiation.

I asked Mr. Khanna to show me the former Master's portrait, and when I saw the picture of Baba Sawan Singh, I saw the glorious Being who had appeared to me with healing in his wings in 1928 and my long search was ended.

In June of 1955 I met the train as it pulled into Union Station in Washington, D.C., which brought His Holiness Sant Kirpal Singh Sahib from India to America....I watched him as he stepped from the coach, the radiant sunburnt Son of Sawan Singh, the beneficent Herald, the emancipator of true soul liberation. He looked exactly as I had seen Him so many times in Sahansdal Kanwal and the higher Heavens with our Beloved Sawan Singh. There was something more than handsome about Him...here was an inner splendor, a singular spiritual magnetism in the flash of His dark eyes, a marvelous sweet-

*ness and kindness in the firm lines of his mouth, a royal grandeur and
bearing of Freedom in the poise of his tall and strong figure...the Saint
from Sat Naam! Who has seen Him? Who can forget Him?*

He held up his right hand: "You see!" He said. I saw![1]

In the present, Mrs. Hughes rambled on, sharing her extraordinary journey:

"In that fresh and magical time after initiation, the Masters took my soul
higher and higher; even to the fourth plane. I was filled with divine intoxication upon experiencing the splendor of those realms. In the second and third
planes, I would see everything happen in this world before it happened. Being
a somewhat foolish and impetuous woman, I began to divulge what I saw. But,
oh, did I pay for my indiscretion, when Master brought down the curtain on
my inner vision. What was once effortless became impossible. For four long
years, I was barely able to see any Light. Things are better now, but I must
guard my tongue!"

I asked Mrs. Hughes about her stigmata, and she replied: "These wounds
manifest in my hands, feet and side only at Easter and Christmas when I relive
a former time with Jesus, and experience the wounding of his crucified body in
mine." I remembered Master's words in India, *"As you think, so you become,"*
and his marvelous story of the buffalo boy and the Saint. If the stigmata seems
implausible, the wary reader is referred to the biography of the late Padre Pio,
a twentieth-century Catholic mystic of Italy, whose bleeding Christ-wounds
were extensively photographed and scientifically documented.[2]

Mrs. Hughes' telephone rang. When she got off, she said, "My, oh my! That
call was from a man just released from the hospital. He was in with double
pneumonia; the doctors declared his case hopeless. Today, Master appeared,
hoverin' over his bed, and passed into his body, jest like he did to me in 1928.
He pushed away the oxygen tent and walked out of the hospital. If you want,
you can meet him before you leave." Unfortunately, I had to catch the bus.
Standing tall on the porch, she called out in her Kentucky drawl, "Honey,
there are angels of Light flyin' round your haid. You take care, now." I felt her
blessing. Not long after, Mrs. Hughes left her body for the last time.

After visiting and speaking to several hundred people in various towns across
America, I returned to Vancouver with barely seven dollars to my name. Piara
and Kuldeep Nagra graciously let me stay in their basement while I struggled
to get established.

---

1. Bhadra Sena, editor, *As They Saw the Master,* (Delhi, India: Ruhani Satsang, 1956), p. 7-
   10.

2. Nesta De Robeck, *Padre Pio,* (Milwaukee, Wisconsin: The Bruce Publishing Company,
   1958).

Before leaving India, I consulted the Master about right livelihood, a way to earn without compromising ethics, in an environment conducive to spiritual practice. I searched for words: "There is, I feel, a crying need in North America to provide wholesome, artfully prepared vegetarian food. Once people find out how delicious, healthy and inexpensive it is, many will embrace a compassionate diet. For those already vegetarian, there are no places to dine out. I'd like to establish a vegetarian restaurant and earn an honest livelihood."

"Good idea!" he replied, and added, "Master Power will be extending all feasible help, both inside *and* outside!" I knew about the inside help; it was comforting to know about the outer. And, it all came to pass.

Back in Vancouver, a *For Rent* sign in a defunct second-hand store caught my eye. Within moments of entering I began to experience a slightly blissful state. While not normally prescient, I was certain that *this* was the place. I was about to discover how clearly fixed mental images can manifest in the objective world through unrelenting effort.

A lease for the store and a four-bedroom suite upstairs was negotiated on a hope and a prayer, for I was broke. Those with means whom I initially approached had no interest in investing in my risky scheme, but a humble bank-teller saw the vision and agreed to co-sign a $1,000 loan. Another $500 arrived unexpectedly in the mail from a family friend. After settling the modest rent, phone and utility deposits, I negotiated the purchase of the entire assets of a failed restaurant nearby for $500. Within two months the Golden Lotus— Vancouver's first vegetarian restaurant—came into being on a $1,500 budget and lots of elbow-grease. Many unique and wonderful people were drawn like bees to honey, some as customers, some as employees. The comfortable quarters upstairs housed the growing circle of workers and the big living room became a communal meditation space.

The late sixties saw Vancouver swarming with war protesters and hippies. The threat of nuclear war loomed. The disenchanted took up the refrain: "tune in, turn on, drop out." A few were serious seekers who responded to the message of the Masters, which emphasized tuning in to a higher principle and the performance of work and service as a form of devotion. The Lotus was not merely a business; it was a refuge from drugs and junk food, a transformative catalyst for positive redirection, a tent in the caravan of *Baraka*.

Baraka, or Grace, requires a focal point, a place in the material world from where transcendence finds ways to manifest. Like a trader's caravan, tents are pitched, wares displayed, sold and bartered. When the job is done, the tents are folded, the caravan moves on, and sets up shop again elsewhere. The *wares* are the seeds of change, seeds of renewal. That is *Baraka*.

Intrinsically I was a loner and my naivetè in the art of administration resulted in valuable, if not difficult lessons. Quitting was not, however, an option, no matter how tough it got. Whenever the spirit triumphed over human foibles and limitations, the result was pure joy—the joy of service to one's brother or sister, no matter how humble or fallen. In the fine balance between work and inner practice, grace transformed many lives.

As with most new, undercapitalized ventures, particularly the restaurant genre, the finances of the Lotus were frequently uncertain. In the early days when nary a soul showed for dinner to eat the many varieties of delicious foods so carefully prepared, I would ask my one or two helpers to join me in meditation in our spotless kitchen. Within ten to fifteen minutes of focusing on the all-surrounding Light, a crowd would inevitably appear at the door. Our vocation was a front for love, not love a front for business.

It wasn't uncommon for customers to feel exhilarated and unusually peaceful after eating our *satvic* fare. *Satvic* is a Sanskrit term for pure or true. Hippies would ask, "Hey, man, what are you puttin' in the food?" The secret ingredient was simran, loving, mental repetition of the charged names, while preparing and serving. Master once told me, "Whatever you say simran over, with full attention, becomes parshad." Sacred thought has profound effects; like wind, it is invisible, but the effect can be seen on everything it touches.

After a well-known food journalist wrote a complimentary feature article, the Golden Lotus became the "in" place to eat and "be." Along with the ever-expanding clientele, many seekers arrived at the door wanting work and a place to stay. As long as everyone agreed to follow the rules, they were welcome to visit or stay upstairs. Amazingly, the rather monastic rules were accepted and followed. Like all others, I drew no wage in the first year although everyone's basic needs were well taken care of and the bills and loans were repaid with interest.

The numbers attending our weekly satsangs outgrew the upstairs, and the venue shifted downtown to the YWCA. Walking through the neighborhood, I could relate to the quandary of the user, the turned-on, the tuned-in, and the dropped-out; I had been there. Every poor lush, every desperate junkie, every paramour and thrill-seeker is intrinsically after bliss. But true bliss cannot be found through the senses or drugs. When the Emperor Babar offered Guru Nanak a goblet full of *bhang*, a preparation made from marijuana, he demurred and sang:

> *The intoxication from opium, bhang, and wine*
> *Leaves one poorer in the morning,*
> *But the intoxication of Naam is such that*
> *Day and night, Nanak is absorbed in its ecstasy.*

According to the Masters of *Sant Mat*, drugs and alcohol impede spiritual unfoldment, and addiction often leads to an animal rebirth, until one eventually gets the human form once again.

In the beginning, my hostess Mrs. Nagra generously shared her delicious Indian recipes and culinary skills. By trial and error, I learned the art of cooking and nutritious food preparation. The first full-time helper to appear was Norah B. Lee, one of "God's originals." Then in her fifties, Norah had varied successful careers behind her in real estate, as a horseback tourist guide, a plumber, and a bulldozer operator (*Time* magazine ran a full page photo-article on her in the early 1950's). Several years earlier, Norah had been bankrupted when a slick promoter left her with a large loan, which she had trustingly guaranteed. In the aftermath, her only possessions were a little Nash Rambler car, which she lived in, a set of clothes, one pair of shoes, and her songbook. When the shoes wore out, come ice or snow, Norah went barefoot. Cheerful, yet snarky, this remarkable woman moves through life, frequently helping others in need.

Before coming to the Golden Lotus, another teacher had initiated Norah, but the absence of spiritual experience kept her seeking. "When I was at Yasodara Ashram by Kootenay Lake," she explained, "I came across Kirpal Singh's book, *Naam or Word*. That night Master entered my soul, filling me with his marvelous splendor and love." I asked Norah, "Wouldn't you like to be initiated?" She replied, "It's not necessary; Master has already done it." I assured her that he had established his spiritual connection with her, but to be able to develop it to a greater extent would require formal initiation.

Norah was very skinny, but strong as a big man. Once she went on a forty-nine day fast while working ten hours a day in the kitchen. Her only food was the juice of half a lemon every two days. Forty days into the fast, Norah decided to re-organize the storage room, and was throwing around 100lb. sacks of brown rice like they were only 25lbs.

Whenever I tried to pay her, she wouldn't hear of it, saying, "The good Lord has directed me here to be of service to my fellow man. After all my money was gone, I decided never to work for material wages again. I'll be happy to just have a little corner to stay in, and if there's anything I can do, that would be a blessing for me." I assured Norah that if it were in my power, she would always have a home and never want. Embodying the spirit of the *faqir* or renunciate, Norah often spent entire nights in meditation, her scrawny neck enclosed by a cardboard collar of pins to waken her in case she nodded in sleep. (This is not a practice the Masters endorse, and Norah gave it up after awhile.)

David Leeworthy was one of many seekers who also came through the Lotus, contributing to, and gaining from it. After our first meeting, he described a turning-point experience, "...when I was walking down the hill on Fourth Avenue, looking westward towards the Lotus, I saw Kirpal Singh sitting cross-legged—about the size of a pea—right where the restaurant is located. His form kept expanding, until it filled the sky."[1]

In 1964, the year that I had come to the Path of Light, brought with it a new way of thinking, speaking, and living. With a daunting vow of celibacy, I tried to see all as sisters and brothers. After three years, the benefit of what the saints call *Ojas*, the power accruing from transmuting base energy into meditation and service, began to manifest. *Ojas* reduced my requirement for sleep and eating, and enabled the achievement in seconds of concentration of what would otherwise take many long hours. It allowed the body to work without fatigue, and cuts healed within hours. Ojas, which is gained over a long time, is, however, easily lost in a burst of anger or a wave of lust.

Such commitment does not go untested, especially amongst the young and vibrant. Carnality sometimes entered my mind, but I dared not forget that the Master within was watching everything. His personal and specific advice in Kashmir, "Avoid being alone in a room with the opposite sex," saved me on at least one occasion, when I felt like a canary about to be devoured by the cat. I was given a new life, and if this body which had been consecrated were to be given, it would have to wait for its life-companion.

Intimations of Returning: In early September of 1968, an architect friend and I drove to the interior of B.C. in search of reportedly free Crown land in the hopes of eventually establishing a permanent meditation center. After the second day of exploring, we camped by the roadside under a canopy of brilliant stars and rolling sagebrush hills. After meditating for an hour, I fell asleep. In the early morning came an auspicious dream:

> *It is India; my job is sweeper in the courtyard of the Master. This courtyard, however, is that of the sixteenth-century Saint, Kabir. My broom is the Indian type, short of handle, and I use it in the Indian fashion, squatting. The dust, sacred dust, billows 'round, becomes bright, flying into and through my eyes into infinite, luminous space...*

Upon waking, my consciousness was suffused with wondrous possibilities. As soon as I could find a telephone, I called the Lotus to discover that a letter had arrived from the Master granting permission to return to India.

---

1. In 1970, David went to India and studied with the great Master. After a personal interview, Kirpal Singh commented to a bystander, "*He will become the source of many books for many people.*" David, who later changed his name to Kolin Lymworth, founded Banyen Books in Vancouver, which grew to become one of North America's finest and largest alternative bookstores.

36

October 23, 1968: Two days before departing for India, a friend and I visited Ram Dass, the former Richard Alpert, in retreat at his father's large New Hampshire estate. He had recently returned from a life-transforming trip with his Indian guru, Neem Karoli Baba. We found Ram Dass alone and unpretentious, in a small white cottage surrounded by rolling lawns and trees. As fellow wayfarers who had both gone East for wisdom, we discussed many commonalities of the spiritual journey.

Neem Karoli Baba, a powerful and enigmatic Hindu holy man, had shaken the foundations of Alpert's existence. He even renamed him Ram Dass (servant of God). The former Harvard professor and psychedelic pioneer turned to the path of devotion, spiritual practice, and *seva* or service—of the blind, service of those incarcerated in the prison system, and service of the dying. As Ram Dass explained to us, "LSD opened doors for a lot of people, which was important in the context of the evolution of a materialistic, up-tight America, but acid could not take one to the Goal of self-realization."

While discussing particular spiritual practices, I asked Ram Dass if he were familiar with the little-known *Surat Shabd Yoga*—the yoga of the Celestial Sound-current. He affirmed that he had come across references to *Naad Yoga* in the *Naad Bind Upanishad*, one of the major Hindu scriptural commentaries, which declared that the *OM* or *aum* sound issued from *Brahma* and created the three worlds. *Nirguna bhagats*, or worshippers of the formless, meditate on *aum* as the most efficient means of returning to the Causal-Creator. Ram Dass was experimenting with a variety of meditation techniques, including Naad Yoga, considering it acceptable to listen to any inner sounds, including those coming from the *left* side.

I respectfully pointed out that the Gurus in the ancient Sant Mat tradition had enjoined the practice of listening to the sounds coming from the right side or from the center of the forehead only. According to their teaching, the inner Melodies heard coming from the right or center take one back to the Positive Power beyond Brahm *[Par Brahma]*, while sounds emanating from the left side were debasing. We talked about *samadhi, bhakti yoga, karma yoga*, and Sri Ramakrishna' allegory of the cotton doll and the salt doll. Ramakrishna had likened the meditator's *savikalpa samadhi* experience of God to a cotton doll—when it enters the ocean, it becomes saturated, yet still retains its form; the higher samadhi—known as *nirvikalpa*, Ramakrishna likened to a salt doll—when it enters the ocean, it dissolves its separate identity, and becomes one with it.

I found Ram Dass warm and sincere, his presence quietly joyous. The company of those on the Way, regardless of outer labels, imparts a unique delight. After a while, we parted company.[1] As much as I would have wished it, Ram Dass never met Master Kirpal.

None blows fire into our hearts but him,
none makes short the path to him but him.
If all the world became our doctor still
no one could cure us of him but him.
—*Awhaduddin Kirmani,*
Persian mystic, thirteenth Century.

---

1. *I was working on this piece about Ram Das in a Baltimore hotel room in September of 1993. At about 2 AM I stopped and went to bed. Eight hours later, I unexpectedly encountered Ram Dass in the lobby of the Baltimore Natural Foods Expo Hall! In the midst of a crowd of conventioneers, we enjoyed an unfettered sharing. This was our third meeting, and our previous one in Vancouver in the early seventies was unsatisfactory, for fame had seemingly affected him. Now I encountered a humbler, more down-to-earth, and joyous Ram Dass. We embraced. Later in the afternoon, at a packed public lecture for members of the natural foods industry, Ram Dass scattered food for thought and "being here now." Spiritual practice and sincerity develop compassion, detachment, honesty, integrity, and dedication to service without thought of reward. While hilariously poking fun at himself and at established social values, he helped show the relevance of integrating eternal values into one's being and one's livelihood, regardless of vocation. Ram Dass has become increasingly imbued with a Buddha-like compassion, even after a stroke in 1998 rendered him partially paralyzed.*

37

A fateful telegram arrived one day before my scheduled departure for India:

I WILL BE ON CONSTANT TOUR DURING NOVEMBER DECEMBER AND TILL END OF JANUARY WITH EXCEPTION OF FOUR DAYS. BETTER POST-PONE YOUR AND OTHERS TRIP TILL END OF JANUARY PLEASE. KIRPAL SINGH 10/25/68.

In numb shock, I read it over and over. The hand of the Beloved moves in mysterious ways; obedience meant forfeiture of my prepaid ticket. Worse, I would remain a fish out of water, far, far from the Master's presence.

That entire night I was kept awake by a titanic struggle: to go or to obey. By the first flush of dawn, I felt resigned to my fate and sent the following telegram in reply:

...FLIGHT POSTPONED FARE FORFEITED.
IF ONLY I MAY PLEASE THEE, TIS PILGRIMAGE ENOUGH...

The last line, a quote from *Jap Ji*, expressed my struggle and submission in a single phrase. By bus, I headed back toward the West Coast three thousand miles away. I was met at the Columbus Ohio depot by David and Pat Hughes, and accepted their kind offer to stay overnight. The moment we arrived at their apartment, the phone rang. Judith from New England was on the line with an urgent call for me: "I didn't know if you would be there or not. I don't know how to begin, or even if I should be telling you this, but..."

"But what?" I asked, my heart in my throat.

"It's not going to be easy on you, but another telegram just arrived from Master and he says,

YOUR TELEGRAM RECEIVED ON RETURN TOUR. YOU MAY COME...
KIRPAL SINGH

What a quandary! I was down to my last $100. David and Pat came to the rescue, loaned me $600, and drove me to the airport at breakneck speed. My hastily boarded plane reached England's Heathrow Airport several hours later, alas, too late by five minutes to connect with my charter flight! With the last of the money, I bought a one-way ticket to Kuwait, hoping to intercept my party which was scheduled to stay overnight there before departing for India.

When this fatigued wayfarer arrived in sweltering Kuwait, he was arrested and interrogated by the military, under suspicion of being an Israeli spy. Admittedly, it did look rather odd—a white man in a turban with a Jewish-sounding name, a one-way ticket, and no money whatsoever. With bright spotlights shining in my jet-lagged eyes, I tried again and again to explain, but no one listened. Questions, accusations, and threats were shouted at me. Initial fear turned to resignation as I began to do simran. After several rounds of the holy mantra, I looked over the heads of the crowd which had gathered to gawk and noticed a BOAC stewardess making her way towards us. She spoke urgently in Arabic with the officials. After listening to and translating my story, she convinced the authorities that I was okay, that my story must be checked out. After some tense moments, I was released. The stewardess confided, "They were about to take you to a prison in the desert. No one would ever have heard from you again. Very fortunate."

The familiar faces of Bruce and Misha from Vancouver bobbed through the crowd of burnooses and veils. (Bruce & Misha had decided to disregard the Master's previous telegram asking us to postpone coming). On the way to the charter group's hotel, we stopped in the bazaar to purchase a branch of the most delicious fresh dates I had ever eaten. It is said that Prophet Mohammed lived off dates, camel's milk, and barley bread. Such morsels are truly Allah's blessings in this sea of sand and barren rocks. After more adventures, Misha, Bruce, and I finally reached Delhi, starved for darshan.

How blessed it was to pass again through the gates of Sawan Ashram, into its timeless and bright dimensions. As we approached on foot within a hundred yards of the porch, the Master "happened" to step outside to an awaiting car. Turning from the car's open door, he suddenly looked in our direction. His powerful glance took away my breath. My storm-tossed boat again found its harbor. How happy, how loving this reunion! I could feel his gentle pat on my back. For my ears alone, he confided, "When your telegram arrived, I felt pity on you."

That night, he shared an episode from his own life, illustrating how love can change the mind of the Beloved.

"Once Hazur left Dera with the instruction, 'No one should follow me to Dalhousie.' Many others did not obey him but I considered that I was bound by his orders. After two weeks I was deeply feeling the pangs of separation.

"In the madness of that separation I wrote a poem to the Master. It was the season of springtime, of Basant. I wrote, 'For others this is the season of Basant—of springtime and happiness; others are enjoying the eternity of your existence, but for me this is Baas-aant.' Baas-aant is a play on the word, changing its meaning from 'springtime' to 'the end of happiness.' This poem was duly conveyed to Hazur, and on hearing it, Hazur suddenly announced he was returning. He came straight to me in Lahore. You see, the slenderest strands of love are more powerful than thick ropes of steel. Just on these few words, the Master changed his plans and came to me."

RAJI AND MATAJI

38

Not long after returning to my spiritual home in the ashram, I watched discreetly from the porch as the Master in the adjoining room spoke with his son Darshan, daughter-in-law Harbhajan Kaur, and a handsome Sikh gentleman in his early twenties. Catching me out of the corner of his eye, Master beckoned me over. He had just placed a flower garland around the young man's neck. Beaming at me, he asked, "Do you want to know what I looked like when I was a young man? See here to Raji! He looks exactly like me. I too was a little plump like him! The only difference between us is that Raji ties a fashionable turban and I always tied a simple turban!"

Raji, Master Kirpal's eldest grandson, is about to leave for America for further studies.

His mother, Harbhajan Kaur, shared what transpired later that night:

"On the day Raji was to leave India, I went to the ashram to find out if the Beloved Master was going to accompany us to the airport to see him off. When I got there I asked the Master if he would be free that evening. Master said, 'Oh, I am very busy. I have no time.' After he said that I did not dare speak further, but in my heart I was feeling sad and dejected that he would not be able to accompany us. After a moment the Beloved Master looked up and said, 'Don't you know I'm very busy tonight! I have to go to the airport to see Raji off. If I don't go, who is going to wipe off your tears?'"[1]

When the first child was born to Darshan and Harbhajan in 1946, Master Kirpal Singh traveled by train from Lahore to Delhi especially to see him. The child was four days old, and when Master first saw him, he touched the baby's cheek with his index finger, saying, "Yes, there are many old memories with this one." Then the baby grabbed Master's finger and put it into his mouth. Baba Sawan Singh personally selected the name Rajinder, or "King of Kings." He was known affectionately by his nickname "Raji." As Raji grew up, he was noted for his exceptional intelligence and gentle nature. He attended one of India's finest engineering universities in Bangalore, graduating with highest honors, and was accepted for graduate studies at the Illinois Institute of Technology, near Chicago. Master Kirpal himself selected the university.

Master Kirpal Singh told Darshan and Harbhajan to have Raji's things packed and ready to go 15 days before the date of departure. He then had Raji come and stay with him at the Ashram those last 15 days, where he personally instructed him in the finer aspects of mysticism, meditation, the teachings of the Sikh Gurus, and comparative religion, so that Raji would have a better knowledge of the teachings of the Saints.

RAJI AND MATAJI

Raji's departure to America, 1968
(left to right: Raji,.Darshan & Master Kirpal)

On the last day, Master had a pair of his own shoes put down on the floor in front of Raji and told him, "Let us see how they fit you." Raji gingerly put his feet into the Master's shoes. They fit perfectly. Then Master said to Raji, "Now your feet are in my shoes. So when you go to America, you should always walk on the purest path. Remember, people will judge me by your behavior."[2]

Mataji—the Master's Wife: Several times I had noticed a very elderly woman, all dressed in white, silently entering or leaving the Master's bungalow in the mornings. I discovered that she was Mataji Krishna Wanti, the wife of Sant Kirpal Singh. Mataji was the picture of piety. Each morning she went quietly from her separate room to pay obeisance to the Master, whom she no longer considered as worldly husband, but as the manifestation of the Lord. I respectfully greeted her with *"Sat Sri Akaal*, Mataji" A lovely smile lit up her face, and she responded huskily, "Sat Sri Akaal ji, *betta* (son)!" Incredible sweetness flowed from her presence.

Mataji returned to her spiritual abode on April 3, 1970. Her frail form had suffered from cancer for about four years. On this subject the Master afterwards remarked, "Many people who have experienced this sickness have suffered greatly and have screamed aloud with the agony that it causes, but with the grace of God, through having direct contact with Him within, Mataji was spared the pinching effects..."

Eventually Mataji was unable to get around anymore, and while the Master was on tour in the latter part of March, her condition worsened. On March 30, (1970) the Master asked her if she was ready to leave and she replied, "Yes, in three days." The Master thought for a moment and then said, "Well, three days, that means April 2nd—I will be very busy that day (due to the commemoration of the death anniversary of Hazur Baba Sawan Singh). The 3rd would be better, in the early afternoon, say 1:30 p.m. I will be more free then."

Mata Ji (Master Kirpal's wife)

At about 1:00 PM on the third it was noticed that Mataji's condition had become very serious. When told about Mataji, the Master said, "I know it." The Master went to Mataji and looking down at her very kindly, asked, "Are you prepared?" She looked up and said, "Yes." The Master said, "Are you sure your heart is absolutely clear—with no hatred for anyone?" She replied, "Yes, I have nothing against anyone in my heart." The Master asked, "Then why are you not smiling?" With this, her face...began to glow with joy. Ripples of laughter came forth and she looked radiant with happiness. Taking hold of the Master's hand she said, "Forgive me, if I have ever done anything to offend you." The Master smiled compassionately. She said, "Both forms are here—I am seeing you outside and inside." The Master said, "All right, now close your eyes and relax," and with these words he returned to his room. Within ten or fifteen minutes, Mataji had left.

---

1. Young Rajinder obediently lived up to his grandfather's expectations. After moving to the Chicago area in 1968, he graduated with highest honors in electrical engineering, and earned a distinguished career with Bell Laboratories. His noble qualities and equanimity of heart and head endeared Raji to his new friends and colleagues in America. He was able to maintain a fine balance between his worldly and spiritual responsibilities, while keeping in frequent contact with the Master and his parents. In time—twenty-one years to be exact—it was not surprising that this gentle, loving, and intelligent grandson would be chosen to inherit the mantle of the Satguru and his global spiritual mission.

2. *Portrait of Perfection: A Pictorial Biography of Kirpal Singh*, (Bowling Green, VA/ Delhi, India: Sawan Kirpal Publications, 1981), p. 189.

Love leads into the world of light!—Sadhu Vasvani

*T*he next five months are spent in close proximity to the beloved Master. Misha, Bruce, Leonard (who arrives from New York), and I accompany the Master on several long tours. On occasion, Father encourages me to sing and share a story or two with the Sangat. (Prior to, and during this period, he gave a series of superb intimate talks to visiting Westerners, forty of which were published as *Morning Talks*). His specific replies to unvoiced questions never cease to amaze. Heart-whispers are heard before being clumsily voiced.

Devlali: We stay a few days in a humble ashram on the edge of a dense jungle in south-central India. The Sabarmati flows less than half a mile away. Getting to the river involves trekking through wild gullies and jungle. Every day I go there both to swim and meditate. Strewn along the banks of the Sabarmati are millions of smooth round pebbles ranging in size from small marbles to large plums. On closer inspection, I discover them to be semi-precious agate, tiger's

eye, lapis, and amethyst...however, I am after the jewel of great worth, and so leave these baubles in the dark sands.

A simple farmer has attached himself to the Master for the last three tour stops. He has attained such a high degree of receptivity, that he leaves his body within minutes of being in the Master's presence. Today is like the others, which finds

Master, Misha, the writer, and Indore sevadars, 1968. Bruce King, photo.

our farmer flat on his back, corpse-like. On his way back from blessing the *langar*, Master stops for a closer look. With much amusement, he directs words to Bruce, Misha and myself, "What should we do with him? Shall we bury or cremate the body?! Is he not a dead man?" After several hours in the higher planes, this meditator's soul finally returns again.

Mouni Baba: A colorful personality from Devlali joins our caravan. Mouni Baba is a renunciate monk, swathed in orange *gerua* robes. Straight-backed, short of stature, broad of brow, shaven head, toothless, pot bellied, and about 65 years of age, Mouni Baba has taken a vow of silence and communicates by writing on a chalkboard.[1] We become close friends, and I learn his story, as he scribbles, shows and erases.

"As a child, I was more interested in God than anything else. I became learned in Sanskrit, practiced *Ashtanga* yoga, performed many austerities. By age twenty, I had studied with different gurus and had quite a number of my own disciples. By forty, several thousands acknowledged me as their guru. As I progressed in *pranayama* (breath control), the fire of *kundalini* awakened suddenly. My whole body and head felt like it was burning in fire. Much heat! This happened about twenty years ago. Day and night for several years this kundalini fire was burning me. I went to so many saints for help. Although they prescribed cures and mantras, nothing worked. About fifteen years ago Sant Kirpal Singh Ji came, but since he was a *grehasti* (householder) and I was a sadhu (monk), I felt very hesitant to accept him. But I did go and explained my difficulty. He made me sit down for meditation, put his holy hand on my head, took me high up, inside. Kundalini was finished, just like that! (He snaps his fingers). Kundalini is dangerous. Surat Shabd Yoga goes much higher."

I ask, "Mouni Baba, you know Master's rule about not initiating those who live off donations. How did Master accept you for initiation? What were his conditions?"

Mouni Baba replies, "Maharaj Ji told me I would have to earn an honest living and asked what profession I could take up. I told him 'Maharaj Ji, the only thing I know by which I can make a living is palmistry.' Then he advised me to carry on that line of work."

Sadhu Vaswani & the Mira School: On the way to Poona, in south-central India, Master invites Bruce to sit on the front seat beside him. Bruce is overwhelmed with this honor and reluctant to obey. With a poker face, Master says, "If you think that by sitting by me, your clothes will be soiled, you can take a bath later!" He laughs heartily.

Sadhu Vaswani of Sindh was a renowned educator, philosopher, humanitarian, author and mystic, revered as a saint by tens of thousands from both the high and low castes. In the early days of India's struggle for independence from the British, Vaswani was almost as widely known as Mahatma Gandhi. At the height of his fame, at the age of 40, he left his post as principal of one of the largest colleges in India, and renounced the world, as he said, "to announce the Eternal." After several years of esoteric study and practice, he settled at Poona, and established the Mira School for Girls, at a time and place when females were considered unfit for education. He opened the doors of his school to many who were destitute, and taught those of means through his own example, to serve the lowly and needy, as though they were serving God Himself.

To Sadhu Vaswani, spirituality included the practice of deep prayer and meditation, as well as service to the holy and the needy. He churned out over 40 books in English and 200 in the Sindhi language. In his heart of hearts he knew that someday God would lead him to a perfect Master. By the time he was in his eighties, the Mira Schools were well established and recognized internationally. One day, while browsing through the major daily newspaper of Poona, he saw for the first time, a picture of Satguru Kirpal Singh and an advertisement for his impending visit. Sadhu Vaswani exclaimed, "This man! This man will give me God!"

Sadhu Vaswani passed away not long after, and was succeeded by his able nephew, Dada J.P. Vaswani. On our visit to Poona in January of 1969, we are treated to the remarkable sight of Dada Vaswani and the Master touching each other's feet.

Vaswani Ji personally escorts us through the entire campus, articulately fielding our questions. In honor of the Master and guests, children sweetly sing verses from several traditions in Hindi, Marathi and English. We are deeply inspired by Dada Ji's words:

> "There is darkness in the world today—the darkness of selfishness and strife, of cruelty and hatred and pride. And, again and again, in hours of silence methinks, I have seen Mother Humanity shed tears while her children grope in the dark, busy preparing nuclear weapons, preparing to destroy themselves. Humanity is as an orphan crying in the night, crying for the Light.
>
> "..Sant Kirpal Singh is the very picture of love and renunciation. To draw near him is to bask in the sunshine of love. And for the love of God, he has renounced everything. I have nothing, he says, except the Name of God!
>
> "A man came to him, one day, and saying: 'Sir! My daughter has had a brain illness for several years. Can you heal her?'
>
> "In humility, Sant Kirpal Singh answered: 'I have nothing except the Name of God. And the Name of God is a great healer!'"

From Poona we drive further south to Satara. It is a strange and beautiful land of hot, fertile plains, farms, villages and dramatic up-thrusting ancient rock formations. Here, Master's Hindi discourses are translated into the local dialect. It is said that in India the dialect changes every fifty miles. Satara is a small town nestled at the base of a mountain butte that rises several hundred feet above the plains. When the morning meditation is finished, Maharaj Ji asks everyone what he or she saw within. When it is Master-ji's turn, he just looks up into Gurudev's eyes, folds his hands together, quietly laughs and replies *"Aap!"* ("You!")

Lenny, Bruce, Misha and I climb to the summit of the flat-topped mountain crowned with an ancient fortress and ramparts, which encircle the entire area of several acres. Here, brave Shivaji, the Mahratha prince and his warriors held back northern invaders. The view in all directions is spectacular, God-inspiring. As we explore the lofty and heavily treed plateau, we wander into a cool, circular glade of Banyan trees. The tangle of roots and trees form a kind of veil to the world, inviting one to meditate. There, in the almost perfect circle of the glade, I sit and enter infinite space between the eyes.

Meditation in the circular banyan grove at the top of Shivaji's mountain fortress.

---

1. Several years later in Vancouver, I had the good fortune of meeting another famous silent Mouni yogi, Baba Hari Das, who also communicates by means of a chalkboard.

40

The systematic study of palmistry had been a fascination since my eighteenth year. I had sufficient proof that the lines of the palm often reveal an uncanny window into each person's past, present and future destiny, as well as their hidden character. I had since discontinued reading palms, considering that that practice, along with astrology, to be inconsequential for travelers on the path of the Masters. Those who have come under the protection of a perfect Adept, and who have crossed the stars, sun and moon on the inner journey, are no longer controlled by astrological influences.

One night in November of '68, somewhere on a tour-stop in central India, I passed by the open door to Master's temporary quarters and saw him talking to Tai Ji, who was sitting on the floor crying. He looked up and beckoned me in from the dark. "Tai is crying. She thinks she is going to die, but I'm showing her that her life-line is long!" he said with amusement. "Do you know palmistry?" he asked. "A little," I replied. He showed me her hand, and of course he was right. Tai Ji, distracted from self-pity, asked, "You like read Master's hand?" How many times had I hoped for this? "Oh, yes!"

I cradled that magnificent hand in mine. The skin was a golden-brown on the back, while the palm was pinkish, with graceful, deep, flawless lines. I recalled the historic meeting with Raghuvacharya, the yogiraj of Rishikesh, and my glimpse of the Master's hand then, but it was not so close and studied as this present opportunity:

A peculiar large star/lotus-like configuration of lines crowned the top of his straight, deep, and very long Destiny line, beneath the middle finger on the mount of Saturn. On his forefinger Jupiter mount was a perfect Ring of Solomon, symbol of self-mastery; a perfect Mystic Cross appeared between the Heart and Head lines; and the Sun Line prominently passed across all major lines. His intellect line swept from one side of the hand to the other. Such marks accompanied by an almost symmetrical balance indicated the *Murshid-i-Kamil*, or Perfect Man, with fully developed potential. After tracing the major lines, I began to look for minor ones and discovered two or three tiny superfluous "worry" lines, possibly indicating betrayal from individuals close to him. But could I presume to speak to him of the human side of the divine? I became tongue-tied. My knowledge was limited, and what if I were wrong? As the moments stretched in silent struggle, full knowing that my mind was an open book to him, I began to experience a spiritual tingling of consciousness and a

receding awareness of normal time and space. His hand was very close to my face; I was aware of nothing else.

An extraordinary experience then took place: tiny little balls of white light appeared, traveling continuously along his lines, leaving minute glowing trails like fading phosphorescence. It was like seeing a simulated atom with electrons spinning about the nucleus, only here, a Godman's hand was the nucleus, and the lines of his life, head, sun, heart, and destiny were the electron paths of Light-energy. I kept watching this cosmic play, until the Master brought me back with a clearing of his throat. Reverently, I took his hand and pressed it against my forehead.

"Master," I gasped, "I am incapable of reading your palm!" He smiled knowingly.

I confess to having developed my own morbid fixation, convinced that I would die of or suffer a serious head injury around my thirtieth year. At least that's what my palm indicated. One evening, as mind continued deliberating this possibility, I happened to walk into the Master's living room, which suddenly erupted into laughter. About twenty regulars were sitting around him.

"You are going to live a long life!" Master said. I looked at him, uncomprehendingly. He repeated it, and added, "We were just talking about you. There is a saying in India, 'If someone whom you are discussing appears, he will live long!'"[1]

One day, as several of us sat around him, the Master mirthfully addressed me, "You look like a Pathan! Who are you? Are you an Easterner? A Westerner?" He turned to the others and said, "He was born in the West by mistake!"

The words of a poem by Rumi welled up, but, finding no path of speech, remained inside:

> *I am not of the East and not of the West,*
> *Not of the land and not of the sea;*
> *I belong to the soul of the Beloved.*
> *I have seen the two as One,*
> *And One I see,*
> *One I know,*
> *One I adore!*
> *The First, the Last,*
> *The outward, and the inward too!*

He then asked, "Do you wish to die in India?" Who could fathom him? A few words stumbled out in reply, "Yes, with you, Master." He chuckled.[2]

---

1. This occurred more than thirty years ago. The Beloved Master left his mortal coil for the last time in 1974, in my thirtieth year, which was a form of trauma/death/rebirth for me.

2. On each of my three stays with Sant Kirpal Singh in India, he asked me this same question. Each time, the reply was the same.

41

February 7, 1969: The day after Master's seventy-fifth birthday, the ashram is still overflowing with humanity. During a program lull, my friend Hasmukh Vyas approaches: "Arran-ji, you would like to marry an Indian girl? She is Master's disciple from a very good family. She is M.A. degree! She is lecturer at a girls' college in Moradabad, you see."

Surprised, I reply, "Well, I don't know...Whatever is His Will, but she must be devoted to the Path."

"Oh yes, very qualified—nice girl, M.A. degree, college lecturer. Very qualified!"[1]

We formally meet in the evening in the presence of Tai Ji and others from the proposed's family in the Master's dining room. As we file through the doorway, I am introduced to a pretty, modest, and determined young woman of twenty-two. *"Namaste Ji.* How do you do?" She speaks with a strong British-Indian accent. "My name is Rattan Mala Bagga."[2]

We sit on opposite ends of the long dining table looking at our plates. Mutually shy and awkward, we ask a few guarded questions of each other. While conversation passes around, I find myself stealing a few glances in her direction and am surprised to catch a few returns as well! Eyes then quickly and properly avert to the plates.

Too soon dinner is over; Rattan Mala and family prepare to leave for Moradabad, a hundred miles away by train. Her granny, Mela Devi, or "Baeji" as everyone calls her, is a wise old initiate of Hazur. She confronts me outside and expresses a well-justified fear of the *feringhi:*[3] "I have heard the Americans leave their wives. This is my daughter, my most priceless treasure! What have you to say about it?"

"Baeji," I reply, "in my life, there is only one woman; only one marriage. See, even my hand says so," showing her the single line there. She hugs me, and with a huge toothless grin exclaims, *"Shabash!"* ("Very good!"), proudly showing off her future son-in-law.

The family had once been powerful, with confectionery factories, mansion, and many servants, but in recent years, hard times fell and the factory and mansion were auctioned off. Due to this, I am told, there won't be much dowry. "No dowry!" I insist. "A good and loving wife; a life-companion of noble character is more than I deserve."

"Namaste Ji," we say to each other in sweet parting. After the passage of days, head swirling with gripping implications, I am struck by cupid's arrow—the kind that cannot be extracted. Although I know hardly anything about this young woman, I'm certain of our intertwined destiny. Simultaneously, unbeknownst to me, in the old city of Moradabad, she is struck by the

same arrow—I am the one she wants to marry—but in her case, she faces the wrath of the more conservative elements of her prominent high-caste family.

"You want to marry a *Bhangi* [a low-caste sweeper]), a *Chamar* [those who handle the dead]! This will defame our noble clan!" While she is harangued and tormented, I am blithely unaware of her trials. She later confides, "Master was supporting me, and for one time in my life I completely surrendered to His Will. Otherwise I couldn't have done it. Although my mother, grandmother, aunts, and uncle Hira Lal who were initiated understood and gave me support, Bau Ji [her father] and two of my uncles were strongly opposed. Fortunately, Baeji ruled the family. Once I had made the decision to marry, no one could change my course." During the stress of these two weeks, she loses 15 of her former 110 pounds.

I go to the beloved Master, seeking assurance. "It is God who puts such like thoughts in you," he says. "...*Tai! Tai ko bulao!*" He calls in Tai Ji, who then hands me a folded Nehru-style coat of fine grey material. "This' Master coat—for you. You wear on wedding!" she orders.

Master urges, "Try it on; I wore it once. Let us see how the coat fits!" Naturally I'm overawed, not knowing whether to wear or revere it. *I first revere it.* After more encouragement, I try it on. Despite my near six feet height, the coat is very large in the shoulders. After all, it was tailored for the broad-shouldered Master. "You can go for a re-fitting," he said. *My whole life is being refitted*, I muse silently.

Rattan Mala and family are summoned back to the ashram in late February. The British-educated Princess Khukhuji calls me over to where she and Eileen are standing under a tree, "Because you are a Westerner, I think you should get to know your future wife a little better. I have arranged for both of you to meet in my house for one hour. This is not done in India, and especially here in the ashram! I will stand guard outside the door while you sit apart and ask whatever you want to know about each other. Only one hour, mind you."

In that brief interlude we get to share some history, poetry, dreams and goals. We are then called to the Master's house, with a few relatives and well wishers. A big suitcase is brought forth, from which saris, suits and scarves of many colors and descriptions are given to Rattan Mala by the Master. He is playing the role of father to both of us, and will not see his daughter married without dowry! If the Master were only a renunciate, he would never have understood nor participated in this side of his disciples' lives, but he is the Complete Man, the *Insaan-i-kamil.*

The Princess then presents a classical Indian filigree necklace and earrings, and Brij Mohan and Mohini Sharma warmly add a gold bangle. When I protest this extravagance, he lovingly insists, "Dear brother, you have no say in the matter. She is also our daughter!"

Master raises his hands, eyes upturned: "O God, I was running towards You like anything! Then You bound my legs, my arms and neck with chains! With manacles and handcuffs! And I was running towards You like anything!" he chuckles. Behind the mirth is portent of great changes ahead. With my ascetic tendencies, he sees my need to experience through marriage and family life the tender bondage of responsibility and human attachment before further inner development is possible.

"When Socrates was pressed by family to be married," Master continues, "he agreed on one condition, 'Give me the most disobedient wife! That will be the best for me.' And one night when Socrates was up late discussing philosophy with his friends, his wife became so angry she poured his supper on his head! That was good for his progress, you see!"

Engagement: On the evening of March 3, Master calls all Westerners, a few close Indian disciples, and Rattan Mala's family to his living room.

Master, chuckling: "Who is the minister of all this?"

Groom: "You, Master!"

Master: "What is the ritual or custom amongst you about marriage?" (He points to Stanley.) "You know better."

Stanley: "No ritual or custom, Master, for the engagement."

Master: "What is 'engagement'? Any special thing to be done?"

Edna: "No, Master, he just puts a ring on the girl's finger, that's all."

Master: "That's all? Only a ring? And if the ring is lost?" He chuckles, "The ring which has bound him—which binds both souls together—is stronger and cannot be broken. Anyhow this is a memento, hmm? How will the marriage be performed? By some church man, or whom?"

Stanley: "A Sikh wedding, I think."

Master: "Look here, I never interfere with the 'isms.' All are dear to me. So, how would you like to conduct your marriage? If according to the Church, we can arrange for a missionary to come over here, or there in a church."

Groom: "Maharaj Ji, I humbly request that it be done in the Sikh way."

Master: "I'm not converting anybody to Sikhism. What about marriage?"

Tai Ji: "Tomorrow morning."

Master: "One day's engagement only?" he says with the sweetest, most incredulous look. "They last for months, is it not?"

Stanley: "Normally, yes, Master. We didn't have an engagement, Edna and I—we just got married."

Master (to Stanley): "Would you like a priest here to conduct the marriage, or what?" (As Master keeps directing his questions to Stanley, the situation becomes ever more hilarious.) "How would you like it?"

Stanley: "Arran's getting married—not me!"

Master: "I'm just inquiring whether you would like to have your marriage conducted according to the Christian rites or what? I have no objection."

Groom (stammering): "If...if Master has no objection I would prefer the Sikh...."

Finally, Master seems satisfied: "That means the marriage is to be performed before God through the hands of some blessed people in the presence of many. So, you desire to perform it according to Sikh rites?"

Groom: "Yes."

Master: "I am a man; I love all. Alright, where is the girl?" Rattan Mala comes forward, and we both bow spontaneously. She gets his right foot, I the left. "Knock your heads!" he says. Intoxicating mirth envelopes all. Master holds up the bride's ring, which is encrusted with nine jewels. Examining it closely, he asks, "One pearl? Alright, take it."

He places gentle hands upon our heads, saying, "Alright, God bless you! That's alright. Now tomorrow, you want to be married according to Sikh rites? Do you all agree, you people? He wants it to be done according to Sikh rites— with no imposition from me, not in the least. Our blessings are there. It is the unseen hand of God working behind the scenes which unites them. This union comes about as a result of the past. He's an Indian! [pointing to the groom] His great-grandfather was a General of the Punjab in India. So unfortunately, or fortunately, you were born there (in the West) and you have been brought back to India! Your great-grandfather was here in the Punjab, in what year?"

Groom: "He lived here from 1840 to 1875."

Master: "So it is these reactions which have brought you back here.[4] Alright! God Bless you, with all best wishes. In the morning, sharp at eight, all you friends be there. He's already bound, you see, but he'll be bound by the silken bonds of love, which cannot be broken—which are stronger than iron chains, is it not? Alright, God bless you. Go and take your food please, and goodnight to you all."

How palpable the joy and peace which fills my last solitary night! The Holy Spirit descends in force several times, touching, blessing, showering a normally world-bound consciousness with ecstasy and supernal awe. Behind diaphanous veils awaits the Spouse of all souls.

The Lord, the Bridegroom, has entered into my soul
...and I have known the loveliness of His beauty.

—*St. Bernard of Clairvaux*

Holi Wedding: March 4, 1969: Our wedding day coincides with Holi, an Indian festival that celebrates the triumph of good over evil. Astrologers consider Holi to be inauspicious for weddings, but Masters are above such superstition and convention.

We meet again, as sacred hymns from the *Granth Sahib* drift across the courtyard from the meditation hall, where the marriage knot is to be tied. Everything feels strangely familiar and marvelous, as though this drama has been enacted before. The bride is wrapped in a red and gold sari, her large dark eyes lowered. Master ties a fragrant veil of fresh flowers upon my pink wedding turban.

He says: "You are having a big load on your life now. You're not to run all alone but you have a big load to carry!" He sweetly laughs. "All responsibilities, of course. This ceremony shows that you are entering into the householder's life. You're not a bachelor anymore. Now others will know you have true matrimony and will have respect for you. A life-companion is an asset to be with you in weal or woe. The ultimate goal of both of you is to know God. The real union of the soul comes only then. Now it is a union of physical body with physical body in this earthly sojourn."

Master hands us fragrant flower garlands: "First, she'll put the garland around your neck and then you'll put one around hers, signifying that you accept each other. First she accepts you, then you accept her." The garlanding is done. "Bow your head. Remain devoted to her! Now you [to Rattan Mala]. That's alright. God bless you."

Four Stages of the Soul's Matrimony with God: I am led separately to the Meditation Hall, which selfless hands have transformed into a Gurdwara, or temple. The sacred *Adi Granth* sits on a specially draped platform at one end, read aloud with great reverence by Gyani Ji. Soon the Sangat breaks out in joyous refrains, accompanied by Hari Singh on dholak drum, Ram Singh on harmonium, and another keeping time with jingling cymbals. Several hundred well wishers have already gathered by the time Master enters. He sits on the floor near the front, but respectfully to the side of the scriptures.

Gyani Ji then selects relevant verses on matrimony, while the Sangat chants: "*Palley tanday lagee, O pallay tanday lagee...*" ("Take hold of the Beloved's hem..."). As a symbol of our union, my bride and I hold the ends of a long scarf while slowly circling the *Adi Granth* four times. At each pass we bow with full hearts to the Satguru and receive his blessing. When the fourth circling is completed, the congregation showers us with rose petals.

In the *Char Lavan*, the Marriage Hymn of Guru Ramdas, the four circlings are related to the soul's stages of matrimony with the Lord, or divine Beloved, of which earthly marriage can be a reflection.

The Master stands before the assembly, now filling the entire hall. He first speaks in Hindi and then in English:[5]

> *"Marriage means the taking of a life-companion, to be with one another in weal or woe, enabling both to meet God, their ultimate*

goal. Both should live very amicably, in a loving way, as God has united them, not any earthly power. The girl was born in the East, the
man in the West, and now the unseen hand of God brings them together.
Whom God unites, let no earthly power separate. Husband and wife
should work as one soul in two bodies for a happy life in this earthly
sojourn.

"If any mistake is committed, we should seek forgiveness, as forgiveness washes everything clean. If anything comes from Above, we should
submit to His Will; then there is no conflict...And, we should be humble; 'Blessed are the poor in spirit, for theirs is the Kingdom of
Heaven'...All virtues should abide in us; virtue or Righteousness means
good thoughts, good words, good deeds. Sweet tongue, honeyed with
humility, is the remedy for all ills in life.

"Ever since leaving our Father's Home, the desires of the world have
attracted us here again and again, with the result that the world has
been imbedded in our hearts, in the subconscious reservoir of mind...
Let mind be depleted of the world and become filled with sweet
remembrance of the Lord, so much that it overflows...

"Many names have been given by Masters to denote that Power
which is One, which resides within every heart, reverberating everywhere... When you see God's Effulgent Form with your inner eye, you
will begin to hear the Music of the Spheres resounding in all creation.
This Music is the Bread of Life, and the more you come in contact with
It, the more love will overflow within you...When the state comes where
you remember God by any name, you'll be full of joy and sweetness.
For instance, when you have eaten one very sweet mango, later on
when you just hear the name of mango, you'll again feel sweetness
within you. God-man gives you contact with the sweetness of the Elixir
of Life, the Priceless Jewel within; then naturally when you say, "God!
O' God!" you'll have sweetness within you. That is the first stage of
your communion with God...

"The second stage will come when the Sound Principle or Music of
the Spheres becomes audible all twenty-four hours of the day, without
closing your ears. When you have developed the Light within, you
begin to see the same Light outside too. Then the second stage of your
soul's matrimony with God arrives.

"The third stage will come when you see the Lord within, without
and everywhere! You will see the whole world as His expression, and
you'll go into raptures! Then, while in the world, outer things won't
attract you; you'll be detached. A time will come when you will see
virtues and evils—everything—and yet you'll remain unattached. This
is when the third stage of your communion with God is developed.

"Last of all, when the fourth stage arrives, inside, outside, everywhere, you will see the Lord, and hear His Melody of the Music of the

Spheres reverberating throughout all creation. You'll sometimes be so absorbed, you'll forget your own self and all ego will go. That is the soul's permanent Matrimony with God, about which Mira Bai has said: 'Mira Bai sada sohagan, Vaar paya abhinashi. Now I have the eternal matrimony with God.' That is the highest aim in life, and what is meant by the four turnings 'round the scriptures. This is the marriage ritual amongst the Sikhs, started by Guru Ram Das under the instructions of Guru Amardas in 1637 AD, and has been the custom until now.

"First turn, second, third and last of all when you reach the final stage, we throw flowers. Then you have attained success in life. Throwing flowers means you are a good couple, you have reached the ultimate goal. And this is before both of you. You are my children! I wish you happy life here and hereafter."

Great radiance flows. The poor bride and groom...well, what can be said of them? They are intoxicated without wine and their happiness is beyond bounds.

When the marriage ceremony is completed, we move back to the porch and sit cross-legged before our Father. He leans forward in his wicker chair to offer advice:

Listening to the Wedding Discourse. Bae-ji is on the right.

"Hear me, what I have to say! You are a bridegroom now. Nobody can deny—so many witnesses. Not one, hundreds!" He looks around at the gathering, "So many responsibilities now on his shoulders." He turns back to us, "God has united you; *remain united until the last breath.* In this life, and even hereafter, let no power disunite you. Behave nobly, in such a way that people may respect you. Like a flute, be vacant from within so that the Master may make sweet music of your life. Be of service, not only to your own self, but to all others as well. This human form is the highest rung in creation, with quadrupeds, birds, and reptiles as your younger brothers and sisters. Love all, and be the source of happiness to them. And whomsoever has brought you up in life, serve them to the best you can.

"Last of all, you have to leave the world, say in a hundred years or so. Remain in contact with God so that you may be blessed here and hereafter. My wishes are always there. God Power never leaves you until He unites you with God. And this book, *Gurmat Siddhant*, I give you, although it is in Punjabi. It gives the practical side of spirituality. Do you know how to read *Gurmukhi* [Punjabi script]?"

Rattan Mala replies, "No."[6]

"Oh my Lord! Anyhow, it is a treasure of what I have found, depicting the practical life on the spiritual way, and verified by the sayings of all Masters from every religion. The theoretical part is in a separate volume, each volume comprising about one thousand pages. This will be your guiding principle in life. So I give to both of you. Take!

"This is no conversion. As a man to man! I love everyone here; those who want to perform marriage according to the Arya Samaj, Sanatan Dharma [Hindu)], Muslim, Sikh, or Christian viewpoints, may do so... So, be a man and turn out to be a perfect man in due course."

"Thank you, Master, thank you."

"What for? It's my duty."

Married Walla: The bridal room is beautifully decorated with fragrant flowers and garlands. The young bride—intelligent, beautiful, determined and innocent—is far more than her husband deserves. The next morning, he approaches the Master, uncertain of response. Master laughs heartily and gives him a big slap on the back, saying, "That's alright! That's alright! Normal married life is best."

In the frontispiece of the specially bound volume of *Gurmat Siddhant* he had given us the day before, Master wrote our names, curiously changing her spelling from Rattan Mala to *Ratana*, or simply, "Jewel." As this is Master's change, we both accept Ratana as her new name. Ram Saroop, an expert on Sant Tulsi Das and a sweet joker, says, "Sahib! Ratana wife of Tulsi Das! You very lucky sahib!"

My young bride and I entrain for Moradabad to seek her father's belated blessings. Some family friends had concocted a charade that I was actually a fair-skinned Kashmiri Sardar of the Kapoor-Khatri sub-caste, in order to lessen Bauji's stated hostility. I refuse to participate in the deception. We are apprehensive, but when I touch Bauji's feet, he weeps and embraces me as his own son. He apologizes for not having given anything. I remonstrate, "You have given the most priceless treasure of all—your own daughter, whom I have sworn to honor, protect, and love—for always!"

Bauji then confides, "One year ago, I had a dream that one in your form would carry Rattan off to *Amrika* [America]!"

After Moradabad, we travel to the beautiful Taj Mahal.

Mum and Dad telegram their

Bride and Groom—after the wedding.

blessings from Canada, accepting their new daughter-in-law with love, and the Golden Lotus staff send hearty felicitations, curious to see the bride and curious to know if the sadhu has changed.

---

1. Actually, she had her M.A. in English Literature, a B.A. in Psychology, and a B.A. in Sanskrit from Agra University.

2. *Rattan Mala* translates as "Necklace of Jewels."

3. *feringhi*—foreigner.

4. We have often speculated about this tape-recorded remark when the Master hinted at my being my great-grandfather. He repeated it once again on the following day.

5. The Master's discourse has been lightly abridged.

6. We both learned to read and write Gurmukhi, albeit imperfectly.

42

Two weeks after the wedding, a huge booksellers' convention took place on the Ram Leela grounds of Delhi. The Master invited us to accompany him there to see/participate in his progressive land-based project for change: *Manav Kendra*. *Manav* means humanity, and *Kendra*, home. Pictures and words spelled out his vision: nature and land service—through sustainable farming; animal service—treating animals humanely; service to humanity—providing homes for the aged and indigent; education—ethically-oriented schools for children; free medical treatment using a variety of allopathic, homeopathic and ayurvedic systems to alleviate suffering; and universal library on spirituality and the world's religions, to help lift the veil of ignorance and superstition from the mind of man. The Kendra would be a teaching vehicle for ethics, service, love for all, and spirituality. Manav Kendra's foundations would be the cultivation of higher consciousness through effective spiritual practice.

For the previous two decades, Sant Kirpal Singh had worked unceasingly to bring the heads of various religions and spiritual groups together to understand their commonalties and lessen sectarian strife. In the early fifties, the Jain sadhu Muni Shushil Kumar founded the World Fellowship of Religions (WFR). Sant Kirpal Singh Ji was nominated and unanimously elected by all religious heads from dozens of countries as its president, year after year. As such, he presided over four major world conferences. While much progress was made in gathering religious heads together, he noticed the tendency among the leaders "to erect water-tight compartments of their own faiths."

> *Good work has been done through the World Fellowship of Religions. Now men can mix with others—but one danger is ahead. Leaders of the World Fellowship of Religions are wanting to strengthen their own formations, in spite of the fact that the inner way is the same for all... To combat the danger of religious chauvinism, it was thought necessary to start the work of regeneration from the roots. Man-making must take precedence. This can only be done by inculcating in people... the humanistic idea of unselfish love and selfless service, with special emphasis on man-service, land-service and animal-service (animals being our younger brothers and sisters in God). This idea took concrete shape in 1969 with the decision to set up... Manav Kendras.[1]*

In the midst of the teeming book bazaar, the artistic Kendra booth displayed the Master's many written works in more than a dozen languages, plus many volumes on world religions, yoga, mysticism, Persian poetry, and spirituality. While browsing through, I was surprised and delighted to find several rare volumes from the Master's personal library. I pulled out an old tome on esotericism, and as

I opened it, some folded papers slipped out and fell to the ground. When I picked them up, I soon realized their significance. These were original hand-written letters from Dr. Julian Johnson (a former missionary and surgeon who became a devoted initiate of Baba Sawan Singh) to Kirpal Singh, and two letters from Kirpal Singh, dating back to the 1930's dealing specifically with Dr. Johnson's major literary work, *Path of the Masters*. They revealed Johnson's great esteem for Kirpal Singh, his fellow-deciple, and the in-depth involvement the latter had in the preparation of the *Path of the Masters* manuscript. At Kirpal's insistence Dr. Johnson made numerous changes, toning down his criticism of various world religions, however, some missionary zeal remained. The letters contained numerous margin notes in the Master's pen.

Dr. Zakir Hussain, the President of India, dropped by the Manav Kendra display. The Master, who was on close terms with the President, introduced me and we shook hands. We discussed Islamic mysticism and Sufism in some depth. The fact that Dr. Hussain, a Muslim, was President is credit to the broad-mindedness of predominantly Hindu India.

Master explained to Dr. Hussain that uplift of the human spirit was the focus of Manav Kendra, and it would not be the exclusive territory of Ruhani Satsang, Sawan Ashram, or any other organization, It was to be truly accessible to all. (After the bookseller's fair was over, the Master worked ceaselessly to actualize the inspired concept and established Manav Kendra on a large acreage in the picturesque Himalayan foothills of Dehra Dun).

Spirituality, Future's Only Hope:
Independent India's first Prime Minister, Jawaharlal Nehru, was an avowed agnostic most of his life, and as a secularist, was remarkably free from religious and racial prejudice. Nehru became recognized as one of the twentieth century's great political leaders, men of letters, statesmen, and humanists. He was singularly dedicated to the welfare of his country, and had little time for personal religious or spiritual considerations. Towards the end of his illustrious career, however, Nehru met privately with Sant Kirpal Singh on several occasions, seeking his counsel. After one of their last meetings, Nehru thoughtfully remarked to all within earshot. "Spirituality is the only hope for the world."

I asked Maharaj Ji, "Did Pundit Nehru ever receive initiation from you?" Looking at me with a slight smile, he enigmatically replied, "Yes... we have talked about these things, you see."

Nehru's sister, Vijaya Lakshmi, also deeply revered the Master, as did his daughter Indira Gandhi, who became India's first woman Prime Minister.

Around the time of our wedding, the Indian Government gave an unusual recognition of Sant Kirpal Singh's contribution to the nation and the world at large, inviting him to an all-political party outdoor rally. As he addressed the huge throng, I was struck by two keynotes, which I jotted into my journal.

While encouraging citizens of the world's largest democracy to exercise their voting franchise, he urged all to evaluate the ethical character, honesty and service record of the candidates, and vote on that basis—not not along party, caste, race, or religious lines.

"In ancient times," he said, "rulers sought the guidance of Saints and Sages whenever their nations were faced with grave crisis. Because political ambition or desire for personal gain does not sway the angle of vision of the wise, they are often able to intermediate and bring peace to warring factions. Politicians can affect the minds of the people but not their hearts," the Master declared. "The heart is the domain of the Saints."

The Masters draw no distinction between initiate and non-initiate, saint or sinner, 'high' and 'low.' Their message calls for a spiritual revolution and transformation within each individual.

After nearly six months in India, my thoughts began to turn towards Vancouver—and a much neglected restaurant. I didn't have enough money for my bride's airfare, but kept quiet about it. The Master, however, divined the situation and insisted on arranging her plane fare (subsequently repaid).

Obtaining passport, ticketing, exit visa, clean bill of health and immigration approval is a lengthy process under the best of circumstances. For an Indian citizen in those days, this was a monumental challenge. As my ticket could not be changed, I dreaded the probability of leaving my young bride behind. She and I raced through Delhi—first to the passport office. When we arrived at the huge government complex, anxiety mounted at the sight of long, slow moving queues. We were delighted and grateful to see Darshan Singh, the Master's son, walking out from an adjoining room. He led us into his office and called for chai and biscuits. Darshan happened to be one of the highest-ranking civil servants in the Indian government, but he was the essence of self-abnegation—a center of calm in the midst of this hectic beehive. Somewhere between the third biscuit and the second cup of chai, all of Ratana's paperwork was done. We tried to thank Darshan, but he abnegated, "It is all the beloved Master's doing, brother and sister!" By scooter, we dashed over to the Canadian Embassy, where we encountered more long line-ups. Ratana's visa was the last approved that day, and I had to leave India that night—with or without my bride.

A Master is a human father-teacher, and simultaneously above and behind the stage, pulling many invisible strings with impeccable timing. We were blessed and sent off to our new life together in the West.

---

1. *Portrait of Perfection: A Pictorial Biography of Kirpal Singh.*(Bowling Green Virginia/Delhi India: Sawan Kirpal Publications, 1981), p. 168.

43

My sari-clad bride was welcomed with showers of rose petals at the Vancouver airport, then embraced by Mum and Dad, the Nagras, and my Golden Lotus co-workers. We settled into a little room above the restaurant, sharing a bathroom with fourteen others. It took quite some time for Ratana to adjust to life in the West, as she deeply missed her family, friends, and the rich traditions of India. We worked an average of twelve to sixteen hours a day to get the restaurant firmly established. Ratana and the rest of the workers earned .75 per hour. As owner-manager I made $1.00. Room and board were free for all.

A tavern for divine grace: We soon received a personal letter from the Master, which offered profound inspiration and guidance in our enterprise:

> *You should be fair yet firm for the dear ones working with you... If all of you will work in a team spirit with renewed zeal and enthusiasm there is no reason why the business should not flourish and earn rich dividends...Try to manage the affairs in such a manner that everybody is kept cheerfully busy with proper work for which he or she is best suited. This will prove very much helpful for maintaining their morale high...I wish that your restaurant should serve as a tavern for divine grace...when every visitor should carry a pinch of divine fragrance by your kind, courteous and generous behavior... — May 27, 1969*

In three months we had saved $1,000 to make a down payment on a little two-bedroom house with a garden. Ratana was already pregnant with our first child, and we had had our fill of communal living.

Two more letters came in which Master wanted to set me straight:

> *One thing of great importance, which I would like to stress, is that you must not meddle with the affairs of others directly or indirectly... Everybody has a right to seek improvement in his or her own chosen manner, and should never be interfered with unless they seek your personal guidance or assistance...Never look on the faults or shortcomings of others nor hear any idle gossip or censure...*
>
> *I am sorry to say that I have received letters...stating that...you are too dictatorial and show little regard for the suggestions of others.*

How my ego needed trimming! How abysmal, my people skills! I had spent too many years as a virtual ascetic. His last letter left me feeling despondent and unappreciated for all the work I thought I had done. I contemplated a move to a new city. While repenting thus, I felt a glowing presence in the living room. Master's astral form appeared out of the very air, solidified and embraced me. All was forgiven in love! He seemed to pass or absorb into my entire body until he disappeared. Despondency changed to delirious joy.

In his next letter of December 10, he said,

> *The love of the Master... sometimes has to take the form of a mild reproof for the child's own good. It was a mark of his grace and love for you that the Master's form appeared before you when you shed tears in remembrance. I am pleased that you are continuing as group leader...and wish for you to forget what has happened in the past.*

Considerable agitation began among the more left-leaning workers to turn the Golden Lotus into a commune. After a lot of soul-searching, we decided to make a clean break, and sold the restaurant to the group for a paltry $3,000, wishing them all success. Ironically, the commune became so unwieldy (too many chiefs), that it was again privatized by those who had earlier vehemently clamoured for the co-op. Soon after, the Golden Lotus went into hibernation. On the bright side, several of my former Lotus compatriots went on to found successful enterprises of their own.

I opened a little store, selling Indian bedspreads, clothing, classical musical instruments, and healthy and organic foods. Food soon edged out the other wares. It became obvious that my destined vocation was connected to organic foods. and wholistic living

Into our lives came a beautiful baby girl. During the miracle of birth, while repeating simran aloud, my wife received the vision of Sawan and Kirpal in blazing light. Master telegramed his congratulations and in answer to our request, bestowed a beautiful name/reminder: "You may name the baby *Shanti*."

Shanti is the ancient Sanskrit word for "peace."

*Babies are
bits of star-dust
blown from the
hand of God.*[1]

Om Shanti!

---

1. Larry Barretto

44

*Try not to become a man of success but rather
try to be a man of value.—Albert Einstein*

By the late sixties, Western society had traded in its wholesome heritage for refined junk foods, preservatives, and additives. The use of highly toxic pesticides, herbicides, and synthetic fertilizers in modern agriculture was widespread, dangerous, and non-sustainable. The winds of change began blowing fresh ideas into the collective mind as nutritional research demonstrated time and again the vital link between poor diet and degenerative disease. Rachel Carson's *Silent Spring* first alerted the scientific and lay communities about the disastrous effects of agricultural chemicals on the environment, as well as a precipitous and related rise in the rates of cancer and other ailments in humans and animals. Research by others strongly corroborated her findings.

During this time and into the early seventies, a handful of socially-conscious individuals in various parts of the continent pioneered the first large natural foods stores (as distinguished from small "health food" stores, which focused mostly on supplements and herbs). Forging alliances with organic farmers, these young radicals developed and popularized difficult or otherwise impossible-to-find unadulterated organic foods and fresh organic produce, whole-grain breads and cereals, yogurt, sprouts, soyfoods, herbs, fresh juices, vegetarian entrees, natural supplements, and hundreds of other products which ultimately improved the health and eating habits of the Western world.

At the forefront of the early organic foods trailblazers were Robert Rodale of *Organic Gardening*; Paul Keene, venerable founder of Walnut Acres, who established a large organic farm and mail-order business in Pennsylvania in the 1930's; Fred Rohe of New Age Natural Foods in San Francisco; Michio Kushi and Paul Hawken of Erewhon, Boston; Bob Kennedy of Chico-San, California; Frank Ford of Arrowhead Mills; and LifeStream. My Dad's early experiments in organic farming have already been mentioned in Chapter 1.[1]

On January 1, 1971, it was my privilege to open LifeStream, Canada's first large natural foods store. It was Dad who suggested the name. Free fresh carrot juice drew in crowds; an electric-powered 20" stone-buhr mill, visible through a window from the street, ground tons of fresh whole-grain flour every day; alfalfa sprouts were grown nearby; fresh nut butters were roasted and milled to order; natural candy bars and cookies; egg-free cakes and muffins; pies, granola, bulk foods, and wholesome breads were baked and sold. These were all firsts in Canada.

Inspiration came from such diverse sources as: Hippocrates: "Let food be your medicine and medicine be your food." Genesis: "Lo' I have given you every herb bearing seed which is upon the face of the earth, and the milk of animals that feedeth on it; to you it shall be for meat." *Back to Eden*, a book on self-healing using inexpensive natural herbs and diet. Like the Golden Lotus, Lifestream manifested at the right time and place.

Teachers brought classes of school children on tours to see how wholesome foods were made. The store became so busy that it was often difficult to wade through the crowds of shoppers and hangers-on. On impulse, I gave half the business to my friend, who became a working partner. Sales doubled every year for seven years, and the business quickly branched out into wholesale distribution. Another partner joined, and we three became equals; I was president.

A separate small vegetarian restaurant in the rear of the large store was started by Victor, another one of God's originals—a gifted pianist and carpenter who built and slept in a coffin, "To remind me that I have to leave the body someday!" Victor couldn't take the rigors of being a businessman, and convinced me to buy his no-profit, no-loss cafe. Ratana ran it like a tight little ship, and that's when I began to discover how astute she was. Her cafe which did only 15% of the big store's volume, soon outperformed it in terms of profits, underscoring the Japanese proverb: "Grow a small garden well."

The natural foods revolution was a significant part of an emerging societal paradigm specific to the Americas and Europe. The people, especially the younger generation, wanted and demanded better quality and more wholesome alternatives to mass-produced supermarket choices. People were getting sick and diseased in large numbers—not by starvation, but by over-consumption of meat and other unhealthy foods. The time for change had come. But what was the power, or the hidden hand behind this new paradigm, which included a growing and widely spread belief in non-sectarian spirituality and global awareness? I would posit that it is nothing less than the hidden workings of the Adepts, who function as conscious co-workers of the divine.

Far apart from the development of LifeStream in Canada—admittedly a worldly enterprise, the Master's non-commercial, spiritual and charitable work was growing throughout the world. In Vancouver, large numbers of young people came to our discourses and meditations at the YWCA—sometimes more than 150. The community was strong but undisciplined; some had problems staying drug-free. The Master had been clear about my responsibility not to meddle and judge, but to exercise both detachment and compassion when my brothers and sisters slipped or deviated, or when their negativity was directed at me. It was a difficult line to walk. There were, however, great rewards whenever someone was raised up and their life transformed, which happened with ever-increasing frequency.

I would like to reiterate that the path of the Masters was and is not a cult. The Master made it very clear that he wished his students to be part of, and meaningfully contribute to society; to not change their outer religion; to get a good education and work diligently; to be ethical, honest and kind; and maintain loving relations with one's parents, family and neighbors—while enjoying the benefits of meditation on the inner Light and Sound-current. The Masters never interfere with anyone's freedom to choose.

Bauji passes—from critic to devotee to freedom: In 1971, Ratana and one-year-old Shanti visited India. Bauji—her father had become terminally ill with tuberculosis and was slipping fast. Prior to our wedding, he had vehemently opposed the Master, and even stamped his foot on his picture (Bauji was an orthodox Hindu), but his hostility gradually softened and his vision expanded. Bauji had five daughters and desperately wanted a son to carry on the Bagga name, but every time a male child was born, he died. His prayers to the gods and goddesses were in vain. One night he had a beautiful dream in which Master Kirpal appeared and presented him a basket of fruit. His wife then conceived and a son was born. From that moment on, Bauji began to develop faith. On his deathbed, family members gathered close around and he humbly asked for their forgiveness. His following testimony surprised everyone:

"For some time I have been thinking of going to Delhi to take Naam from Maharaj Ji, but now that is not possible. Hazur and Maharaj Ji have now appeared within; they have come for me. They tell me I must go with them." Bauji paused, blessing his family with his eyes, and repeated aloud his favorite name of God, "*Ram, R..a..m, R..a..a..m..m...*" and was gone. At the moment of Ratana's personal grief, her tearful presence manifested in far-away Vancouver while I was driving to work. Even her sobs were audible in the car. Not for nothing is it said that *"heart-strings play in unison."*

---

1. By 1999, only a few of the founders of these visionary companies still head them, as pioneers usually catch the arrows first. From several thousand acres farmed organically in North America in the sixties, more than 1,500,000 acres are currently committed to sustainable agriculture—a number which continues to grow rapidly. In Europe, the growth is similar. The move to sustainable farming and ecological management is essential for the future of the planet. Within an average of four years, organic farming yeilds are comparable, if not superior to conventional agri-chemical methods. Ref: Rodale Institute; Organic Trade Association (OTA): www.ota.org

In 1972, Sant Kirpal Singh blessed Vancouver on his third world tour—which included Europe, North America, Mexico, and South America. Before his arrival in Vancouver, Ratana and I witnessed his historic tour stops in Boston, New Hampshire, Vermont, and Montreal.

The True Language: Quebec was undergoing strife over French/English language issues. Addressing a large Montreal audience, Kirpal Singh said,

> *"I am glad you have love for your France and your French language. I beseech you to have love for your Home, the language of which is love. God is love. Love is innate in our soul, because we are of the same essence as that of God. And the way back to God is also through love...So speak in love, think of love, let all your affairs be saturated with love...No language is sacred, no language is not sacred. All are sacred in which you speak of love."*

Back in the lobby, outside the elevator, Master stopped to talk to several visitors, his back to me. On the shoulder of his black coat I espied a loose hair, a beautiful long white beard hair with seven perfectly formed curves. My only thought was to snatch it without being seen. I waited and waited, heart pounding, excited, fearful. Would he notice? Would I get caught? Suddenly my hand shot up and plucked its' treasure!

Vancouver Arrival: Hundreds jammed the airport, waiting to catch a glimpse of the Param Sant. In their wisdom, Canada Customs officials held up the Master for over an hour, despite his physical age and impeccable international credentials. When his white turban was finally spied moving through the crowded terminal, word spread like wildfire. There was jubilation and weeping. When the authorities and other passengers asked and were told that a great spiritual Master was arriving, all clustered around, wanting to see him, adding to the congestion. When he passed through the glass doors, his hands were joined together and his brilliant eyes swept the crowd. The airport suddenly became silent, holy as a cathedral, and supercharged.

At his hotel suite, a reporter from *The Sun* newspaper conducted an extensive interview, but the reporter became so uplifted in the Master's presence he forgot himself, and after a while gave up writing altogether. The others who had packed the room were thrilled to hear his illuminating responses to a wide variety of questions or just to sit and watch. My mother who was present was reduced to tears. At one point I asked, "Mum, can you follow Master's answers?" With eyes overflowing, she just smiled at me and cried some more, following on a level more sublime than words. Dad, on the other hand, was fidgety and wanted to leave. At the conclusion of the interview (which was never printed), both parents stood up to leave. As the Master passed by, mum grasped his hands and held them for a while, thanking him for all he had done for her son. "That's alright. God bless you. God bless you," he replied, looking into both parent's eyes. When she released her grip, he turned and went to the kitchen.

I felt a twinge of regret that their meeting had been so brief. As they moved-out the door, Harcharan ran from the kitchen, saying, "Master sends this to your dear mother and father as parshad!" It was a gift of an apple and an orange. That evening on the ferry back to Victoria, Dad, an apple connoisseur, carefully peeled his fruit and slowly ate it, slice by slice. He commented, "You know, that was the best apple I have ever eaten in my life." He was thoughtful for a long time, then added, "It must have been because the Master blessed it."

Kirpal Singh's first public talk was given in the Kitsilano High School auditorium, which proved insufficient to hold the more than one thousand who had come, including the mayor of the city. The next day, the venue shifted to the larger Unity Church on Oak Street. Every seat was filled, and several hundred sat on the floor, in the aisles and up on the stage. There was no room to move, and fire regulations were ignored. I drove the Master to the church, and we were running late. "Master's here!" someone shouted. Some whom I knew and many others, surged forward, just to be near, to touch the sleeve of his coat, to catch his eye. In this regard, there was no difference between East and West.

Upon his entering the crowded hall, all rose spontaneously from their seats, returning his silent *namaste*. The silence was a stunning teaching in itself. He slowly glided through corridors of happy, wonder-stricken, tear-filled, and curious faces; eyes wordlessly searching eyes, greeting, smashing conceptions and misconceptions with every glance. His discourse was widely published.

Five acres of boggy, forested land twenty-five miles from Vancouver were donated for the purposes of developing an ashram. The Master stated carefully: "It is easy to start ashrams, *but difficult to **maintain** them.*" Although it had been raining for days, several hours before his visit to the site, the sun broke out and warmed the atmosphere. Once there, he put more than three hundred into meditation for about half an hour, and then, to everyone's delight, chucked apples to every person, laughing as they clamored for the blessed fruit.

During one of the question-and-answer sessions, a local representative of a popular meditation organization stood and asked, "Kirpal Singh, what do you think of (teacher) and (the meditation practice)?" There was a lot of attention, because maybe half the people here had already tried this technique. Master Kirpal replied, "(____) is a very good psychologist, but not a Master of the inner way of spirituality. I would say that he has failed to demonstrate the experience of the Self and the Overself."

After this two-hour session, the Master was about to enter the car. I held the door when he turned to Ratana: "Aren't you going to invite me to your home?" We hadn't, due to his whirlwind schedule, but had been secretly wishing. Ratana quickly replied, "It is your home, Maharaj Ji!" At his command, we detoured to our little two-bedroom house. Walking into the kitchen, he noticed his picture on the wall and asked, "Does he eat?" Ratana replied, "Yes, Maharaj Ji, he is the Giver." He just chuckled. We sat before him upon the new Indian rug we had just bought, in the remote possibility of his visit. He was silent, savoring the atmosphere. After a few minutes, he commented, "That home is beautiful wherein the love of God abides."

Being a relatively new father, I asked, "I was wondering how to best bring up children in the West." He replied, "Children are spoiled first in the home, in the schools, and then in the streets. If you want to control your children, see who their friends are. Don't let them run wild in the streets. As parents, set the best example in your own home. See to their friends."

"Master, I was wondering about the business, if we should try to limit its growth." He drilled me with a puzzling glare, "Why? It will provide more opportunities for more people!"

I asked, "But what about the responsibilities? I feel the burden weighing heavily on me." With a chuckle he replied, "Then distribute your responsibilities!" I felt that burden lift and thereafter never looked back, nor felt any further guilt about building a successful business.

Initiation: On November 12, two hundred and twenty-two people assembled in the Unity Church for initiation, the largest number at any stop on his North American tour. Master sat on the dais and seemed displeased. "Weed out!" he said to me, but I didn't know what he meant, why, or how. Finally, he tapped the microphone and asked, "Who here is the follower of another Master?" Some rustling took place in the audience. Finally a young woman stood and walked up to the dais. He asked her, "Who is your Master?" She replied, "Lama Kalu Rimpoche" (a renowned Tibetan Buddhist teacher).

"Why have you come?" "To have your blessing." The Master politely turned her away. Apparently there was some reason he could not initiate this soul. The very second the big doors boomed shut, initiation commenced.

A devout Quaker from Bellingham, who had received a very good initiation experience, later approached me in the hallway: "Will you please tell Kirpal Singh that I would like him to take back the initiation. I feel that it may be in conflict with my concept of the Christian faith." I listened incredulously, but before I had a chance to respond, the Master emerged from his room down the hall! I gingerly conveyed to him the Quaker woman's message.

He looked at me with a mixture of great authority and compassion. "You tell her," he said, "that the Christ Power, God Power, or Master Power has taken possession of her life and will never leave her! She may leave the Master but *Master will never leave her.*"

And the Enlightened Shall Reign:

After Sant Kirpal Singh left Vancouver, he spread his message and grace to thousands in California, Texas, and Florida. When in Dallas, I invited my Texan friend Frank Ford to meet him. Frank was a large-scale organic farmer, and as the founder of Arrowhead Mills, was a true pioneer of the natural food movement; he was also a born-again Christian and a devoted family man. After the public discourse, Frank and I found ourselves alone with the Master in his hotel suite. "So glad to meet you!" Master thrust forward his hand in Western greeting. By way of introduction, I mentioned that Frank had run for Texas Senator against the former American President, Lyndon Johnson, but, disillusioned with politics, Frank turned to farming in harmony with nature. Kirpal Singh focused full interest on Frank and stated, "To grow a blade of grass is more than a patriot's work!"

We moved to the bedroom, where the Master sat cross-legged on the bed while Frank and I sat nearby on chairs.

Frank then leaned forward and sincerely asked in his Texan way: "Kirpal Singh, sir, I certainly recognize and appreciate the great spiritual work you are doing which is helping so many people throughout the world. Sir, I was wondering; do you consider that the great work which you are doing, and the work which I and others are doing, witnessing for Christ and healing the land with natural farming, will help to bring about the New Age?... a rebirth of Man's consciousness to a more spiritual life?"

Master pushed back his turban a little and stroked his long white beard. A few moments of pregnant silence followed; the atmosphere around and flowing out of him was practically dancing with Light. "I tell you," he said, "the day will come when the *Khalsa*, not necessarily those who have the outer form of *Khalsa*, but those in whom the Light of God is fully effulgent, shall reign over the world!"[1]

I didn't quite catch or believe what I heard, so I asked, "Master, they shall *what* over the world?" He spelled it out so there could be no room for equivocation: ***"R.E.I.G.N. Reign over the world!"***

---

1. The origin of the idea of the *Khalsa* has been dealt with in chapter 21, *"The Ancient Legacy."* *Khalsa* literally translates as "pure, effulgent, without stain or blemish."

Master Kirpal on his '72 World Tour

45

I behold a myriad glittering stars;
deliver me from their beauty, O Maker,
take me to the strength of suns.

February 1, 1973: In the midst of labor pangs, Ratana's mind turns inward with great focus, and she once again beholds the Master's radiant vision. While calling on God's Name, she gives birth to our second daughter, the bright-eyed Gurdeep *[Lamp of the Lord]*. In October, we again pilgrimage to India.

Diary, October 18: I arrive at Pathankot by train, most eager to see Father again (Ratana, Shanti and baby Gurdeep stay with family in Delhi for now). The picturesque Pathankot ashram sits by the side of a river, surrounded by wooded foothills, beyond which are the mountains of Kashmir. I proceed straight to a freshly white-washed columned building. Under its porch sits the Master, a large retinue of Indians and Westerners at his feet. I secretly pray for inner receptivity. A few minutes after greeting, I settle amongst the crowd. Any open seams between the present and our last meeting are soon sealed. Master is jolly; questions are invited and I ask, "Is there an ebb and flow to Grace?" *Silence.* His attention is fully on me. I continue, "Spring, summer, autumn, or winter? Sometimes grace overflows, and at other times it's difficult to become receptive to even a tiny drop."

He replies indirectly, "The physical presence of the Master has some effect... the radiation is very strong there. Others at a distance can have the same benefit when they develop receptivity. Even those who are not very receptive, can become so. If stones are put near water, they *become* cold, you see."

Increasingly intoxicated by his proximity, I boldly ask, "How can stones *become* the water?"

His eyes understand my craziness and its cause. He replies, twinkling, "Yes... slowly they are worn down." Long pause. Suddenly he asks, *"Why become a stone?"* The Master-power engulfs me.

This tour proceeds southwestward from Pathankot through many towns and villages of this region of Punjab. At every stop, the Master faces throngs of seekers. The demands on him are enormous. In one place, not wanting to be separated, I literally walk in his footsteps as large crowds swarm in. Suddenly turning, he looks me in the eye and finishes the answer to my question of the 18th: **"Grace is always there, but sometimes it gushes forth!"** Once again I am awestruck by his timing and prescience.

During a discourse in Dasua, a farming town, I am especially moved by just two lines from his comprehensive, two-hour discourse:

> *"As a child has come out of the mother, so our individual soul was born out of God, who is love. If the love of God becomes the ruling passion of our life, then that will affect the heart of God."*

The next morning, Master is racked with a terrible cough. While coughing, he puts everyone into meditation, and asks us to sit without moving. He continues to clear his throat (near the microphone) as he sits before the silent congregation. I have a bottle of homeopathic cough remedy in my pocket and while sitting with closed eyes, struggle between the compassionate urge to offer it, and the desire to follow his instructions to meditate. It is a quandary. After some indecision, I get up and hand Master the medicine. To my surprise he shakes out a handful of the tiny pills and swallows them, thanks me and returns the half-full bottle as parshad. His coughing stops. When I return to an abbreviated meditation, inner grace is sudden and profound. It was the right action, after all.

Is it the Bulb, or the Light?

Later in the day, an American asks, "You have said that when we meditate, we are not supposed to concentrate on your physical form. Is that right? We're supposed to concentrate on the Light?"

"When you see the bulb (Master points to an electric light) from which light is coming, do you see light or the glass over it? What attracts you? *Light*, I think. Not the glass."

47

Mansarovar, Manav Kendra

Kendra Diary With a large contingent of visitors from many countries, my family and I travel all day by bus over the bumpy, chaotic road from Delhi. We arrive after nightfall in the Shivalik hills, a few miles south of Rajpur. In the chill morning, I sit on a treed knoll overlooking Manav Kendra. Lush flower gardens, mango trees and terraces frame a perfect oval pool, 350 feet long by 200 feet wide—the *Mansarovar*. Like some beautiful turquoise eye opening to another world, the Mansarovar reflects pure blue sky overhead—an invitation to contemplation. This pond replicates the shape of the inner Mansarovar of the third grand spiritual region, where soul is distilled from mind.

The Master's wide, columned, white residence is set back from the pool, approached by low terraces and a broad stairway. Several huge, lush trees, recipients of his protection, pass through the house which has been built around them. To the left stands a four-story water-tower; to the right, a freehospital and dispensary; behind that is a school for poor children; next to it a home for the aged and indigent; langar and visitor's residence. Here and there are neatly tended vegetable and flower gardens, a fruit-tree nursery, inter-religious library, cows, grain fields, nightingales, wild parrots, sparrows, cicadas—clean, orderly, spacious, harmonious. In the distance are the foothills, foot-steps of the gods.

This land was acquired four years earlier when it was nothing but arid bush and a few trees.

At the time Manav Kendra was being constructed all the experts were searching for a spring to supply water for the project. The Dehra Dun Valley is faced with a great shortage of water, and after much research it came to the Master's notice that the engineers were unable to locate any spring. Then Master got up and requested the engineers to try digging at a certain spot. This spot is believed to be the one in which Guru Gobind Singh's horse became stuck three hundred years ago. Upon digging, water was found and it seemed to hold great potential for a powerful source. All the drilling machines were set, and the digging began. However, the spring was not supplying enough water. The work continued but all efforts to draw the water out with the intensity needed seemed of no avail. Again it was brought to the Master's notice that they were not succeeding. Master came to the spot where the digging was going on and asked everyone to sit in meditation for half an hour. Then the engineers once more attempted to draw the water out. The water came up, but still it was not strong enough. When everyone was at the point of giving up, the Master took out one cupful of water and drank it. To the relief of all, the water then started to gush from the spring with great force. The supply was enough to not only fill the Mansarovar and meet the needs of the Kendra, but also to help the surrounding area whenever it was faced with shortages.[1]

The Mansarovar's waters are calm, mirroring the white stone rim, shrubbery and flowers, palm, neem, cyrpress and banyan trees, mountains, and surrounding graceful buildings. When mind becomes as clear and still as the Mansarovar, unrippled by thought-pebbles and wind, thus will it reflect the Self, clear and bright.

The Guru Gobind Singh Tree: On the Kendra is a magnificent ancient tree. From its massive trunk emerge five different varieties of trees. Three hundred years ago, the Tenth Guru tied his horse to this very tree and camped under it's branches. He prophesied that one day a great Saint would establish a spiritual community at this beautiful spot.

Manav Kendra was built with tremendous effort and selfless service. The Master guided the work day and night, as thousands toiled to bring the noble project to fruition without the assistance of heavy machinery. He told the visiting Dr. Giri, President of India, "God is my banker, and I'm spending like anything!"

November 17: Master's health has been very poor of late. His body is undergoing pains in the back and legs. Many of us have come to the understanding that he is vicariously working off our karmic debts. His suffering mysteriously disappears, or lessens enough that it does not interfere whenever he is called upon to conduct satsang or provide succor to the endless stream of humanity at his door. After informal satsang tonight, I sit alone under the Gobind Tree, praying to the Master-power to allow me the privilege of sharing, and thus lessening his pain. As if in answer, shooting, fiery pains develop in my back and legs. The suffering becomes unbearable! After several hours, I gaspingly beg the Inner Power to take it back, and it is graciously, and instantaneously lifted. Ordinary humans are incapable of shouldering such a burden as his.

I stagger over to his residence, not knowing if I can get in. Ganga Ram, one of the sevadars, asks if I know how to give massage. I say, "A little." The next thing I knew I am gently pushed into his bedroom where Master is working on correspondence. Despite my bashfulness, I am impelled to stand behind him, and begin massaging his back and shoulders. I am struck by the sight of two small loose hairs and a fleck of lint on the lapel of his black coat, exactly as in an earlier dream. When I mention it Maharaj Ji comments, *"It is better to massage the Master in dream."* As I continue massaging, a note of tragedy is struck when he comments, ***"It is time to exchange these limbs for new ones."***

I involuntarily exclaim, **"No!** Master!" Heart is writhing. Tai Ji, on hearing me, looks up and asks in Punjabi *"Ki gal hai, Maharaj Ji?"* ["What is the matter?"] He translates what he just said to me. Tai Ji begins to remonstrate vociferously, "Maharaj Ji, you cannot go! You mustn't talk like that! Who will look after us? You mustn't go!" He keeps silent.

In the morning, we learn that the raging war between Israel and her neighbors is over. The likelihood of the world becoming incinerated by nuclear holocaust over Israel has been frighteningly real, and the Master has been monitoring it daily. This morning, his countenance is the picture of health and joviality, in sharp contrast to the night before. With a sigh of relief he says, "Thank God it is over." He would never take credit for such an intervention.

Massage and medicine seem to afford his body some relief, but it is the opinion of the writer and others that he accepts treatment not for himself, but for blessing the ministrants. By shifting their attention, Masters can turn pain off and on at will, but some payment is exacted, exchange for the tremendous burdens they willingly shoulder. These are the karmas of the initiates and of others, for the Masters sometimes compassionately intervene to prevent humanity from destroying itself, if not the planet. The *Power* which sustains and keeps the world intact, also works through the Saints to bring about necessary change. That is why it is acceptable to pray to God in the form of a Godman, and why such prayers bear abundant fruit. Baba Sawan Singh used to say that a disciple lives by prayer.

Four year old Shanti boldly approaches the Master and demands parshad as though it is her right. He says "How about *phul* (flower) parshad?" Flowers are brought and given, first to the girls, then everyone else. After shooing away the local sevadars, Master warns us not to give them any presents or tips.

He emphasizes the need for *selfless service*, and that gifts will spoil them and their seva. He also alludes to Jesus having lived in India, lending substance to ancient legends and records existing in Kashmir and Ladakh.

November 19, back in Delhi: As Master passes through the crowd, he turns to baby Gurdeep cradled in her mother's arms. He looks into her eyes and she looks into his, beaming and exulting as he pats her little brown cheek. In Hindi, he says, *"Asi purani yaar,"* [We are old friends]. Then, turning to the crowd, he asks, "Wouldn't you like to be like this?"

Diary, November 25, 1973: Question and answer session:
   Q. "Master, sometimes when sitting in bhajan I become so absorbed in the Abstract Sound, my body becomes numb and falls over, and I cannot move it for some time."
   M. "You don't feel numbness when you are absorbed?"
   Q. "No. But the body just falls over and I can't move."
   "That is but natural. When you come down, come slowly... The Power within will send you back. He's watching your progress..."
   Again, he asks me, "Do you want to die in India?" And he chuckles, his private joke.

December 10, 1973: One of the senior sevadars tells me I am to accompany the Master in his car to Ajmeer, Bombay and Baroda to serve as masseur, whenever necessary. For the next twelve hours continuously I dwell on this seva in my mind as we make the long drive from Delhi. However, to my chagrin this duty is transferred to Master's simple servant, Hayat, with the words, "Let Hayat. He knows better." The Saint's holy body tosses in pain, but no complaint passes his lips. He does not rest, day or night. He knows best. Perhaps some distance is better. Despite the distance, inwardly he shows many wonderous things.
   Tonight, in satsang at the home of Kartar Chand—*Ajmeer-walle,* so much spiritual Light emanates from the locus of the Master's form, washing over the sangat, I find its ecstacy almost unbearable. While sitting motionless in the gathering, soul flutters across the no-space between us, to dash against, and be enveloped by the emanating Flame. As Master's temporal form wears away with age, the divine in him becomes more palpably transparent and luminous.

> *The moth was speechless, and the*
> *Flame was silent,*
> *In the entire assembly there were*
> *Only two who shared this secret.*[2]

After being put off a number of times, I finally get an opportunity to query him about the ashram project back in Canada, and of the non-Satsangi architect who offered his services for the project. He strongly replies, "Satsangi, or no satsangi! I tell you, **all** are satsangis! Satsangis have just been put on the way, that's all. The same God Power operates in all. I tell you, many of those who are not initiated behave better than so-called satsangis." Whenever my limited mind begins differentiating between the initiated and the non-initiated, this enlightening reply comes to my rescue.

December 24: Several South Africans are about to depart, and are understandably sad. One asks, "How can one 'Go Jolly' naturally, Master?"

"When you become in tune with Nature! Go into the open air! How long will you continue to remain in the dark room of the body? 'Take heed that the Light within you be not darkened.'"

Christmas: The Master, with his full white beard and rosy cheeks is just like Father Christmas. He asks, "How many candles do you think there are on the birthday cake of Lord Jesus Christ?" And answers himself: ***"One Big Light!"***

January 22, 1974: Ratana and I have come for a private interview, to ask Master's opinion on the advisability of adopting Rakesh, her eight-year old brother. We are brought to the upper story. *Obeisance.* Father-Master touches our heads with his hands. I'm silently thankful to see his daughter, my wife glowing and growing. I become lost in the majesty which is his, and Ratana nudges to remind me why we came. I explain the loss of Rakesh's father, the family's situation and dim prospects.

He says, "Why don't you adopt me?"

She says, "You have already adopted us!"

He indicates that adoption would be cumbersome. We ask his advice about boarding schools, but he is not in favor and suggests that if Ratana's sister Girish immigrated to Canada she could help the family twice as much. Then he says: "If you think that because you have only two daughters and are going to adopt him because you have no son, that is not the way...Don't worry!" He smiles knowingly. Mutually, silently we wonder if he means what is passing through our mind.[3]

I ask what we can do to correct our child's behavior. He replied, "It is because one of you is strict or gives an order and the other excuses her. She becomes spoiled." He directs a sharp look at us. "You know very well how to beget children, but not how to bring them up. If one disciplines the child, the other parent should cooperate and not contradict."

Q. "As a father, how much time should I give to the children, as my first duty is meditation?"

M. "Until they learn to stand on their own legs. Until they are at least twenty years." Master then warns that if our children become westernized too much, they won't listen and will do as they please. He therefore advises that they should maintain connections with India and her time-honored cultural, familial and spiritual traditions. We take leave, both awed by his hint about a future son.

Make out your will! Perhaps two hundred foreign guests are seated about the Master for a heart-to-heart discussion on meditation. The conversation picks up:

M. "It is always better to make out a Will before you sit for Bhajan! The other day one man said that he was dragged up inside and his thought was of dying. I told him to 'Make a Will before you sit for Bhajan. After all, you have to leave the body someday.' That power drags us up and out."

Q. "Someone asked me the meaning of the words, *Bhanwar Gupha.*"

M. "That's the cave from where the Light is sprouting forth like a waterfall, shooting out. *Sahansdal Kanwal, Trikuti, Daswan Dwar, Bhanwar Gupha* and *Sach Khand: Bhanwar Gupha* is the Gate into the True Home of your Father. *'Bhanwar'* means Whirling Light, *'Gupha'* means 'cave;' whirling cave of Sound and Light!"

Q: "One time when attuning to the Sound Current, I heard the plaintive melody of Flute. Prior to the Flute, the inner music *sarangi* (Oriental violin) came with full force, filling my soul with rapture."

M: "Yes, yes."

Q. "And then appeared an infinitely huge whirling cave, from which the Flute was playing... reaching out and simultaneously drawing my tiny soul across great distance into its vortex...incredible, awesome, intoxicating!"

M: "Yes...*Make out your will!*" (Much laughter).

---

1. *Portrait of Perfection: A Pictorial Biography of Kirpal Singh.* (Bowling Green, Virginia/Delhi, India: Sawan Kirpal Publications, 1981, p. 173.)

2. A poem by Sant Darshan Singh

3. The son he predicted arrived on Remembrance Day, in 1981.

48

There is only one religion—the religion of Love.
There is only one dharma—the dharma of truth.
There is only one God—The Omnipresent,
The Omniscient,
The Omnipotent.
There is only one language—
the language of the heart.
—Kirpal Singh

The ashram committee members were crestfallen; they had been pressing for a grand celebration of the Master's eightieth birthday, but he would hear nothing of it. At their lowest moment, he turned the tables. If a conference were organized where the main focus was *humanity*, not religion or *his* birthday, only then would he consent.

Sant Kirpal Singh was the foremost 20th century pioneer of interfaith dialogue and peace work on a global scale. Several conferences had been convened in the past but as he explained, this congress would be all-inclusive. Thus the doors were flung open and invitations extended to all corners of the world. The ashram underwent a massive building program. More than a hundred new rooms were rapidly constructed, and the banging, sawing, hammering, plumbing, electrical, brick-laying and painting went on twenty-four hours a day for several weeks. More than 350 guests arrived from twenty countries. Each room held as many beds as could be squeezed in, all of which were immediately occupied, even if plaster and mortar were still wet. All visitors were housed and fed at no charge. Thousands began arriving from all parts of India. Every available hall outside was rented and local disciples shared their homes with people they had never met before. The entire ashram perimeter was built up, and second and third stories were added to existing buildings.

It was sad to see half of the beautiful rosegarden covered by new construction, but the fragrant blossoms sacrificed their existence for a greater cause, a teaching in itself.

Oh, how we Westerners love our privacy, order, and silence! It was hilarious to see preconceptions of serene ashram life blown! There were profound lessons

Unity of Man Peace March, 1974

amidst the chaos, especially for those sharing crowded rooms. In the large meditation hall, talks and meditation sittings were given for the foreign guests on one side of a thin, six-foot-high canvas screen, while on the other, a group of local carpenters busily constructed wooden beds, doors, and window frames for the unfinished rooms. Normally the work stopped during talks and sittings, but one day, as more beds were urgently needed, Master allowed the carpenters to continue while he put the crowd into meditation. The hall, being made of concrete and plaster, caused every sound to be amplified and echoed. The screen was certainly no muffler. Over the din, Master raised his voice, *"This is your examination!"* He then left the hall to attend to other things. His wonderful dry sense of humor was at play. For the next two hours, the majority sat through the din. If one surrendered to the Divine working through these carpenters, each hammer-blow was a kind opener of inner vision, their laughter and joking a joyous wash.

When Master returned and tapped the mike, we opened our eyes. About seventy-five percent of the people remained sitting peacefully as he had left them. "Leave off, please! Now, your examination is over! How many of you saw the radiant form of the Master?" A very large number of hands went up. "How many talked to the inner Master?" About fifteen. "How many of you saw bright Light?" Practically every hand went up.

This calls to mind an incident from the life of Sri Ramakrishna. A devotee used to spend his mornings in meditation at Dakshineshwar Temple. Every morning at ten, a loud whistle from the other side of the river would go off, causing him great irritation. After several weeks, the whistle drove him almost insane with anger. He went to Ramakrishna, and told him how bothered he was by the noise. Ramakrishna lovingly explained that the whistle was really a manifestation of the Divine. *"Meditate on the whistle; surrender to it."* When the devotee followed Ramakrishna's advice, he was quickly transported to a deep state of bliss.

An Italian woman arrived who would leave her body quite frequently and easily. All she had to do was look at the Master, and the life-currents would evacuate through the eye-center, and her body would slowly become immobile. Sometimes she would be gone for hours.

Yogi Bhajan, the founder of the 3HO Society, arrived at the ashram with a large retinue of American Sikh converts. Yogi Ji was of gigantic stature, with a big beard, flowing robes, jewelled rings, necklaces, and a commanding personality. Master Kirpal was also a big man, but Yogi Bhajan physically towered over him. When Master spoke of withdrawal of sensory currents versus yogic breath-control methods, Yogi asked to see someone who had completely left the body. We all followed them to a little room where the Italian woman had been out of her body for several hours. I squeezed through the crowd and slipped past the guard into the room to see what was happening.

The Italian lay in bed, with a blue shawl about her blissful face, looking just like the holy Madonna. Yogi Ji tried to bring her back by vigorously rubbing her neck, but to no avail. He then asked one of his followers to rub her feet hard which he did for several minutes, but her soul remained in the higher planes. Master had a sweet smile and remained non-judgemental.

Two hours later, her soul returned of its own accord. She wandered over and stood outside the Master's gate. While looking at him for a few minutes, her body gently collapsed to the ground, as again her soul winged into the Beyond.

Mind your own business: A few days later I flipped on the tape-recorder and asked a loaded question: "What will be the role of your ashrams in the future?" It was my veiled attempt to draw the Master into possibly revealing something about the future of the Mission after he was no longer among us. I had heard others ask him directly, but he would put them off, telling them to mind their own business.

He saw through my ruse and replied strongly: "Mind your own business!" My heart sank. After pausing to let that sink in, he then continued in a barely audible voice: *"No king wants his son to be a minister, mind that. He wants his son to be a king like himself."*[1]

The Conference: More than one hundred thousand people responded to the call to participate in the World Conference on the Unity of Man, which was sponsored and funded by Sant Kirpal Singh's non-profit, non-denominational spiritual organization.

A huge throng more than a mile long, headed by the Master and religious leaders of various faiths, walked in peace through the old streets of Delhi from the Gandhi grounds to the Ramlila grounds, along a main thoroughfare. The spiritual leaders and participants bowed before the historic Church of St. Stephen, Fatehpuri Mosque, Gurdwara Sis Ganj (the Sikh Shrine where Guru Tegh Bahadur was beheaded), a large Hindu temple, and a Jain temple.

Countless (so it seemed) luminaries, dignitaries, religious leaders, swamis, bishops, lamas, bhikkus, pundits, priests, maulvis, yogis, and shaykhs addressed the throng from a huge platform for the better part of three days.[2] India's foremost political leaders, including Prime Minister Indira Gandhi, delivered insightful addresses that were surprisingly spiritual in nature.[3] Darshan Singh Ji recited several of his Urdu verses, including these two:

> *All places of worship are symbols*
> *of the One Beloved.*
> *Bow your head when you see a temple,*
> *and salute when you see a mosque.*

> *When the flowers of the church,*
> *mosque and temple gather together,*
> *Spring will blossom forth*
> *in Your garden O Lord.*

The Remodeling of Our Destiny: (Keynotes of Kirpal Singh's address):

> *"Truly speaking, unity already exists...We have forgotten this unity—the lesson has only to be revived...The challenging task before religious and spiritual leaders is to bring about a radical change in the ethical, educational and economic status of humanity. Economic uplift is essential, because 'a hungry man is an angry man, and to talk of God to him is a mockery.'"[4]*

The highlight of the conference was at four in the morning on the Master's 80th birthday. His friend, Pir Vilayat Khan of the International Sufi Order, spoke of this profound moment in history as an opportunity to ignite peace and divine unity. Swami Ved Vyasanand dramatically intoned ancient Vedic hymns, and Yogi Bhajan gave a rousing speech. The three of them flanked the Master as bhajans from the past Masters were rendered in classical raga by Bibi Harbhajan Kaur—the Master's daughter-in-law, and by the Yogi's Sikh followers. I gathered together a group of about fifteen Westerners to sing *Amazing Grace.* These bhajans and songs awoke a unity of yearning, and opened the gates of receptivity. The last presenter was Darshan Singh:

> *With the wave of a hand*
> *from the Beloved Cupbearer,*
> *the tavern is humming with life*
> *and the cup is ever on the move...*[5]

For those who understood the language, and here the Easterner was at a distinct advantage, each line brought forth sighs, clapping and exclamations of "Wha Wha!" amongst the 100,000 beneath the tent.

At 5 AM, the Master began with a verse from Baba Farid,

> *Kala merey kapra, Kala mehnda veysh,*
> *Ganahi pariya mai phera, Log kahey Darvesh.*
> *Black is my cloth, black, my raiment;*
> *Full of low qualities am I, yet the people address*
> *Farid the sinful, as Darvesh...*[6]

He spoke from the heart, expressing his shame at this praise of mortals, claiming that he was nothing, but for the grace of his Master Sawan. He then recounted in intimate detail his first meeting with Hazur in 1924, as though it had just happened yesterday. Kirpal's face was aglow, filled with a beauty indescribable. He added that just as a Commander sends forth his errand boy to do his work, he was nothing more. God sends the water of life; he was nothing more than a conduit. *In his nothingness, he was everything, and the very spring of existence.*

Dawn of the Golden Age: Later in the day, he spoke again to the vast throng in Hindi, with words of prophecy:

> *"People say that we are in the Kali Yuga, the Iron Age of darkness,*
> *and that before we enter Sat Yuga or the Golden Age of spirituality,*
> *there will be pralaya or destruction and dissolution. But no, we are*
> *entering the Golden Age, and already I am seeing the rays of its dawn-*
> *ing on the horizon...****The Golden Age will not drop down from the***
> ***heavens, but will be born in the human heart."***

Approximately two thousand seekers came for initiation on the last day of the conference. I shall not forget the spiritual power under the walled-off tent as the charged Names were given by this Man of realization, then repeated over and over by the new, and what unwordable mysteries no doubt were revealed in the following hour of silence.

1. Neither I nor anyone else in the room, to my knowledge, made the connection that the Master might possibly be referring to his own son, Darshan Singh, whose role in ashram affairs had been consistently prominent, but unobtrusive. While transcribing this particular tape in the eighties, I was struck by the dimensions of his veiled answer.

2. Some of the many religious and spiritual leaders present were Catholic Archbishop Fernandos of Delhi, Pir Zamin Nizami (head of the Darga Sharif [shrine] of Hazrat Nizamuddin Aulia), Muni Shushil Kumar of the Jains, Nichidatsu Fuji (Buddhist leader from Japan), Pir Vilayat Khan (International Sufi Order), Rev. McWhirter (Anglican) of London, Lama Lobzang Bakula of Ladakh, Swami Ved Vyasanand of Rishikesh (leader of 50,000 sadhus), and Yogi Bhajan.

3. Other political leaders of prominent stature who took part in the conference were Swaran Singh (Indian Minister of Foreign Affairs), G.S. Pathak (Vice President), Jagjivan Ram (Defense Minister), Gyani Zail Singh (future President of India), and Dr. Karan Singh.

4. *Portrait of Perfection: A Pictorial Biography of Kirpal Singh*, Bowling Green, Virginia/Delhi, India: Sawan Kirpal Publications, 1981, p. 250, 256.

5. Darshan Singh, *Cry of the Soul: Mystic Poetry*, (Bowling Green, VA: SK Publications, 1977, pp. 70.

6. *Darvesh* is the Sufi equivalent of *'Saint of God.'*

49

Love burns the lover, but devotion
burns the one he is devoted to...

Last minutes: We have been waiting awhile in his living room, anxious to say our good-byes, anxious not to say good-bye. The taxi waits, purring in the courtyard outside.

I take Tai Ji aside to another room, and ask, "Would it be possible to have a pair of Maharaj Ji's old shoes?" She looks at me curiously and says, "Ik mint," [one minute] and leaves to speak privately with the Master. She comes back with a musty shoebox, bound with string and says, "Here. Master say you have! You very lucky. I never throw away Master's old shoes."

I thankfully accept, untie the knot and look inside the box to my treasure. There are the shoes, covered with mold and dust. I take my handkerchief and wipe them - size 9. Once the layer of dust is removed, the leather is amazingly shiny; the more I rub, the more they reflect like new. *These shoes have been the altar of a million hearts.*

A terrible foreboding is growing within me that we might never see the beloved Master again. He calls Ratana, Shanti, baby Gurdeep and me into his bedroom to gift us with meditation shawls, each shawl a different color, and parshad.

Leaving him has always been intensely difficult for me. At the physical level, separation is inevitable, though we may pray it not be so. And these last moments with the Merciful Lion are definitely the hardest ever. Heart is being wrenched and dragged. We turn to go, but I run back again and collapse on his feet, hugging them, wetting them with tears.

His hand is upon my shoulder, gently patting. "Please," he says, the last words he will ever speak to me in person, ***"My heart is also not made of stone."*** His eyes glisten with tears. We walk backwards from his court, trying to cup and hold unbearable beauty within the heart forever.

This was our last meeting in the world, as we knew it.

THE LAST DARSHAN

The Last Darshan—the following is a brief account of the last days of Sant Kirpal Singh before he conesciously entered Mahasamadhi:

> *Master allowed nearly twenty Western disciples to be with him at the end... There were moments of such beauty, of such peace; they transcend the memory of his suffering. His humor at other moments was so subtle that any feeling of hopelessness that we might have felt never took hold. Yet there were moments also of terrible foreboding. On the evening of August 2, a disciple asked if she could see the Master privately after the darshan. He said, "Yes, as long as there is breath..."*
>
> *On August 6, he told us, "When you look at the Master with devotion, you are repaid in kind. The realm of the Saints is that of all-forgiveness." Then there was a spontaneous moment of lightness when Master suddenly leaned forward and thrust out his hand towards a German disciple who had expressed some doubts, "Touch me," He said, "I'm a man like you." The young man grabbed hold of the outstretched hand...*
>
> *Master's last darshan talk was held on the roof-terrace just outside his bedroom on the evening of Saturday, August 17. The weather was hot and oppressive. Master was on a white bed, sometimes sitting, sometimes lying, sometimes almost unable to speak. There were long pauses. There were moments of radiant beauty...*
>
> *He started by asking us gently if we had any questions; he looked at everyone, but no one wished to speak. After a long silence he then said pointedly, "No questions anyone? No? Any doubts...?" After a while, he made this statement, "These are selections by God. They send the fruit—certain people to administer certain things. They know when to come and when they are going back. They won't let you down, mind that."...*
>
> *A young American asked, "Master, why don't you heal yourself? You are all-powerful." Master repeated, "Why don't you heal yourself...?" Then a radiant smile appeared on his face and he asked so sweetly, "Anyone whom you love, if he gives you something, would you refuse it? Tell me. What does he hope for you? He should gladly accept it."...*
>
> *After answering the few last questions he drew out of those gathered around him, Master concluded this last session with his great commandment, "**Go jolly!**"*
>
> *Towards the end, when Master was asked by one of his close attendants if Baba Sawan Singh had come; He replied, "**When has He not been here?**" Later, this attendant again asked if Hazur had come, and Master replied, "**Everyone has come!**"*
>
> *His last known words, in response to a question about his welfare, were: "**Bahot achaa!**" ["**Very good!**"]* [1]

---

1. Department of Records, *The Last Darshan*, 1974, *Sat Sandesh*, Delhi, India

Sant Kirpal Singh Ji Maharaj (1894-1974)
Photo taken during "the Last Darshan."

50

Listen
to the sound of the flute,
hear its tale of lamentation;
ever since it was cut
from the reed-bed,
the flute has been wailing its separation.
I want a heart torn by separation,
that I may unfold to such a one
the pain of love,
for everyone who is separated
far from his Source,
wishes back the time
when he were one with it.

— *Jalal U'din Rumi*

August 21, 1974: I was busy at the bakery when the phone call came. A quavering voice in my ear became the harbinger of the unthinkable: "Master has left the body!" Beloved Mentor, Father, truest friend, and now...*he was gone from this world.* I sank to my knees, orphaned; life cut at the root. Minutes passed. Then, a palpable, loving glow began mingling with the pain. Kirpal, humanity's true and irreplaceable friend, was released, free forever. I was glad for him, yet sorry for myself, for everyone. Life now seemed like a sentence to be served.

The first available flight from Vancouver refueled in New York where I was joined by friends who held key positions in the Master's North and South American organization. Despite our common grief, we could not avoid the question: *Who* could possibly bear the vast spiritual mantle of Param Sant Kirpal Singh Ji?

Not only is the need for a living Guide pivotal to the teachings, but in his letter dated 31 August, 1966, Maharaj Ji personally assured me, "...God willing when I leave this plane, that Power will continue to work at some other human pole...whose company will afford you all guidance outside."

Convinced that his successor would be revealed to me, little did I realize how long and convoluted my path of discovery would be. In truth, in the divine plan there are no blunders, victims, or villains; whatever transpires, *must.*

A dead Master is not dead to his initiates. The disciples on Earth have lost the benefit of his physical form, no doubt, and for that they must go to his successor. His astral form remains with them and if they have access...they make contact with that form and get guidance from it on the inner planes. In case they have not entered the eye center, and their attention is confined to the physical plane, their efforts should be to reach the eye center, while receiving encouragement from the successor. Dead Masters are not dead for their initiates, but they cannot make new initiates. This is done by the living Master.
—From a letter by Sawan Singh to a disciple

August 22: We arrive in Shakti Nagar, propelled through sweltering streets and dusty lanes clogged with thousands of mourners. From Sawan Ashram we are directed to Kirpal Bagh, one mile east, where the cremation is in progress. The Bagh or garden is a five acre wooded area surrounded by a perimeter wall. When we arrive, the searing otherworldly air is filled

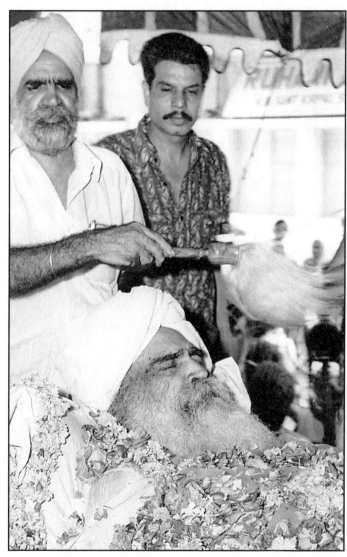

Sant Kirpal Singh Ji Maharaj returns Home, August 21, 1974.
(Darshan Singh is holding whisk)

with wailing as the multitude freely expresses its grief. More arrive continuously from all parts of the world. In a delirium, I am moved through the mob to a brick platform, which serves as the funeral pyre. On the center is a heap of smoldering ashes. Too late! *Oh, how could the Deathless die?*

Sitting on the pyre's edge is Darshan Singh. According to ancient custom, it is the eldest son's duty to perform funeral rites for his father. Darshan poured milk and water over the ashes to cool them, as a long lineup moves forward to receive a small portion from his hands. These are then transferred to brass urns for later immersion in India's sacred rivers. "We call the Master's holy ashes 'flowers.' We do not call them ashes,'" someone says, as my Western friends and I await our turn.

Suddenly, I am before the pyre, tears flowing. Darshan, tears also streaking his cheeks, places our Lord's *flower-ashes* in my hands. Amongst the moist ash is a slender, hollow piece of bone, stark and white against the gray. It is too much to bear. Falling to my knees, I moan, "This is not my Master," hoping the earth will engulf me. Above the din, I hear a responding inchoate cry from Darshan himself.

The passing of the Merciful Lion has wrenched the very heart and soul of the vast multitude. It is a gesture of his greatness that has moved humanity to so passionate a response. *"He first loved us; our love is only reciprocal."*

Leaving the pyre's desolation, I search the Bagh for a place of quiet and aloneness, but in vain. Dust and smoke are thick in the air as we walk back to the ashram. Everywhere, brothers are hugging each other and crying; sisters are embracing their own. Some poor souls clutch the window gratings of the Master's house, sobbing.

A wounded heart asks: *How can your orphans exist, when You, O' true Existence, have gone?*

For You, it is only a question of a single glance;
For me, it is my entire existence.

51

Diary, August 23: While temperatures hover above 110F in the shade, I retreat to my stifling room...The swarming, phantom images of all the forlorn souls of this day disturb my inner gaze...

The next five days and nights were sleepless, feverish, and filled with unspeakable sorrow. Confined to my bed, I was yet aware of increasing and unwelcome agitation within the ashram. A swell of support was rising for Darshan Singh, while another group threatened violence if he ascended the dais. Many, myself included, were divided. Darshan was a *good man*, but I was not as yet able to recognize him as the Friend in a new garment. Who could possibly bear the mantle? Who could fit the shoes of Kirpal?

A mad, hot wind was stirring, about to sweep dust over the world of unity. Whoever it would touch would temporarily lose their wisdom.

> *...And so these men of Indostan*
> *Disputed loud and long*
> *Each in his own opinion*
> *Exceeding stiff and strong,*
> *Though each was partly in the right,*
> *And all were in the wrong!*

> —*John G. Saxe*

August 26: Darshan Singh enters my sickroom and sits on the edge of my cot, offering words of comfort and a gentle hand on my shoulder. I turn my back, for I am not in his orbit, and frankly, beyond caring. Without a word, he leaves in silence. The following day, most of the 30 or so Westerners depart for Rajpur to escape the oppressive heat.

At the old Rajpur estate I continue to grieve but find some peace in the light of meditation. To my chagrin, however, the inner Master is elusive. Master's old gardener, Baba Khetu Lal, disappears under a blanket *for several days*, lost in meditation. He is deeply in love with the Cosmic One and wants no part in our speculations. Whatever Khetu Lal receives in meditation, prompts him to leave for Delhi and seek out Darshan.

Still weak with fever, I slowly walk up the winding Rajpur Road to the Tillis' house, perched on a steep hill. Malcolm and Kate Tillis have been residing in India for the past two years, assisting the Master with literary service. When nobody answers my knock, I enter and take the liberty to lie upon the cool kitchen floor. When I close my eyes, Master Kirpal's form immediately appears in blazing light, infusing balm into my wounded soul. Overwhelmed by his majesty, I forget to ask about the thorny issue of succession. Too soon, alas, that beautiful vision subsides, leaving me stranded in the world of opposites. Malcolm and Kate enter at this moment, surprised to find me on their floor.

After sharing our loss with Kate and Malcolm, I return down the hill to 207 Rajpur Road. Andrew Vidich of New York sits in a corner of our large room in a full-lotus posture, impervious and aloof, like one carved in stone. From sunup to sundown, he remains unmoving like some archetypal, unshorn yogi.[1]

Through extra hours in meditation, each in our little group seeks all-important inner direction as to the Master's Will for the future, but the divine revelation of one cannot be forced or hurried on another. Empty-handed and clouded, I return alone to Delhi, and after booking my return flight, make one last visit to the ashram. At dusk, I watch Darshan walk barefoot across the compound; he turns and looks my way, a glance which lasts but a second. Modestly averting his eyes, he continues to the opposite side and disappears into a doorway. Resisting the puzzling syncronistic resonance, I turn away, once *again*.

* * *

A Parable: GOD SPEAKS TO MOSES [and to all of us]:

God one day said to Moses in secret: "Go and get a word of advice from Satan." So Moses went to visit Iblis and when he came to him and asked for a word of advice, "Always remember," said Iblis, "this simple axiom: never say 'I,' so that you never may become like me."

So long as there remains in you a little of self-love you will partake of infidelity. Indolence is a barrier to the spiritual way; but if you succeed in crossing this barrier, a hundred 'I's will break their heads in a moment.

Everyone sees your vanity and self-pride, your resentment, envy, and anger, but you yourself do not see them. There is a corner of your being full of dragons and by negligence you are delivered up to them; and you pet them and cherish them night and day. So, if you are aware of your inner state, why do you remain so listless! 2

---

1. Andrew did write three months later, claiming inner confirmation from Kirpal and Sawan that Darshan was the spiritual successor. At least five other similar letters came, including one from Malcolm and Kate, but I was unreceptive and threw them away.

2. Farid ud-Din Attar, *The Conference of the Birds*, 1974 (London), Routledge & Keegan Paul Ltd., pp. 87.

52

This anecdote, familiar to those of the Punjab, illustrates the confusion that often arises around an ambiguous succession:

> When the eighth Sikh Guru, Har Krishan (1656-1664), was dying from smallpox in Delhi, disciples anxiously inquired where his successor would be found. He replied, "I will be ever with you; none should weep for me. I will be found in Baba Bakale." Baba Bakale is a small village near Goindwal, on the banks of the Beas River. Subsequently, twenty-two impostors set up shop at Bakale, gladly soliciting donations from the unwary and creating confusion.
>
> Makkhan Shah, a wealthy trader, was at sea when a terrible storm arose, threatening to sink his ship with all aboard. As a devotee of the previous Guru, he fervently prayed for his Master to save the ship and all aboard, and promised to donate five hundred gold coins to the langar. A great saint miraculously appeared and pushed the ship safely through the storm to the nearest port. Makkhan saw that the saint's shoulder was injured in the effort before he disappeared. When he reached Delhi, Shah asked the Guru's whereabouts and was told of Har Krishan's recent passing and his prophecy that he would be found in Bakale. When he reached Bakale village, Makkhan Shah was dismayed by the profusion of gurus. He thought, "I will give each of the claimants five gold coins. If the real Master is here, he will ask for all five hundred." Accordingly, each of the twenty-two gladly accepted his five gold coins. Realizing that none of them could be the true Master, Shah became despondent and asked, "Is there any other saint in this village?" One man told him, "Oh, yes, there is Tegha, but nobody ever sees him. He remains shut up in a hut and meditates all the time."
>
> For Makkhan Shah, this was a ray of hope, and he hastened to the home of Tegha, but when he reached there a sign on the door warned, "Whoever enters through this door is no disciple of mine." The clever Makkhan broke a hole through the rear wall of the hut and entered so as not to technically disobey. When he confronted the meditating Tegha, he presented five gold coins at his feet. Tegha opened his eyes and asked, "You were supposed to give five hundred. Where are the other four hundred and ninety-five you promised?" After seeing the Guru's wounded shoulder, Makkhan Shah ran to the rooftop and shouted out in all directions, "Guru ladoray! Guru ladoray!" [I have found the True Guru! I have found the True Guru!"

An unbiased study of the well-documented *param-para* or lineage of Sant Mat over the past five centuries shows great diversity of expression; often the Saints publicly announced their successors, smoothing the way, but sometimes not.[1] Eight of the ten Sikh Gurus were blood-related, but Guru Nanak chose Angad over his sons. Rarely, if ever, did Mastership remain in one physical place (i.e., in the same dera or ashram) for longer than two spiritual generations.

> *Spirituality is not the exclusive possession of any family or place, but it is like a scented flower that grows wherever Nature has ordained, around which the bees gather from far and near to sip its nectar.*[2]

Whenever succession wasn't clearly defined to the majority—as happened after the demise of Har Krishan, Gobind Singh, Soami Ji, and Sawan Singh, their followers were tested. In every case, the true successor emerged, for a fully illumined soul cannot remain hidden for long. *Long* is a relative term, however, because the new successor doesn't always emerge immediately. Perhaps this is a winnowing of grain from chaff. Bound by inscrutable will and the orders of Hazur, Sant Kirpal Singh never publicly declared his successor. Before the embers of his funeral pyre had cooled, opportunists began to arise, possibly as many as in the time of Makkhan Shah.

> *Whenever Sat Purush [the Supreme Being] comes into the world in the garb of a Satguru to save...the souls in their misery and trouble by giving them the secret of the True Home, Kal...follows suit in different forms to mislead, so as to...prevent an easy escape of the souls in his domain. His agents set up schools resembling those of Sant Mat, use similar language, and adopt similar terminology to ensnare the naive and unwary aspirants. Hence the need for great caution... —from a letter by Kirpal Singh*

Based on a rumor from Harish Chaddha—of a saintly stranger who had visited the ashram after the Master's passing and then disappeared, I cancelled my return flight. Following scanty information, I traveled by train, bus and jeep into a primitive, remote area of western India, questing for the true successor, like some hopeful latter-day Makkhan Shah. About ten days after the Master's passing, I discovered and became attracted to a virtually unknown, unlettered, and magnetic ascetic whom I thought might be the true one. Unwittingly, I became his herald to the world.[3]

I returned to home and business, and as time passed, I underwent several puzzling experiences. The first was a dream of great clarity, which took me inside the apartment of Darshan Singh. Every detail was indelibly etched—the color and patina of the walls, framed pictures, and neatly stacked books on low shelves (I later discovered from a photograph that the dream was accurate in every detail.) Dressed in a short-sleeved Western shirt and pale blue turban, Darshan was smiling, bestowing gifts upon a number of happy recipients. I stayed as far to the back as possible, critically observing. When he moved towards me, lovingly offering a gift, I recoiled and awoke in a cold sweat. Almost immediately following this strange encounter, I received a telegram from Darshan inviting me to come and see him. I dashed off a rude reply, castigating Delhi as "the graveyard of the guru." As much as I aspired to be free of partisanship, I wasn't, for I too had been touched by the mad, hot wind. My wife chided: "I don't want to hear anything against Darshan Singh Ji. He's Master's son after all. You should remember how much respect our Master had, even bowing to the feet of Hazur's relatives, just because they were related to him. He would never speak against anyone." She was right, of course, but I wasn't prepared to listen.

The second experience took place towards the close of a group meditation when an immense vortex appeared in the center of my inner gaze, dragging me headlong into it. Surprisingly, Darshan's form began to coalesce and solidify within the whirlpool, unwillingly drawing me deeper and deeper, even though I was mentally repeating the five charged names. Panic set in. I broke contact, and cried aloud, "No!" disturbing a large room full of meditating initiates. Although I was unable to admit it, these experiences embarrassingly contradicted my opposition to Darshan Singh.

The other experience came in the form of a heavenly sounding voice, which thrice proclaimed the name of the desert sage, towards whom I was predisposed. This auditory experience was convincing, however it wasn't validated by the *simran* acid-test. According to the Masters, if any form appears within, or if any voice is heard in meditation, one is to ask the speaker to appear and then repeatedly test that form with the sacred initiation mantra. If the vision remains, only then may it be relied upon as genuine and helpful for the homeward journey. Alas, this I did not do.

My focus turned from the confusing enigma of succession, to prayer and Light. I might have *seemed* to have been other—a successful businessman responsible for more than a hundred employees, a husband and father, etc.—but for the next two years, not a night or day passed without being involuntarily seized with the pangs of separation. I missed Kirpal more than life. Like a tree, I was being hollowed out from inside. This was not empty despair however, for divine longing unfolds to its sufferers profound dimensions of the spiritual journey, and one would not trade it for any treasures of this world.

> *Even after a hundred years of Bhajan one does not get so purified as*
> *by an intense longing for darshan... —Baba Jaimal Singh*

In the summer of 1977, a form resembling the one whom I took to be the new master appeared within several times. This form continually oscillated and I observed that the eyes had fine yellow lines around them. I blamed my concentration and prematurely accepted these experiences as evidence of succession. I had forgotten Hazur's letter to Dr. Brock:

The Master is within, at the eye focus. Below this stage Kal sometimes appears in the form of the Master, but is distinguishable from him by his narrow forehead, and eyes having yellow and red lines. The Master has a broad forehead, and his eyes are bright and shining. The form of Kal disappears when the Holy Names are repeated.

Hazur described an experience during his own period of discipleship:

One day when I was meditating, Baba Ji's form appeared before me. Baba Ji, or rather what seemed to be his form, said: "If, in a case of emergency, meat and drink are used, there is no harm." But when I repeated the Five Names, he got up and walked away...

"There are *more* deceptions on the inside," Kirpal Singh often remarked, and encouraged his initiates to validate their experiences in person with him or by letter, but that option was no longer available. The great Rumi warned:

Find a Master-soul, for without his active help and guidance this journey is beset with untold fears, perils and dangers.

For one year I faithfully served the new claimant to the mastership as one of only two initiating representatives for the entire Western world. Significant resources and several ashrams were unequivocally surrendered and bequeathed under the claimant's directorship, and a large number of Westerners were drawn into his fold. However, as one inconsistency after another emerged, I began to secretly question and analyze the mounting evidence, external as well as subjective (the reader will be spared the details). Despite brief hope, I had to admit that the impeccable character, universality, and realization of Kirpal Singh were becoming distant memories.

In 1978, I returned to India with my family, seeking clarification and resolution to my doubts, but I was to be sorely disappointed. In spite of the successor-trap, heart still burned intensely for Kirpal. Desperate hopes and the living Presence were my only sustenance.

If soul were to melt in the crucible of the test, that would be a small price for truth. Everything as I knew it was about to be dramatically and forever changed; philosophical understandings were irrelevant. One gracious aspect of my plight was that I proceeded through the valleys of anguish, helplessness, and guilt (for having misled so many), to intense remembrance, to surrender, to Light, and back again. I could sense the hidden hand of the Beloved behind the veil. Something was about to give. It *had* to give.

"When your grief transends all bounds,
it becomes its own cure."
— Ghalib

1. Scores of accounts, often called *Janam Sakhi* ("Life Stories" of different Saints) exist. These accounts were often written by disciples during various dispensations. MacAuliffe's *History of the Sikhs*, Vol. 1-6, is one of the more complete histories, although not entirely reliable.

2. Kirpal Singh, *Man, Know Thyself*, SK Publications, 1980, Bowling Green, VA, p.22.

3. All souls spring from the One Source and have their purpose. I have chosen to protect the anonynimity of the desert ascetic, although my association was no secret to many.

53

October, 1978. I returned to Delhi after a ten-day retreat with the desert Baba. My purpose in coming to India this time was to remove persisting doubts, but now I had even further evidence of a growing web of fictions, into which I and many others had become ensnared. I was desperate for the truth of succession, as well as for forgiveness for having unwittingly played a pivotal role in leading others into his web. In a state of restlessness, I flagged a taxi and requested to be taken to Sawan Ashram. As we neared and then passed through the familiar neighborhood of Shakti Nagar, my pulse quickened in expectation, but somewhere along the way we took a wrong turn. About a mile eastward, the cabbie drove through a narrow twisting lane and stopped before high walls and an open wrought-iron gate. Arching overhead was a sign, *"KIR-PAL ASHRAM."* What was this? Then it suddenly dawned: this had to be the headquarters for Darshan Singh, my imagined adversary. The driver had taken me to the "wrong" ashram! Irked, I barked, "No! No! Sawan Ashram! Turn back!" Somewhere half-way between the two ashrams, I got out. Like one deranged, I wandered the crowded streets and bazaars, yet for me they were all empty. In every small and large shop, I hunted in vain for a familiar face. In happier times, many a shopkeeper proudly displayed our Master's picture, but on this day he was nowhere to be found.

To the side of an old and busy bridge which spanned the Gunda Nala, a half mile east of Sawan Ashram and under a banyan tree stood a fodder-dealer's shop. A slightly tattered calendar bearing the face of Kirpal hung on the wall, gently moving in the turbid breeze. I stood transfixed, while the cacophony of traffic roiled dangerously around me. An old man with curly gray hair was squatting on a bench on the sidewalk, a friendly twinkle in his eyes. Years earlier I had seen him at the ashram, and we smiled in mutual recognition. Pointing to the slightly tattered calendar, I proclaimed its beauty in Hindi.

The shopkeeper smiled, affirming. He then asked, "You are going to the ashram, yes?" and I replied, *"Hanji,* yes!"

In a questioning gesture, he shrugged his shoulders, turned his hand up, and asked "Which ashram?" "Why, Sawan Ashram, of course. It is a place of pilgrimage for me," I replied.

He looked puzzled. "You mean you're not going to Kirpal Ashram, to see Maharaj Darshan Singh, the living Master?" he asked. I vehemently stated, "No Kirpal Ashram! No Darshan Singh!" That irrational fear surfaced again. I wandered away, agitated that fate kept shoving me in the "wrong" direction. I finally ended up before the iron gates of old Sawan Ashram, but it no longer possessed the sparkling radiance I cherished. Its once-immaculate structures were showing signs of neglect and disrepair, and there was no Master here, only another pretender, soliciting money and surrender. I was not about to give either.

My quest took me to an old friend in another part of the city, a government employee who had accompanied the Master on his 1972 world tour. Harcharan and I broke bread and spent much of the night discussing the maelstrom of events. He was bursting to share new information.

"You may be aware that after Hazur Baba Sawan Singh Ji left the body in 1948, our Master retreated to Rishikesh where he spent most of his time in deep meditation. When not meditating he wrote down his inner spiritual experiences in a diary in a coded language. Our Master devised this code so that he could send confidential letters and poems for the eyes and ears of Baba Sawan Singh only, whenever he was unable to go himself, during Hazur's lifetime. He taught this language to Tai Ji, as she and her husband were frequent visitors to Hazur, and could read these confidential messages to him. Master kept these diaries—comprising over six hundred pages in three volumes—absolutely secret. They have been lying unnoticed and neglected in a cupboard at Sawan Ashram these last thirty years."

Yes, I had heard rumors of these manuscripts, but no one except Tai Ji had reportedly seen them.

Harcharan continued, "Tai Ji is convinced that only the true successor will be able to decipher them, but no one has yet turned up who can. She says that she is not going to live much longer, and decided to orally translate the manuscripts to me, before it is too late. Just yesterday I had written down the first installment as she translated it into Hindi. These few pages come from a portion dealing with our Master's conversations with various Saints in the higher planes. You are the first to see and hear any portion of this rare revelation. It begins with a conversation between our Master and the departed Baba Jaimal Singh, or Baba Ji, as we know him:

> *The Being Who is called God*
> *never deceives anyone.*
> *When separated from all untruth,*
> *He (Raab) unites that soul with Him.*

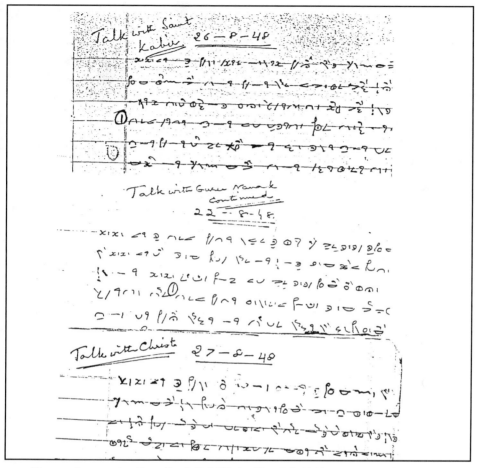

Three sample excerpts from Master Kirpal's Coded Diaries. These deal with his conversations with Saint Kabir, Guru Nanak and Christ on the Inner Planes, August, 1948. The English notes are also in Kirpal Singh's handwriting.

Addressing Baba Ji, I asked Him, "In this world, where illusion reigns supreme, there are many clever people posing as Masters, Sants, Satgurus, Mahatmas and Faqirs, who deceive innocent seekers, claiming access to higher regions, or that they have realized God. Preying on the susceptibilities and naiveté of seekers after truth, they imitate saintly behavior and quote the scriptures. How may one determine the actual stages they claim to have attained?"

Baba Ji replied: "The following questions should be put to any Sadhu, Sant, Faqir, or Master, when the need arises, to determine the extent of their inner ascent. Outer appearances and saintly behavior can be imitated to some extent, but only one who has traversed all the inner regions, who is fully conversant with every secret, will be able to answer all these questions correctly.

There were fifty-two unusual questions concerning the inner topography of the subtle planes. Beginning with visions and passages through the Astral plane, each question led to higher and higher planes, culminating in Sach Khand. But there were trick questions and unless one had personally traveled to those regions and passed through them, the one being questioned would be exposed. While copying them into my journal, I experienced an unimaginable thrill. "It has to be more than coincidence that this has fallen into my lap at such a critical juncture," I thought. "Before anything leaks out, I'm going to put these 52 questions to all the successor-claimants! Then we will see who, if any, can answer them competently."

I sensed the immense purpose behind these questions and the responsibility to employ them as intended, as quickly as possible. At the very least, I was being provided a touch-stone by which a mystery that had confounded many wiser than I might be resolved. I was determined to dig out the truth, no matter the personal price. New hope and fierce determination surged through my veins. Paralleling this optimism was a compelling, ominous sense that a race between the positive and the negative power was taking place.

I added several questions of my own to the fifty-two, based on higher spiritual experiences I had on rare occasion been blessed with since '65. Each of these visions had been confirmed and verified by Master Kirpal in person, and no one could fool me about their nature and authenticity. This outer validation became important, as again, my credibility would soon be on the line.

Discussing the problem of discriminating between the true and false, Kirpal Singh warns the seeker:

> [Those] who pose and act as Master Souls not only deceive themselves but misguide the masses at large. In this category are included persons who are either greedy and selfish or those who are after name and fame. In innumerable different ways and wiles they practice deception on the unwary and simple-minded seekers after Truth with a view to serve their own ends.
>
> It is because of such impositions that Guruship is being looked down upon by most people, and no wonder that the science of Spirituality is being stigmatized as a mirage and a fool's paradise.1

In his first English booklet, *Man! Know Thyself*, he advises:

> To believe in a thing or fact without troubling to investigate it does not in any way do credit to an intelligent man. On the contrary, it reflects adversely on his ignorance or credulity.

To honestly question is healthy and not a sign of disrespect. In this spirit, I returned to the desert area of Western India. While waiting for an opportunity to pose these questions to the one whom I had proclaimed and supported, I sat on an irrigation dike bordering a parched cotton field. Aspirations beyond my quandary percolated to the page:

> *What does it say, the bubbling froth?*
> *'Fling me back from whence I came,*
> *For I am beached and strengthless!*
> *I implore the Lord of ocean's Light,*
> *Draw me to Your immensity again.'*

Later that night, I disclosed the mystery of the fifty-two questions to Richard, Joan, and Alan, three Western initiates of Master Kirpal who were also on retreat in Rajasthan, struggling with their own questions. Richard, a staunch ten-to-twelve-hour-a-day meditator, approached me with a smile that wouldn't stop, and divulged, "You won't believe who came to me in meditation today." I flippantly asked, "What nonsense are you talking about?"

Richard continued smiling, "Darshan Singh appeared out of nowhere, surrounded by radiant Light. He stayed with me for an extended period of time while I repeated simran. What's interesting is that I wasn't thinking of him at all, and haven't thought of him for months. I think you should definitely put these questions to Darshan as well as the others." I assured him I would.

My interview with the desert Baba took place the next day in a private room, but he skillfully and completely evaded the Master's tough questions. Surprisingly, however, he did directly answer my own relating to the one time my soul was taken up to the Fourth stage. "Other than the sound of inner Flute," I asked, "what is the predominant feature of this region?" He replied "*Sona*" (beauty), but his answer was simply not correct. Earlier, I had carefully looked for the mystic sign of the Lotus on his feet, but it just *wasn't there*. When our interview was over, I expressed my thanks for his kindness and whatever good I had received, for Baba had always been quite loving to me and I bore him no ill-will.

Peaceful at heart, my way now felt remarkably clear. A long jeep ride across the hot, sandy waste left me at the Ganganagar station.

November 5, 1978: I reach Delhi, tired and sooty from the all-night train. Ratana and children have gone to Agra to see the Taj Mahal. So much the better, as one thought possesses me: "I *must* see and question Darshan Singh."

Ratana's aunt sweetly insists on my eating and resting, but I have no appetite and conspire to escape. Without pausing to change my sooty clothes and unable to explain, I thank her and call a taxi. Uneasy about my unannounced reception with Darshan, I have to let go of my inclinations, ego, prejudice, fear and preconceived notions—*everything* in the interest of knowing the *truth*.

"*Kirpal Ashram jao!*" I instruct the taxi-walla and proceed to our predestined rendezvous.

---

1. Kirpal Singh, *Godman—Finding a Spiritual Master*, SK Publications, Bowling Green, VA, 1992, p. 21-22.

One of my preconceptions is that whoever succeeds Sant Kirpal Singh Ji will be just as grand and imposing as he. But now I am having second thoughts. I consider the story of Raja Janak—a great king of ancient India—who desperately wanted the immediate experience of God. Of all the great sages and intellectuals of India who had been summoned to his court, only Ashtavakra, a humpback, had the power to deliver the goods in the form of bestowing a first-hand inner experience of divine awakening on the king—when no other holy person was able to do so. This time, I am determined to look beyond the form.

The taxi-walla drops me at the main north gate of Kirpal Ashram. It is a bright Sunday morning, and the in-lane is filled with crowds heading to satsang. My heart is pounding, and I recognize many a familiar face from the old days amidst the new. The atmosphere is quite exuberant and festival-like, in sharp contrast to the desert ashram from where I had just come. As I diffidently move along, I spy a multitude sitting in a large open area. A muffled din, then, sudden silence indicates that the awaited one has arrived. I hesitate as Darshan Singh briefly appears in the sunlit opening at the far end of the lane, gliding slowly past with folded hands, blessing the audience. His silver-gray beard is flowing naturally. (I will learn that Darshan Singh had just retired from government service and November 5, 1978 was the first date he had ever appeared in public with open beard. As a traditionalist, I had hitherto harbored a prejudice simply because he used to tie up his beard. This now seemed irrelevant to the quest). This is a new Darshan, quite different from my recollections. I confess I'm struck by the impeccable timing.

In my present troubled and expectant state, I'm grateful not to be recognized. After Darshan passes by on his way to the dais, I slip into the crowd, and sit on the ground near the back. Perhaps 15,000 are in attendance. I close my eyes, wishing for invisibility. After about fifteen minutes, there is a tapping on my shoulder. Sethi Ji is leaning over, looking into my face. (he was the main personal secretary of Master Kirpal). "Hello, brother Stee-fun! "Master wants to see you up at the front."

"Oh, no, please!" I say, and continue sitting, not knowing what to do next. At the far end of the large crowd is a white dais and on it, diminished by the perspective of distance, are two tiny figures. One stands and slowly descends the stairs, moving into the crowd, slowly moving towards me. I wonder if I should try to beat a quick escape! Instead, I close my eyes and wait anxiously. Soon I feel a strong presence, and open my eyes. Darshan is standing right before me, beaming from ear to ear.

"Hello, my dear, dear brother!" he says. I stand and am quickly embraced. "Welcome to your Father's home. This is your home! We have named it Kirpal

Ashram after our beloved Master." His arms are wrapped strongly around me, and he isn't letting go. I didn't expect this! A delicate and heady jasmine fragrance engulfs me. Darshan then quietly takes my hand in his, slowly leads me through the huge crowd, and up the stairs to the dais. What am I *doing?* Up front is the last place in the world I want to be. "My dear brother, we would be most indebted if you could share with us some sweet remembrances of our beloved Master. Please!" His bright eyes are full of sincerity. Helpless, I accept. Twice, while introducing me to the crowd, I inch away and get up to make a run for it. Twice, his arm shoots out, incredibly strong and fast—and pulls me firmly, gently to his side, while an altogether mischievous smile plays upon his face. I am trapped; there is no escape. *How many times over the past four years have I struggled to escape?*

After sharing two bhajans and a personal remembrance, I sit a bit back as Darshan delivers his discourse to an obviously enchanted crowd. His bare right foot rests on his left knee. Naturally curious, I look at the sole of his foot and see there a very deep and pronounced lotus mark, very similar to Master Kirpal's. I begin to experience a heady intoxication, and the air is filled with jasmine-lilac fragrance. I cease fretting whether anyone has seen me or not; the heart of my soul is filled with radiant joy.

When satsang finishes, Darshan leads me by the hand into the clamoring crowd. He is so giving with his chaste touches and pats, so patient in his listening to those who approach him, that it takes at least forty-five minutes to cross the compound. Here, unlike some other well-known holy men I've met, there are no access restrictions and no body-guards. He gives me a personal tour of Kirpal Ashram's 2.5-acres, which include langar, library, free medical dispensaries, meditation hall, and visitor's quarters. Finally we ascend a narrow worn stairway to his apartment. "Darshan is very sweet," I tell him. I haven't seen such spontaneous devotion from any congregation since 1974.

He introduces me to his life-companion, Mata Harbhajan Kaur, whom he identifies as "Auntie." He takes me by the hand to a spotless bed and makes me lie on it, saying, "You must be very tired from your journey. Please make yourself comfortable, brother. Remember, this is your own home. There is no difference between you and my family, as we are all part of the greater family of God and the Masters."

I am delightfully overwhelmed, but on guard and determined not to be subverted from my real purpose in coming. He won't leave until I lie down. Once he is out of the room, I realize that I am lying on *his* bed, and, in my sooty clothes. I reason, "I don't know if he is a Master or not, but he is the elder son of my Satguru. I can't sleep on his bed; it's not respectful," and slip to the floor. *How have I now become so respectful?*

Later that night, he returns and invites me to eat with him. "I don't know

how to address you," I say. "Just call me Darshan. We are brothers..." he
replies. It is a delicious dinner, delicately prepared under Auntie's supervision,
and I am hungry! After the dishes and guests are cleared, only three remain:
Darshan, Chachaji ('Uncle' Gupta), and myself. We move to the bedroom/liv-
ing room, which has clean white sheets spread over the floor.

As we sit cross legged, I focus cautiously on Darshan's form about six feet
away. Compared to Master Kirpal, his physical stature is shorter and smaller.
His beard is thick and curly with a lot of gray, and his facial features are
decidedly different from his father's. Several long moments pass, while
Darshan slowly plays with his fingers and toes, seemingly absorbed inwardly
and slightly bemused. No words pass between us. The energy level in the room
is tangibly rising; the atmosphere begins to dance with a hidden music. Then
his head bows over, deep set eyes shadowed by bushy brows. His head rises up
to look directly at me, into me, but it is no longer Darshan. None other than
Kirpal Singh's bodily form is sitting before me! A brilliant golden Light pours
out from his body, encircling and engulfing us both, leaving not a trace of
Darshan. The eyes are Kirpal's eyes...those eyes which I never thought I'd see
again in this world. My soul begins to sing, and heart soars. The being before
me, with the precise *form* of Kirpal but the *voice* of Darshan quietly asks, "You
have some questions, brother?"

Over the next five and a half hours, I ask all the questions brought for the
task, and more. During this entire time, the physical form of Master Kirpal
remains, and out of it Darshan's voice definitively, and without the slightest
hesitation, answers all fifty-two questions, going into considerable detail. One
of the more interesting answers is to question #16, "How many steps lead into
the Mansarovar (pool) located in the Third Region?" Darshan answers, *"There
are eighty-four steps."* Each step is linked to the purification of karmas accu-
mulated throughout the great cycle of 8,400,000 lives in various forms.

He speaks with the natural authority of experience, dispelling hundreds of
my old doubts along the way. While elaborating on features of the inner
regions hitherto unrecorded in any books, he obviously knows them as intimately as those of this finite world.

My own four inner questions are answered accurately, without hesitation and
in great detail, and many more which spontaneously arise. This is the most
esoteric and fascinating question/answer session of my life, yielding more inner
secrets than I had ever gleaned from the writings of Kabir, Tulsi Sahib, and
Soami Ji. Darshan also shares mysteries of the *maha sunna*, the region of pitch
darkness that lies between the third and fourth planes; of the great souls who
are suspended there; and how they are eventually liberated by the living Param
Sant of the time, whenever he visits the remote vastness of this region. They
become engulfed in his great Light, and his magnetism draws them through

Sant Darshan Singh Ji, during our November 1978 meeting. Photo by Jamie Smith.

the stygian darkness and into the great radiance beyond. Darshan also speaks of the *Majdoob*, or God-intoxicated, God-mad souls, and more. When he describes minute details of the soul's entry into *Sach Khand*, and what takes place in that eternal region in the presence of the Supreme Being, I can almost imagine what it must be like.

The golden-white light halo surrounding him continues radiating intensely, without any fluctuation, throughout our entire interview. At one point I ask, "When did Master first take your soul to Sach Khand in this lifetime?"

He replies: "It was in 1967 when the Beloved took me up from this earth-earthy plane, through the astral, causal, supra-causal planes, and ultimately brought about my merger with Him in Sach Khand. He then absorbed my soul further, in the *Alakh*, the Ineffable; *Agochar*, the Incomprehensible; and the *Anaami*, the Nameless Absolute. After this experience, I wrote a poem attempting to describe it."

Darshan spends a few minutes looking through a tied-up bundle of his poems and pulls out an old, yellowed piece of paper with neat, careful blocks of verse, hand-written in Persian script. Putting on his specs, he first reads the verses in Urdu and then translates for my benefit. I recall the occasion when he had recited exactly the same poem to me, outside the porch at Sawan Ashram in 1967. The significance of its meaning, lost on me then, now explodes in my consciousness.

After a while I ask, "Tai Ji has said 'Master's Successor will be able to read and understand the secret coded language he wrote his poems and manuscripts in.' What do you have to say about this?"

He replies, "The beloved Master taught this language to both your Auntie and I, when he called us from Delhi to be with him in Rishikesh in 1948. Actually, there is no great mystery to it. He just substituted certain symbols for the letters of the Punjabi alphabet. If you want, Harbhajan or I can teach you the language."

Astonished, I ask, "Really, that's all it is? You mean, even I can learn how to read his coded manuscripts?"

With Darshan Singh, November, '78— J.Smith, photo.

"Yes, of course." He calls Harbhajan into the room, who looks at some of the characters of the original script, writes out the key to decipher it, and gives it to me. Using this key, a small portion is painstakingly transliterated.

The Forgiving Nature of Saints: It is now 4:30 AM on the sixth of November. After seeing Master Kirpal sitting before me all this time, I repent for my blunders over the past four years, and for all the negative thoughts and words I expressed towards or about the One who had always been kind, loving and true to me. *Seven* times I had rejected Darshan's benevolence, but he never gave up on me. How could I have been so wrong, so blind?

With a beauty simultaneously delicate and divine, he folds his hands together, rolls his eyes upwards, and whispers, "Our Beloved Master is so merciful, so forgiving..." Again, through his eyes, Kirpal is looking at me...no doubt about it. A huge load is lifted from my life. I wonder aloud about the many whom I have led to an imperfect Master. I'm concerned about where they will end up.

"You know," he continues, "our Master initiated approximately one *lakh* [one hundred thousand] souls into the mysteries of the Beyond, but that doesn't include the millions of souls he benefited just by His gracious, lyrical glances...When Master is carrying the burden of all the universes, then what is it to Him if He takes the burden of a few hundred or a few thousand more souls across the ocean of existence? That's no burden for Him. Please don't worry dear brother, Master is very gracious."

He then reveals that the commission he has received from Sawan and Kirpal also involves initiating a large number of souls. I ask, "How do you find the burden?" His eyes open wide and he proclaims loudly, *"Burden?* What burden, dear brother? When one is commissioned by the Perfect Master, authorized by Him, then there is never any burden. He takes all the burden! He does all the work! If He wishes, He can even make the stones dance in ecstasy and carry on His work. But others, they feel the burden. This is God's work. *No man can do it and no man can stop it!"*

Obviously Darshan has undergone a tremendous transformation spiritually and physically since his days as a disciple. Before me sits a most *beautiful* Being, a *Paramhansa*. The veil hiding the jewel is rent, and the metamorphosis is awesome. It may *seem* like *his* metamorphosis, but in reality, the myopia of the onlooker's vision has finally cleared.

How Kirpal Ashram Came Into Being: Until early 1978, the Indian sangat had been without a center since 1974, as Sawan Ashram and Manav Kendra had been usurped by yet another false claimant to the Mastership. I have been out of the loop for more than four years, and Darshan kindly fills in for me the missing pieces: "...What started as a trickle became a flood as more and more came every day...As I have written in one of my verses,

> *I started alone on the journey of love,*
> *filled with faith and zeal,*
> *At every step travelers joined me,*
> *And soon we were a caravan.*

"Those who controlled Sawan Ashram and the accounts were not content with their gains. When their support from the sangat had virtually disappeared, they tried their utmost to thwart our mission at every step, calling the police to try and stop our peaceful satsangs, launching frivolous lawsuits, and the like. But they were not successful despite all the resources at their command. I received many death threats by phone and by letter. They even tried to create trouble in my place of work, but my supervisors, peers, and subordinates knew my character and supported me through thick and thin. I never took retaliatory action, nor did I permit anyone else to do so on my behalf. Those who campaigned against the mission were misguided, but there is always the hope that they will have a change of heart.

"For your information, I recently retired as the Deputy Secretary of the Indian government, where more than twelve thousand officers worked under my jurisdiction. I held three portfolios: Supplies, Vigilance and Human Relations. By the way, I still have in my possession those letters threatening your Auntie and I. You are welcome to see them. However, I never felt any fear, as the two great Masters are guiding and protecting me."

The property for Kirpal Ashram had been acquired and dedicated in November of 1977. Indeed, this place feels like home, as Sawan Ashram once did. It had previously belonged to descendants of the great Punjabi Sufi saint, Bulleh Shah, who sold it to the Sangat the previous year. This same family described to Darshan an incident from the 1960's when an elderly saintly gentleman happened into the large compound, admiring the profusion of unusual fruit and berry trees. He discussed with them Bulleh Shah's life and teachings with great knowledge and affection. Their mysterious visitor was none other than Master Kirpal, for whom they ever after maintained the greatest respect.

In an earlier talk, Darshan Singh revealed the secret of his spiritual merger with the Absolute. Fortunately, someone had the presence of mind to record it:

"He has taken me above body-consciousness...to the higher planes, leaving the stars, the moon and the sun behind, making me one with him in his radiant effulgent form. He has taken me into moments of eternity, beyond the limitations of time and space, and then, giving me a glance of love, a boost...he has taken me...into the highest realms of spirituality. On the way he has introduced me to the various Masters who have blessed this earth since time immemorial, and arranged for our conversation. We have conversed in a language which has no tongue...no words...no alphabet...in a language which is eternal. We have conversed in the language which was in the beginning...which was made Word, in the language which [divine] lovers even now speak. This is the language which will continue to the end of all time...
"And after taking me to our Eternal Home, Sach Khand, he has taken me on to higher realms known as Agam and Agochar, those regions

which are fathomless...beyond human imagination. And after that we reached Anaami, the ultimate vast region which has no shores...no limitation...no name..."

The physical transformation of Darshan from 1974 to now was staggering. There was now a palpable Masterly essence exuding from him, and whenever I became still, that essence became very clear. Frequently whenever I put my eyes on him, his eyes, face and body would transform into that of Kirpal.

For the old initiates who came to him, such experience was the norm, rather than the exception (which I verified time and again by questioning them). With awe and wonder I also witnessed Darshan change his physical configuration into that of Soami Ji, the Agra Param Sant. When I related this experience to Auntie Harbhajan, she replied, "In August 1974 when this Master, my husband, entered the living room at Sawan Ashram, Master Kirpal said aloud to several present, **'Soami Ji has come!'"**

5 5

H A L F - C O N F I R M A T I O N

Darshan arranged to have his driver discretely deliver me to my in-laws at about 7 AM. Exhausted but exhilarated, I climbed the steep stairs to the roof, lay down on a cot, pulled a sheet over my body and head and instantly went to sleep. Not really sleep—for my consciousness was immediately transferred into the presence of three Masters—Sawan, Kirpal, and Darshan. For the next four hours, they took turns talking to me. I was comforted, consoled and taken to different places in a radiant universe. At the end of this *endlessness*, Darshan's beaming face came right up in front of me, and said, "Brother, this is **half** your confirmation!"

There are no words to describe the intoxication I experienced upon coming to, which remained for the next twenty-four hours. When Ratana and children returned from Agra, my profound happiness met with great skepticism, but was unaffected. After some time she relented: "You know that I have always respected Darshan Singh Ji very highly. I never spoke against him like you did.

All right, I will go and see him, not as a Master," she said, "but as his son...and we will take our daughters." What more was wanted?, I pondered, still basking in the grace that had been bestowed on this repentant Doubting Thomas.

That night when we arrived at Kirpal Ashram, the Master came down the stairs to greet us personally despite his busy schedule. Ratana and daughters touched his feet. They loved him spontaneously and immediately.

Like a prayer-mantra, Shanti repeated over and over, "Master Darshan is the *real* Master!" As he spoke with us, baby Jyoti curled up and fell asleep with her little head resting on his feet. Some time later, we followed the Master downstairs where several hundred Indians waited. Gurdeep clung to his arm wherever he went. "Master, Gurdeep sings very beautifully," I said. He gathered her in his arms and plunked her down on the dais, asking, "Dear daughter, please let us hear your lovely voice." A big crowd gathered. Smitten by shyness, Gurdeep replied, "I can't, Master, I can't!" No amount of coaxing availed. Master then swept her up in his arms, and said movingly, "Daughter, at least we have heard the beating of your heart!"

What the Sufis refer to as the *tresses of the Beloved* had entangled us too. For several days Shanti was ecstatic. Not wanting to disturb our in-laws nor those still infatuated with the desert Baba, I requested everyone to keep our discovery quiet and secret. "But daddy," Shanti said, with bubbling enthusiasm, "Master Darshan is the real Master."

"Yes, but let's keep that to ourselves." "Okay, I guess," she begrudgingly consented.

At that moment, the big bus pulled into our in-laws' courtyard, loaded with the forty Westerners who had just returned from Rajasthan. The first off was her school teacher from Vancouver. Shanti suddenly broke free from my grip and ran to her, happily exclaiming "Judy, Judy, guess what! Master Darshan is the real Master!"

And the cat was out of the bag.

Karma.

56

My friends Alan and Richard also came to the gentle Saint seeking answers. Joan, who had been entrusted with some money owed to Richard by one of the departing visitors to Rajasthan, went to deliver the funds. Joan shared her experience with us:

"It was with some reticence that I made the trip to Kirpal Ashram where Richard was staying. Disillusioned with others, I had no inclination to see Darshan Singh. However, soon after my arrival, a message arrived, inviting me to meet with him.

"While waiting outside Darshan's room, I experienced one of the best meditations in years, after which Alan and I passed a couple of hours alone with Darshan. I will never forget the sensitivity with which he handled that first meeting. Addressing me as sister, he spoke only of the Beloved Master and his mission, going into detail regarding the planned publication *Portrait of Perfection* devoted to his memory, and of *Sat Sandesh* and the publication of the Master's works in many languages. He also questioned me regarding my own experiences.

"There was a tangible charging in Darshan's presence and I began to experience effortless withdrawal to the eye-focus. I was overwhelmed to see him transform into my own Master for extensive periods, sitting before me a mere yard away. My heart opened and tears flowed, and I realized then the depth of our suffering since that separation, and how, in order to carry on, we covered that pain and our hearts hardened in the process."

Ratana, Joan, the children and I rented a taxi and pilgrimaged to Dehra Dun, but were saddened by the neglect of the once pristine Manav Kendra which, like Sawan Ashram, had fallen into disreputable hands. Darshan had forewarned us, but he also predicted that Manav Kendra would again blossom as originally intended. The 207 Rajpur Road property was still immaculately maintained by one of Darshan's hand-picked caretakers who assisted all who came to pay their respects and meditate there, which is what we did for two days, experiencing a deep spiritual recharging.

We returned to Delhi, where we experienced a joyous reunion with Darshan. After his Sunday public discourse, we dined with him. Richard addressed Darshan explaining that Joan had no specific work to return to in Canada at that time. Darshan turned to her, and transforming into Master Kirpal as he spoke, said, "This is your Father's home, and you are always welcome here." Addressing another who was unsure whether to stay longer, or return to a job, the Master looked around the table with an impish smile, "It depends what you want, *money* or *honey!*"

Joan later commented, "Unable to erase the image of my Master saying I was welcome, I vacillated right up to the customs gate at the New Delhi airport. There I froze, and could go no further."

At the last second, Joan turned around and returned to the *honey*. Her narrative continues:

"Darshan was so loving and open, and made each of us feel a part of the Master's international family. In spite of the sublime experiences I was having in his presence, and the poignant remembrance evoked by the anecdotes and stories he shared, my mind troubled me with residual doubts for sometime. Darshan encouraged us to bring up all questions and would often say, 'There are no secrets here.' He drew out all ranklings that were interfering with our ability to concentrate within.

"One day, in a small group, I told Darshan that many in my area, including myself, had been deeply affected by a rumor that Sant Kirpal Singh had said at some meeting, that his successor would not be from his family, though I had yet to meet anyone that was there.

"He delicately indicated that if the Master had made such a statement, the import may not have been clear, and proceeded to speak of the retreat that Master Kirpal undertook near Rishikesh, after the passing of Hazur. He recalled how during this period, the Beloved Master had invited his family members (including Darshan, Harbhajan Kaur and their son Rajinder) to join him at the old villa he had rented at Rani-Ki-Kothi. Darshan spoke of how intimate and special were these times; how they meditated long hours together, and shared as a family. Master even made chapatis for them.[1] At the end of this period, the Master called his family to him, and told them that from then on, they were not to consider him as their father, for he was now to take up the role of the Universal Father, explaining that in the future they would not enjoy such times together. In the language of esotericism, Darshan then added, 'the family of a Master are *those whom he initiates*.'" [Darshan was initiated by Hazur.]

During my final days in Delhi, Tai Ji permitted Richard and Alan to photocopy the entire hand-written coded diaries attributed to Master Kirpal. The complete copy which Darshan kindly let me keep, contains hundreds of comments in the margins in English, in Kirpal Singh's hand-writing. Several tiny drawings of inner plane features are found along with his words.

Tai Ji was steadily becoming more receptive to Darshan Singh, and made several visits to see him, but she admitted her inability to extricate herself from her unwise creations. She who had been so close to the source of happiness, was now one to be pitied.

Kirpal Singh making chapatis, Rishikesh, 1948.
(Photo by Darshan)

Seekers have always been urged to keep their attention on the Masters, and then graduate to the divine power which works through them, not on the personalities around them, no matter how evolved they may seem. A grateful student will always consider his or her Preceptor's teachings to be their guide, until the Goal of merger is reached.

---

1. Darshan, an avid amateur photographer, captured that special moment on film; the Master, turbanless, is seen rolling out chapatis.

Truth is above all, but higher still is true living. —Guru Nanak

Centuries of accounts by and about the Adepts are conclusive: A *true Disciple* is one whose life is a perfect reflection of the ideals enjoined and embodied by a perfect Teacher. And, every Teacher—no matter how great—was once a Disciple who lived by Truth and *realized* it. True living is nothing less than complete purity in thought, word, and deed every moment of life. By these lofty standards, only a few begin to approach its minimum standards.

In every age and disciplic dispensation, the full transmission of spiritual power was bequeathed to that lone Disciple who had been shorn of any trace of lust, anger, greed, attachment and ego. True living, complete self-surrender, and continuous communion with the eternal Light and Sound Principles were and are concommitants of a God-realized life. Paradoxically, it is this most humble true Disciple who always feels least worthy to inherit the Mastership, and who least covets it.

Only the Writer of Destiny knows why I had to take such a tortuous road to recognition and acceptance. Though none dethroned Kirpal from my heart, I was extremely grateful and relieved that at last I could see what he wanted me to see—the Master working in fullness through Darshan Singh. He, however, was not a mere channel for previous Masters to "work through." Upon assuming the Mantle, the true Disciple *becomes* the Master, and as such, is fully invested with spiritual power and wisdom to guide the many.

Having arrived at this point of understanding, Richard Handel and I put the following questions to Sant Darshan Singh. His answers clarified many delicate points of Mastership and succession. If his style differed from his illustrious predecessors, the message and authority were the same. And, he could call a spade a spade when appropriate.

Question: "Do imperfect masters know they are imperfect?"

Answer: "Generally not. On this Path each step can seem like the end point. Some of the imperfect masters barely see Light, others may go as high as the fourth plane. It is only by the grace of the Master that the disciple can get anything, and this grace can be withdrawn at any time. Sometimes we start to think that we are getting somewhere because of our efforts, then the ego comes in and the grace is cut off. Some think the Master loved them the most. That is a misunderstanding, as the love of the Master is boundless. He has boundless love for all creation. To say, 'The Master loved me the most of all his initiates,' or 'He showered all His grace on me,' is a sign of egotism.

"When the Master sends his grace to a disciple, neither the disciple nor those around him think the grace will ever diminish. Under the influence of his ego, the disciple begins to think he is infallible, or that he knows better than the Master, with the result that he becomes an egoist, or one who thinks he is wonderful; and finally an egotist, or one who tells others how wonderful he thinks he is! However, sometimes the Master's grace does stop flowing to that initiate, although others around him are not always aware of this. Consequently, the disciple often commits many mistakes and blunders.

"Also, even if the disciple is aware that the Master's grace has stopped flowing to him, and even if he knows the truth, his ego may not allow him to come to the right path. The disciple doesn't want to belittle himself before his admirers and colleagues by admitting the folly of his ways, as he is afraid of public opinion and shame. As a result, the errors and deceptions go on."

Question: "What is the fate of imperfect masters who are initiated by a perfect Master?"

Answer: "There was a disciple of Baba Jaimal Singh from Taran Taran named Baba Bagga Singh. He began initiating without authorization. After some time he realized his mistake and invited Baba Sawan Singh to his place. When he met Master Sawan, he bowed down to his feet and repented. In his grace, the Master told him to carry on with his work, and Sawan took over his burden.

"The grace of the Master is always at work. However, if someone goes against the law of nature and starts initiating without authorization, or, if an initiate of a perfect Master starts associating with an imperfect successor, another birth may be required."

Question: "So many people who are much more sincere than ourselves are led to imperfect Masters. Why is that?"

Answer: "We should have in our hearts a similar prayer as the Beloved Master: 'O God, I'm yearning like anything. I want to meet You. There are so many gurus and masters; the world is full of them. To whom should I go, and to whom should I not go? I am afraid if I go to one who has not reached You, my life's aim will be spoiled. In the olden days it is said that You appeared to those who loved You, then why can't You manifest now?' If we cry from the core of our hearts like the beloved Master did, then we will eventually be led to a perfect Master."

Question: "What is the fate of those who are initiated by a perfect Master, but later become affiliated with an imperfect master?"

Answer: "I asked this same question of the beloved Master after Hazur left the body. I asked him if it was their fault. They were only doing what they felt was correct. How could they be blamed? He answered that it is a law of nature that they will have to suffer for their mistake, even though it was committed unknowingly and in good faith. Naturally, since they were initiated by a perfect Master, they will ultimately be taken care of, although they may have to come into the world again [in another rebirth].

"An imperfect master has not completed the Path, and cannot initiate prop-

erly. He may also bind you to himself. This may delay your spiritual progress.
If someone binds you to your Master, it's good, but, if they bind you to themselves, then it's a deterrent on the Path...However, the true successor will open the wound of separation for your Master, and help reunite you with him."

Question: "What about initiates of a perfect Master who don't go to anyone after their Master leaves the body?"

Answer: "That's alright, as long as they keep their Master's commandments, and especially as long as they have love in their hearts for all. As they progress in their meditations, their Master will tell them who his true successor is. The company of their Master's successor will serve as a consolation, and they will derive benefit from his presence."

Question: "If we reach the Master inside even while associating with an imperfect master, will he tell us our mistake?"

Answer: "Definitely, he will tell us everything, *if* we can talk to him inside. However sometimes through auto-suggestion we may see and hear things inside, but in reality they are just a reflection of our mind. Often when our Master or even an imperfect master appears inside, we are so overjoyed that we forget to do simran. In addition, the experience may be of such a short duration that it hardly allows us to start simran. Occasionally it can happen that the Master and the imperfect master appear to merge back and forth into one another, but that also is only because of imperfect simran...It is very easy for someone who is nearer to you in spiritual development to appear within. If you think of your girlfriend for just a short time, then she can appear within. If you look at an imperfect master for even five to fifteen minutes, that can make an impression on you which can be transferred within very easily. But if you look at a perfect Master for fifteen hours straight, even then he may not appear within. You cannot *imagine* in meditation someone who is Perfect. He appears only of his own accord, but an imperfect master can easily be imagined within. Our mind can easily manifest that which is imperfect within, but it cannot imagine that which is perfect..."

Question: "What happens to someone who actively supports an imperfect master and denies the perfect Master before coming around?"

Answer: "A father is doubly happy to welcome home his prodigal son. What you did was done in good faith even though it may have been wrong. Once you realize your mistake, it takes much courage and extra grace from the Master to admit it. It is especially difficult to admit it publicly, as frequently your friends, family and society will all be against you. Sometimes people will realize they have been misled, but because of public pressure or their ego, they will be unable to change their ways. No matter what happens, the Master is always compassionate and forgiving.

ANSWERS FROM A TRUE DISCIPLE

"On my American tour earlier this summer, I told a number of people, "Despite whatever he has said against me, Arran-ji will come around, but our dear brother_____-ji, has so much invested, and is so far entangled, that even if he knows the truth, he will not come out in this lifetime."

Question: "Is it possible for a Saint to ever be unaware of another Saint functioning elsewhere on the physical plane at the same time?"

Answer: "No. Saints are all-knowing."

Question: "Is it better to stay at home and meditate intensely for two or three months, or is it better to use the same amount of money to come to India to be with our Master's true successor?"

Answer: "If you can have remembrance of your Master all the twenty-four hours of the day, then there is no need to go anywhere. But if you keep to yourself, there is the very real possibility of your heart becoming dry and hard like a stone. Also there is the danger of getting a puffed-up ego, because you may start to think that you are accomplishing something because of your great efforts. This is not a path of asceticism. The Master's successor, because he is always suffering the pangs of separation, will create the same state in you, by example. You will be benefited through his thought transference, his radiation and his eyes. This is a path of grace and tears. The successor will bind you to your Master, and not to himself. His company is of great value..."

Darshan cautioned me *not* to recommence as an initiating representative until and unless I had full confirmation from my Master within. Folding his hands together, he turned his eyes up and within for several long moments, and commented, "I pray to the two great Masters that your wish be granted at the earliest possible time. We must have love and respect for everyone. But if someone wishes clarification or direction, we may lovingly share our experience with them." He then added "Maintain harmony in the home. Don't make any hasty decisions. Master will shower his grace and show you."

When I asked about his relationship with Tai Ji and her supporters who had actively persecuted him, he replied, "Whenever my wife or I visit Tai Ji, we always touch her feet, and respect her. In fact she came here when we opened this Ashram, and when she came I touched her feet. I always touch the feet of my elders. The Saints have no fight with anyone. If anyone wants to fight over property, let them have it."

Darshan won those who considered themselves his enemies by his consistently loving ways. In time, Manav Kendra and Sawan Ashram would be laid at his feet, without clamor or dispute.

58

Master Kirpal once shared with an intimate group a profound object-lesson, paraphrased from the life of Socrates. Even now I hear the echoes of his distinctive voice:

*"Socrates was asked, 'Whom do you love most? Plato or Truth?' Socrates replied, 'I love Plato. But, I love Truth **more** than Plato! We are after Truth, you see.'"*

We loved our close-knit community of friends, but when we chose to follow our truth, radical upheaval followed, and the *"I love Truth more than Plato"* took on special meaning.

I know of no higher love than that which a perfect and selfless Master has for his disciples. When the teacher is authentic, Truth is what he represents, and Truth is the eternal verity to which he attaches us. We are also Truth, but Truth asleep. An authentic Master is a living bridge; a door; a boat; an awakened beam back to the Sun.

Everything and everyone can be the mask, veil, or mouthpiece behind which the Divine is trying to reach us, to speak with us. Even so-called misfortunes, which take the form of loss, ignominy and illness, can be our Friend in disguise. If we can see the One behind even the terrible faces, instead of fleeing, we will embrace the test and ultimately pass it.

> *Taunts, reproaches and vilification also strengthen and reform the followers of the Saints, as without them they too would remain as they are. Derision and public opprobrium are the necessary concomitants of true love... In Persian it has been said:*
>
> > *Slander is the watchman of the market of love;*
> > *It cleans love of all its rust and brightens it.*
>
> *—Soami Shiv Dayal Singh—Sar Bachan Prose*

Things would never be the same. Our personal life as we knew it, including the entangled, yet highly successful Lifestream business came to an end, despite best efforts to reconcile. A lengthy partnership struggle left no alternative but to sell to outsiders. As Omar Khyyam reminds:

The Moving Finger writes; and having writ,
Moves on: nor all thy piety nor wit
Shall lure it back to cancel half a line,
Nor all thy tears wash out a word of it.

Selling out was not of my choice, but then, the moving finger writes for all.
Through each test, beyond the ripples, was a delectable heightened awareness,
and the most difficult situations seemed to bring the face of the Beloved closer
to the surface. Each probation was a cleansing of the mirror. Catharsis can
open unprecedented opportunities for growth and change; it caused our little
circle to expand, for we had unknowingly become too narrow. How could a
universal teacher ever wish his pupils to be narrow-minded? What Darshan
lived and asked, was in reality a reflection of his constantly forgiving, loving
nature:

Embrace every man as your very own,
And shower your love freely wherever you go.
—*Darshan*

Too many a time I failed to emulate such unconditioned love, yet I hope and
think there is some improvement. One must tread carefully through the mine-
field of tender hearts.

Excommunicated, as it were, from the community of followers of the desert
Baba, we moved from the country back to the city, drawn to a gracious old
house in a quiet neighborhood, surrounded by a high-hedged secluded garden.
The first time I passed through the heavy front door and into the foyer, joy-
bells were resounding, source unseen. Glancing around, I sensed the presence
of the smiling Master and disciples here in the hallway, there in the living-room
and out back in the magnificent gardens. It said, *home*, and it all came to pass.

59

The cloak of my life has been torn from the very dawn...

In April, 1979, I returned alone to India for three weeks, to fortify and deepen my connection to the Divine working through Darshan, the poet-saint. He encouraged me to share certain experiences with others—experiences which normally would have remained secret. He did this with many in those days, to illustrate, via personal gnosis, the continuation of the power of the great lineage.

Three or four days after arriving in India, a special grace poured out through the successor's eyes to mine. When I returned from his apartment to my room, glorious radiance was constant company, and it assumed the form of the living Master. Whenever these physical eyes would blink, or close even for a few seconds, Darshan's shining eyes and face would be clearly seen in golden, intense brilliance. Sometimes Master Kirpal would appear, flooding my being with joy, but mostly it was Darshan in his transcendental form, communicating simple and profound truths in words, very clearly explaining why things are the way they are. This state seemed unaffected by simran, whether done with full concentration for hours continuously, or not at all. In that intoxicated state I was sometimes careless as a child, and, not knowing whether if this was correct or not, I requested that only Kirpal's form should remain. My own wishes had absolutely no effect and were superseded by the unity of all Masters, contained within Darshan's golden form.

After the second day, saturation set in; there was no room for more. Perhaps complacency, perhaps individual ego intervened, or God decided, *bas! Enough!* Whatever the reason, the visions that had engulfed me unabated for 48 hours, abruptly ended. For the next few days meditation was practically barren, dim, and tasteless. Again the lesson drove home how utterly reliant I was upon grace, that special kindness which flows through a *living* Master.

One may have to work hard for years to catch a significant surge in the divine Ocean of Consciousness, like a surfer who waits long to catch and ride the perfect wave. God, Guru, Soul, Light and the Audible Life-stream are intermeshed and related. It is a living Adept who stirs up the great waves, who makes the difficult Way *effortless.* Paradoxically, the glimpses and the sippings often suddenly give way to *bireh,* the intense pain of separation. Darshan's presence often ripped open the wound of love that I felt for Kirpal.

In the middle of one of his Sunday discourses, I was suddenly overcome by

such a longing, and without showing any signs, I quietly crept through the huge throng, and entered the vacant library toward the back, and shut the door. Wrapping my meditation shawl over my head, I sank to the floor and vented the anguish of my heart.

After a few minutes I heard the door move behind me and shut. The sliding of the lock-bolt followed, but my eyes remained closed. Sensing someone close by, I finally parted the folds of the shawl, and found Darshan himself alone in the room with me. We hugged each other, and wept together in silence, his head on my shoulder, and mine on his. Many minutes passed like this, as I moved from pain to ecstasy. Then Darshan pulled out his handkerchief, blew his nose, wiped his eyes, smiled at me and went out the door, back through the multitude, climbed the dais and took up his discourse as though nothing had happened! He understood the secret delicate pain of the heart.

> *In this world, each is consumed*
> *with his own afflictions;*
> *Only Darshan shares the sorrows*
> *of his fellow man.*

This unique Master rarely takes physical rest or sleep. He passes each night in the assembly of seekers and disciples, a night-owl whose poetry comes to life in the wee hours of the morn. His all night sessions rarely finish before seven AM, when he might take an hour or two of rest, bathe, take breakfast-tea and start the rounds again.

> From dawn to dawn, let us speak of peace
> and listen to the message of love,
> The shower-laden clouds of Sawan
> have enveloped the tavern of time,
> O Cupbearer, let the cup of love
> go round and round and round.²

One night/morning—late, late, somewhere in *no-time*, as five or six of us sit around him, he addresses the omnipresent Beloved in Urdu verse, freely translating into English as he goes along:

> When I am blessed with the intoxication of my Master
> What do I care for the rise and fall of material life?
> For others, life is full of the vintage and the goblet,
> But the very blood of my desires is wine for me.
>
> You scuttle my heart, tear it to pieces
> And the blood which oozes out
> I'll sip with profound gratitude,
> And it will be intoxication for me,
> As the murder of my desires comes from You.

"My poetry has served as an outburst," he says, and then continues his impromptu recitation:

> Please tell the darners of the night of waiting
> that the cloak of my life
> has been torn from the very dawn.
>
> Your life is a chandelier
> of the sleeping chamber of beauty;
> And mine is a candle
> burning in the middle of the road,
> Guiding strangers throughout the night...

Darshan dubs me "welfare officer," and one of my duties is to report to him the condition of the various foreign guests at the busy ashram. One day, a poor, weeping Indian woman leads me to the meditation hall, where I find her husband, reduced to skin and bones, prostrate with high malarial fever. Reassuring her, I proceed to Master's quarters upstairs, where he is engaged with visiting dignitaries. He interrupts the meeting, and immediately comes with me to the dying man.

Despite his filthy sweat-soaked rags, Master kneels beside the invalid, holds him in his arms, lovingly inquires of his welfare, strokes his head and pats his cheek. He calls for a doctor and medicine, and the man is treated. Four days later, we are all happy to see the fully recovered husband and his wife walking about the ashram with beautiful and profound smiles lighting their nut-brown faces.

The Master tells an amusing story about a Russian diplomat who came to India as an atheist, but after one year, he declared himself a believer because, he said, India's conditions were so impossible, so chaotic, that it was only by the grace of a Divine Being that anything ever got accomplished!

Darshan observes the Westerner's difficulties coping with India's heat, noise, smells, insects, spicy food, exasperating delays, etc. With a raised eyebrow and a sweet, slightly mischievous smile he comments, "The Westerner's prayer is, 'O God, grant me patience. But grant it right now!' expecting that the Path to the Beloved should be a velvet path, whereas the Path passes through the thorns. They want a velvet path, and what am I to do?"

His merry laughter, river-like in its intoxicating flow, carries me towards the sea of existence.

> *Begin to live your life according to your aspirations,*
> *And step towards your chosen goal...*
> *You would find that what you take for thorns*
> *are really flowers,*
> *If you but step into my world of faith.*
>
> *This desolate scene will become a haven,*
> *If you fill the world of your heart with love.*[3]

---

1. Darshan Singh, *A Tear And a Star*, SK Publications, Bowling Green, VA, p. 59.

2. Ibid., page 64.

3. Ibid.

60

Auntie-ji, Manohar and I sit in the back seat, while Master Darshan and driver sit up front.[1] Our destination is Rohtak, an industrial city two hours from Delhi. For most of the journey, Master is silent and absorbed in meditation, his upturned left foot resting on his right knee. As I fade in and out of my own meditation, I can't help but notice a large, symmetrical seven pointed star on the sole of his left foot, formed out of his naturally occuring crease-lines. This symmetrical "star" is quite distinct from the Lotus on the sole of his right foot.

Thousands of Rohtak citizens have been awaiting the Master's arrival in the hot sun for more than four hours, lining the roadside for blocks. Our car slowly proceeds through their columns towards the spacious home of Chachaji Rameshwar Das. Chachaji and his wife have spared no effort or expense to ensure everyone's comfort. In spite of his ninety plus years, Chachaji—formerly an advocate of the supreme court, is extremely lucid and sharp.

After the busload of twenty-five westerners and twenty Delhi residents assemble inside, a delicious buffet is served. Master enthuses, "Here you will be served the purest food...only pure ghee (clarified butter) is used and the vegetables come directly from the fields, grown without any chemicals." He eats with us.

We drive to the satsang grounds. As soon as the Master emerges from the car, he is almost crushed by the enthusiastic crowd. Many literally dive for his feet, which he discourages. One man grabs his ankles out of devotion, almost causing him to fall, yet the Master remains unperturbed.

With his arrival, the joy of the Rohtak sangat expresses itself in a holy chant from Gurbani:

> *Darshan dekh jiva Guru Tera,*
> *Puran karama hovae Prabh mera...*
> *In beholding the vision of the Master,*
> *All karmas are fulfilled, my Lord...*

Thousands repeat this refrain over and over. After a while someone stands in the congregation and shouts:

> *"Sawan kay lal ke jayho!* (Victory to the son of Sawan!)
> *Kirpal kay lal ke jayho!* (Victory to the son of Kirpal!)"

After settling on the dais, Darshan humbly bows his head to the floor, to the omnipresent Master visible in the congregation. Only then does he begin to weave his message, annihilating time.

Tavern of the Midnight Sun: Long after the satsang finishes, perhaps around midnight, I walk dog-tired with my bags to the dharamshala eight blocks away where I hope to sink into restful slumber. As soon as I spread my bedroll, a messenger arrives, "Brother, Master wishes to see you right away!"

I groan unreceptively—if not ungratefully, for all I want is sleep. But then, such a request is not to be refused. I gather my things and resignedly stumble back to Chachaji's where a small circle of friends sits on the living-room floor about the Master. Gradually it dawns on me that he is in an extremely gracious state. Desperately struggling for wakefulness and clarity of mind, like one swimming up from the bottom of a dark well, I finally breach the surface, and catch the breath of his rarefied atmosphere. He speaks beautifully of God as the Eternal Beloved and of the Beloved's wiles, the intricacies of the Path...its twists, turns, thorns, despair, sorrow...and also its hope, ecstasy and joy.[2] He speaks of becoming ensnared by the beauty of the Eternal, of becoming undone and remade; of sacrifice, surrender and obedience...of the hopeless and helpless state of the separated lover...a state yet to be understood by the world.

We sit close by his knee, absorbed, awake through the night. His spiritual radiance and reflection is tremendous. This night, the Sun takes off its glove. To describe the ineffable beauty of this shadowless being is impossible, but even crows will croak:

> *Here sits the ancient One—a glowing center*
> *transmitting life into our dust... no dream or fantasy, this!*
> *Out-flowing, in-flowing Light, unfolds Creation's lyric story,*
> *Separation and Union—the song of Everything.*

> *He speaks, and an arching spark leaps from Eye to eye,*
> *to heart, to soul, and back, again & again, one seamless circle;*
> *Timelessness finds its locus.*
> *Light coalescing, translucent, blazing yet cool.*

> *Tell me Whose eyes peer from beneath your brows?*
> *Kirpal or Sawan, Kabir or Namelessness?*
> *You have revealed your secret, O' Darshan!*

> *By comparison, all fortunes are ashes,*
> *for tonight there is no separation!*

Dawn lightens the skies and birds burst into song, signaling the drawing of a veil over the cup-bearer's secret essence. The wine-cask is unbunged and drained. We can hold no more, and leave to rest. Such sessions in the Tavern of the Midnight Sun sustain the seeker for all times.

Who protects Whom? After the second satsang in Rohtak, Master desires to walk through the jubilant crowds and bless the many who have sacrificed satsang to prepare huge amounts of free food for the congregation. Several of us form a wall with our bodies to protect the gentle Master from the undisciplined crowds as he makes his way towards the langar. Halfway, he stops and turns to us, "I have no need of your protection my brothers, as the grace and protection of the two great Masters are more than sufficient for me!" Our eyes connect.

Over the din I ask, "Are you *sure*, Master?" He and I laugh like crazy! We drop our arms. The crowd surges forward, stops within half an inch of his holy body, and parts like the Red Sea. Our Moses goes directly to those in need, with whom he freely converses without let or hindrance from the likes of us. *He leads us from the Egypt of mind, to the Promised Land of the heart.*

Upon returning to the residence, our car is met at the gate by Ramcharan, Chachaji's eldest son. A lively discussion takes place with Ramcharan forcefully entreating, "Maharaj Ji! Please I beg you, show my brothers and me the Lotus Mark on your foot! This will give us faith if you will only show us."

The Master isn't eager to make a public show, but the pleading of these brothers is sincere. He gradually pulls his right foot out of its sandal. A chair and table are brought. With more coaxing in this sweet game, he sits down and places his right foot upon the table. Ramcharan asks me to point out the mark, while the Master looks on with faint amusement.

After I pointed out the naturally occurring mystic sign, the Master retires to his room, and we to ours for meditation.

On my last day in India, Darshan invites me to accompany him on a visit to Manohar's house in another part of Delhi. Master sits between the driver and me. At one point he folds his legs into a half-lotus posture, closes his eyes and quickly withdraws from the body, remaining in deep meditation as the car rolls through the rough and twisting streets. I follow suit, mentally repeating the charged names. The moment I close my eyes, the road, the car, and the city disappear, replaced by the effulgent vision of Kirpal, seated upon a radiant throne. ***"You are to serve my son Darshan!"*** he commands me.

Shashi's Complaint: On the eve of departure, Sevadars enter the Master's room and their spokesperson speaks, "Maharaj Ji? Shashi Bhenji is lying unconscious out in the courtyard." Shashi is a school teacher and librarian who performs a great deal of selfless service around the ashram. Master asks if I would like to come along. While holding my hand he descends the stairs where a crowd is waiting to catch his darshan. One Indian lady has been waiting for several hours at the foot of the stairs, hoping for a glance. When he gives it, her soul immediately leaves the body for higher planes. Someone catches her limp form before it falls to the pavement! Her soul will return after an hour or two.

He leads me out between buildings and into the large open area where, four and a half hours earlier, his discourse on "Spiritual Surrender" had captivated thousands. Shashi lies flat-out on the ground before the dais, surrounded by several women watching over her. Master rubs her forehead, and trickles water on her face. After about ten minutes, life-currents begin to return and an

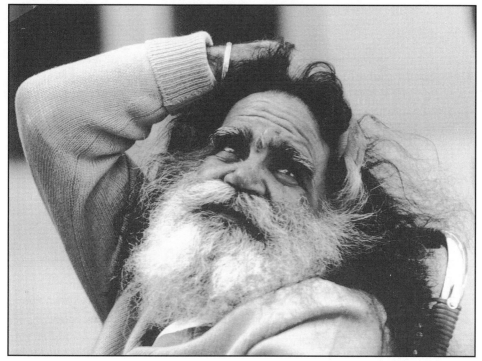

The Tresses of the Friend— Darshan.

unearthly wail emits from her mouth. When Sashi's eyes open and recognize the Master by her side, she wastes no time begging him to allow her soul to be returned to the higher regions again. Master demurs, for she has work to do. With a curious smile he comments, "You see, just yesterday, Shashi complained to me that while others are blessed with higher experiences, she doesn't see the Master's radiant form or much else in meditation." He sweetly laughs, "Now see her state!"

Father and Son: Later, back in his living room, I ask, "What was your relationship with Master Kirpal in the previous life?"

He candidly replies, "...sometimes I have been the son, and sometimes I have been the father. Actually, the Beloved Master and I have exchanged these roles many a time."

If it weren't for my seeing the actual form of Master Kirpal sitting before me in Darshan's place as he divulged this staggering secret, I could never have believed such a thing in a million years.

---

1. Manohar was the son of Sant Kirpal Singh's elder brother, Sardar Jodh Singh Duggal.

2. In the literature of the mystic East, God and/or the God-man are often referred to as the Beloved.

6 1

Despite all that I had been fortunate to witness and receive, knowing on a very deep level that Darshan and Kirpal were one, I still awaited full confirmation directly from the mouth of my own Master inside who his successor was. Both had withstood the inner test of simran, but I just wanted to hear from Kirpal unequivocably that Darshan was his successor. My caution was forged from bitter experience. How long I would have to wait I hadn't a clue, which created a kind of angst in me.

On my last night in India, Darshan and I had an in-depth discussion in the wee hours of the morn. At one point he said, "It is better to let us wait." I turned on the tape recorder.

"Wait?"

"'Till you have had this boon [of confirmation], one hundred percent."

"And if it never comes?"

"The question of its not coming does not arise. We should always be on the lookout, always looking for that. It takes its time. You know the situation, brother, and I'll be the last man to advise you to make a second mistake. You must have one hundred percent confirmation, one hundred percent assurance that whatever you are doing is right and in accordance with the commandments of the Master."

"I want you to know," I said, "that I am very grateful for the wonderful and ecstatic times we have enjoyed together."

"Brother, it is my pleasure also...When we sit together, we think of the Beloved, and the caravan of intense memories starts moving."

"...As I have done in the past, I will work with all love and enthusiasm for Master's work, and if any sincere seeker comes along, I'll send them to you because I know that His power is working through you."

"It would be best if you pass those seekers onto our two Great Masters. That is all I do."

"If the confirmation is given to me, then it would be wonderful if it were also given to Ratana."

"Yes, that's necessary because you have to move as a team. I tell you, throughout life I had never thought I would get entangled like this, but somehow or the other, your Auntie had apprehensions. Whenever the Beloved Master would tell me something or ask when I would retire, she would feel upset about it. He was talking to me alone on so many occasions, but it so happened that the day He told me all about this work, and that I would have to carry on everything, she was by my side. So you know, at least she got the confirmation and this is how the work is going on. I was such a loving husband, and she used to get quite a lot of attention from me, but now...you find our condition. You have seen it, but because she had the confirmation, she is undergoing a lot and is doing her best for the mission, and for that naturally she has to suffer also. If Master also gives Ratana confirmation, then the work can be carried on with great strength. This path is not easy; it is very difficult. If you have conviction and you have grace then you can pull on very nicely...If you did not have that devotion, you couldn't have taken this stand which you have taken so boldly. How many people can take such a stand?"

"There's no virtue in me."

"Because we can't claim any virtue, we can only call it the Master's grace."

Someone interrupts: "Excuse me, Master, but he should be going to catch the plane."

"Right, sir! Your commandments shall be obeyed, sir! If you will only give us five minutes... Five minutes extension!" He turns his attention back to me. "Please convey my love to Ratana, whom I take to be my daughter, or sister— whatever she likes."

"No, she's your daughter."

"Because she is of the age of Raji. Raji was born in '46."

"She was also born in '46."

"Then she is of Raji's age, who was born on the 20th of September. We were all born in September—myself on the 14th and Harbhajan on the 24th."

"I can't relate to you as a brother. You're more a father to me."

"I use the word brother because we are fellow initiates, in that sense. Otherwise you are just like my son Raji, and I have the same love and regard for you. So I treat her as my own daughter. Ask her to devote a little time for meditation. Let us hope for the best."

In the courtyard as the taxi-walla waited to escort me to the airport, I addressed the living Master, who had come to see me off:

"Coming here has opened the wound of separation."

Darshan placed his palms together, rolled his eyes upward, and replied, "He is the healer of all wounds." He and Auntie-ji then blessed me and waved me off into the night.

As the months and years rolled by, many peers were fortunate to meet Sant Darshan Singh for themselves. Most received mystic experience in his presence, if not outright confirmation that this humblest of God-men was indeed the repository of the moral integrity and spiritual grace of all Saints who preceded him. Those who remained aloof, lost out. Ever-increasing numbers of new seekers were drawn in novel and mysterious ways. From the ashes came a spark, a flame, a great Light, a healing.

In November of '79, Ratana and others, curious to meet Darshan Singh, all traveled to India. Usually loathe to speak of her own spiritual condition, Ratana wrote me, hinting of something profound which had taken place in Darshan's presence:

> *"For the first time in my life, I now know experientially what Master Kirpal meant when he talked of rising above body consciousness.*
>
> *"There are so many facets to M. Darshan's personality. Sometimes he is like a child. Sometimes he seems like a giant, all magnificent and beautiful. Last night when he called me in, I began looking into his eyes. They turned golden and bright Light shone from his face. And I was consciousness. Auntie then called from the other room and asked me to request Master to take his food, but he continued talking for half an hour more, mentioning his illness which doctors do not understand. He said, 'I recently initiated ten people who were physically blind. Who is going to take their karma? Sometimes a man comes asking me to take his child's fever. The fever goes away, but who takes it?'*
>
> *"He said, 'We are to bring Cosmos out of chaos.'"*

Janet Judd, one of her companions, related her experience from that visit: "It was during one of those late nights at the ashram with the Master, around 3 AM. He was assuring me that I was a pure soul, filled with God's Light. I was shocked and said, 'Oh no, Master, I'm not. I'm just a sinner and I'm steeped in darkness! You're the one who is all radiance!'

"He again insisted that I was a radiant soul. By this time I was in tears and said, 'I'm unclean; I'm filled with sins and shortcomings. I don't see Light within, but when I look at you I see you filled with Light.'

"He seemed a little impatient with me and said, 'Dear daughter, you are also filled with the very same radiance! Don't say that you are unclean and in darkness! Whatever Light you may see in me, is also in you. I see God's radiance very clearly shining in your face and eyes!'

"Again I insisted that I was in darkness. Master became animated and said, 'If you don't believe what I am saying, then let me show you! I'll take you to that big mirror over there and you can see for yourself!'

"So, I reluctantly let Master lead me by the hand and we stood before the full-length mirror. When I looked up from the floor, I was amazed to see my self reflected in it, glowing like a fluorescent tube, just like the Master! He said, 'You see, daughter, ***the same Light of God is also in you.***'"

FULL CONFIRMATION

6 3

When my experiences in 1978 led me to recognize Darshan's spiritual Mastery, some expected me to resume my former role as an initiating representative. But I had no choice in the matter, being honor-bound to wait until receiving full inner confirmation.

5 A.M., 7th of July 1980: In a vision of remarkable clarity, I was allowed to time-warp back to August 1974, *before* the physical death of my Master, who now appeared in front of me, clad in pure white raiment, reclining on his side on a white-sheeted bed. I kneeled close beside him. After some time he raised himself up to speak. Darshan Singh stood directly behind him, exactly as he had looked in 1974, younger, dressed in Western clothes and with tied-up beard. Simran provided an inner loving-glow as I gazed upon my beautiful, long-departed Kirpal, now very much alive.

I could have passively continued to bathe in the light of this encounter, but an intense need forced the articulation of what I had never been able to ask: "Master, who will be your spiritual successor?" He looked at me mercifully and answered very softly, *"Darshan Singh is my successor."*

After gazing deeply into his eyes and visage, letting those five words sink in, I felt a great excitement and happiness. I saw that we were in a huge hall filled with people, some of whom I recognized. Shepherding them before the Master, I urged, "Now you can ask Master himself who his true spiritual successor is and get the answer directly from him." Darshan continued standing in the background. Then Master sat up and leaned forward, his magnificent face only inches from mine. With great power, he declared, *"I will tell everyone who my successor is!"*

My head lowered, and heart was full of repentance. As a measure of the Godman's merciful nature, the sluice-gates of consciousness were opened; soul and He began to glow, until everything became engulfed in ever-increasing, almost unbearable brilliance and the Song of the Cosmos. The form of the One whom I recognized as Kirpal dissolved in glory and became the portal and catapult to the formless Beyond.

Later, when my consciousness reluctantly returned, every cell of my body was suffused with inebriant joy. The long wait of six years was over. The last restraint removed, I phoned the living Master in India and offered my unreserved services. He was pleased and said that the timing and measure of confirmation were in accord with the divine plan.

Over the next twenty-five years, I persoally met hundreds of old disciples to whom confirmation was mysteriously conveyed in a myriad ways.

6 4

In the summer of 1980, Shanti, Gurdeep and I visited India for a few weeks. Ten-year old Shanti wrote in her diary:

> *August 17: Gurdeep, my dad and I arrived in India at Kirpal Ashram. Master Darshan greeted us and gave me a big bear hug. Master came down every morning to put his thumb on initiates foreheads to help them meditate. We folded our hands in greeting whenever he came. He patted my cheeks a lot. He was very loving. Some nights Master would invite us up on the roof of his house where it was cool. One night he invited all of us up. It was Master and Auntie's wedding anniversary. We had ice cream and talked....*

There is a sweet and joyful Indian festival called *Rakhi.* The ancient customs call for a sister to tie a colored thread on her brother's wrist, feed him sweets, and pray for his long and healthy life. The brother then gives his sister money and vows to protect her honor as long as he lives, regardless of personal sacrifice. If sister-less, he may 'adopt' a sister, who then becomes known as his "*Rakhi-sister.*" In Indian culture, a brother-sister relationship is considered the most pure.

After tying Rakhi on the Master's wrist, he signs and gives Rupee notes to the children (Gurdeep, here).

Diary: August 26, 1980: Our sweetest day yet. The children tie Rakhi threads on the Master's wrist; they also tie one on him for their mummy. He signs and gives both ten-rupee notes and hankies on which their astrological signs are embroidered. He picks a fragrant blood-red rose from a crystal bowl and gives it to me, with the words, "In olden times, the disciples used to tie Rakhi on the Guru. This signified that he was always protecting and looking after them."

The Question of Raji: Before returning to Canada in early September, I ask, "Will your son Raji one day carry this burden?"

"Brother, it is still too soon to say," he replies, and is silent for a minute. "You know, Raji is very obedient to me. Before he got married, he used to phone me from America to get my permission even to see a particular movie or go out to a party!" Such a deep level of obedience and dedication is rare in this faithless world.

"Raji is very helpful to me in the mission," he continues, "and sends me a lot from his earnings. He earns a high salary as an electrical engineer and inventor with AT&T, and if it weren't for his help, how could your Auntie and I possibly afford to feed all those who come to my residence on my modest pension? You have seen how we feed dozens every day from our personal kitchen. The langar which provides thousands of free meals every week is a separate issue, and is maintained by donations from the Sangat; but it is a fundamental principle for the Masters of Sant Mat to live off their own earnings. If retired, they will live modestly off their pensions, and share a portion of it with others." For the next forty-five minutes, he goes into great detail about Raji's exemplary qualities, but falls tantalizingly short of directly answering my question. He assures me however, that he will make it crystal-clear who his spiritual successor will be.

The best investment: Master Darshan reveals his chosen investment:

"In my government position, I earned a very good salary and had every opportunity to invest in property, the stock market or business, like my colleagues, who made a lot of money. But your Auntie and I decided that we would invest in our children, and we spared no effort or expense in their education.

"There are so many arts: the art of music, the art of poetry, the art of painting, the art of sculpture, and the art of dance. But the greatest art of all is the art of raising children, and making them into masterpieces!" His words made me cringe inside for all the times and ways I had not been fully there for my children.

Science of Spirituality:

He freely discusses with me the name of his worldwide organization—*Sawan Kirpal Ruhani Mission.* The name for this unchanging spiritual science had undergone at least five revisions over the past one hundred years, due to the changing circumstances and the fresh approaches of each new Master. One skirts a fine line between presumption and inspiration, but while the Masters are pure conduits for carrying out the will of the Almighty, they often use imperfect others as instruments of His designs. With this in mind, I suggest that *Science of Spirituality* or some other, less foreign-sounding name might be more suitable for the West. The Masters had informally used this expression in their satsangs to describe the empirical nature of the spiritual path:

> *Stripped of all its outer encrustation's, spirituality emerges as a science, as verifiable as any other. Let the seeker take up the necessary prerequisites in the laboratory of the body, and as sure as day follows night, shall he enter into the kingdom of God.*[1]

Not long after our interview, the Master announces his decision to adopt *Science of Spirituality* as the name for his work in the West.

A True Man is like God:

A renowned American surgeon and his twelve-year-old son drop by the ashram while I'm present:

Boy: "How do you meditate?"

Master: "To answer this, can you first tell me how you study?"

Boy: "Well, first I read what I'm supposed to study, then I think about it, and then I say it over, and then I look in the book and see if I'm right."

M: "Yes, when you study you do not think of anything else...that is what is known as concentration. When we say, 'Concentrate on this,' it means think of this alone. You forget everything else. It is similar to when you see a beautiful picture and you become lost in it; you forget yourself. In the same way, when you meditate you think of God alone. You do not think of anything else. There is one Supreme Power, which we call God. When you remember God and think only of Him, then you will start seeing Him. First, you will start seeing the Light of God, then gradually you will see the form of God Himself."

Boy: "People might picture Him in different ways."

M: "...when you see Him for yourself you will see Him in his true colors, in His own true form. Ultimately you will see Him in His...bright form. What have you heard about God?"

Boy: "In church we always hear about Him."

M: "You hear about Him in what respect? What are the qualities of God? How does God behave?"

Boy: "Like a human being."

M: "And how does a human being behave? A good person always does good. God is all goodness; He does all good things. You have not seen a person like God, but you have seen people with the good qualities of God. And we can meet God just as I am meeting you. We can see God. We can talk to God as I am talking to you. In the same way, when we remember God, He will come to us. Just think only of Him. When you read and remember your lesson, you do not think of anything else. You do not think of playing in your school. You do not think of teasing your mummy at that time. Would you like to remember God?"

Boy: "Yes."

M: "That is what you do in meditation."

Boy: "But still can you remember Him in your mind?"

M: "Yes. When you remember Him in your mind, then He comes to meet you. God has made human beings after His own image. A good human being is a carbon copy of God."

At this point, the young lad looked intently into the Master's eyes for several long seconds.

Boy: "So I will think of you like God."

M: "You can think of me only as a good man. God is the source of all goodness; He does all good acts. He is very kind. A doctor may do good only for those who come to him as patients, but God is good to all the people on the face of the earth, whether they are black, white, Indians, Americans, English people, Germans, or any other people.

"When we remember God, and remember God alone, we can meet and talk to Him. Remembering God means we are not thinking of anything else. And that is meditation."

---

1. Kirpal Singh, *Man, Know Thyself!* Naperville, IL: SK Publications, 1980, p. 22.

September 6, 1980: Kapoor Sahib, a disciple and industrialist, invites Master Darshan, Bibi Harbhajan Kaur, and a handful of Westerners to his spacious home for a dinner party. Two blocks from the ashram, the Master calls an abrupt halt, returns to the ashram, and invites the remaining thirty or so Westerners. His tender heart can't bear the thought of leaving anyone behind.

As we settle into Kapoor's living room, the Master is relaxed and charming. With some encouragement, Kapoor begins to share some of his experiences with Satguru Kirpal:

"Once we traveled with Master to Haridwar and spent quite a long time trying to arrange for a suitable building for him to stay in and hold satsang. I was very tired and suffered a severe heart attack. I lay on the bed and Maharaj Ji held my hands for two hours, during which time my heart had completely stopped beating. I revived with his grace. Then he told someone to massage my body that night. In the morning Master came, took my pulse and declared, 'Now no one can say that there is any difference between your heartbeat and mine!'"

I ask Kapoor, "Tell us how you came to Master Darshan." He replies, "Because this is the right place. In November of 1978, when you first came to Kirpal Ashram, you sang Mira's shabd:

> *Gullay toh chaaroh Band'a huu-ee*
> *Guru sae milloo kessay jaaey*
> *All the four ways [directions] are blocked;*
> *O how will I meet my Guru?*

I told you then, "'The way has now been opened.'"

Death makes no distinction: *September 8:* Master calls me to him at high noon. The car is ready and he motions for me to be seated beside him. "Kapoor's eldest son died of a heart attack this morning." We proceed to his home, and are met by the grieved wailing of his wife, brothers, sisters, sons, daughter and other relatives. Master sadly comments, "This physical life is so uncertain. We never know when we have to leave. *'Who knows? The world may end tonight.'"*

We sit around the body, with Master near the head. A distinct smile is on the lips of the deceased, like one in triumph or in blissful meditation. Jyoti, his teenage daughter, poignantly begs the Master for the return of the soul of her father, but Maharaj Ji keeps quiet, comforting everyone all the while. For a long time he holds the bereaved daughter against his chest and strokes her head, easing her beyond the shock. His kind path is one of acceptance, and, *Sweet is Thy Will.*

By constant example, Darshan teaches love and sympathy for the sufferings and afflictions of others. He is the epitome of the dictum *"Love knows service and sacrifice."* For *ten hours* he remains with this devoted family, until the body is washed, swathed, removed to the burial ghats, and finally cremated in the evening.

When she becomes calm, Mrs. Kapoor, the widowed wife, shares with us: "Last night, my husband was telling me, 'Master is showering so much grace on me internally, I don't know if I can contain my ecstasy.' But I didn't understand what my husband was saying. He appeared in perfect physical health and complained of no ailment. After he sent our twelve-year old son Manu to school, he had a massive heart attack. Before his soul left the body, he reassured me that this was the pre-ordained time of his departure, and that he had no say in the matter. I then requested him, 'If you are to die, then please do so with a smile on your lips.' This he did, as you could see by his face, and he exited this world without any pain. Now he is with the Masters...but I am still here," as tears fill her eyes.

How striking that one day is filled with mirth and merriment at Kapoor's luxurious home, while the next is filled with mourning. More than 250 relatives and satsangi well-wishers have come to the burning ghats. Once the funeral fire is ablaze, we move back to sit under a large cupola supported by pillars. No one has taken any food or drink all day. I feel tired and lean against a pillar about fifteen feet from the Master, and enter meditation. After some time, I open my eyes and behold Master Darshan in the dark, though the atmosphere is scintillating. His face turns into that of Master Kirpal. After a long silence, he beckons me to his side and asks, "Brother, please sing some shabd." I sing in Hindi Kabir's seven-versed *Guru Samana Nehi Datta Jag Mai (In this world there is no Benefactor greater than the Guru; He gives that which is unobtainable elsewhere...)*, each line repeated by the large throng. All weeping ceases.

In the car on the way back to the ashram, Master asks me, "Were you able to distinguish the satsangis from the non-initiates at the funeral?"

"Yes, Master," I reply, "the satsangis were composed and resigned, whereas the others were out of control in their grief."

"Yes," he comments, "that is because they have some inner contact. You saw the father, Kapoor Sahib; how composed he was. This death was a great tragedy for his family; the son was a gem of a man. He ran the entire family business [a large factory manufacturing tractor parts]. Of course, the younger son[1] has been groomed for the position but this man was a master of his profession. In India it is very difficult for the wife if her husband dies...Fortunately they are well off and she will be taken care of. All is in the hands of the Masters overhead."

---

1. The younger Kapoor is the same person described in Chapter 28 *"The Vale of Kashmir,"* who fell down the mountain, but was miraculously spared any injury.

SOAMI JI'S TOMB

66

The high-speed Taj Express stops for five minutes at the Mathura station. Mathura is the birthplace of Krishna—the Avatar. Forewarned of our arrival, a large crowd waits on the platform, encircling an empty chair on a white sheet sprinkled with fragrant petals. Master literally hops off the train, meets each person individually, then sits on the chair for a few moments, dispensing parshad and words of love and guidance. Only when the steam whistle blows and the train slowly begins to pull away does the Master reluctantly part.

We are greeted at the Agra station by P.S.Nagpal, the local satsang leader and helpers. While the Master conducts satsang to thousands of local citizens, Nagpal separately arranged for the foreign visitors to tour the places associated with the life of Soami Shiv Dayal Singh, the great Saint of Agra.

At Soami Bagh, a huge marble mausoleum rises up three stories; elaborate marble carvings adorn most of the building, and another four levels await completion. Although this work has been in progress for decades, it likely won't be finished for another fifty years. In the lifetime of Soami Ji, Soami Bagh was a large garden with many fruit trees. Within its sacred precincts, spiritual aspirants were trained in meditation by their Guru. Before he died, the powerful but humble Param Sant specifically stated that no memorials or tombs were to be constructed after he passed from the material world. He considered such to be snares for the gullible and the spiritually naive. In his sayings, *Sar Bachan [Prose]*, Soami Ji declares:

> *A wise man is one, who, having closely examined the nature of existence in this world, has realized that it is all transitory and illusory; wise is he who has consecrated his human form by devoting himself to Bhajan and Simran. He is wise who, taking the fullest advantage of the various spiritual faculties which the Supreme Father has graciously endowed him with, has realized the invaluable jewel within him, which is Surat [spirit], the essence of his being....*

Whatever the living Master wishes for his students is invariably for their advancement. So, I am here to pay my respects to the great Soami Ji. On the ground floor of the mausoleum, his wooden sandals are enshrined on a low white marble altar, the two toe posts aligned in such a way that when one bows (as thousands of pilgrims do daily), they touch one's eyes. The priests claim that this ritual is tantamount to darshan of Soami Ji. A large lock-box with a slot on top is placed next to the Guru's sandals, to receive an endless flow of donations.

After paying my respects to the memory of Soami Ji, I find a quiet corner of the huge building and sit in meditation. A few minutes later, hearing much

Soami Shiv Dayal Singh of Agra.

shouting and commotion directly in front of me, I reluctantly open my eyes to find a *pujari* (priest) shouting and pointing in my direction. I look behind me and, finding no one there, realize that I am the recipient of his outpourings. He is upset because I'm not engaged in rituals like the masses, but sitting in meditation!

At peace, I smile at him, and depart without a fuss. What Soami Ji taught by example and precept, i.e. *"enter within and meditate on Shabd,"* had devolved into a taboo. How soon we mortals forget, and how quickly the guardians and promoters of non-essentials come to the fore. Again, in *Sar Bachan [Prose]*, Soami Ji warned:

> *Religious deeds, austerity, worship and charity ever intensify your vanity.*
> *Give your love now to the Saints, firmly and with heart and soul. Leave*
> *your religious rituals and delusion; and merge your soul in the melody of*
> *the Shabd.*

Punni Gali is a narrow, winding lane, with four and five-storied houses and shops crowding either side, passing through the oldest section of Agra. We pass Gurdwara Mai Than, where Soami Ji gave his first public satsangs in the early 1800s. A few blocks further down the lane is Soami Ji's house. It is said that on the street was a house of ill-repute, and its inhabitants and clients hid in fear or shame whenever the great saint passed by.

Ever since reading about Soami Ji in Baba Ji's biography, a deep reverence for him had grown within me. It is a thrilling experience to enter his home, which has been kept undisturbed and undeveloped, like a museum. A resident guide takes me to the tiny room where the Saint had meditated on a small wooden platform almost continuously for seventeen years. I pray for the possibility of meditating in this realization-soaked room, but the guide informs me, "Not permitted." Before I have time to be disappointed, someone calls from outside and the guide disappears, leaving me undisturbed for about fifteen minutes. My prayer is answered! The atmosphere is profoundly charged, and ingress is practically instantaneous.

Later in the day, we join the Master for lunch, and at 4 P.M. we're off to the Shish Mahal or Palace of Mirrors. Darshan Ji personally escorts us through the palace, its walls decorated with millions of tiny glass mirrors. Lighting a match, he holds it near the glittering walls so we can marvel in its myriad reflections. He then recited some of his Urdu verses:

> *Every grain of sand in the desert*
> *is a mirror;*
> *Amidst your infinite reflections,*
> *Your mad lovers are lost.*

> *O very life of our dreams,*
> *Whoever left your myriad-mirrored*
> *bed chamber,*
> *Did so with eyes that forever*
> *lost their sleep.[1]*

Taj Mahal—the Dream in Marble: Under the arched portals of the ethereal Taj, Master reveals more than its romantic tourist history—the deification of Shah Jahan's love of his wife Mumtaj, who died giving birth to their fourteenth child. Master pays tribute to the unsung blood and tears shed by the thousands of slaves who died in its construction, and to its brilliant but unfortunate architect, whose hands were cut off by order of the Shah so that he couldn't design another building to rival the Taj. Someone in our group adds that the architect, forewarned of the king's plan, sought revenge of great subtlety, building the main dome in such a way that a tiny drop of water would regularly fall tear-like onto the jewel-encrusted marble tomb. To this day, no one has been able to stop the drip, nor unravel its engineering mystery.

Sant Darshan Singh in front of the Taj Mahal, 1980. (AS)
To take this picture, I had to get down into one of the drained reflecting pools.

Darshan Ji adds that when the emperor's son Aurangzeb seized power, he put his siblings to death and imprisoned the aged Shah Jahan in a distant tower on the other side of the river, from where the Taj was but a tragic and distant vision.

In the evening, as our train flies over the rails back to Delhi, Master personally visits with each of us, spread as we are over several compartments. Basking in the glow of this beautiful day, we rename our iron steed, "The Sach Khand Express."

---

1. Darshan Singh, *A Tear and a Star*, Vijay Nagar, Delhi, India: Sawan Kirpal Publications (1986) pp. 9-10.

KIRPAL'S WILL

67

After coming to Darshan in '78 and having had my heart and mind re-opened, I began to dispassionately evaluate the body of evidence supporting his succession, which until then I had deliberately avoided and ignored. When Maharaj Kirpal Singh Ji fell seriously ill in 1971 and underwent surgery, he mentioned before a gathering of thousands that he *had* written a will, but he did not indicate who was his spiritual beneficiary.

The following is a verbatim transcription from the Master's tape-recorded discourse after he returned from Mahajan Nursing Home in August 1971.

> *"I am asked why I fell ill. What a question! Please listen carefully; the law of nature governs us all. One who breaks the law has to suffer the consequences. The way I have used my body is known to all. I have been working, writing continuously in one sitting at a stretch, from six to twelve hours daily. Because of this trouble [illness], I had to postpone my foreign tour. Man proposes and God disposes. Renowned doctors, including the personal physician of the President of India, were consulted. They unanimously decided that I should under-go an operation and, accordingly, the operation was performed. Dr. Mahajan, in whose nursing home I was hospitalized, is a renowned surgeon. After my leaving the nursing home, Dr. Mahajan came to visit me in the ashram and said, 'Now I have come to you not as a doctor but as a devotee...' [The Master laughs.]*
>
> *"Some persons thought that I was leaving this physical vesture and started false propaganda even before my going to the nursing home. I kept on listening. Let such persons know how and when the gaddi [Guruship or spiritual successorship] was bequeathed. This was actually done after my return from the nursing home. If I were to leave the physical body, I would have written the will before admission into the hospital. If I had to leave, I would have done so..." [Again the Master laughs, and continues.] "The Will was executed on my return."*

Malik Radha Krishna Khanna and Sant Kirpal Singh Ji were fellow-disciples, about whom the Master used to say, "Perhaps Malik is the only person who has spent more personal time with Hazur than I." Malik was a brilliant lawyer and served as personal attorney to both Masters; moreover, he was a friend and confidante. Malik also authored *Truth Eternal*, a book on Sant Mat. The following is a copy of his Sworn Affidavit:

I, Malik Radha Krishna Khanna, Advocate, resident of 6/27 West Patel Nagar, New Delhi, hereby declare on solemn affirmation:

That about four years ago Maharaj Sant Kirpal Singh Ji, in the course of his visit to my house, expressed his desire to nominate his son Darshan Singh as his Spiritual Successor after his demise, and I drafted his Will according to his wishes to the effect that his son Darshan Singh shall be his Spiritual Successor after his demise and carry on his work as he had himself been doing in his lifetime.

Gyani Bhagwan Singh, personal Secretary of Maharaj Sant Kirpal Singh Ji, having been sent to me by him a couple of days later for the purpose, took away the drafted Will from me for being made over to Maharaj Sant Kirpal Singh Ji.[1]

I also declare on solemn affirmation that about a month later Maharaj Sant Kirpal Singh Ji paid a visit at my house and told me that he had approved the draft of the contents of the Will drafted by me and had signed it and got attested by the witnesses.

The above is correct to the best of my knowledge and recollection and nothing material has been concealed or withheld.

Deposed to before the Notary Public at Delhi on 25-9-75.

Master Kirpal also informed his friend Jain Muni Shushil Kumar, the sponsor of the World Fellowship of Religions and a prominent religious leader, that he would make Darshan Singh his successor. Although Darshan was easily able to prove his spiritual endowment without the benefit of a legal document, the original hand-written will surfaced when I was in India in 1980, but ironically, it was no longer needed! The will merely corroborated what was already known by the experience of countless recipients of the living Master's largesse.

Because the first will was "lost" by Tai Ji, on August 3, 1974, just eighteen days before Master Kirpal passed away, he got blank papers from Mela Ram and wrote out the will again, in the absence of Tai Ji.

As Darshan Singh was not there, Mela Ram entrusted the written papers to Murari Lal for safekeeping. Murari Lal was a trusted business associate of Tai Ji. After the death of the Beloved Master, Murari Lal left Sawan Ashram and returned to his home in Jaipur. There he had a photocopy made of the will. After two months, he sent a man with that copy to Sant Darshan Singh, demanding 100,000 rupees for the original. This copy was shown, not given. Master Darshan Singh said he could not and would not pay such a sum. That man then went to Malik Radha Krishna Khanna, who also declined to pay the sum. The man went away.

Murari Lal had little faith in his own sons and placed all his legal papers with a friend who was an illiterate ironsmith. Mela Ram, who was faithful to the wishes of the Master, tried to regain the will so it could be with its rightful designee. Murari Lal died in January 1975. After a long time, Mela Ram discovered that the will was with the ironsmith in Jaipur. Mela Ram obtained a photocopy from the ironsmith and gave it to Master Darshan Singh on April 24, 1980, thinking that it was the original.

The Master handed it over to Rameshwar Das,[2] advocate, for necessary action. Rameshwar Das related the following to me:

"I took Mela Ram with me and went to Jaipur. I stayed at Shikar Hotel, which was about four kilometers from the ironsmith's house and shop. Then Mela Ram and I proceeded toward the shop of the ironsmith. On the way, I purchased two containers of burfee sweets, and Mela Ram bought a new pair of sandals. When we reached his shop, I presented the sweets to the ironsmith and said, 'I am the Secretary of Sant Darshan Singh Ji and have come here to give thanks to you. And whenever you want anything or any service, you should inform me.'

"Mela Ram presented a pair of sandals for the wife of the ironsmith's son. After some time, sitting there, Mela Ram requested that the papers should be shown to me. We then went to his house along with him and his son. That package was lying in a trunk on an upper shelf. His son brought that trunk over and opened it. I took those two papers written in the hand of Master Kirpal and told them that they were not of much use, and put them in my pocket. The ironsmith wanted some money for it, but with Master's grace he couldn't open his mouth. Mela Ram stayed the night with his son's family, and I went back to the Hotel. The next day we returned to Delhi and showed the will to Maharaj Ji. Maharaj Ji asked me, 'How much money have you paid for it?'

"I said, 'Not a single penny, Maharaj Ji, except for two packages of burfee and a pair of sandals!'"

The following is a verbatim translation of the will.

I, Kirpal Singh residing in Delhi, have been doing satsang work for the last 25 to 30 years. Human life is uncertain. It is possible that my life's flame may become extinct during this very month. Therefore, I wish to write my Will for the future so that it may be acted upon after my body is no more.

I have two sons: elder Darshan Singh and younger Jaswant Singh. Darshan Singh is fully conversant with all aspects of satsang. He is also internally advanced together with me. He is also devoted to bhajan and simran [meditation]. Therefore, I make this Will authorizing Darshan Singh to satisfactorily and competently carry out all the duties of satsang as I have done in the past.

Darshan Singh and Jaswant Singh shall equally divide my personal property at 207 Rajpur Road and plots as well as my personal accounts in the banks.[4] Other than my personal property, all other properties belong to the satsangis [initiates], and there will be no right of anyone else in that satsang property. Donations received will be spent for the purpose of satsang and Manav Kendra. Satsang money shall be duly entered as such in the account books under the supervision of Darshan Singh. Just as I do not use satsang funds for my personal use, in the same way Darshan

Singh shall not use them for his personal use. All donations belong entirely for the use of the sangat [congregation]. Darshan Singh shall treat my dear sangat with love and affection and he will not do anything which may be objected to or considered wrong by it.

My dear ones in the sangat shall not protest this Will in any way. I had an earlier Will drafted by Radha Krishna Sahib, but, in spite of all efforts, it is not traceable. Therefore, I am writing this second and last Will in favor of Darshan Singh of my own free will when I am in full possession of all my senses and faculties, without any pressure or coercion by anyone, so that it may be on record and acted upon when the necessity arises.

(Signed KIRPAL SINGH)
3rd August, 1974.

Photocopy of Kirpal Singh's handwritten and signed will (in Urdu), dated 3rd August 1974

---

1. In several personal interviews, Gyani Bhagwan Singh who was a witness to the Will confirmed to me everything that Malik had sworn before a notary.

2. Also known as "Chacha Ji."

3. Sant Kirpal Singh's handwriting has been verified by handwriting analysts.

4. The personal bank accounts, and private plots referred to were never traced. Consistent with his non-confrontational manner and incredible patience, Darshan Singh never pressed charges.

Seekers and spiritual refugees from dozens of countries arrived in a steady stream through the gates of Kirpal Ashram. Many found it incredible that such divine power rested in this humble, unassuming Saint. As I was leaving India, my old colleague, Dr. Neil Tessler, arrived at Kirpal Ashram. Neil had been with the desert Baba, and felt that he must satisfy his curiosity about the many reports he had heard, and see Darshan himself.

"At the time of our first midnight meeting, there were six people present besides the Master," Neil later related to me. "However, it was I who had come to probe and question, and so the evening became a conversation primarily between Sant Darshan Singh and myself. After perhaps an hour had passed, I became aware of an energy like a spray coming from the Master and striking me in the eyes. I felt it washing over my face, head, and gradually my body, like an ethereal shower. I experienced a kind of giddiness, which passed into a steadily increasing state of intoxication. In this condition I lost all reservation, all inhibition, all propriety. I asked whatever wild questions and expressed whatever heartfelt emotions came to my mind—primarily my incredible embarrassment for how terribly I had misjudged him. The unconditional, enveloping warmth, the unfailing graciousness from the moment of my intro- duction to my departure from the gates of Kirpal Ashram, the depth and breadth of his words and his way, affected me very deeply. Combined with a palpable, undeniable transmission of spiritual energy from his eyes into mine, I was left in a state akin to shock and was unable to sleep for the entire flight home.

"On reflection, I would also say that, to my small cup, it was a sublime affirmation of the importance placed by Sant Kirpal Singh, and all the Saints, on spiritual transmission through the eyes. As he so beautifully expressed, '*the intoxication of Hazur's glance is still the life of my soul.*'"

Just one question: Within days of returning from India to Vancouver and settling into family and work, I was surprised to find posters plastered all over the city announcing yet another "Swami Satguru" claiming to be the *only* true successor of Sant Kirpal Singh.

I went and sat among the meager audience before a middle-aged, clean- shaven East Indian man with long curls. At the end of his rambling lecture, questions were invited. As no one else had any, I simply asked one of the fifty-two: "How many steps lead into the Amritsar pool in Daswan Dwar— the third spiritual region?"

The Swami was totally stumped! Everyone, myself included, was surprised when his new Western representative stood and said in a voice quivering with emotion,

"Swami, you are not a true Master! You can't even answer spiritual questions properly! I hereby renounce you as a Master!" I had done nothing more than quietly ask just *one* question from Sant Kirpal's manuscript, as he directed!

The following morning, the disillusioned representative urgently requested my presence at the hotel. Her Swami had hastily cleared out of town at dawn, leaving a confused aspirant waiting in the lobby and his representative holding the tab. When I arrived at his hotel room, she showed me the empty whiskey bottle he had left behind.

> *The Masters were once followers, but when they absorbed themselves wholly and solely into their Master, they too became Masters. The trouble is that we want to become Masters, not followers. If you become a true follower and absorb your whole self into Him, mind, body and soul, then? ...Be wholly absorbed into the Master and you will become the Master. You need not ask for it. God will choose you, the Master will choose you...It is a great good fortune to have a Living Master, a true Master. There are many masters, a hundred and one, a thousand and one, but they are only acting and posing, or on the way. Anybody who follows them is led away and those who help them are also led away...*[1]

In the three worlds—physical, astral, and causal—over which Kal reigns, the law of karma or justice rules: *an eye for an eye, a tooth for a tooth, and a life for a life.* The misled innocents are bound to exact their due someday. In the refuge of a Saint of Fifth-plane stature, the cycle of justice is absolved.

I often pondered this story from the life of Guru Nanak, which I had once heard quoted by Master Kirpal:

> *On one of his journeys, Guru Nanak, accompanied by his companions Bala and Mardana, met with a strange sight on their path. A large worm was writhing on the ground as hundreds of ferocious ants were biting it to death. Being tender hearted, Bala asked the great Guru what terrible deeds this poor worm had committed to warrant such suffering. Nanak replied that in a former life that worm had been a false master and the ants were his disciples. They had to be reborn in this form—cruel though it may seem—to balance the scales of karmic justice.*

---

1. Kirpal Singh, *Morning Talks*, 4th edition (Bowling Green, VA: Sawan Kirpal Publications, 1981) pp. 257-258

6 9

On Remembrance Day in 1981, our son was born, fulfilling Master Kirpal's veiled promise to us in 1974. We named him Arjan, in honor of the Fifth Guru, hoping that in his life, the boy might find inspiration in Arjan Dev's great learning, wisdom and ultimate sacrifice. In the winter of 1982, we brought him to India to be blessed by the Master. Our stay coincided with one by Raji, Rita, Rimjhim (their daughter), and one year-old son Kenny (Kunwarjit) from Illinois. A rather grand celebration was held in honor of Kenny's first visit to the ashram. Both boys were about the same age and received a lot of affection from the Master.

One day Master asked, "Would you like to know the etymological meaning of the name Arjan?" He pulled out an old thick book written in Sanskrit, and finding the right page, he read out: *Arjan*: *safedi rang* (fair complexion), *kalota beta* (the only son), and *akh ka tara* ("star of the eye"), meaning some thing like "apple of the eye." The name did fit.

Christmas Eve: On the top floor of Master's house, a joyous Christmas celebration unfolded, with carols sung in English, German, Spanish, Russian, French, and African languages by a large number of visiting disciples. A decorated pine tree contributed to the Yule spirit. Jewish disciples sang wonderful Hebrew songs of Peace in the Hanukkah tradition.

When I poked my head through the door and saw the wall-to-wall crowd, it didn't seem possible that even one more could fit in. Coming to my rescue, Master beckoned me over to sit at his immediate left. Within moments, a barefoot Raji entered and at the Master's bidding, he sat cross-legged on the floor between the two of us. I couldn't help but notice as Raji slipped his right foot up on his left knee in *sidh aasan*. Looking down, I saw on his sole, a perfect *Padam Rekha*, identical to the one I first saw on Master Kirpal in 1967, then Darshan in 1978. Behind this play, by consciously shifting the seat of attention, one begins detecting the inscrutable hand of the Divine—if not the action of Light.

> When...the light of God Almighty comes into view without the veil of soul or heart, it becomes perfectly clear. There is no color, quality, limit, comparison, or contrast to it. It itself is the stability and firm support of all existing beings. Here there remains neither rising nor setting; right nor left; height nor depth; space nor time; near nor far; day nor night; neither earth nor world nor heaven itself. Here the pen breaks; the tongue is tied; the intellect sinks into the pit of nothingness, while understanding and knowledge are lost in the wilderness of amazement.
> —Ibn Yahya Maneri, 1263-1381.

7 0

*That one night spent in Your assembly
was the fulfillment of a lifetime of yearning.[1]*

Sant Darshan Singh accepted a long-standing invitation in August of 1983 to visit Vancouver. For five wonder-filled days and nights (especially the nights), our home was his home, and the Mecca for hundreds of seekers. During this period he gave discourses, meditation sittings, and question-and-answer sessions at Unity Church and the Vishwa Hindu Temple. More than one thousand people met him face to face. By some cosmic play, his arrival at the airport coincided with that of his old friend, Sri Jagjit Singh Ji, the saintly leader of India's Namdhari sect.[2] I was informed that when Jagjit Singh succeeded his guru decades earlier, Sant Kirpal Singh Ji tied his guru's turban on him. Likewise, when Jagjit Singh's predecessor became guru in the early thirties, Baba Sawan Singh tied his turban on him—an act of great significance for the Namdhari followers. Jagjit Singh Ji visited our home where the two holy men met for two hours. Between them was a bond of brotherhood, love, and respect.

Prior to Darshan Singh's arrival, notices were sent to our neighbors and the police that a renowned spiritual leader would be our guest. We explained that none should be alarmed at seeing a large number of people coming and going throughout the day and night. Sixty out of town guests slept on the floors, in hallways, closets, garage, and in the basement. Our kitchen became a langar, where food and chai were served night and day. Throughout, it was a fantastic, joyous, intoxicating experience.

After a public meditation at Unity Church for over three hundred and fifty people, the Master fielded a wide range of questions. Many new seekers and skeptics who had followed his detailed instruction, were amazed and uplifted upon experiencing powerful inner Light along with the living Master's radiant form within. At one point, Paul Hurst—an old initiate—called out from the back of the packed church, "Darshan Singh!" I wondered what would come next, for as far as I knew this man had no interest in the successor. "When I was a child," he proceeded in a clear voice; "I often had visions of Kirpal Singh—who subsequently became my Master. He would appear with a younger man at his side, whom I now recognize as you. All this occurred many years before I had even heard of your names. Then I saw you in the form of a young man. Today I see you as the Living Master." Darshan lowered his head, gracefully lifted his hand and turned it, finger pointing up to the unseen Facilitator.

Wherever he went, Darshan was in a state of gracious surrender, like an innocent child. His manner was kind, patient, and compassionate with everyone. A distinct jasmine-lilac fragrance emanated from his body at all times. I had the privilege to be constantly at his side, and I'd just direct and introduce him to the many whom I knew. He was like a ray gun, and as I guided his elbow to this or that person in a crowd, love and light flowed out from his eyes and countenance. He was always bowing slightly, hands prayerfully joined, and the ecstatic recipients would bow back, never taking their eyes from his. In the process, he passed kind and insightful comments to those in his path. All were his brothers, sisters, mothers, fathers, daughters, and sons. No purer love could be found in the world.

"Master, our daughter is very intelligent, but she does not study," said the parents of a ten-year-old girl. Looking deep into her eyes, with kind but firm love, he gently asked, "Daughter, what is the use of such profound intelligence without diligence?" Thereafter, she consistently graduated with highest honors.

On one of the days as I was driving the Master to various disciple's homes, he asked to see our vegetarian restaurant. When he walked into the eatery unannounced, more than forty customers were dining; amongst them happened to be five or six initiates. Someone exclaimed, "Look! Master's here!" He glided through the place slowly, glancing at the sumptuous buffet, radiantly smiling at the servers and customers with guileless affection. Every single person in the restaurant silently and spontaneously stood, respectfully acknowledging his presence. Not a word exchanged as his hands joined together in greeting; every eye met his, and returned his smile. Without further ado, he bowed to all, turned and departed.

> *Woodlands that the winter's sadden*
> *The leaves of spring again shall gladden;*
> *So toils an undiscouraged God*
> *And covers the barren fields with sod,*
> *And I know nothing that the good, the true,*
> *The gentle, cannot do. —Anonymous*

The Sleepless Saint takes a forced rest: Prior to Vancouver, Master Darshan literally hadn't rested in weeks. For four days and nights at our home we were witness to the fact that he took *no* sleep at all. As the *Saqi* or "Cup-bearer," his awakening attention was distributed with no let-up. Those of us who assisted in his work were likewise imbued with great energy and required little rest—maybe one or two hours per night at the most. On the last night it seemed that even he had pushed his physical carriage beyond all limits. I felt compelled to make an announcement to those gathered well past midnight in the large living room:

"Master has a physical body, and even though he is super-human, his physical frame also requires some rest now and then. Please forgive me, Master, but I'm going to insist you take rest *now*. I'm also going to insist that everyone allow Master to take leave, so that he can be refreshed for his next tour stop in Mexico and South America."

"Whatever you say, dear brother. I am at your service," he said, as he allowed me to shepherd him through the crowd and up the stairs. This took another twenty minutes as he insisted on blessing each person individually. Halfway up, he turned around to again infuse the atmosphere and the congregation. When at last he was alone, the soft bed was ignored for the futon on the floor. In moments he was gone for eight hours, his body resting, yes, but where his soul did go only the Highest of the High would know.

After blessing many, including strangers at the Vancouver airport (one of the airport officials was moved to tears after she received a special glance, and a gentle touch of his hand to hers), Darshan Singh left for Latin America where he was swarmed by thousands, and the number of new initiates there grew by more than two thousand. Sant Darshan Singh was awarded with the Medal of Congress of Colombia and given the keys to several major cities where huge audiences flocked to his talks. Carlos Sardi, President of Congress of the Republic of Colombia told the Master, "Your tour will impress the necessity of looking inside, for the world within is so rich that in reality it is the only one that can make man a true man." For the next ten days the Master took little rest, if any. Certainly he would get none back in India. He was truly the Sleepless Saint.

The Friend of God: After his departure, we held a special gathering at the Unity Church where all were invited to share something of their experiences of the past few magical days. Towards the end of the program, a middle-aged woman stood. "Hello, my name is Mary," she said. "I was wondering if it would be all right if I could add something. I'm the Unity Sunday school teacher and I'm not an initiate." I invited her to the microphone where she spoke guilelessly about her wonderful experiences. The following is a transcription from tape of her sharing:

> *"I don't really know how to start this because I've been sitting in on these things, and I think they are fantastic. I like being with you, although I'm not belonging of you. I was upstairs [in the church] getting some stuff for the children's church school downstairs and there were people pouring in, pouring in, and I didn't know what was going on. I thought maybe there was some new religion going on or something. I found out that the beloved Master was here—Darshan Singh, am I right? So of course, we all came down from upstairs and sat in with you. I was astounded, absolutely astounded at the vibrations that*

our church suddenly took on. I can't explain it. You people know about it, you people are part of it; you are this, I know. It was just like the whole church was velvet. The air was velvet, you were velvet, and I was velvet. I sat in on that and I listened to him and began to think, 'My gosh, I've never meditated in my life before.'

"I didn't know what to do properly. I sat there, and I had done this 'quiet stuff' before, but never meditated. So when he was sort of guiding us through this I began to think, 'Oh, that's right, I do see a sun, and it's right here, and it's in me!' And then I felt this incredible warmth. Then there was a moon; I saw a moon, and I thought, 'Well, this is nuts! I'm absolutely bonkers. I'm just imagining this, because he said this.' And this went on and on.

"I came back that evening [for the satsang], and the same thing started up again, during the meditation, and then at the final time on Friday, he had a very intense meditation. As you know, he was sitting here on a little raised dais. I saw him there and closed my eyes. I was getting these incredible vibrations from this dear little man. I don't know if I should call him that to you people, but he was the dearest little man I ever saw in my life. And I could feel all this vibration between us. I was meditating and meditating and then I saw this same thing, and then finally, I just seemed to...I don't know, but I didn't take any kind of an astral trip or any of that sort of thing, but I just was absent, and I was right up in the universe. It was a big experience! I was right in this universe, and I could see stars, I could look around, and all this sort of thing. And the next thing I knew, I could see a Master, and I thought, 'This is ridiculous,' because I had looked at those pictures, and I knew that my mind was doing something to me. However, in came this picture...the Master..." [She points to a picture of Baba Sawan Singh Ji Maharaj.]

"Then, after a while, Darshan Singh appeared, right there. He was just there, in me, somehow. And that was absolutely incredible, because he is such an intense human being...then I was in this state of total meditation, total feeling, and the whole place was just absolutely alive with something. And then I heard sort of a noise, and a bit of rustle, and here was Arran and several other people, and the Master was walking down here. And I looked up here [to the dais] and he was gone. He had left so much energy, right there where he'd been sitting, and I was meditating to his energy that he left. I nearly fell out of the seat, because here he was walking down the aisle, and he'd gone downstairs.

"I'm not able to be initiated, it would be very wrong of me to be initiated, I do eat meat. I hope I haven't offended you people, but I do eat meat.

I interjected, "We all ate meat at one time."
Mary continued,

> "So, I couldn't go through with the initiation. Friday evening, when I
> was at home...it must have been ten or eleven at night, I was sitting on
> the chesterfield, and I was sort of thinking over the experiences I had
> had. I was in that frame of mind. I wasn't meditating, but I was think-
> ing. And all of a sudden I had the most incredible prickly—like little elec-
> tric shocks—right here [she points between her eyebrows], it came right
> in here to my eyebrows, like pins and needles. And then next thing I
> knew, Darshan Singh totally appeared right before me, and he sort of
> talked to me about things pertaining to me and my life.

> "And then, on the Saturday when he left, I was standing out there,
> and Arran introduced me to him. And he was so darling, and Arran said,
> 'This is one of the ladies who is involved with the church...' And the
> Master did this [placed his palms together in salute] and said, 'Thank
> you very much for having me here. This is a lovely building, and all the
> facilities were excellent...' He was absolutely great in saying thank you
> about us having him here. Our church and our meditations and every-
> thing have just grown intensely, because Darshan Singh was here."

I'll conclude this endless tale with the young American Sufi dervish, Jaami
Travis, a student of Reshad Field, who spoke so eloquently of his meeting with
Darshan:

> "The time spent with the Sufis served me well. On the eve of initiation
> I beheld the Beloved in the love-drenched eyes of the living Master,
> Darshan Singh. As I gazed into his eyes, he became transfigured and
> radiant with light. He possessed such a beauty that I can never forget
> that evening, for truly I beheld the glory of God...

> "My eyes will not turn from your face and I ask nothing of you but
> your beauty. Your perfume intoxicates me and I swoon from it. Truly you
> are Hu Dost, friend of God."

---

1. Darshan Singh, *A Tear and A Star*, Bowling Green, VA: SK Publications, 1988, pp.12.

2. The Namdharis have been historically referred to as *Kukha* Sikhs. They follow a vegetarian
   diet and are pacifists. The mostly hereditary followers of this movement number several
   hundred thousand, and may be identified by their all-white cotton garb and turbans worn
   flat across the forehead.

*A*fter the 1983 Tour, by my own choice, I decided to remove the turban I had been wearing for many years. It was time to more so outwardly blend with the society I had been born into. Nothing, however, could change the inner self and its relationship to the Divine, for that is independent of socio-religious labels.

Three years passed. An excessive workload and intense financial pressures had steadily drained away much of my inspiration and zeal (but fortunately, my connection to the Light and Sound remained intact). Gripped by duty, fueled by expansive ambition, and stung by financial loss, I felt impaled upon the thorns, unable to contact the Radiant Guide within.

My emotions were a jumble as I checked into Montreal's Hotel Dorval on June 12, 1986. Not more than twenty feet from the check-in counter, Master Darshan passed by, surrounded by a cluster of happy and laughing devotees. Conflicting emotions kept me at a distance. Later that night when he passed only a few feet away, he looked near me, but without a flicker of recognition! He embraced or patted others, but for me, *nothing*. I was reminded of a similar incident with Master Kirpal on his 1972 Tour, when *apparently* he too did not recognize me. Alone in my room, I tossed, turned and burned through the long night, pining for a vision of, and nearness to God's Saints. Darshan's presence often summoned the caravan of such intense, all-consuming memories and aspiration.

Why are profound transformations almost always prefaced by periods of turmoil? Nanak has said:

> *Live in sweet remembrance of the Lord;*
> *In pain we remember, in pleasure we forget;*
> *If in pleasure we'd not forget*
> *Then pain would never arise.*

At 7 AM, I was fortunate to be allowed access to the Master's room. When I entered, Darshan, who had been up all night with seekers, was dreadfully tired, but roused himself from the couch where he was lying, turban and beard askew. Feeling guilty for disturbing his rest, I nevertheless complained of my lack of inner contact with the coveted One:

"Brother, you have read Milton's *Paradise Lost?*" he asked. "Paradise lost and Paradise regained are sometimes regular features of the Path. Not to worry, dear brother, our Masters are very gracious." With infinite patience, he poured tea and moved a plate of biscuits towards me. His hands were trembling and he seemed desperately weary. As we drank and munched together, I felt my burdens lifting. Within forty-five minutes, my heart was singing! Amazingly, Darshan's countenance completely changed. All indication of weariness disappeared, his cheeks were rosy, and he bubbled with joyous energy and humor. "Oh! It's after 10!" he said. "I must go for the meditation sitting. Would you like to accompany me?"

After tying a new turban and combing his beard, he led me down the corridors, holding my hand all the way to the auditorium where about six hundred were waiting. There he let go, greeting and blessing the crowd that enveloped him. I found a seat half-way back, watching as he gave instructions. After everyone closed their eyes, I continued gazing at him, and he looked long and deeply back. My eyelids then closed of themselves, and what came made up for the barren spell. His power drew me within very quickly. In brightest Light, Darshan's form appeared; simran was repeating itself; then his full face moved up close. With immense spiritual force, he commanded, more strongly than the famous remark by Winston Churchill, *"Never give up!"*

A remarkable vision: When he inquired if the inner Gurudev had spoken to anyone, about eight or nine raised their hands. With a nod from the Master, Sethi Ji scribbled down their interior audio-visual experiences. Ellen Nardiello, a local writer, reported such a remarkable vision that Mr. Sethi asked the Master if she could share it with the audience. Permission granted, Ellen came to the podium and shared the following:

"Master Darshan showed me each of the Masters from Nanak and Kabir to the present...manifesting God's power and love. Then Master Darshan's form changed into that of his son, Raji, and he said that Raji was his successor; that when he would leave, Raji would be the Master and administer existence with the same love that he himself has shown. Master Darshan added that his departure was not imminent, saying, 'I have much love still to give my children, but when I am gone, Raji will distribute this same love. You should not fear that time.'"

Sitting before us was the living Master, and as no one apparently thought of Raji as the next Master, this public revelation generated a mixed response. Some were jubilant, some were incredulous, some questioned its appropriateness. The Master himself pretended not to hear.

In the winter of 1986, Sant Darshan Singh made an unannounced trip to the United States, ostensibly for medical treatment. Eminent specialists were consulted, and it was found that his physical heart was only operating at fractional capacity. The asthma of his early years had also returned. Both these medical conditions were undoubtedly vicarious, and his earthly spiritual mission was coming to a close. He hardly ever rested or slept, for his habit was to unceasingly minister to the endless human stream at his door. Yet no one, to my knowledge, heard even a murmur of complaint from his lips.

Back in 1978 he showed me his amazing palm and allowed me to analyze it in detail. Darshan Singh's palmistry lines indicated immense intellectual and artistic attainments and self-mastery. Perhaps one of the most unusual markings was a prominent lotus-like constellation on the Mount of Saturn under the middle finger, attached to his long and deep line of Fate or Destiny. Like Kirpal before him, other signs were evident, such as a perfectly formed Ring of Solomon, Mystic Cross, lines of Sun and Intuition...again reflecting the *Insaan-i-Kamil* or Perfected Man. His palm reflected the many obstacles and burdens he would have to face, and the ultimate triumph; he would emerge from obscurity and his renown, like a perfumed crown, would be world-wide.

After patiently hearing out my commentary on all other aspects, when I stated that he would live into his eighties, he interrupted, "Whatever else you have said, dear brother, is quite correct, but you have allowed too much time. My time in this world will be brief." He even went on to say that his life was extended by a special grace from Master Kirpal in 1973, when the latter included him on his last tour of Kashmir. Darshan described how the Master sent him to fetch a packet of medicine from an herbal doctor in Jammu. When he returned and gave it to his father, Kirpal held the herbal mixture a moment, then returned it. "Darshi, this medicine is for you," he said. Darshan's chronic asthma was cured from then on. If that hadn't happened, Darshan said, he would never have had the stamina required to carry on the Master's mission.

Although it was attempted to keep Darshan's winter visit and its purpose secret, word leaked out. Over a month went by with no news, and anxiety amongst the world-wide sangat was rising. I had to pass through Chicago on some pretext of business, and had a burning desire to hear directly of his welfare. From my hotel at O'Hare Airport I phoned Raji, who lived in the suburb of Wheaton. Raji answered my concerns very kindly, but he was justifiably protective of the Master...who was also his father. He explained that due to his weakened physical condition, Master was resting and hadn't seen anyone, not even the local initiates for the past several weeks. I mentioned that if by any chance he wanted to see me even for a minute, I was in town—if not, that was fine also, and left my number. An hour later, I received a call from Raji, saying, "Arran, this is your lucky day. Master is feeling better and he would like to see you."

I found myself at the door of a well-kept house in the suburbs. The door opened, and there stood Maharaj Ji surrounded by his family. After a warm embrace, he led me into the living-room where we sat together on the couch for over an hour, the Master holding my hands the entire time. I had never seen him more radiant and beautiful, but his hands were trembling. "You are the first person I have seen so far, outside of immediate family and the doctors," he said. Our conversation touched on his health and treatment, the mission, family, business and such. He then homed in on the progress of my manuscript

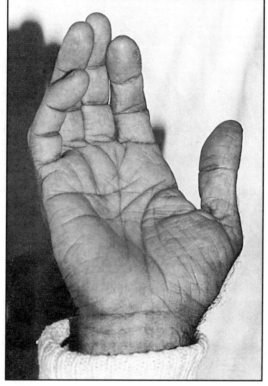

Darshan's palm, 1978
—photo by Jamie Smith

which I began in 1967. "At the present rate of progress," I facetiously replied, "it will probably be published posthumously."

"Brother," he exhorted, most seriously, "I humbly implore you in the name of the two great Masters that you complete your manuscript in the shortest possible time. This book will be of benefit to many, based as it is on your first-hand experiences...As such it will not merely be the parroting of others."[1]

---

1. In June 1989, I asked the new Master, Sant Rajinder Singh, "When did the Master take you up to Sach Khand, and when and where was the mantle of successorship passed?" He replied, "This took place when Master Darshan was at our home in the winter of 1986. The gracious Master took my soul with him to Sach Khand. Afterwards he informed me that I was to carry on the spiritual work after him." The eternal flame of Mastership was transferred in the suburbs of Middle America, two and a half years before Sant Darshan Singh left the world. Perfect Sants are the conscious co-workers of the divine plan, who are fully qualified and prepared by their Masters well in advance of taking on such an onerous role.

7 2

Why should I fear; when was I less by dying?
—*Rumi*

Several weeks before Dad passed in 1976, he shared the following dream:
"A long black limousine entered our driveway and drove right up to the
kitchen window where I was sitting. I couldn't see the chauffeur's face under
his cap, but then he turned and looked me directly in the eyes. The driver
was Kirpal Singh! I can't erase the image of his face nor his penetrating
glance."

Although his yearnings for fame and fortune went unfulfilled, Dad once
confided, "You know I'm not religious, but I do have three prayers. First, I
don't want to die in a hospital or an old-age home; let me pass away in my
own space. Secondly, when I go, it should be sudden, and not by some horri-
ble, drawn-out disease. And thirdly, I don't want anybody around to see me
die. These are my only prayers."

On the day of his actual death, Mum was away in Arizona with her sister.
Hale and hearty in his eightieth year, Dad had just returned from his daily five-
mile walk. While alone and crossing the living room, his heart stopped and he
collapsed, striking his head on a shelf as he fell. My brother discovered him
that evening. As no blood flowed from the resulting cut, the coroner deduced
that his heart had ceased beating instantaneously. Thus his three prayers were
answered.

Mum had developed emphysema in 1976, caused by a forty-year smoking
habit, despite having quit in the early seventies. Her suffering over the next
fifteen years steadily progressed, as did her dependence on debilitating steroid
medication and breath-inhalers. In November of '87, Mum asked if she could
meditate with the group which was then meeting at our home. I was amazed,
for she had rejected all my previous invitations in that regard for twenty
years.

She elected to sit on the stairs outside the room where thirty-five people
gathered for silent meditation. After forty minutes, a loud commotion erupted
from the hallway. I found her on the stairs, surrounded by our four children,
all crying. "Mum, are you alright? What's wrong?" I asked.

Trembling and barely coherent, she said, "They'll think I'm crazy!" With
eyes wide open, and tears flowing, she pointed a trembling finger towards an
empty space in the hallway. She stammered, "K, Ki, Kir, Kirpal, Kirpal Singh
just walked through the front door. He passed through the solid wood, and
stood right there, in the hallway. He stared at me with his blazing eyes. But
who will believe me? They'll think I'm crazy!" After assurances that we
would not, she continued, "The Master stood there in the hallway for about
ten minutes gazing into my eyes! There were no audible words, but a language passed from him to me, from his eyes to mine, and entered my soul. It

was incredible! Power was blazing from him. I don't know what to say. I'm afraid whatever I could say will be understood as the ravings of a lunatic... Oh, damn, who cares! Please now do as I say; promise me that you will be the first person to stand right there where the Master stood a few minutes ago. Now go out the back-door and come around through the front, and stand right there."

I indulged her wish and stood where she indicated. I closed my eyes for a few minutes and felt a powerful, spine-tingling presence. It was not difficult to intuit that her soul would soon gain permanent release. When I returned to the gathering of friends, I related her strange experience in the electrified atmosphere.

In December, Mum gathered her grandchildren around her wheelchair and broke the news that this would be her last Christmas and we had best take advantage of the little time left. For the next week, thirteen-year old Gurdeep faithfully served her night and day, administering oxygen and massage whenever her beloved granny was unable to breathe.

More than once Mum confided to me that immediately after Christmas she would discontinue all medication, and consciously die. Her emphysema was now complicated by pleurisy and shingles. Loathe to live artificially by drugs

Mum and grandchildren, Christmas 1987.

and machines, she expressed a clear wish to die with dignity, in full control of her faculties. She sought my moral support. Repeatedly she begged the Master Power to take her from this world of suffering. Repeating "Kirpal, Kirpal," she would gain relief. Her prayers focused on God and the Master, whose identity she realized as indistinguishable.

Via telephone from India, Sant Darshan Singh Ji advised me to encourage Mum to surrender completely to the Master Power, but if she were 100% set on dying, I should respect her wishes. He conveyed his love and blessings in the name of all the great Masters, strongly assuring that she would receive full protection.

A wonderfully warm and loving Christmas gathered the extended family clan around the Yule tree—Ratana's mother, grandmother, sisters, husbands and children, her brother Rakesh, our kids, and my brother Godfrey were all present. This unlikely collection represented several generations of family life, and contributed a richness and diversity which had been sadly missing from my culturally narrow white background.

When I accompanied Mum on the ferry to her home on Vancouver Island on New Year's day, all medication had been discontinued, yet strangely all physical discomfort had ceased. Body and mind were at peace. She again saw the Master with her open eyes—this time walking towards her in the hallway. "Whenever his turban brushed the ceiling, sparks of light showered," she exulted.

Many were her questions concerning life after death, and the experiences awaiting her. She was happy to talk of these things, and displayed a remarkable absence of fear. As she was hungry for the truth, I inwardly sought guidance from the Masters and shared highlights of the stages of the inner journey, and the fate of those lucky ones who come under the protection of a perfect Master. I then related the story of *the Landlord and the Saint*, which Hazur and his successors have been fond of telling in their satsangs:

> *Once a miserly moneylender went to the home of a poor tenant farmer in a village, and demanded immediate payment of a loan, plus a huge amount of usurious interest. The farmer was able to pay the principal, but asked for leniency on the interest, which was beyond his meager means. The moneylender turned a deaf ear, for his heart was hardened with greed.*
>
> *"I see you will not pay me," he told the farmer. The money lender evicted the farmer and took all his land, cattle and grain. The farmer and his family were ruined.*
>
> *There was no one about to carry the moneylender's luggage back to his own village. He looked around wondering what to do, as he was too proud to carry it himself.*
>
> *A Saint was sitting nearby and witnessed all that had gone on. He approached the moneylender and offered to carry the luggage, on one condition. When the moneylender asked what the condition was, the Saint humbly replied, "Either you talk to me in praise of the Lord, or you listen to me as I speak of His praises."*
>
> *The moneylender agreed to listen to the Saint, but in his heart he didn't think much about it. The Saint shouldered the luggage, and as they walked to the train station, he spoke of nothing but the Lord and His greatness.*
>
> *When they reached their destination, the Saint looked into the moneylender's eyes and spoke with great seriousness:*
>
> *"I have seen that you are destined to die in a few days. In your life you haven't done a single good deed, with the exception of this past hour, which you spent in the company of a Saint, listening to his spiritual discourse.*

"Listen carefully," he continued. "When you die, the angels of death (Yamdoots) will appear and ask if you wish to enjoy the fruit of this one satsang now, or later on. You must tell the Yamdoots that you wish to enjoy it immediately. Ask them to take you into the presence of the Saint. You must then sit in meditation with him, and you will be safe.

As the Saint predicted, the moneylender died, death's angels took his soul to the Lord of Judgment (Dharam Rai) where the record of his good and bad deeds was examined. The one and only good deed was the brief time which he had spent in the company of the Saint, listening to his words of wisdom. When the Yamdoots asked if he wanted to enjoy the fruit of this good deed at once or later on, the moneylender remembered the Saint's advice, and replied:

"Let me enjoy the fruit of satsang at once. Take me to the Master now."

He was brought to the Saint, who was absorbed in meditation on the holy Naam. Overcome with gratitude, the former moneylender addressed the Saint:

"O Master, thank you for your mercy and grace. But I fear that this time with you will soon come to an end, and the angels of death are waiting for me outside."

The Saint bade the moneylender to continue sitting with him in meditation on the Lord. So long as he continued doing this, the angels of death could not come near nor claim him. And the longer he stayed with the Saint, the more his account of merit increased.

Defeated, the angels of death returned to the Lord of Death, and explained why they were empty-handed. Death replied, "Forget the moneylender, as he is lost to us forever. We have no dominion over the true Saints nor any who take refuge in Them. We have many others to catch."

I assured Mum she was far better off than the miserly landlord, for she had not only lived to bring joy to strangers throughout her life, but she also had the protection of the Master-power. Nevertheless, it was vitally important that she keep her attention on the Master's radiant form when she departed.

On January 2nd, her spirits were exceptionally high. She phoned her old friends, her sisters Margaret and Everald, and wound up loose ends. She made peace with everyone. She stipulated that she wanted neither funeral nor fanfare. "I'm not coming back to this world, she stated firmly. "I'm going to be one with the Master forever."

When I commented, "Maybe you'll meet Dad on the other side," she surprised me by saying, "He might not be there. He has probably reincarnated; he was very attached to what he hadn't completed in his life." We had never discussed reincarnation, and as far as I knew, she had no interest nor belief in the subject. She again reiterated her Home-going with Master; her desires for this world were finished. What son could not feel joy in the face of such surrender and wisdom?

I asked if she would like a satsang held in her honor. "I would like that very much," she answered. In the afternoon my brother and I sat around her bed, and we again spoke of the real purpose of life. Godfrey, who had been resisting the Master and his influence since 1967, said, "Somehow, we are all inextricably bound up in Kirpal Singh and his Power. Mum, if he is a Godman, then you don't have to worry. He will take care of you."

Around 5:30 p.m. her serene face was traced by a faint smile. While holding her hand, I asked if she would like to meditate. She nodded, and together we entered the golden brightness. After some time we opened our physical eyes. Her face was aglow. I asked, "Did you see the Light?" She replied, "Yessss...!" I asked her to look again within the Light and seek the Master's radiant form. Her eyelids closed. Moments passed. Then her lips moved and she asked, "What is the meaning of '--- ----?'" Startled, I replied, "'--- ----' means the Absolute Truth...which is within you. It is the highest name of God, given by the Master at initiation." This was a supreme gift from the inner Master. Her last sound in this world was an effort to repeat the holy Name, "Saaa...Saaa...Saa..." and she became unconscious. Around 1:50 a.m. on January 3rd, 1988, she breathed her last. Her appearance was delicate and pure, like a fragrant, wilted lily.

I caught Master Darshan by phone. With profound surety he declared "Your dear mother is in the radiant realms of pure consciousness, enjoying the full bliss and protection of the Masters." He added sympathetically, "Dear brother, she is my mother too."

> *I died as mineral and became a plant,*
> *I died as plant and rose to animal,*
> *I died as animal and I was a man.*
> *Why should I fear?*
> *When was I less by dying?*
> *Yet, once more, I shall die as man,*
> *To soar—with angels blessed,*
> *But even from angelhood*
> *I must pass on;*
> *All except God doth perish.*
> *When I have sacrificed my angel soul,*
> *I shall become what no mind e'er conceived.*
> *Oh! let me not exist, for non-existence*
> *Proclaims in organ-tones,*
> *'To Him we shall return.'*
>
> *— Maulana Rumi*[1]

---

1. *Mystery of Death* by Kirpal Singh. Delhi, SK Publications, Bowling Green VA. p. 22.

Love is a Candle, O Darshan, that consumes life itself![1]

After Mum's transition from the "vale of tears," Ratana and I are irresistibly drawn to India. The Master's health is reported as fragile, and we are mindful of the poet Browning's saying, *"Who knows, the world may end tonight."*

During our first two days at the ashram, I experience a rare bout with depression. Jet-lagged, breathing Delhi's increasingly polluted diesel air, bombarded by the cacophony of noisome squalor beyond the gates, I attempt rest in our freshly constructed room—the plaster yet damp on the walls. Am I getting too old for this, too pampered by Western convenience? Worst of all, I feel disconnected. "This is the last time I come to India," I confide to my spouse, with an edge of desperation.

Two more days pass. Such is the effect of Darshan's company, my negativity is replaced by a delirious joy, which accepts all and embraces all. Even the walls and trees, the cows and crows, have become dearest of friends. The imperfections transpire into perfection, and the squalor beyond the gates and the milling humanity assume a divinity all their own. How did we stay away for three long years? In the presence of love one cannot complain; grumbling and ingratitude arise only in its absence. We rise to a new octave. It is at this time during a meditation that Mum appears, free from the ravages of age and illness. Her smiling countenance is full of radiance; she smiles, waves to me and rises up, disappearing and becoming one with the Light forever.

The Saint's perspective: Ten of us sit around the Master, with whom we share the common floor. I relate the following parable, seeking to draw upon his wisdom:

> *"A disciple walks down a familiar street. He's beset with temptation and revulsion at every step. A little later, his Master takes a walk down the same street. What does he see? What does he know? 'O God, I see you here in all—in the sinner and in the virtuous. Everywhere is Your beauty. Thanks, for I see You, and only You!'"*

Sant Darshan comments: "The Masters see everything bathed in the Light of God. In their eyes nothing is inherently evil; everything is inherently good. There are two schools of thought—one, which states that the nature of man is basically evil, and the other which believes in the basic goodness of man. The Saints always take the latter course, as they see the Light of the Lord who is all goodness radiating from every living being. Looking at man from such an

elevated angle, it is no wonder that the Saints of the higher order always over-
look our faults, our sins, and our shortcomings. We should always try to look
at things from this angle and ask the Master for the grace to be able to do so
ourselves."

He continues: "Despite the prophecies of doom and gloom, our Master Kirpal
foresaw the dawning of the Golden Age, when there would be peace between
man and man; when love would reign supreme...Usually when one Age or Yuga
ends, the new age is preceded by cataclysms, Dissolutions or Pralaya, and
Grand Dissolution or Maha Pralaya. The difference with the dawning of the
coming Golden Age is that it will come about by a change in the human heart.
So, my brother, it all depends on our angle of vision. We should always try to
see the basic goodness in our fellow man, and thus, with a transformation in
our own heart, help bring about the Golden Age."

Over the following weeks, we participate in another intimate slice of the divine.
In the normal world, we are bound by patterns of habit and desire. In the fluid,
sleepless, spiritualized sphere of Darshan's world, these are transubstantiated,
altered and subsumed. As he approaches the sunset of life, the filament of his
essence and beauty constantly emerge through the surface, magnetic and
incandescent, as it was in Kirpal's last months on earth.

On many a random midnight, comes a greatly coveted knock on our door
and the summons, "Brother Steefun and Sister Ratana; Maharaj Ji calling!
Come quickly!" Knowing that at any time we might be called, we go to bed
fully clothed to be at the ready. The Gracious Master— as he is known—
shares sumptuous vegetarian dinners with guests, relatives, and a few locals at
the craziest hours—2, 3 or 4 AM—his normal supper-time. While passing mul-
tiple servings of delicious food about the table, he jokes and makes witty
repartee, himself eating sparingly of *kicherdee* (unspiced rice and dal), plain
chapati and spinach *subje* without chilies. He delights in mystic poetry and
reminiscences, which flow through the nights and the dawns. Rather than tir-
ing, we are imbued with passion for more and more, released only after the
chirping of awakening birds and the rousing neighborhood.

Sleep? Around the Sleepless Saint, who sleeps? Who wants rest? Regularity?
Hah! Meditation? Wherever one is, whether with him or waiting, one can close
the eyes and ears and attune. With Darshan, grace flows freely and discipline is
never imposed, but arises from within. If lax in spiritual practice, however, *one
misses the best of what he has to give.* At daily sittings in the meditation hall,
he often places his hand on the foreheads of meditators, pressing thumb gently
over their third eye, firmly moving it upward once or twice, before moving on
to the next in line. Sometimes he will only touch three or four out of many.
These are wordless sessions, and after his departure, one can sit for hours
absorbing the surges cascading down from higher planes.

Time, in his presence, is suspended, and in that boundless chaos one discovers rare order, perfection, and enchantment. We witness how much he accomplishes each day; how many people he sees, what burdens and pains of others he shoulders, the scores of urgent phone calls he answers, all at the price of his own failing health. Darshan, the tenderhearted, refuses none while he has breath.

What pretensions can a would-be disciple have when the Guru has none? He bows to the feet of the elderly while dissuading others from touching his. He possesses a child's innocence. Tears of compassion and tears of remembrance spring readily to his eyes.

> *This quivering, glistening tear on your eyelashes*
> *is a star falling from the azure sky;*
> *A drop of mercury, sparkling and full of warmth,*
> *or a lustrous pearl emerging from its shell...*[2]

Humor and laughter are also his instruments. Though extremely knowledgeable on practically any topic, he often asks our opinions and listens closely. He might start off on a mundane theme, but always ends on a profound mystic note. One must take care not to be lulled by the relaxed familiar, nor take his friendship for granted, for behind the human is an awesome spiritual power.

This afternoon, while sharing tea, he becomes absorbed in a newspaper, underlining and circling certain articles. Like a professor, he lowers the paper, raises his ample eyebrows, peers over reading glasses and says, "I keep up to date on the latest developments locally, nationally and globally by reading the newspaper for fifteen minutes every day. Articles which interest me, or which I want to know more about, I mark for later reference when I have time. If I don't have time personally, I'll ask one of my friends to check up on them, and research the facts, which I will review later. In this way I can be up to date with current events, trends and developments. It is important to be well informed.

Master further relates: "*Mysticism* is not *escapism*. I coined the term 'Positive Mysticism' which teaches us to lead balanced lives. That path which teaches us to abandon our worldly and social responsibilities is what I call 'Negative Mysticism.' That is not our path. We need to develop all-round in every sphere of life—mundane and spiritual, as integrated men and women. We are to shoulder our family responsibilities. Our level of consciousness should expand from the individual level to the family, from the family to the national level, from the national to the international, and from the international to the cosmos."

As a scholar and a stickler for details, every quote *has* to be accurate, never exaggerated. And while kind, he sometimes corrects the misinformed or misguided with humorous wit and indirect irony.

Darshan Singh carried out the onerous responsibilities of Mastership conferred upon him in 1974 while concurrently working full-time as Deputy Secretary of the Indian government until retiring in 1978. On his way to and from work each morning and evening while riding on the back of his cousin's scooter, hundreds would wait to have his darshan-glance. During those four years where his duties as Master and civil servant overlapped, he discharged his worldly duties by day and ministered to the ever-increasing sangat by night and on weekends. Many of his co-workers became ardent devotees.

"On my final day of service," he told us one night, "your Auntie asked me, 'What are you doing?' I replied, 'I am praying to the two great Masters and offering to Them my profound gratitude, because today I am leaving my service—which is a very sensitive position—without one spot on my clothes. They are quite white, and I am all gratitude to Them for protecting my honor.'"

Professor Janak Raj Puri: One of the frequent nightly visitors is the erudite Professor Puri, author of many fine books on mysticism, and an old disciple of Baba Sawan Singh. Puri Sahib, although aged, has found elixir in Darshan's presence, where years and weariness simply fall away. One night, the professor arrives with Sohan Singh Bhandari and Jaswant Singh Chabbra, two venerable disciple-friends.[3] Bhandari was in charge of the huge langar at Beas. What a foursome—Bhandari, Puri, Chabbra and Master Darshan—as they pass the night singing and sharing the glories of their Hazur! I sit in a corner, observing, delighting.

During the month-long preparations for Master Kirpal's 94th birth celebration on February 6, 1988, more than 2,000 *sevadars*—selfless, unpaid volunteers—are organized into committees to accommodate and feed more than 60,000 people for three days, and about 15,000 for ten days. When the celebration arrives, every nook and corner of Kirpal Ashram, Kirpal Bagh, and Sawan Ashram are used to provide free shelter, bedding, food and medical assistance for out-of-town visitors. Imagine the huge quantities of food, blankets, and medicine! During the 5th and 6th, the crowd overflows into the street outside, where television monitors are set up so all can see the program. I say to the Master, "This place is too small." And he replies, "The Beloved has room for his lovers...and he will also make accommodation for them too."

On the night of the 5th the ashram resounds with beautifully rendered *Gurbani* by Professor Satnam Singh Sethi, one of India's greatest singers. (His tapes and records can be found in Indian music stores not only throughout India, but also in London, Vancouver, Toronto, Los Angeles and New York.) An initiate of Sant Kirpal Singh, Professor Sethi was blessed with good inner experience, but after 1974, he lost contact. Several years later he came to visit Sant Darshan Singh, seeking the boon of reconnection. Master Darshan

Left to right: Sant Darshan Singh, Professor Puri, Jaswant Singh Chabbra, the author, and Amar Nath Sharma, 1988

humbly offered his services in the name of his Predecessors. Escorting the famed singer to his private office, he sat him down, touched the point between the eyes, and left the room. Whatever had been lost was quickly restored; thereafter the Ragi became a regular visitor to the ashram. His superb performance tonight is followed by a troupe of singers, wearing gold brocade caps in Muslim fashion. Mukesh and Handa Sahib lead the ensemble with a *Qawwali* rendition of one of Master Darshan's *ghazals*. The cadence begins slowly, but as the tempo picks up, the talking drums, the ching-ching of cymbals and the harmonium's rippled flight punctuate the night. Rhythmic clapping is taken up by the sangat. And as the ensemble sings, our *Murshid* often raises his arm, hand gracefully turning, forefinger up, eyes partly closed, glowing, joyful, swaying. Qawwali goes on and on, releasing us, lofting us:

> *O' Saqqi-ah, jam challey, jam challey, jam challey!*
> *O' Cupbearer, let the goblet of divine intoxication*
> *go round, and round and round!*

The meaning of Qawwali: Around 2 AM after the program winds down, we retreat to the Master's house. At one point he turns and addresses me, "Qawwali is part of the tradition of Sant Mat, or the Path of the Masters. It is when the disciples sing the mystical verses of Sants like Maulana Rumi, Maulana Dard, Khwaja Hafiz, Bulleh Shah, Chisti, Khusro, and others to their Master, their Murshid. Actually, Qawwali is a reflection from the inner realms when the lovers gather around their Beloved in the inner planes in a circle and sing paeans to him... Hazur was very fond of Qawwali and often held Qawwali *Darbar* [the Court of Qawwali] on the roof of his residence at Beas. Sometimes fifty to two-hundred would gather there on his roof, and Qawwali would go on into the night."

I ask if Hazur ever employed Qawwali in his satsang. "No," Master Darshan replies, "but the Beloved Master did so on several occasions."[4]

Servant of the servants: Each night after a long day's service, most of the two thousand sevadars collect outside the Master's residence. When he appears, he listens to their difficulties, dispenses advice, and distributes parshad. Also met are individuals and groups from all parts of India, as well as visitors from more than thirty foreign countries. When the function winds down, Master spends hours personally handing out bundles of clothing, books and parshad to each volunteer.[5] His zeal and love are inexhaustible, growing in the giving.

Typically, over a hundred people per day are fed from the Master's personal kitchen. His house is not his own; all have staked their claim. In his kitchen service is a young woman from a very poor family. Since her teens, she has quietly and efficiently served under Auntie's supervision. As she blossomed into womanhood, Master arranged for her wedding to a suitable young Indian man and himself bore more than ninety percent of the marriage expenses. The river of giving and receiving is never static; the Masters are what kings were meant to be.

The Disciples of Pakistan: I have the good fortune to meet a small band of Muslim disciples from Pakistan. Abdullah of Peshawar introduces me to his brother. Among them is Bibi Khan, a young woman who shares her remarkable story:

> *"Two years ago, my father and I were on pilgrimage to Mecca. We stayed near the shrine of the Kaaba—the black stone of Abraham. One night I had a vision of the holy Master. I wondered why I would see someone in the Sikh form when I, a Muslim, looked only to Prophet Muhammad, blessed be his name, and to the saints of the Sufi path. He directed me to return with my father to Pakistan, and look up one M. Shaukat at such and such address. I knew of no such person. Father shared faith in my vision, and when we returned to Lahore, we went to the street mentioned in my vision, and found Shaukat Sahib*

waiting for us. He inwardly knew of our coming. He explained the inner way and directed us to the Master."

More than five hundred initiated families reside in Pakistan. They address the Masters in their own beautiful way: Hazur as "Sawan Shah," Kirpal as "Shah Jamal," and Darshan as "Shah Deedar."[6] Since few Pakistanis are permitted to travel to India, the Masters, unbound by time and space, come to them, each in their own way.

Tennyson: A few nights later while about twenty Westerners wait in his living room, Master Darshan enters and spontaneously begins his favorite subject—poetry and poets. "Some," he says, "enter this life with highly developed backgrounds and are just natural at what they do—natural poets, natural sculptors, natural musicians, and natural saints, merely picking up in this life where they left off in their last." He used the example of the great Tennyson, who, at the tender age of nine or ten began writing exceptional poetry. His brutish father, who didn't want such a promising son to be an impractical poet, beat him whenever he caught him writing. Under such duress, Tennyson promised, "Alright father, I'll never write again!" A few days later the boy was again caught writing verses, and as his father began to beat him, Tennyson cried out, "Papa! Papa! Pity take; verses I shall never make!"

The Master speaks on relationships and chastity:

"The main reason husbands and wives cannot pull on together is our eccentric ego. If one partner wants to be chaste, and the other wants to indulge in sex, then sometimes the strict partner should give a little; there should be adjustment. If it comes down to the difference of saving a marriage, I always advise the partners not to be too rigid. It is always better to support and save the marriage. It is the ego that causes disunity, fighting, and separation...I always try to patch them up, whenever my brothers and sisters, sons and daughters, are having their marital difficulties. This problem is particularly acute in the West. It is not so bad in India. We have to learn the art of adjustment, and to prune our egos, our eccentricities. Life is not a solo play. We have to be part of the orchestra!"

Keeping context: One night while joking at the back of the Master's living room with Sohinder and Dr. D.Singh from Ontario, I quote out of context a verse from Farid: *"Bhagrey, bhag, Faqir bal ke, kanch aur kamini bhaga laga."* [*"O meditator, flee from woman and gold; run, run away fast!"*] The Master notices three of us chuckling like truants. He raises his eyebrows and asks for an explanation, which I lamely give.

"You know, people often tear things out of context," Master comments. "For example, there's a famous saying among the Sikhs, *'Satguru sikh ke bandhan kaatey,*' which translates as '*Satguru cuts off all bondage of the disciple.*' It means the Master cuts off all your bonds, but they don't bother with the next line: '*Gur ka sikh vikhar sae hatte,*' or '*Provided the disciple of the Guru remains away from all failings or evils.*' They only want to quote the first line, but not the next. I have heard the first part of this verse from hundreds of disciples, 'O Master, you will take care of me,' but they did not take the next line, the next step— 'When we refrain from evil.' We only quote what suits us."

One evening Darshan privately discusses with Dr. Neil Tessler and I the process and varieties of Guru-succession. Some have only apparent legality but no real power to elevate the souls of others, and while Master Kirpal, Baba Ji (Jaimal Singh), and other Param Sants had full *spiritual* authority and power, they had neither wills nor the benefit of their predecessor's property. When *both* exist side by side, as in the case of Baba Sawan Singh and several other past Saints, their work faces little impediment, he says. Master Darshan also has both, but as we know, the hand-written will disappeared for six years. At this point, I express hope that the next succession will be crystal clear. He assures me that he will indeed make his succession unequivocal, and the mission of the one to follow him will flourish on an unprecedented scale.

Tonight he reminisces over Hazur, who was regal and an elegant dresser. Everything about him was of the finest quality: "Normally people could not get within six feet of Hazur, and I only know of one instance when the great Hazur embraced anyone. This lucky fellow happened to a former friend and colleague from his earlier years when they were military engineers. This old friend hadn't seen Hazur since their earlier days, but when he came up the stairs of Hazur's house, he shouted out at the top of his lungs, 'O Guru! O Guru! O Guru!' And when he reached the top of the stairs, Hazur warmly embraced him!

"Hazur always carried a walking stick with him, and if the devotees tried to touch his lotus feet, he would threaten to give them a whack. Several were the lucky souls who actually got a tap from his cane. His court was full of splendor— despite all that, Hazur's beauty, humility, and magnetism were incomparable."

Early devotees are unanimous in saying that Master Kirpal lived very simply and was totally accessible. He did not copy Hazur's regal style, clothing or mannerisms; rather he manifested his essence, and spent every breath in Hazur's service. M. Kirpal was not so meticulous about his clothes and didn't care if his turban was sometimes askew. When someone once advised him to change his shirt because of a small food stain, he retorted, "are the people coming to see my shirt or are they coming to see me?" If a pickpocket comes to a Saint, he may see only his pockets. However, there have been instances when thieves came to satsang, and found their hearts picked by the Master.

While Darshan's language is poetic and ornate, Kirpal's was brief and simple. Kirpal's magnificent physique and commanding personality made him appear awesome and austere. The transmission of awakening from him was often sudden, while with Darshan, grace seeps slowly into one's every cell, every atom, imbuing the spirit with intense intoxication—the end-result is the same. Personalities, body-types, complexions, status, education, styles and habits of the Saints vary greatly, but the fundamentals of ethical character, stages of realization, integrity and the competence to grant experience on the Path of Light and Sound remain constant throughout the millennia.

In Darshan we have seen an Adept who is naturally a most caring husband to his wife-companion and loving father to his sons—dimensions which the more austere Master Kirpal rarely revealed. All these years, Darshan's apparent meekness has been his cloaking device behind which God mischievously played hide-and-seek with devotees. Master Kirpal sometimes patted the arriving and departing disciples on their backs or on the tops of their heads. On the other hand, Master Darshan has been most liberal with his chaste affection. This verse of his is no exaggeration of a constant example:

Embrace every man as your very own,
And shower your love freely wherever you go.

Of himself, he deprecatingly says: "I am only a collared dog of the two great Masters, and I go wherever they send me... Beside the towering personality of the Beloved Master, I am just a clerk..."

I try in vain to conceive of anyone alive whose qualities match the pristine purity of this kind, totally accessible, magical, and unpretentious being.

---

1. Darshan Singh, *A Tear and a Star*, SK Publications, Bowling Green, VA.

2. Darshan Singh, *Love at Every Step - My Concept of Poetry*, 1989, S.K. Publications, Bowling Green, VA, p. 60.

3. Jaswant Singh Chabbra is mentioned in Chapter 35, *The Vale of Kashmir*. He became the fortunate father-in-law of "Bawa Ji," Master Darshan's youngest son.

4. *"Qawwali" literally means "utterance" and qawwali is the mouthpiece of Divine Power. This art-form is the devotional music of the Sufis...intended to elevate the spirit and bring both performer and listener closer to God...Music is the vehicle to reach the heart and attain a state of grace.*—Dr. Adam Nayyar, whose jacket notes appear on the CD by Nusrat Fateh Ali Khan *Traditional Sufi Qawwalis*, Navras Records Ltd. 22 Sherwood Rd. London, NW4 1AD

5. By October 1997, this number more than tripled.

6. Sant Rajinder Singh is also known as Rajan Shah.

7 4

What does it matter if I am called a man?
In truth I am the very soul of love;
The entire earth is my home
And the universe my country.
—Darshan Singh

Valentine's Day, February 14, 1988: After a long drought, heavy downpours drench the Delhi region. Many assume the Sunday satsang will be canceled due to the chill and rain, but at 1 PM the ashram is suddenly bathed in hot sunshine. Steam literally rises from the earth, puddles disappear before our eyes, and the air sparkles with clarity.

The crowd is rather small due to the rains—less than five thousand. The Master often arrives late and today is no exception. Lateness is one of the "dogs" he keeps at his door to test our patience and maturity, if not to prime our yearning. Just the other day I had the temerity to say, "I have only been able to find one fault with you, Master." He looked at me and asked, "Yes, my brother, and what is that?" "You have no concept of time!" I replied, as we both dissolved into laughter.

The gracious one sits on the white dais, silent and reflective for long minutes. Inspired by his Muse, he extemporaneously composes a new Urdu poem on the seasons. As my attention focuses on his eyes and forehead, his physical stature seems to grow; a humble form metamorphoses into glowing royalty. Many, myself included, are rewarded with ravishing glimpses of past Masters emerging from his form, while a golden-white nimbus dances around him. In order to gain this blessing, it is essential to sit very still with *unwavering* attention (as in meditation).

Harish Chaddha sits to my right. At the satsang's conclusion I ask him, "Did you see Master Kirpal sitting on the dais today?" He answers, "Actually, I saw only my Master Sawan sitting there!"

In the evening Darshan invites Ratana and I into his office, and unbidden, translates highlights of his Hindi discourse into English while I furiously scribble in my notebook:

> *"Keats has said, 'A thing of beauty is a joy forever, its loveliness increases, it fadeth never.' Our so-called physical love fadeth—it is not real love. External beauty reaches its zenith in youth, but intoxicated by it, we do not realize how temporary it is. A poet has said, 'Youthful beauty is a shining dewdrop on the rose at dawn; come the day, it evaporates and is gone.'*

"As a child, I would build fine castles from wet sand on the banks of
our river. When the moisture evaporated in the sun, my sandcastles
would crumble and become just a pile of sand again. Is this not the
fate of all physical beauty? Rumi in a poem asks us to observe the
artist's painting. Don't just look at the picture; look within to know its
beauty. If you wish to find eternal beauty, you have to seek within.

"Only that love which exists between the lover and the divine Beloved
lasts forever. It alone is real love. When the poet Yeats said, 'A desire
which can be fulfilled is not a great desire,' he was speaking of all
world-worldly loves and desires. A thing of worldly beauty is in reality
not a joy forever, cannot be a joy forever, as everything of this world—
even the magnificent Taj Mahal—will sooner or later wither or crumble
and fall to the ground. Only a thing of spiritual beauty can be a joy
forever, and that eternal beauty is the Beloved.

"When a true Sufi or lover looks into the mirror, he will not see his
own face, he will see only the reflection of his Beloved—the Master.
The test of a true lover is when he looks into the mirror, he will behold
therein none other than his Master, and he will behold that form in
every atom, in every flower, every bud, every tree, in all animals, in
every man, and in all creation.

"When the love in our heart for the Master is ripe, then his form must
appear. It is said that our love should be so intense, so one-pointed
that our heart will be like a shining mirror. And in that mirror our
Beloved should always be shining. The moment we wish to have a
glimpse of the Master, we just bow our head, look into the mirror of
our heart, and find him there before us.

"Every wrinkle of a lover radiates divine love. A Sufi Divine has said
that if you cut the veins of a lover, instead of blood, you will find only
love pouring from his veins. A lover will always think, 'I will not mind if
my physical beauty dwindles, so long as the beauty of the love of my
Beloved is within me.' The love of the eternal Beloved beautifies the
lovers even as they progress in years. Such a love keeps their heart and
soul evergreen, ever-blossoming. As I have written in one of my ghazals.

> Your love is the very rise and fall of my life;
> Love is the name
> Of a continuous restlessness of the heart.

As Darshan continues, he shares remembrance after remembrance of Hazur,
and his countenance become suffused with an inner beatification:

"Once Hazur made what appeared to be a very revolutionary statement
in one of his satsangs: 'It is the Master who gives birth to God.' Several
eyebrows were raised. Since I was a student of Persian language and
literature, Hazur asked me to explain his revolutionary statement. I

said, 'The word *paeda* used by Hazur is a Persian word, which commonly means "birth," but its real meaning is "manifestation." Hazur's utterance meant that the Masters are beyond birth and death, and they bring the manifestation of God down on earth.' Hazur was pleased and accepted this interpretation as correct.

"I remember that when the great Hazur went to our village (Sayyed Kasran), the local ministers of religion gathered together and invited the beloved Hazur. They asked him many questions, which he answered to their entire satisfaction. At last when there were no more questions their chairman got up and said, 'It is alright if you distribute your gift of divinity and immortality, but kindly give it only to the deserving ones. You bestow that divine gift on every Tom, Dick and Harry!' And the great Hazur came to his own...sometimes these Saints just give us a glimpse of their greatness. He said, 'If a rich man is prepared to distribute his wealth to whomsoever he likes, why should anyone bother about it?' And he added, in all humility, 'If it was a question of only the deserving ones, then even I didn't deserve this divine gift. It was just the grace of Baba Ji that He blessed me.'

"So, none of us is deserving of the lyrical glances of our Masters which give a boost to our soul. When we get that boost our soul flies from this human launching pad into the inner space, where the Master pilots us into regions of higher and higher consciousness. Just as dangers exist in outer space where the pilot makes sure his ship won't fall into the gravitational pull of any other planet, there are also many temptations and dangers on the inner path as well. When the Master-Pilot keeps us under his protective wings we are saved from all dangers. Throughout successive stages of the journey, he escorts us ever onwards and upwards towards our final goal—communion of our soul with the Creator. And for this grace we pay our obeisance trillions and trillions of times, expressing immeasurable gratitude to Him."

Around 10 PM Master calls all 119 of the visiting Westerners to his spacious living room to meditate and later to participate in a joyful party. An earlier Valentine talk is read aloud, followed by poems and songs written and sung by Germans, French nationals, Austrians, Africans, Canadians and Americans. Someone presents a big garish balloon in the shape of a heart, arms protruding from the sides with the words across its front: *I love you this much!* For a moment I consider how hokey this is but I admonish my mind, *flow with it.* Fortunately the Master's child-like innocence and joy in sharing with his disciples permeates us all; when flash-floods run down the mountain into the desert of barren hearts, all roads and all irreverencies are washed away.

Before leaving that same night for Canada, Ratana and I are again called to his inner office. He had written to our daughter Shanti, who was missing the Master and despairing of ever finding a suitable match. "Tell Shanti," he says, "that I will find her a suitable husband! What kind of husband does she want? Which nationality? How tall? How old? What kind of education? Dark or fair complexion? Tell her that she should not despair, as I will take the responsibility for finding a suitable companion for my daughter!"[1]

"Thank you, Master, your message will be conveyed. On another subject, someone has been advising everyone here that we should not give advice to others." He smiles, yet serious, "We should give our advice whenever it can be of use to others. A doctor will give advice, an engineer will give advice a teacher will give advice; however, we should not give unauthorized advice for inner spiritual progress or experience. That is in the hands of the Master because he has traversed all the stages of the inner journey; he is the only one who can give correct guidance within. Others can only give advice to the extent of their experience and training, and even then it may not always be correct...Sometimes Master may give a piece of advice to a particular individual. That may be for them; it may not be for all people."

Weary of our ups and downs in business, Ratana urges me to ask Master for his advice to help set my feet firmly on the path of consistent profitability. He laces his fingers together, plays with them a little, and says:

"Brother, you know that I have never entered into the business line, but when my son Bawa wanted to go into business, this is the advice I gave him, and as you are also like a son to me, the same I give to you:

"First, *keep to quality*. Quality should never be sacrificed either for quantity or money. Be honest.

"Second, we should expand our business to the extent that we can *control it personally*. Most of the problems in business come about because we expand beyond our control.

"Third, we should be *progressive*, do our best, and make the most of our business but not be too ambitious. Be very cautious—expansion is very easy; retreating is very difficult. We should be contented with whatever the Master blesses us."

He elaborates further about the difficulties that even great generals and leaders faced when they had to retreat, using the example of Britain's evacuation of India in 1948. While I have attended many seminars and read numerous books on business and personal motivation, the Master's extemporaneous and free advice captures the quintessence of what is taught in sophisticated and costly seminars.[2]

If this pilgrimage to India, my tenth, could be compared to previous ones, I can only say that it has been one of the best. Not because of any great spiritual visions, for such was not my lot. Rewards came in the form of a much-needed course in man-making, and the continuing and ever-deepening realization of the Master's competency and humanist wisdom. Something was righted deep inside. His constant example of how to *live* love in a practical way pointed towards the means to not only improve our lives, but also to help bring peace to a troubled world.

And, this is the very first time I don't feel sad upon leaving. As we cross his threshold for the waiting taxi, sweet Darshan hugs me to his bosom. He is wearing the oversized coat Master Kirpal had given him fourteen years earlier. His arms wrap around me, and my head buries in his shoulder. There we remain for what seems like many minutes; I feel his long silky beard on my face. I continue standing, transfixed, enveloped in darkness, then light, bodiless and infinite. *"Master will be always with you,"* he says, gently returning me.

When he blesses Ratana with both hands on top of her head, Richard Handel snaps a Polaroid of the event. We watch as the Polaroid develops itself, and a mysterious bright light appears in the photo above the Master's hands on her head. The best meditation of this pilgrimage comes while sitting with closed eyes in Amsterdam's bustling airport. The stilled heart is the mirror; in the mirror is the Beloved; in the Beloved is everything.

He is hidden in every instrument,
in every song and melody.
All creation reflects His glory.
There exists not a sparkling wave
nor a fiery star
that does not owe its radiance to His Light.[3]

Two nights after we returned from India, ten-year-old Jyoti came to our bed crying, "Daddy, I just had a bad dream about monsters chasing me. I'm so scared." I groggily advised, "Pray to Master and He will help you. There's nothing to be afraid of; his protecting hand is over your head. Now go back to sleep." About half an hour later, Jyoti came back and woke me up a second time.

"Daddy, Daddy! Again the monsters came. Then I remembered what you said. Master Darshan came and told me to repeat *Sat Naam* if I ever have any bad dream, and all bad things will go away, and they did!"

Two days later, as I was leaving for work, the car nudging into traffic, I saw a crowd huddled over a limp figure on the busy intersection across the street from our house. I thought, "Oh no, some child has been hit!" There, lying on the ice-cold pavement was little Jyoti, looking up with tears in her wide-open eyes, spasms working the corners of her mouth.

Jyoti had been struck by a car, which tossed her more than seventeen feet to where she now lay on the pavement. Ratana was frantic. Soon an ambulance whisked her off to Grace Hospital. After an examination, she was released. No broken bones, not a scratch, no pain. Her only injury was a light bruise over the kidney area; otherwise she was perfectly fine.

Dr. Masterson, the urologist approached me and said, "Amazing that your daughter wasn't badly injured. By the way, I think we're related. My mother is the daughter of your father's sister." We had never met before.

When we called the Master to express our gratitude for Jyoti's safety and all other blessings in our lives, he said how much he missed and loved *all* the dear ones abroad, wishing them to be regular in their practice. I asked for the strength to live up to what we had received, adding, "Your love is a fragrance all around us and we don't want to lose it."

He replied, "I'll pass on your prayer to the two great Masters and I'll certainly add to it my own prayers. Master is always with you. Your Auntie and I send you our love and best wishes."

I said, "I think of her as Mother, not as Auntie."

He replied, "In India when we say Auntie, we mean like a Mother."

---

1. When the gracious Master passed on in 1989, Shanti was heart-broken. Not only did a very strong bond of love exist between them, but she was still unmarried. She thereafter met a bright disciple from Germany, Markus Schramm and became engaged. The Master fulfilled his promise through his spiritual successor in August 1994, and blessed the marriage in person.

2. By following his advice carefully, our future labors began to bear abundant fruit.

3. Darshan Singh, *Love At Every Step*, Bowling Green, VA: SK Publications, pp. 30

75

*A sublime heart receives more light from love
than from the beauty which the eyes behold...*[1]

July 31, 1988, New York: Against doctor's advice, Sant Darshan Singh Ji undertook another world tour. Thousands came to meet him in New York City; some to renew their covenant with freedom, others to begin it. His inspired discourses were followed by initiation into the mysteries of the beyond. During the inner sound portion, an elderly woman interrupted her meditation and laid a hand on his arm. He led her outside, inviting me along too.

"Dear Master," she said, "I have been seeing the radiant form of Kirpal Singh within, off and on for several years. During your meditation sitting two days ago, I passed through the veil and beheld his resplendent form again. He took me up through plane after spiritual plane, until the brilliance and glory of the Light were beyond my capacity to endure! He then directed me to you for initiation." Suddenly she hugged the Master, and wept on his compassionate shoulder.

He turned to me, and said, "One of my daughters told me last night that she was seeing me in her dreams before she had ever heard of me. I told her, 'We are not new friends; we are not strangers. We are old friends and we are already bound in the divine silken threads. We are not strangers here; we are members of the great universal family of God! You are welcome to come back to your True Home.'"

The woman spoke "I have known you before. Perhaps we are old friends, perhaps from another life."

Master said, "I have seen many, many eyes, but they are all His eyes. Everywhere I look I see the eyes of the one divine Beloved."

After the initiation finished, James, an elderly Greek-American asked, "Master, when Jesus was on the cross, why did he say '*My God, My God, why hast thou forsaken me?*'"

Master replied, "I'm not sure, but I have always believed that he was quoting the Twenty-second Psalm. And when I put that to the Beloved Master he agreed with me."

He then called for a King James Version of the Bible to be brought forth and has it read aloud before the large audience:

> *My God, my God, why hast thou forsaken me? Why art thou so far from helping me, and from the words of my roaring?*
> *My God, I cry in the daytime, but thou hearest not; and in the night season, and am not silent. But thou art holy, O thou that inhabitest the praises of Israel. Our fathers trusted in thee: they trusted, and thou didst deliver them. They cried unto thee, and were delivered: they trusted in thee, and were not confounded...*
> *For dogs have compassed me: the assembly of wicked has enclosed me: they pierced my hands and my feet...They part my garments among them, and cast lots upon my vesture. But be not thou far from me. O Lord: O my strength, haste thee to help me...*

Next he had the Twenty-third Psalm read out:

> *The Lord is my shepherd; I shall not want. He maketh me to lie down*

in green pasture: he leadeth me beside the still waters. He restoreth my soul: he leadeth me in the paths of righteousness for his name's sake.

Yea, though I walk through the valley of the shadow of death, I will fear no evil: for thou art with me; thy rod and thy staff they comfort me.

Thou preparest a table before me in the presence of mine enemies: thou anointest my head with oil; my cup runneth over.

Surely goodness and mercy shall follow me all the days of my life: and I will dwell in the house of the Lord forever.

Bibi Harbhajan Kaur
—the Master's life-companion at his side.

1. Darshan Singh, *Love At Every Step*, SK Publications, Bowling Green, VA, pp. 89

Travelers who come after me
will have no cause to complain
That they found no light nor footsteps
on the path of love.

7 6

On May 30, 1989, I received a call from Raji in Chicago. With an emotion-laden voice he said, "Arran, our gracious Master has just left his body for the Eternal Home..." We had already endured much for Kirpal, and now...our beloved Darshan. Thankfully, this transition would be peaceful, for the Master had taken precautions to ensure that his succession would be crystal-clear to all.

By coincidence, Ratana and I arrived in Delhi at the same time as Raji and his family. Enormous respect was paid to him from all sides as we moved through the airport. Cars whisked us over to Kirpal Ashram, where the Master's body was resting on a white bed, covered with mounds of fragrant jasmine and marigolds. His still form, his open face crowned with turban, was the essence of serenity and dignity. Later in the afternoon, the body was placed on a platform and, accompanied by his sons and hundreds of thousands of well-wishers, transported to the burning ghats by the Yamuna River, several miles away.

The funeral procession wended through the capital of India peacefully and without mishap. With his family and several close disciples, we stood atop the cremation platform, which was about twelve feet high and twenty feet across. As far as the eye could see in all directions was a sea of weeping humanity. The heat in the midday sun was extreme. Along with family members, the few foreigners present were given the honor of placing fragrant sandalwood logs upon the pyre. Raji, dignified in his sorrow, lit the pyre, and as the flames leaped up, a great cry arose from the multitude. Soon the searing heat forced our retreat.

Back at the ashram, sacred hymns filled the air. Sorrow co-mingled with divine peace. Most affected was Auntie-ji, but she somehow managed to maintain supreme dignity. When I asked if she were seeing Master inside, she sweetly replied, "Arran-ji, if I weren't seeing the Gracious Master within, how could I carry on?"

The following morning we returned to the pyre. Milk mixed with water was poured on the Master's ashes to cool them, then they were collected in brass urns. Raji found a circular bone from the Master's skull and showed it to us. "Master Kirpal said that from this piece of bone, one who knows can read many things about the past and future of that person," he commented. None loved the gracious Master more than Raji, but he was the essence of equipoise and clarity.

For thirteen days, scriptures were sung in the Ashram, offering peace and inspiration to the bereaved sangat (as it might have been after Master Kirpal passed, if, if...). On the last day, Darshan Singh's sealed will was opened and read, and as expected, Rajinder Singh was declared the new living Master. He was no longer to be referred to as Raji, his nickname, but by the name Hazur had given him, *Rajinder* which means *King of kings*.

There was great rejoicing, as turbans from Hazur, Master Kirpal and Darshan were tied on Rajinder's head. During the ceremony, hundreds of old disciples, eminent holy personages and religious leaders came up on the huge dais to garland and bless the new Master for his great work ahead. As he sat, his quick, large, luminous eyes searched out the eyes of everyone in the vast assembly. In his eyes was a powerful similarity to the great ones whom we had earlier known.

We accompanied the new Master to Rishikesh for immersion of the sacred ashes, and then to Niranjan Akhara, an ancient Hindu religious order where he was honored by hundreds of India's most eminent sadhus. Here by the banks of the Ganges, Sant Rajinder Singh Ji gave and received the *tilak* or sacred forehead mark to a seemingly endless procession of orange-robed holy men. It was an exceedingly rare spectacle.

Upon returning to Vancouver, I drafted the following article which was published in *The Link* newspaper, and the *Common Ground*.

> *At 8:00 AM, on May 30, 1989 Sant Darshan Singh left for his Eternal Home. 200,000 people of all religions and creeds from India and 14 other countries, attended his funeral on June 1. More than a million people witnessed his funeral procession as it passed through the streets of New Delhi—one of the largest gatherings since the death of Mahatma Gandhi. Yet, this was no politician, priest or king; it was the great poet-saint Darshan Singh, loved by millions throughout the world...*
>
> *For several weeks, Sant Darshan Singh had been hinting to those around him that he would not be with them much longer, but most thought he referred to his leaving on a world tour. Dr. Scotti said, "Master, we'll meet in four weeks time in Germany." Master replied, "That will be in eternity." To his assistants, he asked, "If the Bridegroom does not proceed forth, where will the marriage party go?" To Allan Jacobs, who phoned from Alberta, he confided, "We will not meet again. Raji will take care of you." To another, he said, "Instead of repeating the Names, catch hold of the Named One." Sometimes the persons of God appear to speak in riddles, but behind their remarks are many a profound truth.*
>
> *At 2:00 am on that fateful morning, Raksha, one of the attendants*

*asked if she could take away his tea cup. He replied, "Yes daughter,
take away the cup. From now on, you will have my shuksham darshan
(inner radiant vision)" She said the Master looked healthy and radiant
and at the time she couldn't fathom the depth of his remark.*

*At 3:00 AM he telephoned Dr. Jay and Ricki Linksman in Florida,
both of whom had worked diligently for many years on the publications, profusely thanking them for their contribution. He added that he
wanted to make one last change in the manuscript of his forthcoming
book,* Love At Every Step. *The original version stated: "I have always
written as inspired, and will continue to do so in the future." He said
to delete this line, and the change to be inserted would be arriving by
mail shortly. The change was:*

> The Ocean of Light is limitless;
> It is life that is so short.

And then he added the following from his book of verses, A Tear
& A Star:

> So far I have only drawn a few lines,
> and am preparing a blueprint...

*Shortly before 8:00 am on May 30th, Sant Darshan Singh lay peace-
fully on his side. His wife, Bibi Harbhajan Kaur was asleep on the
couch nearby. An attendant in the room stood watching the Master
and noted nothing unusual. The Master then sat up, composed himself,
and lay straight on his back, took one deep breath and exited consciously
from the body with absolutely no sign of travail.*

*Always a perfectionist, Darshan Singh took precautions to ensure a
smooth continuation after him. The following is an extract from his
will dated November 17, 1987:*

> I...hereby nominate Shri Rajinder Singh...as my sole spiritual
> successor, in view of his strong spiritual attainments and mani-
> fold qualities of head and heart, who will become the next
> Living Master and will take over the spiritual tasks of Naam-
> Initiation and of conducting satsang after I leave the physical
> body...

*According to Sant Rajinder Singh, it was on November 5, 1986 in
Chicago that the Master transferred his spiritual power through the
eyes to him in the time honored way.*

*The blueprint which Sant Darshan Singh prepared will continue to
manifest in the coming years, and no doubt, his spiritual successor will
play a key role in bringing about the Golden Age as foretold by many
great seers and saints.*

*The lyric verses of Darshan, the gentle poet-Saint, reveal his mystic
vision and shall inspire humankind always:*

Love has only a beginning;
It has no end.

Sant Darshan Singh—Taj Mahal (AS)

7 7

Nothing is lost in nature.

As we move into the new millennium, the unfolding sequence of events continues to deepen my sense of awe and gratitude. Whatever I thought was lost, returned full-circle, plus interest, transformed. Through new forms and faces the same principles and essence became manifest as a spiraling progression.

Life-Path: Dedicated work is worship, and physical existence is the crucible by which our spiritual transformation is made manifest. In my wee world, when the Lifestream business was reluctantly sold in 1981 due to a partnership impasse, I went from executive to waiting on tables at our vegetarian eatery. While undoubtedly good medicine for hubris, this soon became an under-challenge.

I had long been inspired by *The Essene Gospel of Peace*, a two-thousand-year-old Aramaic manuscript attributed to the Essene brotherhood which once flourished by the Dead Sea, before the community was dispersed by Roman legions. Dr. Edmond Bordeaux-Szekely, scholar and translator of this obscure work, several Dead Sea Scrolls, and author of more than fifty books, moved to British Columbia, and we became friends before his death in 1978. I recall a delightful afternoon with the venerable professor and his wife, Norma, at their home in the Fraser Valley. In his student years, Dr. Szekely had unlimited access to tens of thousands of ancient manuscripts and scrolls buried within secret Vatican libraries. Here, and in the Library of the Hapsburgs, Austria, he discovered the Essene teachings and the hidden origins of Christianity. His discoveries made palpably evident the fact that Jesus, the Essene Master of Life, was an Adept of the Light and Sound. This following discourse of Jesus is from Book Four of *The Essene Gospel of Peace*:

> *I tell you truly, your body was made not only to breathe, and eat, and think, but it was also made to enter the Holy Stream of Life. And your ears were made not only to hear the words of men, the song of birds, and the music of falling rain, but they were also made to hear the Holy Stream of Sound. And your eyes were made not only to see the rising and setting of the sun, the ripple of sheaves of grain, and the words of the Holy Scrolls, but they were also made to see the Holy Stream of Light. One day your body will return to the Earthly Mother; even also your ears and your eyes. But the Holy Stream of Life, the Holy Stream of Sound, and the Holy Stream of Light, these were never born, and can never die. Enter the Holy Streams, even that Life, that Sound, and*

that Light which gave you birth; that you may reach the kingdom of the Heavenly Father and become one with him, even as the river empties into the far-distant sea.

More than this cannot be told, for the Holy Streams will take you to that place where words are no more, and even the Holy Scrolls cannot record the mysteries therein.

The *Essene Gospel* also contains compelling evidence of the vegetarian and natural healing science of Jesus, as well as the following recipe:

Moisten your wheat, that the angel of water may enter it. Then set it in the air, that the angel of air also may embrace it. And leave it from morning to evening beneath the sun, that the angel of sunshine may descend upon it. And the blessing of the three angels will soon make the germ of life to sprout... Then crush your grain, and make thin wafers, as did your forefathers when they departed out of Egypt, the house of bondage...[1]

Inspired by this two thousand year-old recipe, my helpers and I developed a line of organic nutrient-rich sprouted, whole grain loaves which we called Manna, and thus Nature's Path—our future business was born. Manna Bread became popular with health enthusiasts across North America.

In 1989-90, Nature's Path built North America's first certified organic cereal processing plant, located in British Columbia. Daunting challenges had to be overcome, for I had no technical experience in large-scale factory production, no partners, and limited capital. For seven trying months the machinery refused to cooperate, and it appeared that the enterprise was about to be engulfed by a sea of red ink.. All possible human efforts were made, but obviously that alone wasn't enough. I was reluctant to ask the Master for worldly help, but then, so much and so many weredependent upon a breakthrough. Ultimately I had to surrender my burden before the Divine and ask for Divine assistance, for it is said, "prayer succeeds where all human efforts fail.". And only then did the gleaming new machinery begin to cooperate. Delicious cereal flakes and shapes began cascading off the assembly lines into bags and boxes, into stores and homes, and hearts. Debts were paid, and we moved forward, garnering several prizes for quality, taste, packaging, exports and ethics along the way. Thanks to excellent employees, and my wife and children's unfailing support, the company survived, even thrived. By 1996, independent research confirmed Nature's Path to be the number-one organic cereal brand in North America.[2]

In 1995, fourteen years after losing Lifestream, we re-acquired it from Kraft Foods/Philip Morris. Although Lifestream possessed little of its former vitality, one could still detect a flicker of a heartbeat and a promise.

In the spring of 1999, Nature's Path opened its second certified organic processing facility in northern Washington state, to serve the expanding global market.

Dad's advice to me as a child: *"Always leave the earth better than you found it"* and Master Darshan's three universal business principles given on our last visit to him in India continue to inspire and underpin the enterprise.

In the cycle of growing an enterprise, then and now, my wife and I surround ourselves with talented, self-motivated associates more capable in their particular fields than we, who believe in and practice the principal of excellence. From difficult experiences with the early Lifestream, we learned that building a company with individuals who espouse a shared spiritual orientation is *not necessarily advantageous.* Spiritual and business associations are kept separate, but without compromising ethics or losing sight of the larger vision. Each company team-player holds diverse beliefs and follows different personal paths, like a mini-U.N. Maturity must embrace diversity, tolerance, and mutual respect, and never forces one's viewpoint. Success in any worldly enterprise is an outcome of higher principles, diligence and hard work. The business is not the trunk, but a branch, albeit a far reaching branch, under which, many find shelter and sustenance.

In our fast-paced society and aggressive business environment, what relevance does the practice of meditation, compassionate diet, service to humanity, avoidance of drugs and alcohol have? Is it possible to balance spiritual progress with professional ambition? Can meditation enhance performance and efficiency? Does a compassionate diet lead to better health? Personal experience leads me to respond with an unqualified yes! Meditation enhances concentration, and concentration is the key to success in every field. Stress reduction, better concentration, improved memory, increased work capacity, inner peace, better health, personal fulfillment, and a modicum of success are not meditation's goals—but they are its natural by-products. A whole-foods vegetarian diet, fresh air, regular excercise and a positive attitude are definite assets for improving health and for living a longer life of quality.

Beyond, yet integrated into the wholesome life is the all-important spiritual connection. The inner Light, once ignited, bestows strength to endure every adversity, engenders humility in the presence of the Divine, and grants patience to realize distant outcomes. Meditation in the morning adds an elevating perspective to the daily challenge, and a brief dip into the Audible Life-stream in the evening washes away weariness, stress, and attachment.

I cannot imagine starting any day without first making a positive inner contact, which sets the tone for everything that follows on the surface. Meditation requires focus and the weeding out of non-essentials—reducing everything to the simplest common denominator—from the many to the one. Tuning into the greater Reality, the Infinite, means tuning out static and the stations of the mind. When applied in our mundane spheres, the results are gratifying, if not mind-boggling. By steady practice and introspection, worldly and spiritual growth become linked like the unfolding upward spiral of a double helix.

A Haven for the Northwest: As the spiritual community in the Cascadia region grew, the need for a tangible, supportive retreat center evolved, like the slow ripening of a fine fruit. In the final moments of the North American leg of his 1986 world tour, I broached the subject with Master Darshan. We were in the Los Angeles Airport, and more than a hundred and fifty had gathered to see him off to Mexico and South America. I further shared with him that in 1974 Sant Kirpal Singh predicted, in my presence, that a major center would take shape in our region. Master Darshan exclaimed: "Retreats are the order of the day! I support your wishes to have a meditation center, which will be so helpful for all the dear ones in your area...Establish your center and I'll rush headlong to it! *I'll be with you there.*" The wine was dancing in his eyes as he again exhorted, "Go ahead, my dear brother, and the two great Masters overhead will be extending all help and protection." He added that this project was not to be the work of only one or two; it was to be carried out in the name of the mission and required the whole-hearted support of the community.

Upon returning home, an awaiting letter described an intriguing ten-acre property one hour south of Vancouver, located in Birch Bay, Washington. Orchard, gardens, meadows, several well-kept buildings, and a park-like setting surrounded on three sides by lush forest overlooked the Gulf Islands. When my wife apprehensively sought clarification from the Master by phone, he sweetly commented, "Daughter, we should have our own place," and she was satisfied. With the help of many, the Sawan Kirpal Meditation Center of the Northwest came into being, providing a peaceful nature-haven for visitors from various parts of the world. The vision, which arose with Kirpal, was given new life and form by Darshan and Rajinder.

- - - - - - - - - -

1. Edmond Bordeaux-Szekely, *The Essene Gospel of Peace*, International Biogenics Society, (1981), Box 849, Nelson, B.C. Canada V1L 6A5

2. According to SPINS Information Systems, Inc.

> *Prayer is when we talk to God, and*
> *Meditation is when we listen to God.*
> —Sant Rajinder Singh

After the spiritual coronation of Sant Rajinder Singh in early June, 1989, Ratana and I met briefly with him alone at the ashram. He gave me one of Master Darshan's fresh handkerchiefs as a parting gift, and blessed us with a pat on our heads and backs. In the taxi to the airport, Rajinder's subtle countenance began to appear clearly in front of me, but transparent enough to see and function in the world "normally." Although we passed through customs and many worldly environments on the return journey, his large yet luminous eyes and face never left me alone for the next twenty-four hours. Despite this vision, several dreams of him, and the certainty that Rajinder Singh was the true spiritual successor, I had a great internal struggle to develop depth of receptivity to his person. To my limited eyes, Sant Rajinder was more like a friend, a spiritual brother (not a father), and no amount of wishing or several visits over the next 19 months succeeded in opening the door of my heart.

The desperate struggle to get the new cereal factory open and off the ground in 1989-90 must have added to my internal barriers. After consulting with the living Master, I requested a leave of absence from leadership of the Vancouver group. He agreed, on the condition that it would only be "temporary." For the next 6 months, it was enjoyable to passively sit and observe others do what I had done for more than twenty-five years (they did a remarkable job).

The new Master visited Seattle, Birch Bay and Vancouver (in that order) for the first time in November of 1990, to the joy of many. I, however, felt disenfranchised, and when I arrived at the Meditation Center, Sant Rajinder was at the top of a grassy knoll planting a fruit tree, surrounded by a jolly crowd. I was looking in from the cold impersonal edge. Soon, everyone entered a large tent. Dieter and Barbara Schugt, the center caretakers requested me to speak of the remarkable series of events that led to the genesis of this beautiful place.

Outside, rain and violent gusts of wind began shaking the tent, threatening to sweep it away. I went ahead regardless, relating the center's history, glancing a few times towards Sant Rajinder, who was all peace and calm, smiling at me. When finished, I found a place to sit on a bale of hay towards the rear of the tent. And then, *It* happened...*WHAM!* While he spoke of life's purpose, the wild storm lashing the tent, I became engulfed in a palpable radiation emanating from his person, which had the effect of suffusing my inner being with intoxicating joy. The Master-power was extending unusual presence, and for the next five days, I was smilingly subsumed into his circle, yet, to my surprise, still able to function normally as far as the world was concerned.

A divine power became evident to me and many others throughout Sant Rajinder Singh's Vancouver talks, impromptu meetings, meditation sittings and initiation. The inner experiences had by old and new spiritual seekers were on par with what I had witnessed in the presence of the past Masters. Of 42 adults and 15 children initiated, 19 experienced the radiant visions of one or more of the Adepts of our century. Two saw Jesus along with the living Master—the very confirmation they had been praying for. Practically all experienced at least strong inner Light. The inner Sounds experienced covered the spectrum. Ratana's wizened granny experienced the entire panorama, and later exclaimed, "Rajinder Singh *budda Sant! Mahan Sant!* Very great Saint!"

My own inner droughts and doubts, followed by rains, and deep conviction, have led me to have greater empathy and understanding for others, along with a healthy respect for the mysterious process of each one's unique evolution. Awakening is not a cookie-cutter process. Recognizing one's own helplessness before the illumminating Power always ratchets down the separating ego. Humble prayer bears fruit, but in its time. Secret, anguished cries and fierce longing have been known to draw down heaven's mercy.

On his last night in Vancouver, all tour sevadars got together with the Master in a large room. After singing and sharing stories, a woman arrived around midnight asking for initiation, but when told that it was already given 12 hours earlier, she became very dejected. Maharaj Ji took her outside for a few minutes and returned, without comment. Over the next hour, he left twice more. I went to investigate, and found the Master down the hall in a small room giving secrets of the five holy names and the higher regions to the fortunate latecomer. After instructing her in the art of meditation, he left the room. When we returned an hour later, the woman's sensory currents had withdrawn from her body and only descended very reluctantly to her eye-focus. After about ten minutes, she recovered her normal senses; she had not only witnessed the inner Guru-saroop, but described in great detail her ascent upto and into Trikuti—the second region. She was quite intoxicated by her experience, and had to be helped to her feet.

In the closing hours of his visit, good-byes were shared and tears were spilled—not only from those in the audience, but from the Master's eyes as well. We were given a glimpse of his tender heart—how much he cared for everyone, and how he was already missing his dear ones.

A new initiate next to me in the parshad line informed the Master that he was a palmist, and asked permission to see his palm (while the Masters of Sant Mat are not advocates of astrology or palmistry, they recognize that in certain rare circumstances these may be legitimate tools for verification of specific character traits, pinpointing major life-events, and helping one's self and others develop a

causal understanding of the endless and complex human condition).
Fortunately, we were allowed the priviledge of scrutinizing his palm. While I do
not pretend to be an expert, I was struck by the similarity of the lines of Sant
Rajinder's right hand with those of Master Kirpal's. The same extraordinary
spiritual, intellectual and ethical qualities were reflected there. The palmist may
not have had this comparison, but he was nevertheless deeply impressed with
such a flawless hand, for it is said, *"The face may lie, but the palm never."*

While driving the Master to the airport that morning, I confided my former
difficulty relating to him in the same way I had to the past two Masters, but
that had changed in the past few days. I added, "When I took a leave of
absence 6 months ago," he interrupted and said, "That is why I never had
your name removed, because it was a *temporary* leave of absence."

"Of course, you knew," I said.

"You have to continue in the Master's mission," he chuckled.

Too soon, it seemed, we arrived at the Vancouver International Airport, and
the sangat was introduced to the sweet paradox of parting.

Sant Rajinder Singh,
his wife Rita Ji, brother Manmohan, and others
at the inauguration of Sawan Kirpal Meditation Center of the
Pacific Northwest, Birch Bay, Washington, 1990.

100,000 march for unity and peace, Delhi, 1994.
Sant Rajinder Singh and other holy persons offer blessings.

7 9

As we approach the millennium, what of the work for unity and peace begun by and so dear to the heart of Master Kirpal? *"Don't behave like a frog in a well,"* he often said, exhorting all to be broad-minded and inclusive. Happily, interfaith and peace networking is active across the globe, not as a monopoly of any particular organization or person, but as the expression of an evolving universal wish. Ever since the first astronauts journeyed beyond Earth's gravitational pull, when they viewed and photographed our beautiful, jewel-like, borderless planet from outer space, the general awareness of humanity began a fundamental shift. The idea of planetary citizenry with global responsibility for environmental protection, the ending of war, and a new, non-sectarian spiritual consciousness began to blossom. Some see the workings of God, a divine plan, behind this new paradigm, some see organic evolution, and yet others their Master's hand. Need one exclude the other?

February, 1994: The Seventh World Religions Conference coincides with the birth centenary of Sant Kirpal Singh Ji, and begins with a peace walk through the ancient capital of Delhi. My family and I are here, engulfed in the hundred thousand marchers. Reminiscent of the Unity of Man march of 1974, respects are paid to places sacred to several traditions: Hindu, Christian, Muslim, Jain, and Sikh. Many diverse spiritual leaders have come together to work for the common good of humanity and planetary ecology. Before the towering ramparts of the Red Fort, and at various venues over the next three days, participants share prayers, truths and visions with the multitudes:

Rabbi Abraham Soetendrop, Global Forum, Netherlands:

"Today, we have prayed with our feet! God give us the strength, the humility, and the energy to make this world a round table of sharing and receiving. Make it a compassionate world and let us as religious leaders become compassionate, transcend barriers, and walk humbly in Your Eyes and Your Heart."

Dr. Mohammed Shalaan, Al Azhar University, Egypt:

"How can we be different and yet live together in harmony? How can we be separate and yet strive for union? Not in any museum of modern art can I see such a beautiful picture with so many colors that complement each other as I see here."

Sant Rajinder Singh, Science of Spirituality, President of the Conference:

"Along this historic peace march today...we passed places of worship of different religions. Was it not beautiful to see how many different ways people worship the One Lord? Is not a garden more beautiful when it is decorated with flowers of different colors and fragrances? Similarly, we are all flowers in the garden of the Lord..."

Dr. Karan Singh, India's former Ambassador to the USA:

"I am a worshipper of Siva, who is called the Compassionate One, while Muslims worship one who is referred to as the Merciful, and other traditions all call the Divine by names of peace and love. Yet in the name of these compassionate Deities, we commit atrocities. The religion we need is the one of love and compassion. These know no boundaries. It is the height of hubris to imprison the Light of God in one form..."

Jonathan Granoff, Bawa Muhaiyuddin Fellowship and lawyer with the United Nations Disarmament Committee:

"Separate from yourself that which separates you from other human beings, for that which separates you from others also separates you from God. And those qualities which bring us closer to each other, also bring us closer to God."

Father Maximillian Mizzi, Delegate General for Ecumenism and Inter-religious Dialogue, the Franciscan Order of Assisi, Italy:

"We all came to this conference after receiving a letter or a fax, or somebody told us about it. But I say that something else has brought us here. Behind the letter or fax, or whoever asked us to come here, was

God. God brought us here. He wants to tell us something. He wants us to do something... 'Be an instrument of My peace and reconciliation.'"

Sant Rajinder Singh:

"If our planet with its interdependent ecological systems is to survive, we have to learn to live in harmony with all creation.... If we realize that the soul in us is the same soul that inhabits every being, whether plant or animal, and comes from the same Source...then we would care about and love every being...Unless we find peace within, we will destroy this Earth. We have taken too much and need to give back. Plant trees and flowers and charge the Earth with their fragrance! The path of ahimsa [non-violence] needs to be followed in order to live peacefully. We live in an interdependent world. If we use resources meant for all only for ourselves, we shatter the lives of future generations...We have to make the best use of our time now...to focus on God and go within."

The Centenary: On the sixth of February, a hundred years of Kirpal are celebrated at Kirpal Bagh, before the largest crowd I have *ever* seen. The huge dais is filled with scores of luminaries who share their wisdom. Here are just a few:

His Holiness, the Dalai Lama of Tibet:

"I am very impressed to see people of different colors, nationalities and customs coming from different parts of the world, expressing such enthusiasm. I am very happy! It is important to promote harmony in the religious traditions, where the leaders and the people come together to exchange their deep spiritual understanding. This allows development of a deep respect for the underlying truths of each...

"If we mobilize our emotions positively, it is very useful, but very destructive if not. Small incidents need to either be encouraged if they are good, or stopped when small if negative, to prevent them growing, because they do grow... We cannot separate our own good future from that of humanity. Each must adopt a sense of responsibility and make an effort. Even if we fail, it doesn't matter. Failure with effort is much better than doing nothing.".

Pir Vilayat Khan, International Sufi Order:

"I am sharing with you in the emotion of participating in one of the most important historic events of our time. I do not know whether you realize the very importance for the world of what we are doing here, as we celebrate the hundredth anniversary of Sant Kirpal Singh, whom so many of us have loved so dearly and whom so many of us have revered...

Sant Rajinder Singh and H.H. the Dalai Lama at the Centenary of Kirpal—6th February, 1994.

Each one of us is responsible to find in his or her religion that element which unites rather than divides us. Let us not allow our religions to divide us. Let us not allow the religious leaders to divide us. If you look in the heart of your religion, whatever that religion is, you will find peace. Find the essence of your religion in your contact with God directly. And there you will find inner peace as you turn within. Your spiritual experience is the most important part of your religion. It is the perfume. And then spread that perfume to all those around you."

Sant Rajinder Singh:

"Sant Kirpal Singh Ji came to this Earth with a godly mission and was the personification of all that was divine. Yet he lived among us as a human being to show us how we too could exemplify the highest virtues while withstanding the storms and tempests of earthly life... If we look at each aspect of his life, we will find the model, the teaching, and the practice by which each of us can do what he has done. When he told us, 'I am a man like you,' he was providing positive hope that we too can attain self-knowledge and God-realization as he had."

Door-Darshan, India's leading television corporation, produced a sensitive and masterful full-length documentary of the Centenary, beaming it to millions across Asia and the Middle East.

[When the Dalai Lama made his way from the dais, he and I silently connected, eye to eye. He reached into the crowd and grasped my folded hands.]

8 0

Sant Rajinder Singh encouraged his far-flung spiritual family to arrange Interfaith Dialogues as part of his 1994 European and North American tour program, thus intensifying the work begun by Sant Kirpal Singh Ji in bringing different spiritual leaders and their followers together in a spirit of love, unity and world peace. Many thousands of hearts and minds were opened—including those of us who were narrow-minded within the fold of the Masters. By example, he helped expand our limited horizons to include and accept those who did not necessarily share our own interests and faiths.

Over the next few months, many planned and worked together for the upcoming conferences which were entirely funded by Science of Spirituality and its members. Late one evening, Angele, one of the local volunteers confided,"I don't know why I'm doing all this work, which has become a full-time obsession for me, and as you know I am a mother, a wife and a business-person. I have been involved with the New Age movement for many, many years and I've never given my self to any of the several groups I have been around. I am a follower of Jesus, and Jesus always appeared in my meditations. I was so surprised one day, when Jesus told me to go to and get initiated by Rajinder Singh! It is on the strength of my beautiful experience with him inside, which was so powerful, and because of his gentle, loving, true spirit that I am doing all this. And that is why I have given my heart."

August 11, 1994: Prior to the Master's arrival by sea-plane at Semiahmoo Bay, Washington, I had been busy with a multitude of tasks: coordinating a team of interfaith workers; planning for the conference; making complex preparations for a wedding and an engagement.

As the small aircraft veered across a bright blue sky towards the pier where disciples were waiting, I watched through the glass window of a phone booth, returning an urgent call from Vancouver. "Baeji has just passed away," Ratana's voice in the receiver was choked with emotion. Three hours earlier, I was the last person to be at Baeji's hospital bedside where she had lain in a coma for six weeks.

The Master proceeded to the Meditation Center in Birch Bay where he was received with love and jubilation. He and his wife Rita Ji expressed sympathy for the bereaved family, and sent special parshad for Ratana. I returned to Vancouver to comfort her and join the many excited helpers rushing to complete last-minute errands. The next morning, after signing my company's payroll (the wordly work still has to go on), I rushed to the Meditation Center around noon.

A   WEDDING

With his large dark eyes flashing, Master appeared shortly from the main house. The previous night he had been up late with disciples, discoursing on a hymn of Soami Ji. Today, he sat with hundreds circled around him under a big open-walled tent, sun-dappled orchards and forest to his back. A gentle, warm breeze rippled the leaves. Speaking heart-to-heart, he expressed appreciation for this special place, and for the love of all who had served with no thought of self. I sat cross-legged on the grass, the first time this hectic day I was able to slow down. The moment I looked up towards him with open eyes, there was nothing but brilliant radiance everywhere; his luminous face its center.

Sant Rajinder was scheduled to leave Birch Bay at 1 PM; it was already after 3. I grew anxious about getting to the Interfaith conference in Vancouver on time, as the distinguished religious leaders and audience mightn't appreciate the delay. The publisher of *Common Ground* (readership 250,000) had been waiting at the center since the morning for an interview with the Master who had been constantly assisting seekers and initiates with their needs and questions. As there was still the border to cross, always fraught with possible delays, I was considering the probability of canceling a planned detour. The Adepts, however, have their own immaculate schedule, and possess the ability to stretch time! When the interview was finally underway, Joseph Roberts, the publisher/editor stated, "Master Rajinder Singh, I am an open-minded skeptic." His honesty was heartily welcomed.

After the remarkable hour-long interview was over, Joseph asked, "Why do I always get light-headed in the presence of Rajinder Singh?" "Why? I tell you, there's a special grace at work!" I replied. Joseph continued, "When I was interviewing him, not only did I feel light-headed, but I kept seeing others coming through...his father Darshan, grandfather Master Kirpal, and Baba Sawan!" "Joseph, why am I not surprised?" I asked. (The article was published in the next issue of *Common Ground*.

It wasn't until 4:30 PM before we left the center and breezed through Canada customs. En route to Vancouver, Master visited the home of Dennis and Grace, group leaders for the Surrey region, who had been expectantly waiting. They and their young sons—Gian and Andre were exceedingly proud to actually have the Master in their home.

Interfaith Progress: Master "miraculously" arrived at the five star Waterfront hotel, a full ten minutes before the scheduled Dialogue. As he proceeded through the posh hotel to meet the religious leaders, I was warned that a certain Christian minister had declared his intentions to disrupt the event as he harbored a deep misunderstanding that it was only a "front" for some hidden cult-agenda. Unperturbed, Maharaj Ji went directly to the minister, whom he met very lovingly. The Reverend Father immediately reciprocated, and remained close by the Master's side for the entire program.

As the various presenters entered, more than 800 packed the ballroom. A Cree First Nations medicine man offered traditional welcomes, followed by Rabbi Marmorstein blowing the shofar (a ram's horn trumpet used in Jewish ritual). The Rabbi led all in prayer and a loving Shalom (Peace) chant. Ba'hai representatives shared the inspired universal vision of their creed, along with a poem by Abdul'ba'ha. Rukmini Prameya of the Mahalakshmi Temple eloquently described her vision of Hinduism, interspersed with ancient and melodious song. Anglican Reverend Appavoo held high a large cross, and began with a moving apology for his doubts about the intentions of the Conference. He proceeded to delight the audience with his lively and bright sharing of Christ's love. Red-robed Dhongtok Rimpoche, one of Tibet's most eminent Sakya Buddhist scholars and translators shared the teachings of Lord Buddha. Dr. Abdul Hassam, Ph.D. represented the Ismaili religious tradition of Islam, ending with a verse from the universal Rumi:

> *I am not of the East and not of the West,*
> *Not of the land and not of the sea;*
> *I belong to the soul of the Beloved....*

As emcee, I reminded all of the recent historic peace accord between Jews and Muslims, and asked the learned Islamic doctor if he would take the hand of the distinguished Rabbi. When both warmly embraced, the entire hall burst into applause.

To crown the evening, Sant Rajinder Singh gave an eloquent yet simple discourse on the way to attain peace and unity through deep mystical prayer and meditation. He invited the audience to experience a taste of the inner Light and Bliss inherent within every human being and every religious and mystical tradition. He then led all into a silent meditation for five minutes. Although the time was brief, many experienced a great outpouring of spiritual power. After he closed the conference, even strangers were hugging each other.

> *Embrace every man as your very own,*
> *And shower your love freely wherever you go.—Darshan.*

August 13, 1994: Our daughter Shanti wed Markus Schramm in our spacious garden in the presence the Master, his family, the Unity Minister and 250 relatives and friends. After blessing the food and the occasion, the Master expressed his love and solicitude for the happiness of the couple—in all spheres. Fulfilling Master Darshan's promise to Shanti in 1988 that he would find a suitable husband of her choice, Maharaj Ji said, "Master Darshan gives you His blessing. And this poem of his I now share with you:

A WEDDING & A FUNERAL

'May the orchard of Markus and Shanti
Be blooming and fruitful forever,
And may God bless the flowers of that orchard
With a thousand springs.'

Gurdeep, our second daughter and her fiance, Dr. Pascal Courty then
stepped forward to celebrate their formal marriage engagement, accompanied
by his parents who had just arrived from France.

My 87-year-old aunt Margaret approached Maharaj Ji, standing next to me
in the garden and boldly asked, "I want your promise that Kirpal Singh will
come for me when I die! He came for my sister Gwen. Will he come to take me
over the Great Divide?" Maharaj Ji briefly closed his eyes in concentration,
opened them and replied with a smile, "Yes, Master Kirpal will **definitely**
come for you." She thanked him and heaved a big sigh of relief.

Master left early to lead a meditation at the Waterfront Hotel for several
hundred seekers. His words as they resounded throughout the large hall were
perfectly chosen. He met separately with a large contingent of teens and
answered many questions to their satisfaction. More Q's & A's with adult seekers ensued. Then we returned home to prepare for Shanti & Markus's *second*
wedding of the day, this time following her Indian heritage. For Ratana, the joy
of the occasion was overshadowed by Baeji's passing.

We were not new to 'Indian-time,' but even then, the bride was *very* late to
the large, modern Sikh temple on No. 5 Road, Richmond. The expected delay
was exacerbated when her car missed the freeway exit, ending up in the next
municipality. Finally, Shanti and her bridesmaids, matrons of honor, aunts, in-
laws, cousins, nieces, and friends arrived, all decked out in their finery, while
the handsome groom looked like a prince, bedecked in turban (personally tied
by the Master) and silken Nehru coat, reminiscent of our own wedding in 1969.

After the concluding round of the wedding ritual, Sant Rajinder Singh Ji
delivered a beautiful marriage discourse. Like his noble predecessors, his message went far beyond the mere joining of life-partners; it dealt with the soul's
mystic journey back to Sach Khand, the Eternal Home. A few words to bless a
couple transformed into a full-blown satsang, first in Punjabi, and then
English—for the benefit of more than 600 present. As he stood against the
white wall of the majestic temple, many noticed a golden radiance playing
around his form.

As far as the writer knows, this was the first time in North America that this
Master had given satsang in a Gurdwara. At first, some of the older, more orthodox Sikhs—those who had no faith in the idea of a living Sant Satguru—began
to murmur whether it was appropriate for him to be there at all. I watched with
great fascination as many averted their gazes at the beginning of the discourse,
but soon all eyes were glued on the Master. At the end, even the most staunch
Sikhs and followers of other saints came before Sant Rajinder Singh, bowing
reverently, smiling and asking to be photographed at his side.

I had to get Master back home, and then off to his major scheduled talk. It was a delight to see Rev. Appavoo in the audience, raptly listening to every word. Questions and answers followed, and went on late into the night.

The next morning, Master initiated a good number of new seekers. When it ended late in the afternoon, he ate a light lunch with the new initiates and returned to our residence. In the evening, the Master and his family attended a reception as guests of honor. Markus's mother recalled an outstanding incident from twenty years earlier: "When Markus was seven years old, he traveled with me on a train. A man came into our compartment and sat opposite us. He.had a large red nose, with sores on it. Markus stared at him, and finally he pointed and said, 'Mummy, look at that man!' 'Oh no!' I thought, fearing the worst. But Markus continued, 'Doesn't he have such beautiful eyes!'"

The Master offered practical advice and wisdom to the young couple. One piece was: "We should cover up each other's faults and shortcomings," and he smilingly added, "True marriages are indeed made in heaven!"

My brother Godfrey arrived and asked me to introduce him to the Master. When they shook hands, Godfrey looked into his eyes for several long moments and exclaimed, "Wow! You have the same bright shining eyes as your grandfather. You have Kirpal Singh's eyes!"

Around midnight, Juaneva and Mitch drove Master to the St. James Church where about 250 who weren't able to be at the reception, were longingly waiting, missing him. The Master voiced appreciation from his heart for their love for all the selfless service done, so harmoniously and smoothly over the past few days, especially praising those who toiled unseen and unsung in the background. He stressed the need for unity, harmony and tolerance, urging everyone to make use of the beautiful Meditation Center, further suggesting that summer youth camps be held there. Answering the prayers of Krishna and Rakesh Bagga, he made a surprise visit to their home nearby.

I had the good fortune to meditate and rest on a small couch directly below the Master's bedroom in our home. As a light sleeper, I noticed that by the time he retired to his suite upstairs, it was 3 AM. For the next hour or more I could barely hear the muffled tones of a conversation coming from above; he was on the phone to India, giving others much needed guidance. He was up and about after an hour of silence. We may think otherwise, but whether visible to our sight or away, the Saints are ever centered in the One. As conscious co-workers of the Divine, they are always in service of the Creation with a minimum of physical rest.

In the space of three days, Sant Rajinder Singh met over 2,000 new people from all walks of life, religions, colors and creeds; visited several homes; gave nine discourses, two meditations and scores of private interviews; and connected many new seekers to the Light and Sound of Creation. This is typical of his

Sant Rajinder Singh Ji, scientist and mystic.

tour-stops, and reveals his great stamina and dedication to humanity. Such Saints freely broadcast seeds of light and love to all, knowing that many, if not most of these indestructible seeds will not fully germinate in this life (at least the initiates are greatly benefitted in their next incarnation). They also know that wherever the soil of character is well prepared, watered and weeded, the Naam will grow and bear abundant fruit in the here and now. Saints respond to the hunger in the soul. And they exhort all to "make hay while the sun shines." What good is medicine to the afflicted if it is not used?

While driving the Master, his wife, son and daughter to the airport, I reflected aloud on the calm-centered whirlwind of recent events. I asked, "Does the Master's power increase with the passage of time?"

With surprisingly directness he replied, "Yes. You see, when a father dies, his oldest son assumes responsibility to look after the family [according to Indian tradition]. At first, he may not be fully comfortable with this position, and his younger brothers or sisters may not accept his authority right away. But with the passage of time, he demonstrates his competency, and everyone begins to accept him. Time is a great healer. It is something like that."

"It seems like the power is definitely increasing. I also noticed that towards the end of Master Kirpal's life, the power seemed to increase, day by day..."

As Baeji's funeral was to take place the following day, Master and Rita Ji conveyed their condolences to all family members. On a great positive note he added, "Baeji is with the Masters. As we speak, Hazur is taking her up through the higher spiritual planes back to Sach Khand." Passing through the customs gates, the young, black-bearded Master waved a hearty good-bye to all.

The Story of Baeji: Soon after Sant Kirpal Singh passed away in 1974, Baeji experienced a tumble down a stone stairway at Haridwar on the banks of the Ganges River. She survived unharmed and adamantly maintained that her Baba Sawan, in the company of Kirpal and "Darshi" appeared in bright light and pulled her to safety. Thereafter she was always full of praise for "Darshi," as she affectionately called him. Of course, at that time I used to resent her praise of Darshan, since I was embroiled in the successorship controversy. After 1978, I often took her to see her "Darshi," who always touched her feet out of respect, treating her with great deference, as though she were his mother. Baeji always became ecstatic in his presence.

Ratana said of Baeji:

"She cared for people so much that my uncles used to say that 'even if the dog of Shalimar dies, Baeji will go to its funeral.' If any child were sick, she would go to give it folk medicine. If any one had a wedding, she was there; if there was a funeral or a birth, she was there.

"At the age of eighteen she became a widow with two little boys. Her youngest son was born five months after her husband's death. She brought up her three sons and never married again. One day, her brother-in-law came to her when she was making chapatis over a wood fire. He asked, 'Mela Devi, a certain woman from the village is saying that you and I...' He was in the middle of his sentence, when Baeji cut him off by saying, 'Brother, if you say another word, I will put that burning stick in your mouth! I was married once and that's it!' Whatever strength of character and upbringing I had was mainly due to Baeji, and I'm all gratitude to her."

Because her husband had passed away, Baeji claimed her eldest son's first-born (Ratana) as her own, and when she took the infant to her breast, milk began to flow. She nursed her granddaughter for the first year of her life and looked after her until the day of her marriage to me.

A WEDDING & A FUNERAL

Baeji came to the lotus feet of Hazur Baba Sawan Singh in the 1930's and received the boon of initiation. She had an unshakable faith in the great Saint of Beas. During the terrible days of the partition of India, when more than a million lives were lost, her family had to leave their wealth and property behind in Lahore, arriving in India with literally only the clothes on their backs. They left at night, under the cover of darkness. Fortunately, Baeji had the farsight to sew sixteen tolas of gold (one tola equals slightly less than an ounce) into her undergarments. At that time, Ratana was only one year old.

Managing to escape the wholesale murder and destruction in and around Lahore, she and her family fell into an exhausted sleep by a wide river. Hazur Baba Sawan Singh appeared to Baeji in a vision-dream and commanded her, *"Oot Kako, Oot! Katara Aayainga!"* "Child, wake up! Danger is coming!" She then woke up her family and urged them to wade across the river. When they were halfway, an armed mob of religious fanatics with torches visited the very spot where they had been sleeping, hacking people to death. Had not Hazur aroused them, they too would have been slaughtered.

The Bagga family, along with thousands of other Hindu, Muslim and Sikh disciples, found safe refuge at their Master's Dera at Beas. During the partition of India while all the slaughter in the name of religion and nationalism was going on, Hazur suffered bleeding from the bladder. He took upon himself the suffering of others. It is said that none of his thousands of disciples lost their lives in the partition.

With the sixteen tolas of gold she had secreted out of what became Pakistan, Baeji's family established a new life in Moradabad, where their confectionery business flourished. Baeji had great faith in Sant Kirpal Singh Ji, whom she considered as one with her great Guru. Because she led such a pure life, which is termed in the scriptures as "pavitter jeevan," her blessings had power behind them. She was always wishing family and friends long life, children, health and happiness. Once, Baeji came to me in the early morning in a dream, and placed her hand on my head. With the grace of the Adepts working through her, I received a profound inner experience.

On March 29, 1989, the day Master Darshan breathed his last, he appeared simultaneously to Baeji in a vision, and touched her feet, and bade her farewell (it was his habit, born of humility, to touch the feet of his elders). Later in the day she learned that the Master had just relinquished his mortal coil.

Baeji once taught me this, her favorite verse, and we'd often sing it together:

Meri Sataguru pukkerdi ba
Tey hun dara ka da Khatura ka da...
O' my True Master, take hold of my hand;
Lead me from fear & danger;
Take me to Your eternal Abode.

Manav Kendra—return and renewal, September, 1996:

Two years have passed since the historic Centenary. I write from my humble room at Manav Kendra in the lush Shivalik foothills, presently the only Westerner here. I can hardly see to write, due to severe conjunctivitis, or "pink-eye." Eighteen years earlier when I reported on its sad condition, Master Darshan asserted unequivocally that Manav Kendra, every atom of which was saturated with the divine attention of Kirpal, *must* blossom again. Recently the Kendra was returned to the Mission's care, and although the reversal of twenty-four years of neglect has begun, the project is vast.

When I arrived a few days ago, the former walled-off bathing *ghat* (a 50-by 150-foot semi-circular pool) at the north end of the 350-foot-long oval Sarovar, was entirely choked with chest-high weeds, grass, saplings, bricks, and mud. In disgust, I yanked out a single weed—and then another, and another, unplanned and spontaneous. Soon, I became totally lost in the daunting solo task until it became too dark to see. At the end of the second day, several local children joined in, Tom Sawyer-like, to help, while I chopped out three twenty-foot high trees which had forced their way up through the mortared stones. On the third day, all the growth was cleaned out. Then came the task of removing the large amount of slimy muck and broken bricks at the bottom of the partially drained pool. The first step was to unblock the drainage pipe, and then scoop the muck into baskets and dump it over the six-foot high wall into the bush. Finally, the bathing ghat was clean, ready to be refilled, and looked almost as it did in 1974.

This *seva* became one of my life's most exhilarating experiences, in that while serving, I was symbolically, if not mystically cleaning none other than the Master's feet, and simultaneously, the feet of all. In the weeds, grass, muck and searing heat was the beauty of the Lord. This gut-wrenching labor was done with bare hands and sweat. If these fingers were worn to the bone, or a life given in the process, I reasoned, what more was wanted?

After completion of the repairs and the cleansing, exhausted, tears of joy flowing, clothes and body splattered with mud, I washed in the Sarovar, then poured its benison over my head and sat with closed eyes, plunging into the billowing presence. What came was worth the entire trip—the heat, the cratered and washed-out roads (200 kilometers in eight hours), the illness—just to pull a few weeds and clean the blessed flagstones. But it was *He*, not me. *Seva* can be the fastest way to find the face of the Beloved; besides, it's much easier than meditating! Combine seva with meditation—plus the secret ingredient—Grace, and the inner treasure-house opens with lightning speed.

Man can do absolutely nothing of himself.
He only rearranges things.—Paramahansa Yogananda

The Indian brothers and sisters who live and serve at Manav Kendra full-time have little in the way of worldly goods but are in tune with the rhythms of the land. The rice fields will soon be ready for harvest. Each day begins and ends with praise—in between is simple, honest labor, and family life. The buildings are being painted and repaired in preparation for Master Rajinder's visit on the tenth of October, when the bathing ghat will be filled with pure, clean water for the use of the thousands who will be coming. A thriving school sits on the twenty-five-acre Kendra, providing quality education for more than six hundred lively youngsters. Today, I paced the base of the Guru Gobind Singh tree, which has a circumference of about forty-five feet, then sat beneath it for several hours. My heart breathed easier: *The world is in good hands.*

A vision for the future: I return on the twentieth of September for the fiftieth birthday of Sant Rajinder Singh, exuberantly celebrated on the Polo Grounds of Delhi by an enormous collection of humanity. Due to terrible road conditions, I arrive late, in the midst of an inspiring, passionate address by the renowned educator Dada Vaswani, who calls for a vision that recognizes the moral inviolability of all living creatures. He requests those gathered to go inside in silence, to work in God's loving presence, and to serve His suffering children—humanity, the birds, and animals. When the elderly Dada takes leave of the dais, I intercept him, "Dada Ji, I first met you in 1968 at the Mira School for Girls. I remember Master Kirpal trying to touch your feet, and simultaneously, you were trying to touch his!" He turns to me, smiling and we also try to touch each other's feet! He holds my hands and whispers, "I see the Beloved Master in your eyes!" And the crowd sweeps us apart.

September 22: Three thousand, five hundred receive initiation and a first-hand spiritual experience of Light and Sound. About half report seeing the radiant light saroop of the living Master within.

September 23: Eight hundred visitors from fifty countries join the Indian sangat at a new, verdant ashram site on seventy-five acres of recently acquired farmland half an hour from Kirpal Ashram. Master Rajinder informs me that as soon as a total of one hundred acres is obtained, construction will commence. "This large center will accommodate those who will come in the future," hinting of the millennium.

Tall eucalyptus and indigenous shade trees crown the hill which crosses through the property. Much of the fertile flatland is planted in grains, vegetables, and orchards, to supply the Master's community langar. Healing hues of green and sparkling artesian water running along grass-lined irrigation canals,

is a sight for eyes sore from the ever-increasing congestion of the city. Methinks if the West borrowed India's sublime spirituality, generosity, devotion, family values, and sense of self-sacrifice, and if India borrowed the West's organizational, pollution, and sanitation standards, along with a lower birth-rate, straight-forwardness, and improved roads, then both would be immeasurably enriched, and we'd move that much closer to the heralded Golden Age.

I hike over the forested hill to an isolated brick factory on the other side. It waits to supply building materials for the huge project ahead. Out of earshot of the future ashram, Darshan Academy, a fully accredited international school for grades 1-12 will take shape here, joining eight other flourishing Darshan Academies in various parts of India, with an enrollment of more than 1,000 children—the vast majority coming from families of non-initiates. Along with emphasis on academic and artistic excellence, these schools incorporate a brief morning meditation period and inculcate selfless service and respect for all religions and saints.

The living Master predicts a time when vast numbers will come seeking inner peace and spiritual realization. Architects and engineers have constructed scale models of the future community. In its scope are lakes, open spaces, a meditation hall in the shape of an opening lotus, living quarters for visitors and staff, a library of comparative religions and mysticism, a wellness center, retirement homes, and gardens. This is the most current evolution of the vision of spiritual community expressed by Guru Nanak at Kartarpur, Guru Ram Das at Amritsar, Hazur at Beas, Aurobindo at Auroville, Sant Kirpal Singh at Manav Kendra, and others.

Like his predecessors, Sant Rajinder Singh works and travels ceaselessly to bring the science of spirituality to as many people as possible—including places that no Masters of his lineage have been to before—New Zealand, Australia and countries in Africa, Eastern Europe, and Central America. (By 1999, the number of those fortunate to have received initiation from him already exceeded 250,000—more than any previous Satguru in recorded history). Sant Rajinder Singh is still relatively young and filled with energy. In his presence, new seekers and veterans are having the same sublime experiences as were enjoyed with the Masters in times gone by. The power and purpose of the ancient lineage is very much alive and lucidly communicated within contemporary frames of reference.

Saints and mystics have been able to realize God within themselves, and have shared their knowledge with humanity. They describe to us what God is and how He can be contacted. They tell us that God is an ocean of all Light, all love, and all consciousness... the alpha and omega of all existence. He was neither created nor can He be destroyed. He is all that is.

The soul is a drop of His essence. Thus, the soul's real nature is also sat-chit-ananda, "truth, cosciousness, and bliss." Each of us is actually a drop of this blissful awareness. It is only when we identify with our real self that we become moving drops of bliss on earth. We are moving about on the desert of the earth becoming more and more parched, looking for the ocean. We need to realize that a reservoir of refreshing waters is lying within us. If we can identify ourselves with our true essence we will begin to live in a sublime state of happiness...

Spending two hours concentrating on the eye-focus each day will help our attention withdraw from the body. Generally our sensory currents which give us sensation of this physical world are spread out through the body. As we concentrate at the seat of the soul, the sensory currents start withdrawing from our extremities. They come up from our feet and legs to our trunk. Eventually they are totally concentrated at the seat of the soul. Once at that point, a vista of divine Light and celestial Sound opens up for us. We witness the Light and Sound which emanated from God at the dawn of creation. Like a current, this stream flows out from God through all the regions. It also returns to Him. When our soul comes in contact with this stream, it can travel on it back to the Source.

The journey begins at the third eye. By putting our attention there, the soul begins its voyage to the ultimate source of happiness. This is what meditation is.[1]

---

1. Rajinder Singh, *Inner and Outer Peace Through Meditation—With a Foreword by H.H. The Dalai Lama*, Element Books, Rockport, MA 01966

8 2

Without inner peace there is no outer peace. Peace within is the result of the centripetal return on radiant streams back to the center of unity.

Spirituality has always been the leaven to the loaf of existence. With sustained practice, even the most limited mind begins to soar free from its usual ruts. We then see how we are interconnected with every other being, like points of light in a radiant, networked universe. Human compassion and the desire to serve this expanded Self begin surging in our veins, and in a million little ways, the innate nobility of the soul finds expression in deeds. In a society that flows towards selfishness and sensual gratification, the truth seeker appears to move upstream, swimming against the current of status quo.

In every age and even now, Perfected Ones centrifuge the Light of the divine to others, through whom it has the potential of multiplying. Those fortunate to be connected, even though imperfect, may also become its instruments. The radiance of true existence is invisible to the physical eyes, but it can be seen with an awakened inner faculty. From *seeing* arises *becoming*. On discovering its hidden presence the heart begins to overflow, and bows in adoration of its own accord.

> *O holy Knowledge, by Thee am I illumined,*
> *and through Thee do I sing praise to the incorporeal Light.*
> —The Hermetica of Hermes Trismegistus, of ancient Egypt

The true artist, disciple, or spiritual wayfarer is a conduit, a flute through which the music of the Creator is waiting to be played. The Saints are Master-artists whose craft is the transformation of souls. Like Michaelangelo who saw beautiful forms in shapeless blocks and then chipped away all that did not belong, so the Masters see our perfection and help us release it.

None can presume any credit for the awakening global awareness. One can, however, consciously assist, resist, or hinder the process. In our times we have seen momentous societal changes and transformations, but we remain a culture with a gaping lack of worthy heroes. Our heroes and icons are too often the morally dead.

> *Saints, real saints, are magical. They are luminous, transparent, irre-*
> *sistible. They enchant us, enthrall us, captivate us. They seem to be*
> *qualitatively different from the rest of humankind. They attract us not*
> *by preaching, much less by screeching, but by radiant goodness, irre-*
> *pressible cheerfulness and devastating love. We are compelled to follow*
> *them, not because of what they say but because of who they are. Our*
> *aim is not necessarily to do what they do but, rather, to try to be what*
> *they are.* — Andrew Greeley, Newsweek, September 22, 1997

THE GOAL OF LIFE

Decades have passed since my first tremulous steps across the Master's threshold. Those enchanted times with him remain etched deep and fresh. A line was cast, even before this life began; 'till now the great Angler hasn't let go. Many peers and elders have been harvested from the finite sea, while this fish still dances on its tether, neither totally free nor totally bound. A promise was sealed deep within, and ever since, each tug on the heart-line has been none other than a token of his affection.

These journals safeguarded a hidden garden of intense memories. Despite periods of drought and storm, weeds and blight, ambition and expansion, a few tears kept the garden green; vigilance and practice kept the most persistent weeds at bay. Here, there are no *unthorned* roses. Though poor and tattered, this soul has basked in the shimmering silence of twelve thousand dawns; even then, ego, distance and dirt remain. The pruning, polishing and cleansing by the Inner Light will continue, until 'me' and 'my' and 'I' are no more, and only 'He' remains.

Countless times, heart has asked, *Will we meet the Friend again?* The answer always comes, *we surely will, for He is not apart from you.* It is a waiting game, a seeking, keening, and yearning before the inner door. It is beggary and princely; it is a moth in orbit; an atom spinning toward the Sun of Existence.

In various guises, the Compassionate One comes, not on any worldly timetable, nor to fit any preconceptions, but unpredictably, rare and precious, wild. Like a cosmic teaser, he pulls the veil aside a little, to fulfill in part his promise. And always, the moth swoons in ecstasy, bedazzled in the radiance and beauty of Eternal countenance.

I did not deserve association with the Adepts of our time. There's nothing special about me. It was sheer kindness that the Master plucked me from the gutter, washed and placed me in the sun to cure. In so doing, he proved the redemptive love of God as divine Parent. On the physical plane—all shall pass, but the Resounding Flame, or God-in-Action Power, Word, Naam, or Kalma— is forever. Seek within, and if you go deep enough, you will surely find. And *that* will lead you to the place where All came from.

> *The salt of life is selfless service;*
> *The water of life is universal love;*
> *The sweetness of life is loving devotion;*
> *The fragrance of life is generosity;*
> *The Pivot of Life is Meditation;*
> *The Goal of Life is Self-Realization.*

Kirpal Singh

Etching by Gustave Dore, from Milton's Paradise Lost.

C O S M O L O G Y   A P P E N D I X

T H E   M A C R O C O S M
A N D   I T S
P L A N E S   O R   R E G I O N S

In my Father's House, there are many mansions.

According to many great and enduring spiritual traditions—and validated to some extent by modern quantum physics—the Creation consists of vastly more than the physical universe with which we are somewhat familiar.

Within mystic literature and poetry are innumerable references to subtle universes and varying planes of consciousness within, beyond, or interpenetrating our physical universe. This macrocosm can be accessed through the microcosm of the human form—which the Adepts have termed as the *true* temple of God. Our body-temple contains within it subtle and spiritual essence-envelopes corresponding to similar dimensions of the cosmos. While the corporeal world is experienced through the physical senses, additional planes or dimensions of being can only be accessed when the attention is withdrawn from outside stimuli and focused within at the center of awareness that lies between and behind the two eyebrows. This locus, or doorway is called the single eye in esoteric Christianity, nuqta-i-saveda by the Sufis, and the ajna chakra, divya chaksu, or tisra til by the sages of India. It is also referred to as the third or spiritual eye.

The attention is the outer expression of the soul. Concentration of the attention is required for participation in physical, emotional, and mental activities, but when focused within, through techniques learned from a spiritual Adept or Master, one can enter and traverse the subtle and spiritual regions.

There are six centers or chakras (literally wheels, or lotuses) within the subtle or astral body—which are parallel and concurrent with the physical body, located at the rectum, genitals, navel, heart, throat, and forehead. The Adepts of Sant Mat do not advocate practices involving the centers below the spiritual eye as they are limited and do not help much in the attainment of Self-knowledge and God-realization. The journey to divine knowledge and freedom commences only after physical consciousness is transcended.

With the assistance of a competent spiritual Adept who has realized the full potential of humanhood and traversed all the stages of the inner journey, the student learns to gradually progress within. Guided by the helping hand of a

Master, the aspirant lays the groundwork for spiritual evolution by cultivating ethical virtues and developing regular and accurate meditations. While patiently explaining the way, a competent Adept provides an indispensable series of spiritual boosts to those whom he initiates into the mysteries of the beyond, through the transfer of his attention or consciousness. A sacred mantra of five holy names (appellations of the deities of each spiritual region) are imbued with the Adept's powerful charging,and serve as passwords and a passport to the subtle and spiritual planes. The repetition of these names clears away inner obstacles and protects the individual from inner and outer negative influences.

Like the layers of an onion, the various coverings (physical, astral, causal, and supra causal) which enshroud the soul are gradually peeled away. Through regular practice, the initiate begins to experience in meditation the various lights of the first inner stage in the form of myriad stars, big star, heavenly skies, moon, sun, tunnel, mountains, gardens, rainbows, eye, vortices of light, lightning, radiant reflections of the living Adept and other perfected sages. This gradual process of withdrawal from outer to inner awareness requires practice, patience and perseverance. As concentration and devotion increase, mysterious inner sounds and melodies become audible from the right side or center of the forehead, such as the buzzing of bees, surf, bells, conch, whistle, waterfalls, birdsong, drumbeats, violin, flute, etc. Concomitant with the auditory and visionary experiences, the practitioner undergoes spontaneous ever-deepening states of mystical bliss and peace. The Sound-current purifies the mind of its dross.

When complete withdrawal of the sensory current (the sense of feeling) from the body is attained, the disciple is joyously met by the radiant form of the spiritual Guide (in the mystical vernacular of the East, this manifestation is called "Gurudev"). As receptivity develops, the inner guide may converse with and escort the initiate to the headquarters of the astral plane. This center is known as the sahasrar, the thousand petaled lotus (a pyramidical cluster with one thousand glowing lights, when viewed from the side, or, like a lotus with a thousand luminous petals, when viewed head-on). While the attainment of sahasrar is considered to be the be-all and end-all by several yoga systems and religions, on the Path of Sant Mat, it is regarded as the first stage of a much longer journey.

In the astral plane, one travels with the speed of thought and may encounter many peculiar phenomenon and unusual dream-like experiences. The initiated are urged to ignore this region's myriad illusions and snares, and hold fast to the inner Guide, who leads the soul onward to more spiritual planes.

The Masters of Sant Mat speak of five regions or planes. Reference to these is found in several religious scriptures, mystical accounts and the writings of numerous sages, saints, and their disciples.

COSMOLOGY APPENDIX

Only as a handful of straw do you know your body,
But beneath it flows the ocean of Life;
Outwardly you are a particle, but inwardly
You are more than a hundred suns!
—Shams-i-Tabriz

Maulana Rumi, a renowned 12th century Persian mystic who lived in Anatolia, makes reference to five muqqams or spiritual stations in his Mathnavi. Jacob Boehme of 15th Century Germany speaks of five spiritual planes as do Kabir, Nanak, Paltu, Chisti, and other Sant Satgurus (perfected Saints) of northern India. Sometimes they speak of four grand spiritual divisions: astral, causal, supra causal, and the purely spiritual realm (where the fourth and the fifth plane are combined). All refer to the Overself or Lord dwelling within, who yearns for the separated souls to return Home, and expresses itself as the five-fold melody of Naam or Word, the power that brought creation into manifestation and simultaneously draws it back to its Source.

The five regions or planes are characterized by five primal sound currents, which are different frequencies of the One creative Word or Logos. Each higher region is successively more subtle and enchanting than those it proceeds. According to the Adepts of Sant Mat, in the astral plane the predominant sound is the bell, and the predominant vision is the thousand petaled lotus. This region is far greater in size and power than the physical universe. Above and beyond the astral plane lies the Causal (Brahm, or Brahmand). Here, soul beholds a vast continuous red rising sun which colors this entire region in golden-crimson hues. The sound-current of the Causal Plane assumes the form of pealing thunder, exciting drumbeats, and Om, or Aum. This realm is also called Trikuti (three mountains), because the soul beholds three golden promontories (Mer, Sumer, and Kailash). Trikuti is the headquarters of Kal—the Universal Mind, or *Time*—but the source of the soul is far beyond in the higher, purely spiritual and imperishable realms.

Leaving the mind behind in Trikuti, soul journeys up into the third region, known variously as Daswan Dwar, Par Brahm, or the Supra-causal. Here, the sound current is more melodic and enrapturing, resembling the form of stringed instruments like the sarangi (Indian violin) or the sitar. The Light here is like a full moon that exceeds the light of countless full moons of the physical world. The fabled pool of Amritsar (also known as Mansarovar) is at the center of the Supra-causal, in which the sins and karmas of countless lifetimes are washed away, leaving the soul increasingly purified and powerful. Separating the third plane from the fourth, is a kind of barrier, meant to keep back lesser souls. It is called Maha Sunna—the region of stygian darkness and silence which only the perfected spiritual Adepts can cross, and whomever they wish to take with them (The Maha Sunna can, however, be by-passed altogether, if the Master so wishes to take the disciple directly to the Fouth plane).

In the fourth region, the sound assumes the form of a sweet and plaintive flute. The Light now takes the form of a grand Sun that exceeds thousands of outer midday suns, yet remains cool and enlivening. In this fourth cosmos is a vast, immense slowly rotating cave through which the soul proceeds. Here, one works without hands, walks without feet, sees without eyes, and hears without ears. The soul is stripped of all coverings and shines in its native luminosity greater than twelve suns combined. Soul now realizes that her existence is none other than God, and cries out as did Christ: *I and my Father are One!* And as did Mansur: *Anna'l Haq! [I am the Truth!]*

The fifth stage, the Eternal Realm known as Sach Khand or Muqqam-i-Haq, is reached after the purified and realized soul enters through a great portal. Here soul delights in the sound-current which assumes the song of a continuously playing bag-pipe, but infinitely more melodious and enchanting than anything known on earth. Here, soul comes face to face with the Supreme Being (Sat Purusha), shining with a brightness greater than trillions of suns and moons combined. In this Light-saturated region there is no death, no rebirth, only eternal bliss and joy. Here, pure swan-like souls feed on and swim in rivers and pools of divine nectar. Their existence is perpetual, inconceivable bliss-consciousness.

Finally, the pilgrim soul reaches Sach Khand or the Abode of Truth. Here complete Oneness is realized and it sees all universes functioning according to His Will in devout awe and adoration. Even remembrance of such a vision is blissful, but the vision itself is such that no eye has ever seen, the heart cannot conceive and the tongue cannot describe.
— Kirpal Singh

Sach Khand or the Realm of Truth is the seat of the Formless One.
Here He creates all creations, rejoicing in creating.
Here are many regions, heavenly systems and universes,
To count which were to count the countless,
Here out of the Formless,
The heavenly plateaus and all else come into form,
All destined to move according to His Will.
He who is blessed with this vision, rejoices in its contemplation.
But, O Nanak, such is its beauty that to try to describe it
Is to attempt the impossible.

—Jap Ji of Guru Nanak.

COSMOLOGY APPENDIX

Kabir, Nanak, Kirpal, Darshan, and other Param Sants have spoken of three higher divisions of the fifth plane Sach Khand (the True Home). These have been termed as Alakh (the Incomprehensible), Agam (The Ineffable), and Anaami (the Nameless, Formless, Attributeless existence of God). This ultimate reality has also been termed as Agochar, Radha Soami, Nirala, Nirankar and Akaal. All such names are only attributive and descriptive, and carry no power per se.

Sant is a term for one who reaches Sach Khand, whereas Param Sant is one who reaches the Anaami realm (although such titles are often misused by imperfect masters and their followers). All who attain Sach Khand, along with their direct disciples are free forever. If they come into incarnation again, they come not as prisoners of existence like the rest of humanity, but as spiritual Adepts and saviors. Such a living Master or Adept is the representative of Sat Purusha on earth, sent to bring lost souls back to their Home, or Source. Through the power of their attention, they connect the yearning seekers with the Word, which takes the souls to the astral form of the inner Master, the Guru Dev, or Word-personified. Guru Dev takes souls to the Satguru, beyond the Astral and Causal planes. The Satguru takes the souls to the Supreme Being who absorbs and unites them within Itself in the Nameless, Formless, Wonder region.

No mind can conceive the splendor of the journey, much less, the Destination.

His devotees praise Him, yet never attain
full knowledge of the Infinite;
Like streams tumbling into the ocean,
They know not the depths therein.
Even kings and emperors
With heaps of wealth and vast dominion,
Compare not with an ant filled with the love of God.

-Stanza XXIII, Jap Ji of Guru Nanak.

Sparks fall upon the Flame;
Beams return to the Sun;
Drops merge in the Ocean.
All, all return Home someday.

-AS-

THE INNER PLANES OF CREATION
Various aspects of Divine Light & Sound-current
(an approximation only)

Purely Spiritual Regions

8. ANAAMI
The Nameless, Wonder Region

7. AGAM
The Ineffable Region

6. ALAKH
The Inconceivable Region

5. THE FIFTH PLANE — SACH KHAND
*Sat Purusha—the Supreme Being, dwells in Sach Khand—the **True Home**. Here, Soul merges in God as a drop merges into the ocean.*
Predominant Sound Current:
Bagpipes

Trillions of suns and moons cannot vie with even one hair of the Supreme Being: It is all Light

4. THE FOURTH PLANE — BHANWAR GUPHA
The Rotating Cave
Soul realizes here that it is none other than God

The Sun of the 4th Plane exceeds 100,000 physical suns

Predominant Sound Current:
Plaintive melody of Flute

MAHA SUNNA — The barrier region of darkness & silence

MAHA SUNNA — The barrier region of darkness & silence

3. PAR BRAHM
THE SUPER-CAUSAL— BEYOND THE MIND

2. BRAHMANDA
THE CAUSAL PLANE HOME OF THE MIND

1. ANDA
THE ASTRAL PLANE

PINDA
THE PHYSICAL PLANE

DASWAN DWAR
The Pool of Nectar— Amritsar/Mansarovar Full Moon exceeding 1,000 outer moons

Predominant Sound Current: *Sarangi (violin) and Sitar (harp-like stringed music)*

TRIKUTI
The Golden Mountains: Mer, Sumer & Kailash

Red Rising Sun

Predominant Sound Current: **Thunder and Drum**

SAHASRAR
The Thousand Petaled Lotus

Heavens and Purgatories

Stars, suns & moons

Predominant Sound Current: **Bells & Conch**

THE SIX CHAKRAS OF PINDA

Chakra	Divinity	Color of Light
Behind Eyes	Paramatma	radiance
Throat	Shanti	white
Heart	Shiva	bluish white
Navel	Vishnu	red
Reproductive	Brahm	blue
Rectum	Ganesh	yellow

Transmigration of Souls

The Wheel of 84 Lakhs

Bunk Naal (the curved tunnel)

GLOSSARY

A partial list of Sant Mat or Science of Spirituality terminology:

Adept—Highly skilled expert; spiritual Master, or Satguru (Master of Truth).

Adi Granth—or Guru Granth Sahib—the sacred scriptures of the Sikhs.

Agam—the Ineffable region; one stage below Anaami—the Nameless and Formless Region

Agochar—The Incomprehensible region; synonymous with Agam.

Ahimsa—the doctrine of Nonviolence, or non-injury to any living creature, as expounded by Buddha and Mahavira of the Jains.

Ajna Chakra—the sixth ganglionic center, chakra or psychic lotus located at the point between and behind the eyebrows. Also known as Third Eye, Single Eye, Divya Chaksu, or Shiv Netra. See chakras.

Akaal—The Eternal, the Timeless; synonymous with Anaami, Radha Soami, or Nirala.

Akalis—An ultra-orthodox Sikh sect.

Akbar (1542-1605)—The greatest of the Moghal emperors of India. Akbar demonstrated remarkable religious tolerance, wisdom and understanding. Akbar was an admirer of Hindu, Sikh, Jewish and Sufi Saints, including Mira Bai, Guru Arjan, Sarmad, and saints of the Chisti order.

Alakh—The Indescribable Realm, the region immediately beyond Sach Khand, and before Agam.

Amrit—Nectar, ambrosia, water of immortality. In Sufism, Amrit is termed Aab-i-Hayat or Water of Life.

Amritsar—In mysticism, Amritsar is a name for the pool of nectar encountered in Daswan Dwar—the third spiritual Region. Here, soul is purified of all traces of mind, karma, sin and matter. Not to be confused with the city or outer temple/pool of Amritsar, Punjab founded by Guru Ram Das.

Amir Khusro (1253-1352—Famous Sufi poet of northern India, and chief disciple of Nizamuddin.

Anaami—The Nameless and Formless region. The perfected Saints describe this stage as the be-all and end-all, utterly beyond human description or mental comprehension.

Anna l'Haq—Lit. "I am Truth."

Arjan Dev (1563-1606)—5th Sikh Guru; compiler of the Adi Granth and martyr.

Arjuna—The princely warrior-disciple of Lord Krishna, who, hesitant on the battlefield, with Krishna as his charioteer, received from his master the Bhagavad Gita (or Celestial Song).

Asana—Any yogic posture used for meditation or exercise.

Ashram—Hermitage, refuge in nature, an esoteric school, a center of spiritual teaching.

Ashtanga Yoga—the eight-fold path of yoga as developed by Patanjali.

Avatar—an Incarnation. In Hinduism, Ram, Krishna, and Narsingh were avatars of Vishnu—the Preserver aspect of God, born to bring about the balance between good and evil in the physical world. The role of the Avatar is different from that of the Sant Satguru, who comes to take souls back Home.

Baba—Reverential prefix for an old man, a father, or a Saint.

Baba Jaimal Singh—(1838-1903), the Satguru of Baba Sawan Singh.

Babar (1483-1530)—A descendant of Genghis Khan, conquerer of Afghanistan and northern India. Considered to be the founder of the Moghul dynastic empire. On one of his campaigns, he imprisoned the inhabitants of a village. Amongst them was Guru Nanak, who was ordered to grind corn between two large stones. Nanak started grinding, but in the process, entered a state of oneness with God. The stones continued turning, but no human hand was evident. This miracle was reported to Babar, and after an epic discourse, Babar set Nanak and all other prisoners free.

Baha'Ullah—A mystic saint and poet of Persia, founder of the Baha'i faith.

Baraka—Persian word for Grace.

Beas—One of the major rivers in the Punjab; also the name of the town which sprang up on its banks, around the place where Baba Jaimal Singh meditated and taught.

Bhagavad Gita—The immortal discourse given to Arjuna by Lord Krishna. The Gita is the most popular scripture of Hindus.

Bhajan—Devotional song. In mysticism, bhajan is the meditative practice of listening to and absorbing in the internal Sound-current as heard from the right side or center of the forehead. Bhajan is the third fundamental spiritual practice, and it leads the practitioner to higher states of consciousness. Ultimately, by following the internal melodies of the Word (Naam), union of soul with God is attained.

Bhakti—Devotion to God or to a Godman.

Bhandara—Death anniversary of a Master, followed by a free meal.

Bhanwar Gupha—The fourth inner spiritual region preceding Sach Khand. Bhanwar Gupha means "whirling cave of light."

Bharat—Another name for India, named after King Bharat, who renounced the world and became a hermit-yogi of the forest. Despite his renunciation of society and family, Bharat developed a deep attachment for a deer. Due to his attachment, Bharat was reincarnated as a deer, illustrating the importance of inner detachment from the temporary objects of this world, especially at the time of death, whether one is a king, a yogi or an ordinary householder.

Bibi—wife, polite term of addressing an Indian woman.

Brahm—Lord of the causal plane who controls the two lower planes (astral and physical) as well.

Brahma—One of the three deities of the sacred Hindu Trinity, entrusted with the work of creating the causal, astral and physical worlds. Brahma, the Creator, Vishnu, the Preserver, Mahesh (or Shiva), the Destroyer.

Brahmanda—Egg of Brahm, so-called due to it's egg-like, elliptical shape.

Brahmand, the causal plane, is also known as Trikuti

Brahmcharya—Chastity, purity of conduct; controlling the senses.

Bulleh Shah—(1680-1758) The great Sufi poet of Punjab and foremost disciple of Inayat Shah, the gardener Saint.

Bunk Naal—Curved tunnel connecting the astral and causal regions.

Causal Region—Brahmanda, or the second spiritual region. Here, soul sheds the astral body and works through the causal body. It is the region from which the mind originates, and its ruler is Brahm. Om, thunder and drums resound throughout this region which is illuminated with the light of a continuous red rising sun.

Chakras—Wheels or lotuses; centers in the body through which various energies function. Six chakras of the body are: guda—rectum; indri —genital; nabhi —navel; hridey —heart; kantha —throat; and ajna —third eye. The chakras are connected to the Ida, pingala, and shushumna nadis, subtle pathways through the length of the spinal column. The six chakras of the body lead to the Thousand Petaled Lotus—headquarters of the astral plane. The shushumna continues on up into the higher regions.

Chaurasi Lakh—Wheel of Transmigration through 8.4 million species. According to the Saints of India, the immortal soul passes through the various species until it attains human birth—the roof and crown of creation. Only in human birth can the soul realize itself and return to the Creator, but most often this priceless opportunity is wasted, and the cycle of births and deaths continues.

Chela—Disciple of a guru.

Dacoit—Thief, or robber. In mysticism, mankind is beset by Five Dacoits: Lust, Anger, Greed, Attachment, and Ego. These inner thieves are conquered as the disciple perfects his or her spiritual practice, and when the Sound-current purifies the mind, the dacoits depart in the form of snakes or little boys.

Dadu Sahib (1544-1603)—Poet-saint who composed the *Bhakti Sagar* (Ocean of Devotion).

Darshan—Seeing, vision, meeting the Master without, or within.

Darshan Singh (1921-1989)—Eldest of two sons born to the great saint Sant Kirpal Singh Ji, who brought him at an early age to the feet of his Master, Hazur Baba Sawan Singh, of Beas. Darshan received Naam initiation from Hazur at the age of six, and served his mission assiduously. As Sant Kirpal Singh spiritually succeeded Hazur in 1948, and carried on his mission of Naam initiation, so also was Darshan Singh chosen as the spiritual successor of Sant Kirpal Singh before he passed on in 1974.

Darvesh—Sufi term for mystic or Godman.

Daswan Dwar—Third inner spiritual plane.

Dera—Residence, ashram, or hermitage.

Dharma—Duty, faith, religion.

Dharam Rai—God of death and justice, also called Yama Raj.

Dhun—Tune, inner sound.

Dhyan—The holding, or fastening of attention in meditation on the inner vistas of Light. Dhyan progresses to contemplation on the inner radiant form of the Master Adept, so much so that the self is subsumed. Dhyan is the second phase of meditation, and it leads to the next phase: Bhajan, or inner listening to the inner Music of the Spheres, the Word, or Naam.

Eye Focus:—the point between and behind the two eyebrows. Also known as the Third Eye, Tisra Til, or Single Eye.

Fina-Fil-Shaykh—Sufi term for merger in the Master.

Fina-Fillah—Sufi term for Death in God, Sufi term for the merger with God. This follows *Fina-fil-Shaykh.*

Farid (1175-1265)—Sufi poet and saint of Punjab.

Fakir (FAQIR)—Mendicant, saintly ascetic living on alms.

Ghalib (1797-1869)—Urdu poet.

Ghazal—In Persian and Urdu poetry, a lyric intended to be sung. Each verse represents a complete unit of meaning with well-defined metrical forms. The Urdu ghazal condenses many subtle and grand concepts, either romantic, philosophical, allegorical or mystical, into a few words or phrases with rhyming couplets. Urdu poetry is immensely popular in India and Pakistan.

Gita—see Bhagavad Gita.

Gobind Singh—Tenth and last Sikh Guru (1646-1708). Author of Dasam Granth, Bachittar Natak, and Gobind Geet.

Granth Sahib—Guru Granth Sahib, or Adi Granth—the sacred scriptures of the Sikhs compiled Guru Arjan Dev. Besides the writings of several of the Sikh Gurus, the Granth Sahib includes compositions by well-known Hindu and Muslim Saints. The largest number of verses is by Kabir Sahib.

Gurbani—the sayings of the Gurus, in the form of the Adi Granth.

Gurbhai—a brother in faith; a fellow-initiate.

Gurmat Siddhant —A comprehensive treatise on spirituality in Punjabi in two volumes. The work uses illustrations from most religious traditions and was written under Baba Sawan Singh's direction by Sant Kirpal Singh. Like the nine successors of Guru Nanak, Kirpal Singh signed the book in his Master's name, as he considered it was Hazur's doing, not his.

Guru—Spiritual teacher. Literally, "dispeller of darkness".

Guru Saroop—Inner radiant form of the Guru. The Word-made-flesh.

Guru Granth Sahib—See Granth Sahib.

Guru Dev—The radiant light-filled form of the Master, as it appears in the Astral and Causal regions.

Gurdwara—Threshold, or "Door" of the guru; Sikh temple.

Gurmukh—(pronounced *Gurmookh*) One who has become a mouthpiece of his Master; one who lives in obedience and surrender to the will of God.

Gurmukhi—Punjabi script used by the Sikh Gurus to record their verses. Gurmukhi bears some similarity to the Hindi-devanagri script.

GLOSSARY

Guru Nanak (see **Nanak**)

Hafiz (1325-1388)—Mystic poet-saint of Persia.

Haj—pilgrimage to Mecca, considered sacred and obligatory to Muslims.

Haq—Persian and Arabic for Truth, or God in Supreme State..

Haridwar—Sacred city for Hindus, located where the river Ganges emerges from the Himalayan foothills onto the plains of northern India.

Hatha Yoga—Yoga which seeks spiritual development through mastering various bodily postures.

Hazur—Lord. A term of great respect for someone in a position of authority. Sawan Singh was addressed by his disciples as Hazur. See Sawan Singh. He was also called "Vadey Maharaj," or "Great Master."

HU—Arabic term for the third spiritual region (pronounced "Hooo").

HIndi—the most commonly spoken and written language of northern India.

Ida (Ira)—One of three subtle channels which pass from the head down to the base of the spine, connected to the breath, and which yogis attempt to master. The three subtle channels, sometimes called nerves, are the Ida, Pingala, and Shushumna (or Sukhmana). Ida or lunar current flows on the left side and Pingala or solar current flows on the right, Sukhmana is the central channel in which the Sound current is heard by the serious meditator, when focused in the third-eye center.

Initiation—In Sant Mat, initiation is the process of connecting the disciple's attention with the inner Light and Sound-current, through the agency of a perfect living Adept. Basic requirements involve living off one's own honest earnings, adopting a strict vegetarian diet (no meat, fish, fowl, or eggs), and avoidance of.drugs and alcohol.

Jaimal Singh (1838-1903)—also known as Baba Ji. Spiritual successor of Soamiji of Agra. Baba Ji was the Satguru of Baba Sawan Singh.

Jainism—A religion founded in the 6th century BC by Mahavira—a spiritually realized ascetic who roamed the forests of India. He taught the inner way, along with non-violence and respect for creation.

Jain—A follower of the Jain religion.

Janak—King of ancient India who aspired to spiritual knowledge. Through the grace of the humpbacked Adept—Ashtavakra, Janak attained enlightenment. Afterwards, Janak successfully combined kingship with sainthood.

Jap Ji—Mystic epic poem of Guru Nanak, which begins the Adi Granth.

Ji—suffix of respect.

Jiva—Embodied soul; soul plus mind.

Jyoti—Inner Light.

Kaaba—The black stone of Abraham enshrined at Mecca, Arabia.

Kabir (1398-1518)—Poet and mystic Adept of Banares. Kabir is considered to be 'the grandfather of Sant Mat' in the present millennium. Many Hindus and Muslims were amongst his initiates. Kabir's compositions are found in the Adi Granth.

GLOSSARY

Kal—Time, Satan, Negative Power. While a creation of the Supreme Being, Kal's function is to keep order and justice in the lower, perishable regions— the physical, astral and causal planes. In contrast to Kal, God, the Almighty and Merciful works through the Masters to bring seekers into contact with the Word, Logos or Naam. The Logos permits escape from Kal's domains, and ultimate Emancipation.

Kali Yuga—See Yuga.

Kalma—In Islam, Kalma means an affirmation of faith in God and in his Prophet Mohammed. In Sufism and in Sant Mat it refers to the Holy Word or Sound-current.

Kam—Desire, lust. Of all the weaknesses of man, Kam is probably the most difficult to master. But, it is said that Ego is the last to go.

Karma—Action and reaction, the law of action and reaction; the fruit or result of past thoughts, words   and deeds.

Karma Yoga—The Yoga of right action, performed in a spirit of detachment as a means of spiritual unfoldment.

Khusro, Amir—Scholar, mystic Sufi poet, disciple of Nizam-ud-Din Chishti.

Kirpal Singh—(1894-1974) full title: Param Sant Kirpal Singh Ji Maharaj), a perfect Adept, author, transmitter of ancient truths; spiritual successor to Hazur Baba Sawan Singh (1858-1948); first Sant Mat Master to visit the Americas, Greece and Europe; known to his approximately 100,000 disciples as "the Beloved Master."

Koran—The holy message of God as revealed to Prophet Mohammed.

Krishna—Avatar of Vishnu, friend and mentor of Arjuna; Krishna hero of the Bhagavad Gita.

Khuda—Lit. One who comes of his own accord. God or Allah.

Kriyaman—See karma.

Kundalini—The coiled, dormant serpentine energy situated at the base of the spine. When the kundalini is awakened and rises up to the forehead, the practitioner may acquire miraculous powers, and/or go insane. Kundalini practice is not advocated by the Masters of Sant Mat.

Lakh—One hundred thousand.

Lakshmi—Goddess of wealth, good fortune and beauty.

Langar—The Guru's Kitchen. In India, all who come to the Master's satsang, are fed a free vegetarian meal afterwards.

Lao Tse—Father of Chinese mysticism or Taoism. Author of the *Tao Te Ching*.

Mahabharata—Indian epic by sage Vyas. It centers round a catastrophic war between the Kauravas and Pandavas, in which all civilization throughout the world was destroyed in thirteen days.

Mahavira—Jain Ascetic and saint who lived in the 5th century B.C. in India.

Mansarovar—A lake, high up in the mountains of Tibet. However, in Sant Mat, the Mansarovar (Chashma-e-Kausar in Sufism, or Amritsar) is a sacred pool in the third inner region, whose waters purify the soul of all traces of mind and matter.

Maha Sunna—The barrier-region of great silence and stygian darkness which lies between the third and fourth spiritual planes. Only the perfect Adepts and those whom they take with them can cross this barrier.

Mathnawi (Turkish), or **Masnavi** (Persian)—A collection of the mystical verses of Rumi. His incomparable verse combines mystical allegory, music and sublime language with deep revelation born of God-realization.

Maya—Illusion, the principle of unreality which makes us see the outer universe as real. This illusion (dream) divides us from God or the Real.

Mira Bai (1503-1563)—Princess saint of Rajasthan, famous for her poignant devotional songs.

Moghal—Mongol; one of several emperors of India, or their descendents.

Mohammed, Prophet (C. 570-632)—"The Praised One," Founder and Prophet of Islam.

Muni—Silent one, wise or holy sage.

Muqqam-i-Haq—Arabic and Persian: Realm of truth, fifth inner region among Sufis, synonymous with Sach Khand in Sant Mat terminology.

Murshid—Persian: Spiritual teacher.

Naam—Name, Holy Word, Logos, Kalma, Amrit, Shabd, Bani, etc. The celestial Light and Sound of Creation, Music of the Spheres.

Nad—Sound, in mysticism it refers to the inner Sound.

Namaste—"I bow to the Lord in you;" traditional Hindu greeting/parting.

Namdev (1270-1350)—Poet saint of Maharashtra and Punjab.

Namaz—Prayer of faithful Muslims, performed five times daily.

Nanak, Guru (1469-1539)—First Guru in the Sikh lineage, Nanak was born of Khatri lineage in Talwandi, near Lahore in the Punjab. Guru Nanak realized God and spread the fragrance of the True Name to countless seekers. He traveled on foot from the Himalayas in the north, to Sri Lanka in the south, China to the East, and to Mecca in the West. Author of *Jap Ji* and many important verses found in the Adi Granth. Nanak was revered by both Hindus and Muslims as a perfect Saint.

Negative Mysticism—Term used by Sant Darshan Singh to describe forms of mysticism based on asceticism and the renunciation of a householder's life, see also positive mysticism.

Negative Power—Kal, time, death.

Nine Doors—The two eyes, two ears, two nostrils, the mouth, the generative organ and the rectum.

Nirgun—Without attributes, Formless, opposite to saguna.

Ojas—spiritual power accruing from celibacy when all energies are directed away from the sense organs to higher centers within the brain.

Om (or, Aum, Onkar)—The Sound-Lord of the second spiritual region.

Pundit—Learned priest or scholar. A member of the Brahmanical caste.

Papiha—India's rain-bird. According to tradition, the Papiha will drink only pure rainwater, and will die of thirst before drinking ordinary water. The papiha is used as a metaphor of a pure soul longing for, and accepting nothing less than a glimpse of the Lord.

Paramatma—The Oversoul; Supreme Soul; God.

Parampara—Spiritual lineage.

Param Sant—Supreme Saint, one who has reached Anaami.

Par Brahm—Third or supra-causal region.

Parshad (Prashad)—Anything blessed or sanctified by a Saint; commonly used for blessed food from vegetarian sources.

Patanjali—Author of the *Yoga Sutras* and *Ashtanga Yoga* which outline the philosophy and practice of traditional Yoga.

Pind—can mean either the human body or the physical universe.

Pir Inayat Khan—Twentieth century Sufi mystic, author of *Mysticism of Sound* and other works.

Positive Mysticism—Term used by Sant Darshan Singh for that form of mysticism in which the seeker, while meeting normal family and social responsibilities, pursues lofty spiritual goals. This approach is typical of Sant Mat or Science of Spirituality.

Prana—Vital energy of the body, intimately linked to the breath process.

Pranayama—Breath control, yogic-breathing which harnesses energy for spiritual progress.

Pythagoras—Sixth century B.C. Greek philosopher. Defined God as "Living and Absolute Truth clothed in Light"; also as "Supreme Music, the nature of which is harmony."

Rabia Basri (717-801)—Woman saint of Basra, Iraq, famed for a life of intense spiritual practice, devotion and lofty sayings.

Radha Soami—Lord of the Soul, term used by Soami Ji of Agra for God in the Absolute state, also known as Anaami. Rai Saligram, a prominent follower, founded the Radha Soami Faith.

Raja—King

Ramakrishna Paramhansa (1836-1886)—The mystic of Dakshineshwar, Calcutta. Ramakrishna was a practical mystic of direct realization. He practiced Hinduism, yoga, Christianity, and Islam and discovered that they all arrived at the same goal. Ramakrishna taught the unity of all religions, and had great spiritual powers.

Ramanand—A Saint of mystic devotion, born near Madras. He came to northern India early in his life. He initiated Saint Kabir and Guru Ravi Das.

Ravi Das (1376-1527)—A cobbler by profession, Ravi Das became a great saint of Surat Shabd Yoga. His poetic compositions can be found in the Adi Granth. He was the Guru of the celebrated princess Mira Bai.

Riddhis—Supernatural or psychic powers such as the ability to read minds, see events at a distance, read the past or future, etc. The Adepts warn against the cultivation and practice of occult powers, as they retard the upward progress of the soul.

Rishi—Forest sage.

Ruhani Satsang—Spiritual satsang, term used for the organization set up by Sant Kirpal Singh for disseminating truth.

Rumi, Jalaluddin (1207-1277)—Arguably one of the greatest Sufi poets and saint of all times; author of the *Mathnawi*.. Rumi became the devoted disciple of the wild Master, Shams-i-Tabriz, after the latter revealed to him his divine, all-knowing condition.

Sach Khand—The Realm of truth, the True Home of God and soul, from whence all souls originated. When soul ultimately returns Home and comes face to face with the Supreme Being, it then dissolves its separate existence in the Eternal Being.

Sadhana—Spiritual exercises, inner discipline.

Sadhu—Ascetic or holy person.

Sahansdal Kanwal (Kamal)—Thousand petaled lotus, same as Sahasrar; headquarters of the Astral plane.

Sahasrar—City of a thousand lights, center of the first inner region.

Sahjo Bai—15th century poet, woman mystic and disciple of Charan Das.

Samadhi—State of superconsciousness, when the soul of the devotee transcends the limits of body, self and mind, and becomes one with his or her ideal, at whatever region one has attained. To pass from the Astral to the Causal, or from the Causal to the Supra-Causal, the initiate must become one with the residing Power at each plane, then pass beyond.

Sangat—Congregation, community consisting of disciples of a Master.

Sant—One who has reached Sach Khand (although in reality not all who are called Sants are truly Sants, i.e. those who have perfected themselves and reached Sach Khand).

Sant Mat—Path, or Way of the Masters, another term for Surat Shabd Yoga, or Science of Spirituality.

Sanyassi—One who has renounced the world, wandering ascetic.

Sar Bachan—Title of the prose and poetical works by Soami Shiv Dayal Singh of Agra.

Satguru—True spiritual teacher, perfect spiritual master. This also refers to the transcendental form of the Master when the disciple in Sach Khand meets it.

Sat Naam—The True Name—an appelation of the immortal Supreme Being.

Sat Purush—Lord of Sach Khand, the Supreme Being.

Satsang—Company of truth, a spiritual discourse.

Satsangi—An initiate of a realized Master; literally "One who is in contact with Truth."

Sat Sri Akal—"Truth is Eternal." Traditional Sikh greeting and parting.

Satvik—One of the three gunas or qualities of mind: Tamsik—lazy, negative, Rajsik—energetic, forceful, active, hard-working; Satvik—pure, highest, noble, elevating, truthful. Satvik diet = vegetarian diet.

Sawan—First month of the rainy season.

GLOSSARY

Sawan Singh—Full title: Hazur Baba Sawan Singh (1858-1948), the first perfect Adept to spread the teachings of Sant Mat to the Western world. Hazur initiated approximately 120,000 seekers.

Sensory Current—The sense of feeling. When the sensory currents are withdrawn to the eye-focus, Light and Sound automatically appear.

Seva—Selfless, or ego-less service. Seva may be physical, intellectual, monetary, or spiritual.

Sevadar—One who performs selfless service.

Shabd—The Sound Current or Word which brought everything into being; the vehicle for taking souls back to the Source of its emanation.

Shakti—Spiritual power.

Shams-i-Tabriz (Shamas Tabriz)—Spiritual Master of Maulana Rumi.

Shastras—Ancient Hindu scriptures.

Shaykh—In Sufism, Shaykh is synonymous for Master, but is also used for those who preach in a mosque, head of a religious order, or a learned one.

Shiv Netra—Lit. Eye of Shiva. Represented as a flaming eye in the middle of Shiva's forehead. In Sant Mat, third or single eye. See tenth door.

Siddhis—See riddhis.

Sikh—lit. Disciple of a true Master. Conventionally, a follower of the Sikh religion. According to the Adepts, one only becomes a "disciple" after seeing the Master's radiant form within.

Sikh Gurus—Guru Nanak (1469-1539), Guru Angad (1504-1552), Guru Amar Das (1479-1574), Guru Ram Das (1534-1581), Guru Arjan Dev (1563-1606), Guru Har Gobind (1595-1644), Guru Har Rai (1630-1661), Guru Har Krishan (1656-1664), Guru Tegh Bahadur (1621-1675), and Guru Gobind Singh (1666-1708).

Simran—Sweet remembrance of the Lord. In Sant Mat, simran stands for the inner practice of focused mental repetition of the five charged names received during initiation from a perfect master. Simran is the first phase of meditation practice, and it helps withdraw the sensory current to the third eye. The five Words only have validity or power when conveyed by a realized Adept.

Singh—Lion.

Soami Shiv Dayal Singh, or, Soami Ji (1818-1878) Great spiritual Adept of Agra, author of *Sar Bachan* and Satguru of Baba Jaimal Singh.

Sohang—'I am as Thou art'. The Lord of the fourth spiritual region. A'naal Haq, as uttered by the Sufi Mansur, and 'I and my Father are One' as proclaimed by Jesus in the higher planes, mean the same.

Sufi—The Mystics of Islam. Soof comes from the Persian word, 'wool,' as the early Sufis wore a simple woolen cloak. The great Sufis have always represented the highest form of mysticism within the Islamic tradition, often suffering for their beliefs at the hands of orthodox fanatics. There are several gradations of Sufis—just as in all other spiritual traditions.

Sunna—(see Maha Sunna)

Supra Causal—Region where pure spirit predominates. Same as Par Brahm.

Surat—the Attention, or more specifically, the inner faculty of hearing. In Sant Mat, the attention is identified as the prime attribute of the soul.

Surat Shabd Yoga—the science of uniting soul with the Celestial Sound-current. Considered the highest of all yogas, Surat Shabd leads practitioners to realms far beyond the reach of more commonly known yoga systems, which may not extend beyond the astral or causal planes. Surat Shabd Yoga is synonymous with Sant Mat, Path of the Masters, or Science of Spirituality.

Swami (or 'Soami')—Lord. Can also mean any one who dons an orange robe and who has been initiated into one of India's four monastic Hindu orders..

Swarath—Worldly life.

Tao (or Dao)- the Way of Heaven, as taught by Lao Tsu of China. Same as Naam or Word.

Tenth Door—The human frame has nine apertures through which the attention spreads out into the world—two eyes, two ears, two nostrils, generative organ, and rectum. There is a hidden tenth door between and behind the eyebrows, which leads to the spiritual regions within. There is another Tenth Door or Daswan Dwar in the Third Spiritual Region.

Third Eye—See tenth door.

Trikuti—Brahm, second spiritual stage, home of the mind. Trikuti refers to three golden mountains of this region, which the sages have called Mer, Sumer, and Kailash.

Tulsi Das—Hindi poet of medieval times, author of the Ram Charitra Manas which retells the ancient Saskrit Ramayana.epic.

Tulsi Sahib (1763-1843)—Sant Mat Master from whom Soami Ji of Agra received initiation. Tulsi Sahib was the crown prince of the Peshwas (Puna). He renounced kingship for the spiritual life.

Udgit—Upanishadic term for the "Sound from the Beyond", the Holy Word.

Upanishads—Teachings of the ancient Rishis or sages, containing commentaries on the Vedas (India's oldest scripture), often in dialogue form.

Urdu—A language which developed in Moghul times using Hindi structures and Persian script and vocabulary. Spoken in some regions of India and currently the national language of Pakistan.

Valmiki—Author of original Ramayana in Sanskrit. Valmiki was a robber and illiterate, but, through association with a Saint, he became proficient in meditation and ultimately attained Self-knowledge, and God realization.

Vedanta—The end of the Vedas, a school of Indian philosophy based on the Upanishads (commentaries on the Vedas).

Vedas—Knowledge, the four basic sacred books of ancient Hinduism: Rig Veda, Sama Veda, Yajur Veda, Athar Veda.

Vishnu—Member of the Hindu triad responsible for sustaining the creation. Vishnu and is said to reincarnate as an avatar whenever the balance of good and evil is seriously disturbed in the world.

GLOSSARY

Vivek—Discrimination.

Vivekananda Swami (1863-1902)—Devoted disciple of Sri Ramakrishna, eventually succeeding him. Founder of the Ramakrishna Order, Vivekananda brought India's spiritual philosophy to the West in 1894, when he addressed the World Parliament of Religions in Chicago.

Vyas—Ancient sage and poet, author of the great epic Mahabharata.

Wahi Guru—Wondrous Lord. Another appelation of the Supreme Being

Wheel of Eighty-Four—8.4 million species of life through which the soul transmigrates. While all life is sacred, say the Masters, only in human form can soul seek and attain liberation.

Yama—God of death and justice, Lord of the nether regions.

Yoga—To yoke together, to discipline, a system which leads to or aims at the union of the soul with the Oversoul.

Yugas—Age or cycle, ancient Indian thought sees time in terms of a recurring cycle of 4 Yugas: Sat Yuga—Golden Age; Treta Yuga—Silver Age; Dwapar Yuga—Bronze Age; Kali Yuga—Iron Age. According to Sant Kirpal Singh, we are leaving behind Kali Yuga, and returning towards Sat Yuga.

Zoroaster (660-583 B.C.)—Founder of the ancient religion which bears his name. From his writings in the Zend Avesta, it is evident that Zoroaster was experienced on the inner way of Light and Sound. He taught the path of good thoughts, good words and good deeds, and the worship of the Creator— *Ahura Mazda* whose creative power he called Sarosha—the Word or Naam.

For further information on the teachings of the Masters:

<u>Western Headquarters</u>:
Science of Spirituality
4S Naperville Road,
Naperville, IL 60563
Phone: (630) 955-1200

<u>International Headquarters</u>:
Sawan Kirpal Ruhani Mission
Kirpal Ashram
Vijay Nagar, Delhi, 110009, India

www.sos.org

For more information regarding this book, how to order, including full-color photos and illustrations, the reader is welcome to browse:

www.naturespath.com/luminous

Notes: _____

_____

_____

_____

_____

_____

_____

_____

_____

_____

_____

ORDER YOUR COPY TODAY

Journey to the Luminous by ARRAN STEPHENS

Also available at your local bookstore

USA ORDERS in US$		OVERSEAS ORDERS in US$		CANADIAN ORDERS in CDN$	
____ copies @ $19.95	$_____	____ copies @ $19.95	$_____	____ copies @ $24.95	$_____
Trade Discount	$_____	Trade Discount	$_____	Trade Discount	$_____
Shipping (1st book)	$ 5.00	Shipping (1st book)	$ 6.00	Shipping (1st book)	$ 5.00
Add $3 (for each additional book)	$_____	Add $5 (for each additional book)	$_____	Add $3 (for each additional book)	$_____
State Tax (if applicable)	$_____	Air Mail	$ 12.00	GST	$_____
Total enclosed	$_____	Total enclosed	$_____	Total enclosed	$_____

SEND YOUR MONEY ORDER, CHECK OR VISA CARD AUTHORIZATION PAYABLE TO:

ELTON–WOLF PUBLISHING

5560 BAYVUE RD. BIRCH BAY, WA 98230 USA

PHONE TOLL FREE: 1-877-371-5560 E.MAIL: schugtsos@aol.com

Name	Address	City	State/Province
Country	Zip/Postal Code	Phone (Daytime)	(Home)
VISA Number	Expiry	Signature for Authorization	Thank You

All net proceeds from the sale of this book will be donated to charity